YEATS,
THE IRISH LITERARY REVIVAL
AND THE POLITICS OF PRINT

Yug Mohit Chaudhry

CORK  UNIVERSITY
PRESS

First published in 2001 by
Cork University Press
Cork
Ireland

© Yug Mohit Chaudhry 2001

British Library Cataloguing in Publication Data
A CIP catalogue record for this book is available from the British Library.

Library of Congress Cataloging-in-Publication Data

Chaudhry, Yug Mohit, 1968-
    Yeats, the Irish literary revival and the politics of print / Yug
Mohit Chaudhry.
        p.   cm.
    Includes bibliographical references and index.
    ISBN 1-85918-260-7 (alk. paper) -- ISBN 1-85918-261-5 (pbk. : alk. paper)
    1. Yeats, W. B. (William Butler), 1865-1939--Political and social views. 2. Yeats, W. B.
(William Butler), 1865-1939--Criticism and interpretation. 3. English literature--Irish
authors--History and criticism. 4. Literature publishing--Ireland--History--20th
century. 5. Literature publishing--Ireland--History--19th century. 6. Publishers and
publishing--Political aspects--Ireland. 7. Nationalism and literature--Ireland--History.
8. Ireland--Intellectual life--20th century. 9. Ireland--Intellectual life--19th century.
                                                                                    I. Title

PR5908.P6 C47 2001
821'.8--dc21
                                                            2001017291

            ISBN 1 85918 260 7 [Hardback]
            ISBN 1 85918 261 5 [Paperback]

        Typesetting by Red Barn Publishing, Skeagh, Skibbereen

    Printed in Great Britain by MPG Books Ltd., Bodmin, Cornwall

Dedicated to my late father and to my sister who worked to make this book possible

CONTENTS

ILLUSTRATIONS

ACKNOWLEDGEMENTS

My debts to John Kelly are as varied and large as the personality and generosity of this prince of supervisors. He made Oxford home for me, opened his home and his heart to my needs, gave me a sense of joyful belonging in a place that had initially made me miserable and unwelcome, and above all made the burden of scholarship and thesis writing so light and enjoyable. His unsurpassed knowledge of Yeats and Irish literature worn so lightly and shared so carelessly, and the meticulousness and rigour of his scholarship so belied by his easy and charming ways, deserve greater credit and grander testament than I or my book can ever give.

V. A. Rao, my tutor from St Stephen's, Delhi, has stood by me unflinchingly through personal and professional highs and lows. He nurtured a raw enthusiasm and took it to the doors of an Oxford D.Phil. He kept his faith in me when my faith in myself was flagging. His advice and suggestions have made a huge difference to my approach to literature, and to the writing of this book. I can never hope to repay this debt.

Raphael Ingelbein has seen this book evolve through its many drafts and he rid it of errors that cropped up at each stage. A keener, more perceptive and richly endowed intelligence is difficult to find, and it has been my inestimable good fortune to have him as my friend. Linda Munk and A. N. Katil spent hours trying to teach me how to write good prose. Christine Kelly found me a home when I suddenly found myself homeless in Oxford. Terry Eagleton read and commented caustically on an earlier proposal, thereby saving me from the error of my ways. He was more encouraging when he read an early draft of this book, and later helped it find a berth with Cork University Press. Jon Stallworthy read early drafts of some chapters. Roy Foster was generous with his advice and I have often taken recourse to his encyclopaedic knowledge of thing Yeatsian and Irish. Edna Longley read the thesis, and convinced me of its printworthiness. She was generous in her help and encouragement and this book may not have been published but for her. Ray Ryan taught me what my book tries to teach others and showed me how to market my wares. His generosity and friendship have brightened many a dark day, and I am grateful for his companionship and help. Sowon Park and Shamindra Herat read and improved several chapters, tightened the argument and pointed out its flaws. They have enriched me personally and intellectually in more ways than I can know.

The staff of the Upper Reading Room at the Bodleian have endured my demands with a heroic stoicism, and never complained though they often had good reason to. Being with them each day of my research has contributed greatly to the pleasure I have taken in writing this book.

ABBREVIATIONS

By W. B. Yeats

Auto	*Autobiographies* (London: Macmillan, 1955).
CL1	*The Collected Letters of W. B. Yeats*, vol. I, ed. John Kelly (Oxford: Clarendon Press, 1986).
CL2	*The Collected Letters of W. B. Yeats*, vol. II, eds. Warwick Gould, John Kelly and Deirdre Toomey (Oxford: Clarendon Press, 1997).
CL3	*The Collected Letters of W. B. Yeats*, vol. III, eds. John Kelly and Ronald Schuchard (Oxford: Clarendon Press, 1986).
E&I	*Essays and Introductions* (London: Macmillan, 1961).
Ex	*Explorations*, selected by Mrs. W. B. Yeats (London: Macmillan, 1962).
L	*Letters of W. B. Yeats*, ed. Allan Wade (London: Hart-Davis, 1954).
LNI	*Letters to the New Island*, eds. George Bornstein and Hugh Witemeyer (London: Macmillan, 1989).
Mem	*Memoirs*, ed. Denis Donoghue (London: Macmillan, 1972).
P&I	*Prefaces and Introductions*, ed. William H. O'Donnell (London: Macmillan, 1988).
SS	*The Senate Speeches of W. B. Yeats*, ed. Donald R. Pearce (London: Faber and Faber, 1961).
UP1	*Uncollected Prose by W. B. Yeats*, vol. 1, ed. John Frayne, (New York: Columbia University Press, 1970).
UP2	*Uncollected Prose by W. B. Yeats*, vol. 2, eds. John Frayne and Colton Johnson (New York: Columbia University Press, 1975).
VP	*The Variorum Edition of the Poems of W. B. Yeats*, eds. Peter Allt and Russell K. Alspach (New York: Macmillan, 1957).

Edited by W. B. Yeats

FFT	*Fairy and Folk Tales of the Irish Peasantry* (London: Scott, 1888).
OBMV	*The Oxford Book of Modern Verse* (Oxford: OUP, 1936).
RIT	*Representative Irish Tales* (Gerrards Cross: Colin Smythe, 1979).
SC	*Stories from Carleton* (London: Walter Scot, 1889).

Other Works

Bibl	*A Bibliography of the Writings of W. B. Yeats*, ed. Allan Wade (London: Rupert Hart-Davis, 1951).

BRC   *Book of the Rhymers' Club* (London: Elkin Mathews, 1892).

Famine   F. S. L. Lyons, *Ireland After the Famine* (Suffolk: Collins/Fontana, 1979).

Ireland   R. F. Foster, *Modern Ireland 1600–1972* (London: Penguin, 1989).

Parnell   F. S. L. Lyons, *Charles Stewart Parnell* (London: Fontana, 1991).

PBYI   *Poems and Ballads of Young Ireland* (Dublin: M. H. Gill and Sons, 1888).

SSF   Mary Ferguson, *Sir Samuel Ferguson and the Ireland of his Day*, 2 vols. (London: William Blackwood, 1896).

WBY   Roy Foster, *W. B. Yeats: A Life*, vol. 1 (Oxford: Clarendon Press, 1997).

YA   *Yeats Annual.*

YAACTS *Yeats: An Annual of Critical and Textual Studies.*

Periodicals

BP   *Boston Pilot*

DUM   *Dublin University Magazine*

DUR   *Dublin University Review*

FJ   *Freeman's Journal*

IT   *Irish Times*

NR   *New Review*

NO   *National Observer*

PSJ   *Providence Sunday Journal*

SO   *Scots Observer*

UI   *United Ireland*

INTRODUCTION

'September 1913': Composition, Reception, Interpretation, Misinterpretation

I

This book is part of an emerging practice of reading texts in the contexts for which they were first written. It demonstrates that our understanding of Yeats and the Irish Literary Revival can be enhanced significantly, and perhaps fundamentally altered, by relocating his work in its original bibliographical and socio-historical environment. Restoring the ties that existed between a text and its context humanises the text at its most fundamental level by reanimating it with the materiality and vibrancy that it formerly possessed and by viewing it as the product of human agency in its interactions with its immediate world. Removing a text from this context, from what Walter Benjamin calls its 'fabric of tradition', dims its 'aura', denudes its 'authority' and undermines its historical testimony.[1] It also conceals knowledge of what Pierre Bourdieu has described as 'the self-evident givens of a situation. These remain unremarked and are therefore unlikely to be mentioned in contemporary accounts, chronicles or memoirs':

> Ignorance of everything which goes to make up the 'mood of the
> age' produces a derealisation of works: stripped of everything
> which attached them to the most concrete debates of their time
> . . . they are impoverished and transformed in the direction of
> intellectualism or an empty humanism.[2]

Bourdieu may overstate his case when he proposes to recapture 'everything' in the 'mood of the age', but it is an endeavour that must be encouraged. If we are interested at all in history, in the relationship between literature and society, and what a text tells us about its author, the past, and its relationship to that past, then we need to know as much as possible about the author's

1

milieu, the pressures and motivations underlying his work and how his work was understood by his contemporaries.

The meanings intended by an author may be written into a text linguistically, but, more often than not, they are encoded bibliographically. Terry Eagleton's time-honoured insight has proved invaluable to scholars decoding textual meaning:

> every text intimates by its very conventions the way it is to be consumed, encodes within itself its own ideology of how, by whom and for whom it was produced. Every text obliquely posits a putative reader, defining its productibility in terms of a certain capacity for consumption.[3]

However, in the case of republications, as opposed to original editions and first publication, the conventions, ideology and intended reader are not the author's but the editor or anthologiser's. Moreover, what makes the context of a text's first publication more significant than the contexts of its republication – even if these republications have authorial sanction – is the fact that it represents a text's original purpose and function, as opposed to the subsequent uses to which it is put through republication by the author and his editors. The comparison that is then facilitated between the original purpose and function of a text and the subsequent uses to which it is put by the author indicates the importance of the text's original context of publication for literary and cultural scholarship. This does not mean that the first publication is the most authoritative for purposes of study, but merely that it is the most interesting for what it can reveal about the author, the influences shaping the text, and the historical circumstances to which it may have been responding.

It is in the context of a text's first publication that original authorial intentions are most objectively recoverable in as much as they are embodied in an author's choice of time, place and manner of publication, each of which represents a conscious decision made with a view to generating meanings most closely approximating those intended. However, authorial intention and a given text are shaped by authorial temperament and ideology as well as by non-authorial factors such as the socio-historical context of publication and the tastes of readers, editors and publishers. It is again in the context surrounding a text's first publication that these non-authorial sources of meaning – what Henry James calls 'the contributive value . . . of the *accessory* facts in a given artistic case'[4] – lie embedded. It is at this site that a text carries in its most visible form the imprint of an author's relationships with his publishers, magazine editors and readers.[5]

By limiting our knowledge of texts to their republication in complete editions or anthologies we obscure 'the primitive terror of a modernist text's highly self-conscious origination' and ignore the 'large implied hinterland of knowledge'[6] that are sources of authority and meaning. This concealment has often impaired and distorted readings of key Yeatsian texts, our perspective on Yeats, and even our understanding of important cultural events. It has led to scholarly inaccuracies, historical anachronisms and false conclusions that have skewed biography (the provenance of Yeats's Parnellism) as well as cultural and political history (the dating of the Revival). Such unawareness has also left unearthed the often tacit, sectarian and political assumptions and motivations of his work, facilitating thereby a sanitised and 'international' reading of Yeats as 'the last Romantic'. It has prevented a realisation of how volume publication of texts originally published separately is often, especially with Yeats, a way of controlling meaning, either by creating new meanings or by silencing older ones. To show these processes at work, and as an example of what this book sets out to demonstrate, I begin by focusing on 'September 1913' and on institutionalised readings of that poem. The following chapters relocate Yeats's work of the 1880s and '90s from the collected editions and anthologies, in which they are now read, to the periodicals and newspapers in which they were first published. They examine his engagement with Irish, British and American periodicals and editors, and study the cultural, political and bibliographical contexts in which his work was published and received. They demonstrate the impact of this environment on the composition and reception of his work and on the origin and nature of the Irish Literary Revival. Finally, they highlight how the pressures of the marketplace influenced the course and character of the Revival as well as Yeats's literary and political responses by forcing him to modulate and modify his work to accommodate the often antagonistic attitudes of his editors and readers. That almost all of Yeats's work till the turn of the century, and much of the literary output of the Revival, were first published in periodicals makes it imperative for Yeatsians and Irish cultural historians to take cognisance of this context.

This project derived its impetus not from bibliographical theory but from a personal experience. I first read and studied Yeats in a Pan edition of his selected poetry edited by A. Norman Jeffares. Except that Ireland was once a British colony struggling for independence, I knew little of Irish history. Even so, 'September 1913', an overtly political poem, stirred my imagination. Mediated through my own colonial heritage, the words struck a chord. The roll-call of martyrs, the greasy till, the hangman's rope, Romantic Ireland, O'Leary's grave – dominated my understanding of the poem. Here was a man of letters attempting to revive the revolutionary patriotism of a bygone age by rebuking his countrymen for their mundane middle-class aspirations and exhorting them to emulate their heroic ancestors by taking up arms against their oppressors. This reading, institutionalised by eminent Yeatsians, is widespread among both scholars and students.[7]

During my M.Phil. research on Yeats, I accidentally discovered that the original title of 'September 1913' was 'Romance in Ireland / (On reading much of the correspondence against the Art Gallery)'. Yeats was now seen as hectoring Irishmen for opposing Hugh Lane's proposed art gallery. 'The romantic entity buried with O'Leary', Malcolm Brown claimed, 'was thus not primarily his militance, but his taste; and O'Leary's revolutionary name was invoked not to impel Irishmen to shoulder arms rather than live as "slaves that were spat on", but to enforce another demand altogether, very remotely connected – that is, to compel the Dublin Corporation to build Sir Hugh Lane his art gallery astride the Liffey'.[8] This view sat uneasily beside my first impression. I could not accept that 'September 1913' expressed a bitterness generated solely by the gallery controversy. What had an art gallery to do with a hangman's rope, or Impressionist paintings with O'Leary's grave? Would 'that delirium of the brave' loosen people's purse strings for a collection of pictures they cared little about? Why invoke images of revolutionary nationalism and martyrdom to chastise boorishness and philistinism? Surely, to be a patriot or a martyr it isn't necessary to know the difference between Manet and Monet? Had Yeats really lost his balance, as George Moore's contemporary tongue-in-cheek account would have one believe?[9] Though I was unconvinced, I decided to let it lie. But the matter would not rest there, and a few days later I discovered in Wade's *Bibliography*[10] that the poem was first published in the *Irish Times* (*IT*), Ireland's unionist and most conservative daily newspaper.[11] My bewilderment was now complete, for even my first reading, which I had clung to desperately, seemed hopelessly wrong. Why would the editor of this pro-establishment, unionist newspaper, representing upper-class Protestant views, publish a poem advocating armed rebellion?

And that too in 1913, when many Protestants were cleaning their gun barrels and stockpiling their armoury in readiness to defend the Union.[12] By 1910 the gulf between unionists and nationalists, and by general implication between Protestants and Catholics, had widened considerably. Irish nationalism had become increasingly sectarian and Protestants were denied any authentic claim on Irishness.[13] Their unionism had been radicalised by the constitutional crisis of 1909–11 which had culminated in the removal of the Lords' veto. On 16 January 1913, the Home Rule Bill had passed its third reading in the Commons; on 30 January, it was rejected by an emasculated House of Lords. The next day saw the founding of the Ulster Volunteer Force, an armed militia whose *raison d'être* would be to defend the Union. Even the Conservative party, traditionally the party of law and order, advocated armed resistance as a last resort.[14] Southern Protestants were not far behind in opposing a measure that threatened them far more than it did their northern counterparts. A smaller and more scattered group, they could not organise themselves militarily but, for that very reason, were even more intractable and determined in their opposition. Their influence was vastly disproportionate to their numbers, comprising as they did 86 out of the 104 peers in the House of Lords who had Irish interests, and representing 18 British constituencies in addition to two Irish ones in the House of Commons.[15] Most of them, if not all, would have read the *Irish Times*, which, as the organ of Conservative Protestant opinion, had relentlessly attacked the Home Rule Bill, championed the call for a general election or referendum before the Bill took effect in 1914 and, in the very same issue that it published 'Romance in Ireland', had asserted that for Irish unionists the British connection was 'a matter of life and death'. (Other articles in that issue discussed the possibility of the sovereign exercising his prerogative to veto the Bill or to dissolve parliament.)[16] The unionists' very identity, not to mention security, depended on the maintenance of the Union which, according to a noteworthy body of critical opinion, Yeats's poem demanded be severed, and that too violently, if necessary. Wade's *Bibliography* had called all in doubt.

This book, investigating the original contexts of Yeats's early work, has its genesis in that doubt. Bewildering though it was, that detail about the place of the poem's first publication gradually illuminated long-obscured niches and cast an entirely different light on the poem's meaning. After completing the M.Phil., I set off to exorcise an old ghost. I returned to the library and looked up references to that poem in Yeats criticism. I found that almost without exception scholars' understanding of the poem suffered from two deficiencies: their readings depended on a severely limited and even warped account of O'Leary, and their readings had ignored the poem's bibliographical and socio-historical context. Contrary to popular understanding, O'Leary was not the respected, left-wing, anti-establishment Irish nationalist of the physical force tradition. Furthermore, critics had seemed unaware of the changes in the Yeats–O'Leary relationship. Yeats had a long association with O'Leary and their relationship was more complex and less cosy than has been generally understood. For example, in spite of his highly nuanced psychological understanding of Yeats, Ellmann presents the relationship as static and unchanging. He assumes that Yeats's early allegiance to O'Leary remained intact throughout. Hence, Yeats's absence at O'Leary's funeral – in Ireland, a noteworthy gesture – even though he was in the country at that time, is not even mentioned, let alone explained. Jeffares in his commentary on 'September 1913' characteristically explains Yeats's absence by drawing on Yeats's own explanation from *Essays and Introductions*:[17]

in the grave: Yeats could not bring himself to go to O'Leary's funeral, for he shrank from seeing about his grave 'so many whose Nationalism was different from anything he had taught or that I could share'.[18]

Such uncritical acceptance of Yeats's retrospective explanations for past actions has been summarily dispensed with by recent revisionist inquiry. In his biography, Roy Foster rejects Yeats's explanation and attributes his absence to a loosening of ties after a falling out over the '98 centenary organisations and O'Leary's subsequent backing of MacBride against Maud Gonne in the divorce proceedings.[19] However, gaps remain which can only be filled by relocating an author in his original bibliographical and socio-historical contexts. In this case, it is likely that the Yeats–O'Leary friendship had begun to cool off much earlier than Foster surmises.

In 1892, the *United Ireland* printed an article, 'Irish Nationalists and the Trinity College Tercentenary' (16.4.92, 5), attacking 'this mother of bigotry and foster-mother of apostasy' for having perpetuated anglicisation and unionism. In the next issue, O'Leary defended his *alma mater*, thereby provoking an attack on TCD and on himself.[20] Yeats's sole contribution to this debate was a cleverly balanced mention of TCD in a letter that could be read either way.[21] The discussion and the attacks on O'Leary continued for three months, until 23 July, bringing the total coverage of this matter to 113 column inches. In the next issue (30.7.92), Yeats launched a broadside against TCD, reiterating the arguments against O'Leary's position and introducing some of his own. Trinity is 'but an aspect of the great god, Dagon of the Philistines', and lives 'in abject fear of the National enthusiasm which is at her gates'.[22] Given the background of the O'Leary controversy, Yeats's article was not merely an attack on TCD. The younger Yeats was severely critical of the college for its initial indifference and subsequent hostility to the literary movement. Though O'Leary was Yeats's mentor and felt strongly about his college, this in itself would not have hindered Yeats from expressing his views in print. He had attacked TCD for its West-Britonism and servility to English notions in one of his earliest published articles in the *Dublin University Review*, to which O'Leary was a fellow contributor and closely associated with the management. However, in the case of the *United Ireland*, things were very different. This advanced nationalist weekly had severely criticised and mocked O'Leary almost immediately after his return to Ireland and regularly thereafter. The following excerpts are representative:

> The Irish public are a little weary of Mr O'Leary's querulous complaints as an *homme incompris*. So far as we are aware, the only ground he himself has for complaining of want of toleration is

that he possibly considers the good-humoured toleration for years invariably extended to his opinions on men and things savours of neglect. His idea of toleration is for everybody except the unhappy wretches who may happen to be for the moment doing any practical service in the Irish cause. (23.6.88, 4)

The posturing and posing, the pretensions and the patronising airs of Mr O'Leary in National politics, during the past twenty years, have been fruitful subjects of mirthful comment to those who have had most opportunities of witnessing his peacock-like self admiration. Without a single act of real service to any National, social, literary, or educational interest to his credit (beyond the questionable merits of his *Irish People* editorials), except a comparatively short term of imprisonment this gentleman has for years assumed the *rôle* of censor-in-chief upon every man and movement associated with Irish National or literary affairs! Truly, a most amusing personality in Irish contemporary life and politics is the unequalled 'scholar' and 'gentleman', the 'Blade' O'Leary. (Letter by Michael Davitt, *UI*, 15.9.94, 5)[23]

O'Leary had provoked these attacks by his tactless animadversions on the Land League and the Irish Parliamentary Party, attacks that had been eagerly endorsed by the unionist media.[24] His views on TCD were of a piece with his other 'Protestant' views and provided *United Ireland* with yet another opportunity of ridiculing him publicly. Because O'Leary had been prominently associated with one side of the debate and had been attacked personally because of this – the whole discussion had been carried out under the headline 'John O'Leary and the Trinity Tercentenary' – criticism of TCD also indirectly involved criticism of O'Leary. Yeats must have realised this. He would have also realised that by keeping silent he could save O'Leary the further humiliation of being attacked by his protégé in the very newspaper where he was regularly pilloried. Yeats could have held back out of concern for the old man's dignity but chose not to. During the late-'80s and early-'90s, as we shall see in Chapter 2, Yeats was ingratiating himself with the *United Ireland*, Ireland's most popular and influential nationalist newspaper. He was also establishing his nationalist credentials within this forum of advanced nationalism. His connection with O'Leary, therefore, would have been embarrassing at the very least. The TCD debate was an opportunity to assert his own advanced nationalism and to dissociate himself from the reactionary and conservative views of his erstwhile mentor. His vociferous and unambiguous attack on TCD would have achieved just that. None of this is documented in any of the existing editions of Yeats's prose. Moreover, the editor's critical headnote to 'Dublin Scholasticism and Trinity College' in *UP1* neither mentions the debate that Yeats's article was responding to nor explains the significance of its place of publication. As with most readings of 'September 1913', this annotation assumes that the article, without any explanation of the environment from which it is extracted, contains its own meaning which stands independent of historical and bibliographical contexts.

The second factor distorting most critics' understanding of O'Leary (and through him of 'September 1913') is that they see him as Yeats presented him in *Reveries over Childhood and Youth* – written in 1916 about the period 1885–87 – where Yeats, after the Easter Rising, is rehabilitating himself as a romantic nationalist of the school of John O'Leary. Illuminating a Yeatsian utterance of one period with a Yeatsian utterance of another can on occasion be useful. However, it does have its pitfalls and therefore caution should be exercised by contextualising both utterances. Jeffares in his various editions of Yeats's poetry has this to offer on the O'Leary reference in 'September 1913':

> *O'Leary*: John O'Leary (1830–1907), influenced by the Young Ireland movement, became identified with the Fenian movement which succeeded it. Arrested in 1865, he was condemned to 20 years' penal servitude but released after four years on condition that he kept out of Ireland for 15 years. He lived in Paris, returning to Dublin in 1885; he lent Yeats books by Irish authors and translations of Irish literature, influencing his moving from his father's Home Rule views to more nationalist attitudes. Yeats saw him as belonging to a tradition of older nationalism, that of Henry Grattan (1746–1820), based on the reading of Homer and Virgil, and that of Thomas Davis (1814–45), influenced by the idealism of the Italian idealist and patriot Giuseppe Mazzini (1805–72).[25]

In his *Commentary*, Jeffares supports his annotation by quoting from *Autobiographies* (95–6)

> Sometimes he would say things that would have sounded well in some heroic Elizabethan play. It became my delight to rouse him to these outbursts, for I was the poet in the presence of his theme. Once . . . he said, 'There are things that a man must not do to save a nation.' He would speak a sentence like that in ignorance of its passionate value, and would forget it the moment after.[26]

It is only natural therefore that, in his biography of Yeats, Jeffares should see 'September 1913' as a product of

> the association of memories which John O'Leary's nationalism would call up in Yeats, the loftiness of the old man's ideals and the settings of his speeches where 'sometimes he would say things that would have sounded well in some heroic Elizabethan play'.[27]

T. R. Henn and John Unterecker have similarly based their interpretations of the poem on O'Leary and read it as a nationalist cry to arms.[28] Consequently, the question that sparked off my inquiry destabilises theirs: would John Edward Healy, the editor of the *Irish Times* – a Conservative, pro-establishment, unionist newspaper – publish a poem exhorting his readers to sever the Union? The answer, surely, is no, for it would have been journalistic suicide to do so. Besides, he himself was wholeheartedly committed to defending the Union and was a member of the unionist establishment that was most threatened by Home Rule. Even after Irish independence, he remained staunchly unionist, much to the irritation of the new dispensation. During his editorship (which lasted till 1934) all 'foreign' words were italicised, even 'Dáil'.[29] That he did publish 'Romance in Ireland' indicates that he did not read it as a nationalist cry to arms and that he knew his readers would not either. And surely, Yeats too, by choosing to publish the poem in a unionist newspaper, could not have intended, or expected, it to be read as a nationalist cry to arms. As we all know, and as McGann and others have demonstrated, an article published in two very different newspapers will be read in very different ways because the newspapers are coded 'visually and materially' for different audiences and different purposes, and cater to 'very different reading expectations and procedures'. Newspapers cultivate a consistent readership by taking up a consistent position on issues with which their readers can sympathise. Readers approach the contents of their newspaper of choice already attuned to that newspaper's biases, perspectives and political programmes. This starting-point, as Peter Rabinowitz argues, 'significantly influences the ways in which they interpret (and consequently evaluate) texts . . . what readers do both while they read and after they finish reading . . . are already limited by decisions made before the book is ever begun'. This is not to say that readers' perspectives are one-dimensional or immune to subversion and free play. Periodicals, as Margaret Beetham points out, offer

> their readers scope to construct their own version of the text by selective reading, but against that flexibility has to be put the tendency in the form to close off alternative readings by creating a

> dominant position from which to read, a position which is main-
> tained with more or less consistency across the single number and
> between numbers.

She goes on to add that, despite this availability of alternative readings, 'for
many – perhaps most – readers the desire to be confirmed in the generally
accepted or dominant discourse may be more powerful than the dream of a
different future or the fantasy of alternatives'.[30]

One does not have to be an expert in bibliography or publishing practices to understand this, though Yeats certainly knew enough about both.
Moreover, he also knew the importance of targeting a readership that was
likely to receive his work favourably and in the manner he wished it to be
received. After the commercial failure of *Poems and Ballads of Young Ireland*
(1888), when he edited another Irish verse anthology he knew precisely
where his readers lay and the best way to seek them out. In the 'Introduction', he specified that

> This book differs also from some of its kind, in being intended
> only a little for English readers, and not at all for Irish peasants,
> but almost wholly for the small beginning of that educated and
> national public, which is our greatest need and perhaps our
> vainest hope.[31]

For thus wearing his nationalism on his sleeve, he was rewarded with a
two-and-a-half column puff on the cover page of *United Ireland*.[32] His awareness of the importance of a clearly defined readership is evident also in his
remarks on the failure of the quarterly *Shanachie*: 'I don't believe it is possible to make a good magazine without making up your mind who it is for
whom you are making it and keeping to that idea throughout.'[33] One can
therefore easily accept McGann's claim, at least with regard to Yeats and the
Irish context – where social, political and religious divisions ensured demar-
cated readerships – that 'a great many writers, and all poets, appreciate the
symbolic and signifying dimensions of the physical medium through which
(or rather as which) the linguistic text is embodied'.[34] Students and scholars
reading 'September 1913' in an anthology or an edition of Yeats's poetry are
usually clueless about the expectations and predispositions with which the
poem would have been read when it was first published, expectations and
predispositions that Yeats was well aware of and sanctioned in the act of
choosing one out of a number of possible publishing venues. While analysing
intentions, Shillingsburg astutely distinguishes between the intention to
mean and the intention to do. He quite rightly observes that the latter is
more plausibly recoverable than the former, and 'provide[s] some firm
ground' for those involved in trying to 'construct or reconstruct meaning'.

Even Jerome McGann, a proponent of the historical/materialist view who resists the intentionalist's approach to literary studies, concedes that

> [t]he expressed intentions, or purposes, of an author are also signif-
> icant for understanding a poem. At the point of origin those inten-
> tions are codified in the author's choice of time, place and form of
> publication – or none of the above, by which I mean his decision
> *not* to publish at all, or to circulate in MS, or to print privately.[35]

Though I may not know what Yeats intended 'September 1913' to mean, I do know that he intended to publish it in the *Irish Times*. Using that fact and information that was available to him about what publication in that forum entailed, I can deduce that he knew that the poem would be received in a certain way. That he chose to publish it there and not elsewhere where he knew it would be received differently indicates that he preferred the meanings generated by one context to those generated by another.

All the Yeats scholars cited earlier have made invaluable contributions to our understanding and their views therefore command respect. However, by ignoring the poem's bibliographical and socio-historical context, its unique existence at the time and place for which it was produced and which to some extent produced it, they have ignored the very basis of its uniqueness and significance: its historical testimony, and what Walter Benjamin calls its 'original use value'. In such cases, Benjamin argues, 'what is really jeopardised when the historical testimony is affected is the authority of the object'. The quantitative shift brought about by extracting a work of art from its 'fabric of tradition' results in 'a qualitative transformation of its nature'.[36] With 'September 1913' this has led to a radically flawed understanding of the poem. Daniel Albright's annotation on O'Leary, for example, follows Yeats's portrayal in the *Autobiographies*, and quoting from it at length, describes him as an Irish revolutionary, 'imprisoned for years, whom Yeats admired deeply'.[37] This is meant to inform readers of O'Leary's role in the poem and guide their responses to it. By remaining silent on the poem's social and historical context, Albright's gloss achieves a consistency and inner coherence that passes a superficial muster. Since it does not mention where and for whom the poem was first published, the incompatibility of the O'Leary annotation with the political ideology of the poem's original readership goes unnoticed.

In annotating the O'Leary reference, Albright, Jeffares and others should also have clarified, and perhaps stressed, that he was a non-practising Catholic, an opponent of the Land League and the Irish Parliamentary Party, and a constitutional monarchist opposed to republican democracy and adult franchise in Ireland. His brother describes him as 'quite an Englishman and

. . . a conservative in politics'. Hyde claimed that he 'never came across so complete a Tory as O Laoghaire', and Michael Davitt described him in the *United Ireland* as 'a social Shoneen' (15.9.94, 5). Seen by his fellow Fenians as a 'fossil' and an 'old crank full of whine and honesty',[38] O'Leary was relentlessly attacked and ridiculed in the nationalist press. There were good reasons for this. His political philosophy – 'there are things that a man must not do to save a Nation' (*Auto*, 96) – was derived from the romantic idealism of Young Ireland, 'a movement at its weakest in action', and from William Smith O'Brien's 'cabbage patch' revolution.[39] His aristocratic, high-principled conception of patriotism was hopelessly out of touch with *realpolitik*. It was also too genteel, gallant and ineffectual to have any chance of success. Or, for that matter, of being put to the test. Having shunned boycotting, agrarian violence and acts of terrorism, O'Leary could occupy the moral high ground without ever risking life or limb for the national cause. Though a Fenian, he posed no threat to the unionists. And for the nationalists, he was a liability. This is how J. M. Hone, then a writer for the *Irish Times*, described him in a book published before the Rising in 1915–6:

> He did not, after the failure of the Fenian movement, again take any active part in revolutionary effort; nor did he interest himself, except as a moral critic, in the Home Rule and agrarian agitation of the 'eighties and 'nineties. In this respect he differed from old comrades, like O'Donovan Rossa and John Devoy, who composed with the Irish-Americans an extreme left wing of the Parnellite movement, and kept the powder for the Land Leaguers dry . . . In his old age, at least, O'Leary was a confessed visionary, a transcendentalist, in his politics . . . To O'Leary the methods of the Land League were as immoral as dynamite . . . [40]

O'Leary's public denunciations of the Land League, agrarian agitation and parliamentary politics – the most effective and popular forms of protest against British rule – are characteristic of Castle Catholics or Protestant landlords. In fact, O'Leary was a landlord with substantial holdings in Tipperary and, like other landlords, had seen his rentier income drastically reduced through boycotts. He was in many ways an honorary Protestant and, not surprisingly, Yeats, in 1907, saw him as belonging to 'the generation of Grattan' (*E&I*, 246) and the genteel Protestant culture which had read Homer and Virgil. Ironically enough, O'Leary's 'Protestant' Tory views, from which Yeats dissociated himself in the 1892 TCD debate while siding with the advanced nationalists, had become more congenial to Yeats in 1913, when he had begun asserting his own 'Ascendancy' heritage. It is therefore O'Leary's Conservative, élitist, anti-democratic and anti-Land League attitudes that would have wedded him to the poem's context and struck a sympathetic chord with *Irish Times* readers, many of whom were themselves landlords with similar views. Keeping in mind the obvious fact that 'September 1913' was written by Yeats in 1913 (as opposed to the 1880s) for a southern Protestant unionist reader-ship, it is this aspect of O'Leary, not his Fenian past, which needs to be stressed. A misplaced emphasis on O'Leary's Fenianism, which after 1874 was mostly of the armchair variety, is not only anachronistic, but it also conflicts with the poem's purpose and logic in the context of the *Irish Times* and its unionist readership. If O'Leary had been only what critics claim, then the *Irish Times* reader would have seen him as a threat to his property and person rather than as the repository of Irish romance.

Richard Altick has forcefully demonstrated that understanding a text's his-torical context necessitates a focus on what that text meant to its first readers.[41] Yet, though attempting to give a historically informed reading of 'September 1913', most critics have completely ignored the fact that it was published for a southern Protestant unionist audience. This singular omission on their part has resulted in a radically flawed understanding of the poem. It has led to readings that have politicised the poem on the wrong side. Such readings have also, often naïvely and uncritically, facilitated Yeats's portrayal of himself as a romantic nationalist of the school of John O'Leary, and thereby institutionalised the 'internationalist' reading of Yeats as the last romantic so prevalent in American academia. The poem is not a nationalist cry to arms, nor is it, as Elizabeth Cullingford would have it, Yeats's 'satiric attack on modern cowardice' and a lament for the passing of 'the old romantic Nationalism' and with it 'the possi-bility of armed insurrection'.[42] It is, rather, an affirmation of Protestant superi-ority, Protestant patriotism and Protestant nationality (as opposed to nationalism), as well as a bitter denunciation of the Catholic middle classes.

The poem's original title, 'Romance in Ireland / (On reading much of the correspondence against the Art Gallery)', gives some hint of this. Yeats's views on Irish history illustrate what 'Romance in Ireland' meant to him. His essay, 'A Reckless Century', though published for a Parnellite readership in 1891 (and therefore given an appropriate slant, as I shall demonstrate subsequently), is an early association of 'Romantic Ireland' with the Protestant Ascendancy of the eighteenth century.[43] This association became stronger with time. It was 'Ireland's better self'.[44] It was also 'the one Irish century that escaped from darkness and confusion', and the source of 'everything great in Ireland and in our character, in what remains of our architecture'.[45] Grattan's parliament, an almost entirely Protestant affair, was the high point not only of this period but 'of the whole history of Ireland for the last seven hundred years . . . [the] one epoch that we look upon with entire joy and pride'.[46] 'Had they under-stood the people and the game a little better', Yeats regretted in 1904, they 'might have created an aristocracy in an age that had lost the meaning of the word' (*Ex*, 27–8). Instead came

> the Great Demagogue [Daniel O'Connell] . . . and turned the old house of the noble into 'the house of the Poor, the lonely house, the accursed house of Cromwell'. He came, another Cairbry Cat-Head, with that great rabble who had overthrown the pageantry of Church and Court . . . and the old individual, poetical life went down, as it seems, for ever. (*E&I*, 375–6)

O'Connell also brought Catholic emancipation, eroding the Protestant stranglehold on commerce, politics and society. Catholics, who 'had been without influence in the generation of Grattan, and almost without it in that of Davis' (*E&I*, 250), now gradually gained influence. By September 1913 their social, political and economic standing more accurately reflected their numerical majority.

Yeats attributed the degeneration in Irish public life and the retardation of Irish civilisation to the rise of the Catholic middle classes, the 'badness of Catholic education' and the decline of the Protestant Ascendancy:

> The whole system of Irish Catholicism pulls down the able and well-born if it pulls up the peasant, as I think it does. A long continuity of culture like that at Coole could not have arisen, and never has arisen, in a single Catholic family in Ireland since the middle ages.[47]

For Yeats, this demoralisation and degeneration could only be remedied by the influence of the cultivated classes, by gestures such as Hugh Lane's, and here we come to the significance of the original subtitle of 'September 1913': 'On reading much of the correspondence against the Art Gallery'. For Yeats, the magnanimity of 'The people of Burke and of Grattan / That gave, though free to refuse' ('The Tower,' *VP*, 414) typified the eighteenth-century Protestant spirit and differentiated it from its Catholic counterpart.[48] He wrote and published 'The Gift' in the *Irish Times* to remind Protestants of their caste responsibilities, of noblesse oblige, and to urge them to exercise their prerogative of choice by supporting the gallery. While 'Paudeens play at pitch and toss', he told his unionist readers:

> Look up in the sun's eye and give . . .
> That some new day may breed the best
> Because you gave, not what they would,
> But the right twigs for an eagle's nest!
>   ('To a Wealthy Man', *VP*, 288)[49]

Wishing to highlight 'the possible slightness of "Paudeen's" (little Patrick) desire for any kind of art',[50] Yeats, in the same issue, also arranged for the publication on page 6 of an editorial ('Art and Aristocracy') 'elaborating the thought in the poem'. He had 'suggested very vaguely' the outline of this editorial in his interview with the journalist Joseph Hone.[51] The poem was printed on page 7 alongside the following articles: 'From *The Times* of Today: The Unionist Memorial', 'Conference of London', 'Uniting the Unionists', 'Derry Election', 'Against Home Rule: Women's Demonstration in Dublin', 'A German in Ulster: Covenant Day: The Fighting Spirit', 'Consecrated Meanness.'[52]

Immediately preceding the Hone article in the same column was another editorial on a gathering of 'Unionist Women' held in Dublin the previous evening. It began by calling 'attention to the Home Rule Bill's crudities and absurdities' and denouncing its '"safeguards" for minorities' as 'illusory and worthless'. It urged unionists to do their utmost in pressing for a general election before the operation of the Bill and closing ranks 'for the last stages of the struggle.' 'To work for these ends is the present duty of every Irish Unionist.' The determination of southern unionists was equal to their Ulster counterparts and meetings such as the previous evening's 'remind the Government that in the capital of Ireland, as in every part of the four provinces, unionism is a living force, and a force which cannot be ignored . . . And they remind the British electorate of its duty to the minority in Ireland.'

Hone's 'Art and Aristocracy' adopted another approach towards reinforcing Irish unionism. '[T]he point [of "The Gift"] is clear enough. There is no use in being angry with "the people". We are asked to clear our minds of democratic cant. Mr Yeats's poem lifts the discussion out of the region of sentimentality.' The article contrasted the commonness of the present with the grandeur of the past:

> It is *apropos* to note the report that the Nationalist Party, with due regard for economy, is content to see an Irish Parliament housed in any brand new building suitable 'for all practical purposes.' Our upper classes never were content to associate such house-wifely economies with the far different political ideals of their breed.

Hone interpreted the poem as claiming that, should Dublin forfeit the pictures, 'the gentlemen of Ireland will have lost another opportunity'. It pointed out that, unlike 'Nationalist preachers [who] have delivered themselves *ad nauseam* upon the Irish duties of the Unionist upper class', Yeats's poem 'is really the most subtle of compliments':

> Ercole d'Este, Duke Guidobaldo, Cosimo de Medici, the greatest patrons of the liberal arts the world has known, were more than patrons of the liberal arts. They illustrate for all time an attitude

which must be that of aristocracy if the word has any meaning. *Deprived temporarily of his political power*, Cosimo did not grow embittered, or forget that it was still his prerogative to patronise Michelozzo. *Who can say that Mr Yeats's analogy is impertinent to Ireland today?* (Emphasis added)

The issue, however, as the article averred, is not merely *noblesse oblige*, but strengthening southern Irish unionism.

Irish Unionism, at least south of the Boyne, derives its main strength from the upper classes. Our upper classes have lost a part of their former reputation for taste in learning and books and a delight in the arts, and who knows but that Unionism has suffered thereby.

The argument, urging Protestants to assert their cultural superiority and thereby their superior worth, is underpinned by an Arnoldian logic whereby power lost through the democratic process can be regained through the back door of culture: southern unionism draws its strength from the upper classes; the upper classes draw their strength from their hold on culture; because unionists have relinquished that cultural hold, their political strength has diminished. However, 'they have, one is quite certain, still their chance'. The models suggested are the Protestants of the eighteenth century. 'They, as Mr Yeats has said elsewhere, "had they known the people and the game a little better, might have created an aristocracy in an age that has lost the understanding of the word".'

William Martin Murphy understood the game but played it by different rules. In 1885, he had successfully contested the St Patrick's Division of Dublin on a nationalist ticket, but lost his seat to the Parnellites in 1892. An industrialist and newspaper tycoon and one of the most successful businessman of his time, he was described by Hone as 'a man of distinguished character and appearance, to whose energy in industrial enterprise Dublin was under considerable debt'.[53] Murphy also had close links with the Sullivan family and was the financial head of a triumvirate representing the nexus between finance, the Catholic clergy and politics (Tim Healy) that had scurrilously attacked Parnell. Yeats too had recently been attacked by the same nexus and, in another poem written the same month addressing Parnell's 'Shade', he would refer to Murphy as 'Your enemy, an old foul mouth' (*VP*, 292). Murphy's *Irish Daily Independent* had described an Abbey production of St John Ervine's *The Magnanimous Lover* as 'too foul for dramatic criticism' and more becoming 'a sanitary inspector' (18.10.1912, 6). Following this, an editorial in the *Cork Examiner* (9.1.1913, 4) demanded the institution of a Board of Censors, appointed by the Maynooth Union, the Catholic Truth Society or the Senate of the National University, to oversee dramatic productions.

Not surprisingly, Yeats regarded Murphy as one of O'Connell's heirs: Catholic, ill-mannered and philistine. Though not closely associated with the Land League, as Conor Cruise O'Brien astutely points out, Murphy, through his alliance with the clergy and 'the sullivan gang' (*CL1*, 242), was perceived by Yeats and other Protestants as a representative beneficiary of 'the boycott in its wide variety of forms, as an instrument for the transfer of economic power out of their [Protestant] hands into those of the more astute, energetic and rapacious of the conquered caste, now beginning to form a "new middle-class" '.[54] Its newly acquired social, political and economic strength rendered it particularly repulsive, especially because, as Yeats saw it, it ignored its debt to Protestant Ireland and refused to be led by its betters in literature (Synge), the arts (Lane) and politics (Parnell). He claimed that, in 'the thirty years or so during which I have been reading Irish newspapers, three [the Synge, Lane and Parnell] public controversies have stirred my imagination' (*VP*, 818). Their common feature was the denunciation of a Protestant by the 'new middle class' highlighting 'how base at moments of excitement are minds without culture' (*VP*, 819). In *Autobiographies* he spoke of Lane's 'Irish ambitions', which 'led to his scattering many thousands, and gathering much ingratitude'.[55] In each of the three controversies, Murphy had played a prominent part. He denounced the whole gallery scheme as humbug, an 'exotic fashion', an 'aesthetic craze' (*VP*, 819–20), and in a letter to the *Irish Times* had attacked Lane for demanding an '*ante-mortem* monument': 'generally speaking, benefactors have to depend on posterity for the erection of public monuments to their memory.' While claiming apropos of the pictures that he did not think 'the game to be worth the candle', he took this opportunity of also attacking Yeats's 'contemptuously poeticised' reference to 'Paudeen's Pennies' (*IT*, 18.1.1913, 8). Murphy's response to 'The Gift' represented the anger felt by the Catholic nationalist community at the poem's unabashed élitism and contempt.[56] 'Romance in Ireland' was Yeats's response to what he called this 'Paudeen's point of view' (*VP*, 820).[57] As we shall see, in composing the poem Yeats used Murphy's reference to the candle, harnessed it to its religious connotations to attack middle-class Catholics, and eventually arrived at the image of a 'greasy till'.

Neither was there any love lost between Murphy and the *Irish Times*. Religious and ideological differences apart – in the *Newspaper Gazetteer* (1880), the paper described itself as 'the Protestant and Conservative daily' – the *Irish Times* had enough incentive to endorse an attack on Murphy, especially one emanating from the Protestant quarter. Shortly after its rebirth in 1859, the *Irish Times* became the upper-class paper.[58] It was also Ireland's largest selling newspaper.[59] After 1875, due to increased literacy and interest in the national movement, the *Freeman's Journal* exceeded its circulation.[60] In 1892, the anti-Parnellite *National Press*, co-owned by Murphy, merged with the *Freeman's Journal*. In 1904, at John Redmond's request, he bought over the ailing Parnellite *Irish Independent*. Merged with the *Daily Nation* and renamed the *Irish Daily Independent*, Murphy's new paper was launched as Ireland's first halfpenny daily. At the time of the merger both newspapers were in the red, and it is a tribute to Murphy's considerable skill, acumen and gusto that his new paper soon caught up with the *Irish Times*'s circulation. Its first issue sold 50,000 copies, and by February 1905 its sales averaged 25,000. By 1910, it had exceeded the *Irish Times*'s circulation by 12,000 (45,000 to 33,000) and for the year ending 1913 it was 22,000 ahead. Murphy imported practices pioneered by Northcliff's *Daily Mail*: lavish illustrations, larger and fancier types and borders, shorter and livelier news items, greater spacing, targeting of female readers, introduction of competitions. He also introduced, by all contemporary accounts, a more humane system of newspaper distribution. 'Shoppers' were used to liaise between the paper and the newsboys. Until then, newsboys, often unshod and in tattered clothes, accepted any kind of employment to keep starvation at bay. Murphy's scheme gave them a secure livelihood and was an immediate success. When he died, he left instructions and blueprints ensuring that his new headquarters were designed to facilitate the health and comfort of his employees. He was described as a man of progressive ideas and humanitarian sentiment whose interests were not restricted to filling his coffers.

Despite the *Irish Daily Independent*'s greater circulation, the *Irish Times*, because of its wealthier clientele, remained Ireland's pre-eminent advertising medium. In 1914, its ratio of advertisement rate per 1,000 readers was 2.1d; the *Irish Daily Independent*'s ratio was 1.1d (the same as the *Freeman's Journal*'s in 1887). Nevertheless, its profits were being gradually eroded after Murphy's consolidation of the *Freeman's Journal* and the *National Press*, and more so after the advent of the *Irish Daily Independent*. In 1890 the *Irish Times*'s profits were £37,882; in 1905, the year after Murphy launched the *Irish Daily Independent*, they were £29,466; in 1910 they had recovered to £33,089, they fell slightly in 1913 to £32,920, and more perceptibly in the year ending 1914 to £30,995, largely on account of the strike and the lock-out. As in the social and political world generally, in the newspaper world too the Catholic parvenu was threatening established interests. It is not unreasonable to suppose that Murphy did come up in the conversation Yeats had with Healy over dinner in May 1913.[61] Neither is it purely fortuitous that, immediately below Murphy's letter, the *Irish Times* placed an article entitled 'Foot and Mouth Disease: Resolution by Irish Pig Traders Association'.

Between January and August 1913, while Yeats was toying with the idea of the poem and composing it,[62] he had been regularly denouncing Catholic intolerance and their marginalisation of Protestants, and was being attacked in turn, either directly or through the Abbey productions, by the Catholic press. In a speech delivered on 23.1.1913, to an audience 'entirely Protestant', he announced that they 'were asking nothing but an arena in which the best might come out, and the best might rule' (*IT*, 25.1.1913, 9). A few days later he conveyed to Augusta Gregory an MP's lament that the Home Rule Bill would not include a House of Lords. In other letters to her between January and April 1913, he deprecates Catholic narrow-mindedness and intolerance. He points out that a libel action against a review of *The Magnanimous Lover* (published in Murphy's paper and reprinted in the *Freeman*) would not be successful 'with a Catholic jury'; he reports on the *Cork Examiner* editorial demanding the institution of a Catholic Censor Board to guard against a 'grave national danger'; he claims that 'the dislike of the Gallery can only come from fear of culture which was described by a man called Hacker – who is I believe on the staff of the new University [a predominantly Catholic institution] – as this "enemy of faith and morals" '; he comments on Murphy's letter ('He merely showed himself up by the ill manners of his letters, as my sister says, "*They* always do"' [emphasis added]); he predicts that all 'the Irish orthodoxies – political and religious – are at this moment in fear of dissolvent'; he advocates an uncompromising stand on the latest *Playboy* riots in Chicago ('I should not perhaps be so anxious to free myself from all diplomacies if I had not suffered so much from a series of false positions in the past'); and he confesses that he is fed up with 'diplomatic complications' and is trying 'to free myself from the need of religious diplomacy'.[63] In May, he expresses an always growing 'desire to get away for a time every year from Ireland altogether . . . from all that moves me to criticism . . . My imagination . . . is always the worse for every sight of Dublin'. To Edward Gordon Craig he complains of having to cope with 'a most ignorant press & a priest created terror of culture'. Then in July, by which time his patience is wearing thin and he has already mentioned that he is working on 'Romance in Ireland', he writes to Gregory about a speech made the previous day in favour of the gallery where

> I spoke with him [Lane] quite as much as the possible subscribers
> in my mind. I described Ireland if the present movement failed as
> 'a little huckstering nation groping for halfpence in a greasy till'
> but did not add except in thought 'by the light of a holy candle'.

A letter in August says that he has completed 'a poem about modern Ireland in four verses' but is troubled whether 'the allusion to "the tallow" in the first verse explains itself. I mean those holy candles – it is the result of a passage I had made up for my speech on the Gallery [delivered 15 July 1913] but had to tone down.' Finally, while discussing his plans to publish his poem in the *Irish Times*, he remarks: 'I had not thought I could feel so bitterly over any public event.'[64]

This bitterness, and one particular image ('groping for halfpence in a greasy till') – tempered by the exclusion of 'by the light of a holy candle' – is evident in 'Romance in Ireland', and would have come across to the *Irish Times* readers, for his feelings were shared by many of his caste who would have followed these controversies in the press. Like him, the *Irish Times* too viewed the gallery controversy as a Catholic–Protestant conflict where the former were once again using their democratic strength to dominate the latter. In August ('The Art Gallery Scandal') the paper averred that Murphy's argument, that money should be spent on slum clearance rather than on art, 'deserves no consideration whatsoever':

> Its policy is purely destructive . . . When the small, but noisy, section of opinion which it represents says 'we will not have the bridge site', what it means is 'we will not have the pictures'. Arguments which pretend to be against the bridge site, but are actually against the acceptance of the pictures, are not impressive when they come from quarters which have persistently slighted Sir Hugh Lane's patriotism, questioned his motives, and depreciated the value of his gift . . . We have urged again and again that it would be madness to let this priceless collection go . . . In the manner of that acceptance or rejection is involved our reputation, as a capital city, for civic courtesy, and, we may now say, for civic decency. (*IT*, 12.8.1913, 4)

For Yeats and the *Irish Times*, the opposition's lack of decency and courtesy manifested in their rejection of Lane's offer was a product of ill-breeding and poor education. The *Irish Times*'s attacks on Catholic government and education were similar to Yeats's:

> Except where Sir Horace Plunkett's co-operative organisation has taken root, the rural economy of Ireland is thoroughly unsatisfactory, greed runs riot, the paternal influence of Government Boards does not make for character, a taste for intrigue and conspiracy has been bred into the bone. As to the Nationalist middle classes, their goal is the Government 'post'. Industrial pursuits are tabooed. Every second young man whom the writer saw in Connaught seemed to be employed under the Insurance Act. 'Cramming' for competitive examinations is the end and beginning of education in the Roman Catholic schools. (*IT*, 12.8.1913, 5)

Given the poem's background, its context of publication, and Yeats's own efforts
to make 'the allusion to "tallow" in the first verse explain itself', contemporary
readers would have known that it was only the 'Paudeens' the poem addressed,
not, as Jeffares supposes, 'the people of Ireland' (*Yeats's Poems*, 543). This would
have been clarified by the poem's subtitle, 'On reading much of the correspondence *against* the Art Gallery' (emphasis added), for the opposition came
predominantly from Catholics. An editorial saw Yeats's poem attacking 'those
who have grudged the money and the granting of Sir Hugh Lane's conditions'
(8.9.1913, 6), both of which pointed to the Dublin Municipal Corporation, a
body dominated by the new Catholic middle class. It would have been further
clarified by the portrayal in the first stanza of the commercial–religious nexus
easily identifiable with the same addressee. Nor should we miss a possible allusion to Parnell's relationship with Katharine O'Shea in the accusation, 'You'd
cry, "Some woman's yellow hair / Has maddened every mother's son"', especially since it was the Catholics, led by Murphy and 'the sullivan gang', that had
denounced Parnell, not the Protestants. In attacking Parnell, Tim Healy had
consistently claimed that the latter's actions were dictated by 'the Brighton
Banshee'.[65] In fact, after his fall, he became for Protestants a symbol of yet
another Protestant nobleman done to death by the bigotry and ignorance of
the very classes he had sought to emancipate.

Ascendancy historiography, John Kelly observes, rehabilitated Parnell after
his death as 'a friend of the landlords' 'opposed to land agitation' and as having 'nothing of the revolutionary and little of the radical in him'. Through
sheer 'force of personality and authority of caste' he kept the 'unruly natives
in awe and order' and, as an Anglo-Irishman, he instilled fear and admiration
in patronising English statesmen.[66] A *rapprochement* took place between the
architect of Home Rule and those most threatened by that measure.
'Romance in Ireland' similarly sanitises and rehabilitates Edward FitzGerald,
Robert Emmet and Wolfe Tone – eighteenth-century republican Protestant
revolutionaries who led violent uprisings against the British:

> They have gone about the world like wind.
> But little time had they to pray
> For whom the hangman's rope was spun;
> And what, God help us, could they save? (*VP*, 289)

While Yeats's portrayal emphasises their quintessential 'Protestant' qualities –
passion, recklessness, unworldliness, heroism, leadership and generosity – it is
their ideals and what they stood for – Jacobinism and anti-Protestant hegemony – that are thrown to the wind. It is interesting to compare them with
their Yeatsian prototypes in 'A Reckless Century', an article written for a
nationalist audience in 1891:

> The duellist Whaley going off for a bet to play ball against the
> ramparts of Jerusalem is a nobler sight than the railway king put-
> ting his millions together. Those eighteenth-century duellists, at
> any rate, tried to really live, and not merely exist. They took their
> lives into their hands and went through the world with a song
> upon their lips; and if a curse was mingled with the song they are
> none the less better to think of than had they grown rich and
> much-esteemed, and yet lasted on no more than half alive, toad-
> stools upon the state. (*UP1*, 202)

In both cases, he celebrates aristocratic dash and *joie de vivre*, privileging them
over the middle-class imperatives of pray and save. This was not something
new for Yeats or his readers. A *Daily News* article in 1910 reported him as
lamenting that the 'Ireland of Synge' conspicuously lacked the style and spirit
of the duellist Buck Whaley.[67] The common factor linking those who went
'about the world like wind' and those who went through it 'with a song upon
their lips' is not their political opinions, which are actually antipathetic to
each other. Rather it is their common class background, their Protestantism,
which has bred their *sprezzatura*, their 'boldness in war and sport, carelessness
of cost, the ready meeting of pain and death'. Whether it is Grattan, or Whaley and other eighteenth-century duellists, or nationalists such as FitzGerald,
Tone, Emmet, Parnell and Davis, for Yeats the 'sense of form . . . *of form in
active life*, has always been Protestant in Ireland' (*Mem*, 212–13, emphasis
added). In 'Irish Rakes and Duellists', as well as in 'Romance in Ireland', his
subjects' political opinions are irrelevant. In both cases, they are lionised not
for what they represented or achieved – both of which would have been distasteful to Yeats's immediate audience in each particular case – but for their
Protestant panache.

In the lines from 'Romance in Ireland' quoted above, Yeats reduces the
lives of FitzGerald, Tone and Emmet to the glamour and immediacy of a
fleeting heroic moment whose political import is inconsequential. He elides
the many years they spent in plotting the overthrow of British rule, convincing the French authorities about the feasibility of invading Ireland, and
planning and organising the proposed invasion, the shipment of arms to Ireland and the details of the uprising. By making their ends appear fated, the
poem bypasses the political motivations governing their actions, motivations which would have been antipathetic to Yeats and to his *Irish Times*
readers. It instead emphasises their 'Protestant' qualities – their recklessness,
their generosity and their bravura – contrasting it with the money-
grubbing religiosity of the Catholic middle classes depicted in the first
stanza. By doing so, it makes them 'one of us' and rehabilitates them into
the fold. In point of fact, Edward FitzGerald was a glamorous aristocrat and

romantic adventurer; he served in the British army in America and Canada, made his way through the Canadian forests using just a compass and was formally admitted into the Bear tribe, met Tom Paine in Paris and at a dinner toasted the abolition of all hereditary titles, was cashiered from the army, turned patriot and, with an order out for his arrest, visited his wife twice, once disguised in female attire. Tone, himself a thwarted and frustrated imperialist, had tried enlisting in the East India service after being snubbed over his plans, delivered as a memorial to Pitt's residence, for establishing a British colony in the South Seas. Later, after a second rejection from the Foreign Office and his surrender to and forced deportment by the British, he seriously contemplated settling down permanently first in America as a farmer and then in France as a soldier. Neither went 'about the world like wind'. And further, neither died of the hangman's rope. Tone died of a bungled suicide attempt made after being refused a soldier's death following his capture; and FitzGerald died in a Dublin prison of wounds sustained during his arrest. By suppressing these details, the poem's rhetoric glamorises and transforms them from the desperate Jacobin revolutionaries that they were into objects of Protestant pride and emblematic examples of upper-class Protestant *sprezzatura*, romance, generosity and leadership. Once again, the contrast with the Irish Catholicism portrayed in the first stanza is all too clear.

The next stanza puts this difference into perspective. The poem's mounting rage and indignation culminates in a crescendo of rhetorical questions: 'Was it for this . . .? / For this . . .?/ For this . . .?' Each of these questions points to the picture of contemporary Ireland depicted in the first two stanzas and derides the Catholic middle classes for their apathy, their ingratitude, their amnesia, and above all for their refusal to recognise the value of the Protestants' contribution to Ireland of which they are the unworthy beneficiaries. The opposition that is built up is between a Catholic-dominated present and a Protestant-ruled past.

The view that 'Romance in Ireland' is a Protestant *cri de coeur* and not a nationalist lament is also supported by Yeats's own understanding of the poem, its meaning and its function. As with 'The Gift', he carefully arranged its publication in the *Irish Times*. He knew the editor, John Healy, had dined with him on 10 May, and, when he read the Lord Mayor's statement that 'Lane's gift of pictures would go back to that gentleman' and that 'the matter is at end', he wrote to Hone 'to arrange for publication of my poem in the *Irish Times*'. He also wrote to Augusta Gregory that he 'shall give Hone an interview',[68] which presumably, as with 'The Gift', 'suggested very vaguely' the outlines of the accompanying editorial comment 'elaborating the thought in the poem'. The sectarian, rather than the political, dimension to Yeats's instancing of Emmet, Tone and FitzGerald was remarked upon in this *Irish Times* editorial:

> We are glad to publish a new poem by Mr W. B. Yeats, and not the least so because it deals with a reality of the time. Mr Yeats sees behind the opposition to the Art Gallery project a tendency of mind which he fears may grow on us in Ireland. *Irish Unionists would hardly vindicate the romantic spirit from the historical events to which Mr Yeats refers, but he makes his point quite clear.* He feels that there is danger of our people becoming hardened to the worship of materialism and commercialism . . . We want a prosperous Ireland, but we must not sacrifice to it the sweeter qualities which have formed the character of our people. We have said much already on the subject of the Art Gallery, and we shall not cover the same ground again. But we feel that . . . if the day is lost, the city will deserve the reproach which Mr Yeats makes against those who have grudged the money and the granting of Sir Hugh Lane's conditions. (emphasis added) (8.9.1913, 6)

Yeats's choice of Hone as a *via media* and interpreter of 'The Gift' and 'Romance in Ireland' is in itself indicative of how he wished his poem to be read. An Irish Protestant educated at Wellington and Cambridge, Hone shared many of Yeats's tastes and prejudices, as his obituary in *The Times* (28.3.1959) indicates:

> In many ways a characteristic product of the historic Anglo-Irish tradition and outlook, which he traced through Swift and Berkeley . . . The Irish contemporaries of whom Hone wrote all left their mark on Irish letters, but the new Ireland in no way corresponded to their hopes . . . He was simply an Irish gentleman, who feared the tired and timid simplifications of the recently emancipated.[69]

'September 1913', or 'Romance in Ireland' as it was originally called, far from being a nationalist cry to arms and threatening its Protestant readers in the *Irish Times*, would have validated their sectarian prejudices and flattered their sense of superiority. It denounced the new Catholic middle class that had supplanted them, lamented the lost spirit and authority of Protestant Ascendancy, and contrasted the romance of their heyday with the sordid squalor of the new dispensation. It is no wonder therefore that Catholic Ireland found it hard to forgive Yeats for this poem in particular.[70]

Today, when I return to commentaries on 'September 1913', I realise that Ellmann, Jeffares, Bloom, Cullingford, Albright, and a whole host of scholars following their lead, have arrived at meanings which are incompatible with those arrived at by the editor of the newspaper that published the poem, with those his readers would have derived, and with those Yeats himself intended (as evidenced by his letters), expected and sanctioned by choosing to publish the poem in the *Irish Times* for a Protestant readership.

The importance of the site and form of a text's publication is also highlighted by Shillingsburg's adaptation of John Searle's distinction between product and use, utterance and sentence. Each 'utterance has its intentions and its "social life" (i.e. the purpose for which it was released, and the context, moment and form in which it was designed and launched)'. For an utterance to occur, or a speaker's meaning to be communicated, there has to be a speaker (text) and a recipient interacting within a 'context of presuppositions'. This context 'provides what "goes without saying" for each speech act'; it 'influence[s] and contain[s] ("keeps from running wild") the meaning and help[s] indicate what meanings are operable'. The sentence, on the other hand, is the formal and sequential relationship of words with each other. Because a sentence can be used on separate occasions to mean different things without compromising its integrity, 'sentences are iterable'. However, because 'utterance is the intended meaning in the use of sentence' on 'an occasion in a specific setting', it is not iterable. When a particular sequence of words (sentence) is used in two or more situations, different utterances are generated. These discrete utterances are differentiated from each other by the presuppositions and meanings (things that go without saying) inherent in the particular contexts circumscribing each utterance. There may be an overlap in meaning, but this need not be necessary.[71]

The further a particular utterance is removed from its context, the more this context is denuded and obscured, and the more utterance comes to resemble sentence, which, since it is iterable, can in different contexts produce other different utterances. While utterance relates to the product of an '[a]uthoring, manufacturing or reading performance',[72] sentence relates to the uses to which that product is put. Utterance is born out of a particular situation to serve a particular purpose; sentence can be made to serve other and multifarious purposes. This distinction helps illuminate some salient aspects of the publication history of 'September 1913' that highlight the importance of studying the text in its different contexts.

When Yeats first published 'September 1913' he may not have known for sure whether his intended meanings would be communicated to and understood by his audience, but, given the fact that he published it in the *Irish Times*, he did have a pretty good idea of the meanings and implications that the audience would derive from his text. The fact that he preferred to publish his poem in that and not another venue indicates that he was content for his poem to be read in that way, that he sanctioned those meanings. When he republished the poem in a volume alongside some of his other poems, he knew equally well that his poem would be read in a very different way. With book publication, unlike periodical or newspaper publication, the context of presuppositions and the frame of references that the writer and reader can take for granted and that provide what goes without saying do not pre-exist the publication; they are created – in the case of 'September 1913' and indeed most of Yeats's book publications after the turn of the century – to a very large extent by Yeats himself. Without underestimating the substantial input from publishers, printers, illustrators, etc., I wish to focus briefly on Yeats's own efforts to create this new context that will bring some new meanings into reckoning while precluding some older ones from consideration altogether, and in the process create what is today the standard version of his poems and of himself as a poet.

One example should suffice. The first time Yeats republished 'September 1913' after the 1916 Rising, he appended a note to the edition:

> 'Romantic Ireland's dead and gone' sounds old-fashioned now. It seemed true in 1913, but I did not foresee 1916. The late Dublin Rebellion, whatever one can say of its wisdom, will long be remembered for its heroism. 'They weighed so lightly what they gave', and gave too in some cases without hope of success. July 1916. (*VP*, 820)

The implication of the first one-and-a-half sentences is that it is true of the past, but not the present, that 'Romantic Ireland's dead and gone'. What has revived 'Romantic Ireland' is, of course, the Easter Rising. Since the difference between the 'then' (September 1913) and the 'now' (July 1916) is the Rising, the reader is led to believe that the qualities represented by the Rising are the very qualities Yeats was speaking of in his reference to 'Romantic Ireland': revolutionary nationalism, blood sacrifice and heroic martyrdom for the Irish cause being the most obvious. To this Yeats adds another, namely, romanticism: they 'gave too in some cases without hope of success'. By thus linking Romantic Ireland (and therefore 'September 1913') with Easter 1916, Yeats implies that the absence or non-occurrence of an event like the Rising led to the demise of Romantic Ireland and formed the subject of his lament or taunt in the poem. 'September 1913', therefore, according to this version, yearns for and tries to instil in its readers the revolutionary nationalism exemplified in the Rising.[73] When he says, '"Romantic Ireland's dead and gone" sounds old-fashioned now. It seemed true in 1913, but I did not foresee 1916,' is he suggesting that the Rising was brought about by his poem, as he was later to suggest that it was brought about by his play?[74] Maybe not, but he is certainly implying that Easter 1916 typifies the 'Romantic Ireland' he was referring to and hoping for in his poem 'September 1913'.

There is one other aspect of the appended note that needs attention: '"They weighed so lightly what they gave", . . . success.' The use of the phrase from 'September 1913' links the 1916 martyrs with the men cele-brated in the earlier poem. By thus incorporating them into the fold of Romantic Ireland, Yeats effects a shift in the nature and significance of what romantic Ireland represents, and thereby what 'September 1913' means. He authorises a new meaning, and remakes himself in the process. What is the nature of this shift? The men celebrated in 'September 1913' were mostly upper-class Irishmen, either Protestant or de facto Protestant, who 'went about the world like wind'. The 1916 martyrs are principally middle class and Catholic. They lack the *sprezzatura* and dash of their 'predecessors', and form the subject of jokes Yeats and his kind tell 'around the fire at the club'. In this new, post-Easter 1916, club of romantic Irishmen, class and sectarian divisions have been abolished, Gaelic Leaguers rub shoulders with aristo-crats, and the sole criterion for membership seems to be romantic national-ism, the very quality Yeats is now trying to take on so far as posterity and his international readers are concerned.[75]

After 1916, when Yeats republished 'September 1913', he excised two paragraphs from the annotations to this poem that had been part of his efforts at illuminating the poem's background and meaning. He said he excised them because they were dated and pertained to his defence of Lane. In these para-graphs, among other things, Yeats had attacked the opposition to the gallery proposal, which came principally from the clerical and lay Catholic newspa-pers, as being ignorant, crass and philistine, in essence 'Paudeen's point of view' (*VP*, 820). An added reason for dropping those paragraphs may have been that they illuminated aspects of the poem that Yeats would rather were ignored and that conflicted with the self-image he was fashioning for pos-terity. An examination of the contexts of Yeats's publications of 'September 1913' helps us understand the uses to which he has put that poem, how he has attempted to control its meanings, the role it has played in his projected self-image, the popularity and provenance of the 'international' reading of Yeats and of the stylising of the poem, along with some of his other political verse, into a serial romanticism.

The extent to which scholarship is undermined by an ignorance of a text's historical context, of factors constituting its 'self-evident givens', is demon-strated in George Bornstein's recently published article seeking to unravel the 'thick political codings' surrounding the first publication of 'September 1913'.[76] Bornstein quite correctly points to 'the weakened political invoca-tions' of subsequent publications of the poem in anthologies and collected

editions which 'depoliticise this extraordinarily political poem, finally reducing it at best to an artefact talking about politics rather than incarnating them'
(236). To understand the poem's 'deep embedding', he suggests, 'we need to
read the poem not in the de-politicised context of an anthology or even of
Yeats's collected poems but, rather, in the highly charged codes of its original publication' (240).

The *Irish Times*, he observes, 'also provides a different contextual code for
the poem than do any of its later incarnations'. However, he does not take
cognisance of what this context means. For instance, he spends over ten pages
recreating the poem's socio-historical background and analysing its bibliographical codings. Yet his article, surprisingly, seems unmindful of the basic
and essential fact that the *Irish Times* was a Conservative unionist newspaper,
a fact that queries each of his many assertions about the poem. Surprisingly,
because in the column immediately to the left of that in which the poem was
published, and co-extensive with it, is an article hoping that the royal prerogative would be exercised to veto the Home Rule Bill or to dissolve parliament. Bornstein's omission is also surprising because a periodical or
newspaper's political ideology is a crucial factor and among the first things
one has to consider while unravelling bibliographic codes. Most nineteenth-
century newspapers and periodicals operated as party organs and mouth-
pieces for political propaganda addressed to different vote banks. 'Conceived
in sect and reared in the strife of parties', they served practical ends and permitted 'only so much play of mind as was compatible with the prosecution
of those practical ends'. Literary criticism too was perforce 'political in origin and propagandist in effect' and periodicals boldly proclaimed their different political allegiances.[77]

Noting the date of the poem's publication, Bornstein asks 'What was happening in Dublin at that time?' (237). By examining that day's *Irish Times*, he
notices that the Transport and General Workers' strike dominated the headlines. However, he does not investigate the perspective from which the strike
was reported in the newspaper, something he ought to have done if he was
going to base his reading of the poem on that event. Purely on the basis of
the poem's title, its attached date ('September 7th, 1913'), and the fact that in
the column adjacent to it on the right was an article on the workers' strike,
Bornstein situates Yeats's 'fiery denunciation of the cash nexus in contemporary Dublin . . . precisely at the end of the first full week of the acute phase
of the troubles' (237). He then quotes the poem's first stanza ('What need
you being come to sense . . .') and claims that it expresses Yeats's solidarity
with the strikers:

> Throughout the controversy Yeats stood firmly with the strikers
> (though not always with some of their supporters), the more so

> because their chief enemy was the same William Martin Murphy
> who had attacked Parnell in the 1890s and Synge's *Playboy of the
> Western World* in the 1900s. Yeats appeared on the platform for
> them and even published a letter on 'Dublin Fanaticism' in
> Larkin's paper, the *Irish Worker*, for 1 November. (238)

There is no connection established either between the contents of the first
stanza and the biographical details provided above, or between the rest of the
poem and the strike. Having quoted the *Irish Times* headlines of 1 and 8 September 1913 dealing with the strike, Bornstein simply superimposes the
poem onto this structure while disregarding the tenor of the articles he refers
to, the larger context that might exist, the testimony of Yeats's letters written
while he was composing the poem, and anything the poem itself might have
to say. The result is a host of unfounded assertions, untenable propositions,
inconsistencies and anachronisms. If 'Romance in Ireland' represented Yeats's
efforts to champion Larkin's cause – and Bornstein adduces no evidence
whatsoever supporting this claim – why then did he not publish it in Larkin's
paper, the *Irish Worker*, where he subsequently published his letter denouncing those opposing the strike? Why did he publish it in the *Irish Times*, which
had denounced Larkinism as an 'intolerable tyranny' and had, on the very
same page as it published the poem, condemned the strike as a sign of things
to come should Ireland be given Home Rule:

> Six of these transport workers now sit on Dublin City Council.
> The Transport Workers 'run' Dublin. They hope to run Ireland.
> In any case, these six men are the harbingers of at least half a
> dozen Irish Labour members in the first Home Rule Parliament,
> and, who knows, perhaps, thirty to fifty in the second Parliament.
> (*IT*, 8.9.1913, 7)

Those supporting the strikers were described as 'red-hot Socialists, who are
content to while away Sunday afternoon in listening to ravings of men of the
Ben Tillet type'. If it is contended that Yeats was taking the fight to the opposition by publishing the poem in the *Irish Times*, we are left with the question of why he then published his pro-strike letter in the *Irish Worker* and not
in the *Irish Times*. Furthermore, if the editor of this pro-establishment newspaper had read the poem as supporting the strike, or if he thought his readers might do so, or if he saw Yeats as being one of those 'red-hot Socialists',
or a 'Ben Tillet type', would he have published the poem and endorsed it
with an editorial? And finally, and most importantly, how could even Yeats
have intended his lines to refer to the strike, or to support it, given the fact
that he began thinking about the poem seven months before the strike was
called, and had finished it on 9 August, seventeen days before the strike had

even started?[78] Needless to say, there is no mention of the strike in any of Yeats's letters during this intervening period.

To establish the connection between the poem's title and the strike on the one hand, and its subtitle and the gallery affair on the other, Bornstein links these two disparate events and claims that the whole 'controversy became intertwined with that over the strike and lockout, with Murphy and the forces of capital and propriety opposing the gallery and Larkin and those of Labour supporting it' (238). This is factually incorrect. While Murphy and a large section of Dublin's Catholic middle classes opposed the gallery, the unionists, 'the forces of capital and propriety', mostly supported it. This is clear from the newspapers' editorials and correspondence columns. On the other hand, Bornstein adduces no evidence to show that the gallery project had the backing of the working classes, most of whom were nationalist and Catholic and would have seen the project denounced by Arthur Griffith and D. P. Moran in *Sinn Fein* and the *Leader* and also by Murphy's *Irish Daily Independent*, Ireland's largest-selling daily newspaper, which had a predominantly Catholic readership. What is more, Bornstein's statement that the gallery 'controversy became intertwined with that over the strike and lockout' is neither true for Yeats in 1913 (as his letters testify), nor for the *Irish Times* editorial on the poem (page 6), which makes no mention of the strike. Bornstein relies on a note Yeats appended to the poem when he published it as part of a larger collection in 1914 (*Responsibilities: Poems and a Play*), and later in 1916 (*Responsibilities and Other Poems*, reprinted 1917), claiming that, because Larkin and 'important slum workers' (*VP*, 820) supported the gallery project, the 'purpose of the opposition [that the money should be spent on slums] was not entirely charitable'. In the same note, but this time attached only to the 1916 and 1917 editions, Yeats also vaguely suggested that the Easter Rising was an offshoot of 'September 1913'. Years later he would claim that the Rising was an offshoot of *Cathleen ni Houlihan*. There is no evidence either in his letters, diaries, articles, or speeches, or in the *Irish Times* itself that 'Romance in Ireland' was intended as a comment on the strike. The strike had only been in the news for a week, whereas the issues raised by the poem had a much deeper resonance.

Bornstein's view of the poem begets other oddities. He sees the poem's 'you' as referring to, among others, 'those wealthy members of the Anglo-Irish whom Yeats had attacked earlier in the same venue for failing to support the gallery adequately' (240). According to Augusta Gregory, after her return from America in May, 'want of money was no longer the stumbling block'.[79] This may or may not be true, and documents may emerge that controvert this view. Nevertheless, it is true that want of money, if there was a want, was not the only obstacle, and was in fact the easiest to overcome.

Writing to Augusta Gregory about his decision to publish the poem in the *Irish Times*, Yeats makes it quiet clear that his decision has been precipitated by the Lord Mayor's statement in the *Morning Post* that 'the Gallery Project is at an end as the Corporation will not accept an English architect' (Torchiana and O'Malley, 39). Hence, it was not Anglo-Irish apathy but Catholic bigotry that, according to Yeats, jeopardised the gallery. It was clear to both Augusta Gregory and Yeats in 1913 that the gallery proposal failed, not because the Anglo-Irish gentry had failed to underwrite it, but because the Dublin Corporation – a body dominated by Catholics and nationalists – blocked it on one pretext or another: money, site, design and, finally, because the architect, Lutyens, was only half-Irish. According to Augusta Gregory, the fault lay with 'the system that puts our precious things into the hands of a democracy' (*Sir Hugh Lane*, 103–4). Yeats's diary attributes the nationalist opposition to their reluctance to 'acknowledge in public that they accepted a gallery they could not or would not support' (*Mem*, 198) and to the potential embarrassment they would suffer were it financed by Protestant unionist contributions. Secondly, 'Romance in Ireland' does not attack the Anglo-Irish gentry; it affirms their superiority to the class that grovels 'in a greasy till by the light of a holy candle'. It is difficult to imagine how anyone could connect the *Irish Times*'s unionist readers with the poem's subtitle ('On reading much of the correspondence *against* the Art Gallery' [emphasis added]), or with the images of money-grubbing Catholic religiosity in the first stanza. Finally, in 'The Gift', Yeats did not attack the Anglo-Irish gentry, but clearly flattered them, as we have seen. It was Paudeen, 'little Patrick', left to 'play at pitch and toss', who was disparaged for the 'slightness of . . . [his] desire for any kind of art'.

Bornstein is misleading when he claims, 'The poem [*sic*] subtitle "On reading much of the correspondence against the Art Gallery" appears in the correspondence column of the same paper that had published the attacks that it responds to' (239–40). This implies that the *Irish Times* repeatedly attacked the gallery scheme, that Yeats published 'Romance in Ireland' in that paper as a response to its attacks, and that the issues raised by his poem pertained mainly to the art gallery and the strike. None of this is true. The paper wholeheartedly supported rather than attacked the gallery project and the only attack that was published in its pages was Murphy's letter, which was denounced by the editor's indirect as well as overt comments. Hence, there is no question of Yeats deciding to publish his poem in that newspaper as a kind of rebuttal. He published the poem in the *Irish Times* because he knew that the paper and its readership shared his views. Finally, Yeats's poem was not responding merely to the art gallery controversy but to larger issues of Protestant marginalisation.

Bornstein's failures to locate the poem in its broader context and to deci-
pher correctly the *Irish Times*'s bibliographic codes result in his seeing the
poem as Yeats's expression of sympathy with the working classes. To then
claim, as he does, that the poem is reincarnated in its next publication as a
kind of Yeatsian Socialist Manifesto is only a short step away. According to
him, the 'strongly charged political aura' of Elizabeth Yeats's Cuala edition of
Responsibilities (1914) emanates from the fact that the Cuala Press 'was a fem-
inist and nationalist enterprise' (241). The only evidence he adduces for this
claim is that the 'very name Dun Emer [the original name of Cuala], Irish
for "the fort of Emer" (queen-wife of the hero Cuchulain), indicated both
the gender and the national politics of the enterprise'. What conclusion
would he reach if he applied the same logic today to loyalist gable murals in
East Belfast depicting Cuchulain as a champion of Ulster?[80] He then goes on
to make an even more untenable claim. He points out that the limited edition of four hundred copies used the fourteen-point Caslon Old Style font,
'an eighteenth-century typeface that thus originated in Yeats's favourite
period of Romantic Ireland', that the copies were made from 'special rag
paper from Saggart Mills in County Dublin regularly used for Dun
Emer/Cuala books, and the ink made special use of red highlights (here the
opening and closing poems and the colophon) in the manner of Morris'
(242). QED: 'At the material level of inscription, then, the book protests
against those who fumble in a greasy till and instead gestures towards a more
large-minded conception of nationality; it also gestures toward an ideal of
bookmaking that respects the integrity of materials rather than simply trying
to reproduce linguistic codes as cheaply as possible' (242). Leaving aside for
a moment the fact that there is as much visible connection between élite
bookmaking practices and a 'large-minded conception of nationality' as there
is between an antique dealer and a political martyr, Bornstein does have a
point about élite publishing practices using expensive paper and more labour-
intensive methods to evoke an earlier age. The product is a more expensive,
more exclusive, and perhaps a more attractive book. This contrasts with mass
publishing practices 'trying to reproduce linguistic codes as cheaply as possible', just as romantic Ireland of the eighteenth century does with grubby,
materialistic Ireland of 1913. However, he undermines his own case by asserting that the similarity in Yeats's and William Morris's use of red highlights is
indicative of their shared political ideologies:

> For Morris, of course, was one of the founders of the Guild
> Socialist movement in England and the founder and leader of the
> Socialist League at the time that young Yeats was one of his dis-
> ciples. Use of a format derived from Morris here signals a resist-
> ance to capitalist forms of literary production and an allegiance

> to a countertradition involving art, communal ownership, and alternate social structures. Incarnating the poem in this manner carries particular force in attacking a social formation led by William Martin Murphy, a capitalist tycoon who made his fortune in mass circulation newspapers. The very material form of the poem matches the words in protesting against a corrupt social order and suggesting an embattled alternative. (242)

One despairs at such disregard for history, chronology, context and some hard facts. 'September 1913' is not incarnated in the manner Bornstein suggests. It is not printed in red ink 'in the manner of Morris' and it does not 'use a format derived from Morris'.[81] It is printed in the same black ink used for most of the other poems in that volume. But let us assume for a moment that Morris's spirit does permeate the twenty-odd pages from the 'Preliminary Poem' (xvi) published in red ink 'in the manner of Morris' to 'September 1913' (16–17). By the time this proselytising spirit reaches page 16 it should have already infused its resistance to capitalism and 'allegiance . . . to communal ownership' into 'To a Wealthy Man' (15–16), which flatters the aristocracy, advocates *noblesse oblige* and denounces Paudeen's philistinism. By Bornstein's methodology, we should also be able to detect Morris's egalitarianism in 'The Statues' (*Last Poems* [Cuala, 1939]) and in *On the Boiler* (Cuala, 1939). Morris was Yeats's 'chief of men' (*Auto*, 141) when Yeats was Morris's disciple, but his affinity for Morris was literary rather than political and that did not really last beyond the late 1880s, i.e. more than two decades before 'September 1913'. Since then, there is enough in Yeats's letters, biography and poetry to dispel any fond hopes that Morris's political ideology might have had a lasting influence on him. Further, in 1913 Yeats did have an aversion to modern industrial society, and to capitalism, but his aversion to democracy and egalitarianism was even stronger. The 'alternate social structure' he favoured was not one of 'communal ownership' but a feudal, aristocratic society composed of the beggar and the nobleman. Similarly, the 'corrupt social order' he protested against was not capitalism but one where Catholics dominated and Protestants were marginalised. Besides, one would hope that, if a case were to be made that Yeats was a socialist believing in communal ownership and the equitable distribution of resources, it would present more substantial evidence than merely his use of red ink. (After all, red is also the colour of Her Majesty's post-boxes.) Such an argument would also have to address the fact that Yeats's 'allegiance to a counter tradition . . . [of] communal ownership' did not actually extend to the ownership of the Cuala Press itself, that Yeats's Cuala books were costlier than his Macmillan publications and were sold mostly to private collectors looking for quick returns rather than an enjoyable read.

To restore a text's larger human context, to socialise and historicise it at its point of origin, is not merely to reinsert it into its original bibliographical framework and to stop there. It is rather to study that context in its interactions with the text by bringing to bear on it the vast amount of information available about publishing practices, the political affiliations of periodicals and their editors, prospective readerships, the social and political events making up the 'mood of the age' at that particular point of time and, finally, the author's relationships with and perspectives on different persons and events which comprise this larger human context. Disregarding the historical specificity of 'September 1913' – whose very title announces its rootedness in history and its status as a historical comment – has skewed our understanding of a poem which is seminal to most people's evaluation of Yeats. An attempt to refine artistic sensibilities (Brown), champion the cause of Labour and socialism (Bornstein) or instil a sense of revolutionary nationalism among the middle classes (Ellmann, Cullingford, *et al.*) has little to do with either the founding impulse of 'September 1913' or the way it would have been read by its earliest readers.

II

The importance of studying the context of a text's first publication was brought home to me powerfully by my research into 'September 1913', a poem of Yeats's later phase. It provided the impetus for a journey backwards to the beginning of Yeats's literary career and the origins of the Revival. As I discovered, my initial insecurities were groundless. There was no reason to assume that such a historical and rigorously empirical approach could be productively applied to texts only from his later period and not to those from his earlier, Celtic twilight, floppy bow-tie phase, when he cut such an ethereal and dreamy figure in the eyes of his contemporaries, or only to Yeats's poetry and not to his prose.

Yeats claimed that, while his brother painted to please himself, this 'is not my attitude towards poetry. You must remember your audience; it is always there. You cannot write without it.'[82] William Charvat has demonstrated how, in nineteenth-century America, the 'whole economic life of the nation was brought to bear upon literature and literary life'. He also illustrates the shaping influence exerted by the editor of *Graham's Magazine* on Longfellow's overall oeuvre:

> The editor had agreed to pay Longfellow fifty dollars a poem on condition that he publish in no other magazine. Longfellow consented, but one of his contributions drew a protest from Graham.

The poet had charged fifty dollars for a sonnet. This, hinted the editor, was cheating: it raised the cost of verse to almost four dollars a line, and did not fill enough space for the money. The editor's economy was not the poet's. Graham operated on a budget – so many pages to be filled, so much cost to be paid for filling them . . . One can assume a connection between this episode and the fact that, before the fifties, Longfellow, an excellent sonneteer, wrote few sonnets but many poems in space-consuming quatrains.[83]

In nineteenth-century England, the power and control exerted by Muddie's circulating library on the whole business of novel writing – the size, shape and price of a novel, and sometimes even its contents – is well known. Thomas Hardy protested but had to comply. The influence exerted on his work (particularly in the case of *The Return of the Native* and *Tess of the D'Urbervilles*) by such non-literary institutional factors has been documented. Writing with scarcely controlled 'bitterness' about a writer being coerced into 'arranging a *dénouement* which he knows to be indescribably unreal and meretricious, but dear to the Grundyist and subscriber', Hardy passed his most damning verdict on the nature and force of such pressures:

> If the true artist ever weeps it probably is then, when he first discovers the fearful price that he has to pay for the privilege of writing in the English language – no less a price than the complete extinction, in the mind of every mature and penetrating reader, of sympathetic belief in his personages.[84]

Even an artist as fastidious and highbrow as Henry James described word limits imposed by editors and publishers as 'the governing condition' of his literary practice. The extent to which this 'coercive fact' along with his financial dependence on the literary marketplace compelled him to 'frame his artistic goals in distinctly marketable form' has been the subject of some fascinating studies. Having completed a novel, he was more anxious about securing its periodical, rather than book, publication because the former paid more. But that also compelled him, as we see in his letter to his agent about the serialisation of *The Golden Bowl*, to make 'various heartbreaking excisions' (including 'three priceless gems of chapters'), to '*divide*, & in some degree heroically *cut* it', for this purpose.[85]

Why did these writers deviate from their original intentions and succumb to such pressures? Part of the answer is obvious: despite professions to the contrary, writers write to be read and purchased as well as to fulfil some larger artistic ambition. 'It cannot . . . be too clearly understood', professed Arnold Bennett, 'that the professional author . . . is eternally compromising between glory and something more edible and warmer at nights'. This was reaffirmed by one of Grub Street's most successful authors when he warned starry-eyed newcomers to wake up to the reality of what a literary career entails:

> There is life-long penury in it: starvation: suicide: a debtor's prison: hard and grinding work for miserable pay: a cruel task-master: work done to order paid for by the yard. As for the wished-for life among books, these unfortunate poets could not afford to buy books: as for freedom, quiet, ease, they never had any at all. Even the joy of composition, which one would think could not be taken from them, they could never enjoy, because they wrote to order and what they were told to write: they were paid servants: they lived in a garret: they never rose out of poverty and misery: they were buried in the paupers' cor-ner . . . One has only to look around in order to find out these wrecks: to discern the men who put out from ports, years ago, with flowing sails and flying flags, and now return with the bat-tered hulk which hardly keeps afloat: men who made a bid for success and have failed: who now live sordid lives, doing the lowest drudgery of literary work for the pay that is tossed to a drudger . . .[86]

And if this seems unconvincing, one can always read Gissing's *New Grub Street*. There, Edwin Reardon and Jasper Milvain represent the two extremes: one ultra-idealistic and the other ultra-practical. While it is hardly surprising that it is the latter that succeeds, it is surprising that this aspect of literary life and its effect on Yeats's work have hardly been studied. In the 'Grey Rock' he memorialised the literary intransigence of his fellow Rhymers' Club aesthetes:

> You had to face your ends when young –
> 'Twas wine or women, or some curse –
> But never made a poorer song
> That you might have a heavier purse,
> Nor gave loud service to a cause
> That you might have a troop of friends.
> You kept the Muses' sterner laws,
> And unrepenting faced your ends . . .
> ('The Grey Rock,' VP, 273)

The contrast drawn is between an art that is pure and uncompromising and one that is mercenary. Yeats often rode this high horse of *l'art pour l'art* and urged fellow artists to think of the 'Perfect and the True' (*CL1*, 371) rather than of what their audience might want. This, however, needs to be read in

conjunction with his letter to a young poet where he recommends oppor-
tunism and vouches for the commercial viability of Celtic subject matter:

> You will find it a good thing to make verses on Irish legends and
> places and so forth. It helps origonality and makes one's verses
> sincere, and gives one less numerous competitors. Besides one
> should love best what is nearest and most interwoven with ones
> life (*CL1*, 131)

The aphoristic addendum, probably a face-saving afterthought, is the virtue
he assumed in his literary journalism which itself was often manipulated with
a view to the given political situation and the sensibilities of his intended
readership.

Yeats is neither a Jasper Milvain nor an Edwin Reardon but incorporates
shades of both. To a very large extent, and more so early in his career, Yeats
had to write for money and therefore produce work that would sell with
publishers and editors. Dickens, Thackeray and a whole host of other writers
have freely admitted to writing for the same motives.[87] At the same time, artistic disavowal of economic motives is a common enough occurrence. It is a
type of 'economic rationality' lying, according to Pierre Bourdieu, at the heart
of the cultural world 'governing its functioning and transformation' (Bourdieu, 1993, 75, 79). The world of 'high-art' – an 'economic world reversed' –
is based on 'a winner loses' (7–8) logic which privileges financial disinterestedness and hardship as signs of artistic probity and commitment, and dispar-
ages financial success as evidence of compromise. The only legitimate
accumulation is that of prestige, authority and recognition from fellow artists.
Such 'symbolic capital', which is not without its economic benefits, even if
they are 'misrecognised' and obfuscated, can only be achieved by 'disinterestedness' and 'a refusal of the commercial.' Thus, artists, by 'concealing from
themselves and others the interests at stake in their practice, obtain the means
of deriving profits from disinterestedness' (75). In other words, to be com-
mercially successful in the world of 'high art' one has to first denounce commercial success. However, as Bourdieu argues, this disavowal is not mere
dissimulation but an intrinsic element of the 'bad-faith' economy of cultural
practice in which 'new producers whose only capital is their conviction can
establish themselves in the market by appealing to the values whereby the
dominant figures accumulated their symbolic capital' (76).[88]

The second reason why an artist succumbs to the dictates of editors and
publishers is because he needs their approbation. In the literary marketplace, such literary mandarins function as what Bourdieu calls 'symbolic
bankers'. Having already accumulated literary prestige and authority, they
invest their 'symbolic capital' in consecrating an unknown author by

publishing/endorsing his work, giving it a commercial value and bringing it into the market:

> He is the person who can proclaim the value of the author he defends (c.f. the fiction of the catalogue or blurb) and above all 'invests his prestige' in the author's cause, acting as a 'symbolic banker' who offers as security all the symbolic capital he has accumulated (which he is liable to forfeit if he backs a 'loser') . . . Entering the field of literature is not so much like going into religion as getting into a select club: the publisher is one of those prestigious sponsors (together with preface-writers and critics) who effusively recommend their candidate. (77)

By stamping him with his imprimatur, a banker helps an author attain authority and recognition. Yeats was not oblivious of these benefits, as we shall see. In Ireland, he assiduously cultivated the patronage of the largest-selling newspaper and, in England, secured the backing of W. E. Henley. The latter, particularly, served him well. Others recognised this distinction and after becoming 'one of Henley's boys' his work immediately became more marketable. Notwithstanding the fact that Mowbray Morris, Macmillan's reader, rejected the firm's proposal to publish Yeats's collected works – 'Perhaps since he has taken to playing at treason with Miss Maud Grane [sic] and Mr George Moore he has not found time to cultivate literature' – the letter George Macmillan sent him introducing Yeats testifies to the currency of Henley's stamp: 'Some good critics, notably W. E. Henley, seem to regard Mr Yeats as one of the coming men, putting him for instance above Stephen Phillips. His last little volume, "The Wind among the Reeds", was crowned this year by the *Academy* in its annual competition.'[89] It is worth noting that Henley's approbation is given precedence in order of importance to the *Academy* prize, itself a prestigious accolade.

III

In 1988 Terence Brown predicted that 'further knowledge about nineteenth-century Ireland must enforce re-examination of the origins and nature of the Irish Literary Revival. The degree to which that movement was a part of the history of Victorian Britain in which Ireland played a part must increasingly, I think, stimulate "revisionist" enquiry.'[90] The publication of Yeats's correspondence has substantially furthered such enquiry. Letters written between 1885 and the mid-1890s indicate how deeply the Revival is grounded in the late Victorian periodical culture and its reading tastes. Yeats and other Irish writers of the Revival depended on Victorian readership, periodicals, publishers and reviews for their success and income. Being on the spot and with vested interests of his own to look after, he championed their cause in the English media. The range of periodicals he contributed to is impressive and incorporates various contraries within the literary spectrum: high-brow (*Yellow Book*) and low-brow (*Girl's Own Paper*), Catholic (*Irish Monthly*) and Protestant (*Leisure Hour*), intellectual (*Academy*) and athletic (*Gael*), populist (*Bookman*) and élitist (*New Review*), imperialist (*Scots Observer*) and socialist (*Irish Worker*), unionist (*Dublin Daily Express*) and nationalist (*United Ireland*), decadent (*Savoy*) and anti-decadent (*National Observer*), general (*Contemporary Review*) and specialised (*Vegetarian*), celebrated (*Fortnightly Review*) and forgotten (*Lucifer*).

Within this arena, he participated in the 'war of schools' (*UP2*, 89) fought between literary factions through representative periodicals often writing simultaneously for warring groups. Depending very often on their political and social orientation, these periodicals had varying, and often antagonistic, ideas on what constituted good literature and 'aesthetic value'.[91] Contributions gladly accepted by one editor would have been rejected out of hand by another. To market his writing Yeats had to cater to these editorial and institutional predispositions. By doing so, he published his work and publicised his name. The latter was as important as the former, for in the 1880s, as Nigel Cross demonstrates, there was for the first time 'a direct equation between publicity and sales'.[92] Yeats's insights into the political and sociological underpinnings of periodical publication were keen and he knew what would and would not be acceptable to particular editors. One has only to read his early letters to realise this. He advises Katharine Tynan against sending her more nationalistic poems to the *Scots Observer* because its editor is a unionist and later apologises for being unable to review Ellen O'Leary's poems for the same reason.[93] Later he is seen straining his resources to give Tynan the widest possible exposure. This inevitably involved using the periodicals. The extent to which he did so may justify this extended quotation from his letters which reveals his knowledge of that industry and his dependence on it:

> I see by '**Irish Monthly**' that your 'A Nun – her friends & her order' is out. If you have not been able to keep me a copy get me a review copy at any rate. I can review it in the **Pilot** certainly & elsewhere probably. I can also if I care for it as I feel sure I will, get it reviewed probably in some of the papers over here – the **Anti Jacobin** & the **Star** I think very likely, & perhaps also in the **Pall Mall** & one or two others . . . Owing to the Rhymers Club I have a certain amont of influence with reviewers. I can probably

besides before mentioned papers get you a note in the 'Speaker' at least & certainly can help you with the 'Queen'. 'The Speaker' reviews are unfortunately very few & far between. The notes however are very much in the friendly hand of John Davidson. 'The Academy' must also be looked up. If you like I can myself ask for it there. I must however read it first as it may be a very good book & yet a difficult one – if you have made it very catholic – to review for a churchless mystic like me. I meen that an ardent believer *might* be better for you as far as **Academy** is concerned. I think however that it is important that someone should ask for it or they may bunch it up with a lot of other books. I gather from 'The Irish Monthly' that you have done your work in the very best spirit & look forward to reading it with excited expectation. Your first prose book is a momentous matter & may be the beginning of a new literary life for you.

I am myself busy with a new work. Fisher Unwin are going to print my articles on folklore etc from the **National Observer** with what aditional articles on Irish subjects I can get together this summer & Jack is to make twenty illustrations . . . The book ['Carleton'] has been very well received on the whole – much better received than anything of mine except the poems. The reviews have been longer than were given to the Fairy Tales – a much more elaborate & useful book – or as far as Ireland was concerned to 'Oisin.' There are still a number – 'the Star,' 'the Pall Mall' & the 'Academy' – which are a writing in friendly hands. 'The Saturday Review' is the only hostile paper yet. I am rather anxious about 'Sherman.' It is good I believe but it will be a toss up how the reviewers take it – for if they look for the ordinary stuff of novels they will find nothing. Do what you can for it – for a success with stories would solve many problems for me & I write them easily. (*CL1*, 255–7) (emphasis added)

Yeats used the periodicals not only to propagate the Irish Literary Revival and keep himself before the public eye, but also to create among his readers the taste by which he would be relished. However, this was not a one-way exchange. In propagating a literary sensibility favouring the reception of Irish writers – diverse but herded under the common banner of Celtic – his own work was influenced by his readers' and editors' tastes. While his letters give us an insight into his dealings in the periodical marketplace, it is only by examining the periodicals themselves that one realises how profoundly that relationship is imprinted on his work. Given the significant fact that most of Yeats's poetry until 1900 and almost all the prose he ever wrote were first published in the periodicals, the importance of this context for Yeats studies should not be underestimated.

Yeats's involvement with periodicals was not a matter of choice but of necessity. Book publication, especially of poetry, had small commercial value. New writers, such as Yeats and Tynan, were often compelled to finance their first book themselves. Periodical publication, albeit sometimes unpaid, was the cheapest and most practical way of publicising their work, garnering a readership and establishing their literary credentials. Even if a book did make profits, the delay in payment was considerable. Usually publishers balanced their accounts only once a year, mostly in June, notified authors of the year's sales in October, and settled their dues in January, i.e. almost two years after the book's publication. Moreover, as Brian Maidment has observed:

> the dangers of an outright sale of a manuscript which might meet with an unexpected success, the investment of large amounts of unpaid time in writing lengthy books without any sure rewards, the lack of proper copyright protection, and the uneasy relationships between publishers and authors all made volume publication the reserve of either established writers, or those supported by inheritance, husbands, wives, patron or a non-literary profession.[94]

Payments from periodicals were generally prompt, and, as the work involved was relatively undemanding, journalism subsidised the slower and more risky business of book publication. Besant therefore advised literary aspirants to focus on periodicals, for they could be paid £50–100 for an article and nothing for a book on the same subject.[95] The lion's share of most writers' incomes was derived from periodicals and Yeats was no exception. Anesko shows how in the 36 years between 1864 and 1900 Henry James's income from periodicals always exceeded his receipts from book publication, except for 1893–95, when he was preoccupied with the theatre, 1882 when his father died, and 1885 when a publisher went bankrupt leaving unpaid the £2,000 owed for the serialisation of the *Bostonians*. According to the only published record of Yeats's earnings, almost the entire sum of £27.17s.4d earned between November 1889 and November 1890 was from periodicals.[96]

Besant believed that 'a writer cannot live by contributing to magazines, except in the way of fiction' (137). How then does a poet live?

> Mostly, he lives by journalism of some kind or the other. Sometimes he hangs about a publisher's place and picks up some of the work that is going. If he is wise he goes on in the work by which his parents hoped to see him live, and thrive, and rise even to the making of money. But by poetry he cannot live. (Besant, 79–80)

The Wanderings of Oisin, privately subscribed in the main, had sold only 28 copies on the open market by June 1891. Eventually, the publisher threatened legal action for the £2.3s.10d owing to him. *Poems and Ballads of Young Ireland* fared no better and Yeats's share of the loss was 9s.1d.[97] Since the market for poetry was very small, he had to fall back on literary criticism and, if possible, short stories to make ends meet. Hence his anxiety in the quoted letter about the fate of *John Sherman*, 'for a success with stories would solve many problems for me & I write them easily'. Yeats was dependent on readers' tastes for his livelihood and it is clear that he was quite willing to adjust to their demands. Succeeding in the periodical marketplace was his only hope of survival.

As a young man with neither an income nor a professional training, and a family living in impoverished conditions, his overriding concern during the 1880s and '90s was publishing his work in periodicals and thereby securing a regular income. His early feelings of despondence and inadequacy remained a vivid memory. In 1915, while writing his autobiography, he recalled those days of hardship: 'I had [thought] suddenly, while passing along Fleet Street to call upon a publisher, what could the most powerful soul do against weight and size?' (*Mem*, 19–20). Making the head 'bow a ceaseless obeisance to the heart' had in two years led to 'ever multiplying boxes of unsaleable manuscripts'. In 1888, a chastened and more worldly aesthete wrote to Katharine Tynan: 'Yet I don't know that it is ambition for I have no wish but to write a saleable story . . . However, I am exemplary at present . . . & have written lately everything with a practical intention' (*CL1*, 8, 71). On occasion, practicality necessitated work which he would later deny or suppress.

Compromises were ineluctable. Despite their pretence at objectivity, most editors had their own agenda, and their magazines served definite interests. These had to be catered to if Yeats wished to survive and be successful. The editorial choice of contributors was an important and carefully deliberated one. Articles had to ratify the journal's interests and blend with those they were buttressed by and interacted with. Editors frequently altered an author's text to suit their agenda. From their perspective, James Thorpe argues, the 'author is a tradesman, his work is a commodity which can be made more or less vendible, and the magazine is in a more favoured position in the commercial hierarchy than is the author'.[98] Where editorial revision did take place, Laurel Brake argues, 'the published piece was the result of a collaboration between contributor and editor, sometimes with the co-operation of the author and sometimes without it.' More often than not, the contributor would already have 'pitched it to the style, tone, and taste of the periodical for which it was intended'.[99] In Yeats's case, as I shall demonstrate, nailing his colours to a particular periodical involved mixing and matching his work, sometimes even giving it a different ideological slant, to suit the editor's preferences and the periodical's politics. Hence, the function and meaning of anything he published in periodicals falls to be determined by its context as much as by its content.

Because of the wide range of periodicals he wrote for, Yeats's articles, though expressed with some fervour, betray, when examined in their original contexts, a contradictory and mutually antagonistic character. For example, he wrote regularly and simultaneously both for the advanced nationalist weekly, *United Ireland*, and for Henley's *Scots* and *National Observer*, which were not only unionist and imperialist, but also vehemently anti-Irish and even more vehemently anti-*United* Ireland. In both cases, as I shall show, his contributions were angled to conform with and validate the political programmes of these periodicals. This, of course, has important repercussions on any evaluation of his aesthetics, politics or relationship with Irish nationalism. The considerable extent to which his work reflects this, for good and for bad, often with his conscious connivance and sometimes unconsciously, has not been explored in Yeats studies.

IV

The conviction underlying this book is that a historically informed approach to literature is enriched by an understanding of the conditions in which a writer worked and the contexts in which his work was published. Ignoring the context of a text's creation and publication can result in distortions of the kind that inform and prop up an entire perspective on an author – as I have shown through the publication history of 'September 1913' – and even on literature, as D. F. McKenzie brilliantly demonstrated through Wimsatt and Beardsley's use of a Congreve (mis)quotation in their seminal essay 'The Intentional Fallacy'.[100]

By establishing the bibliographical and socio-historical contexts of Yeats's early publications, this book explores the consequences to our understanding of Yeats of the generally accepted notion that meaning is a product of both form and content, the linguistic and the material text. It reinserts Yeats's texts into their environment of publication and examines his interactive exchanges with the periodical industry; the influence it exerted on his literary practice; the opportunities, temptations and constraints it created and his responses to them; and his attempts to create among his readers the taste by which he would be relished. This book shows that a good deal of Yeats's work, which we rightly consider literary criticism or artistic production, was 'market led' and 'market-friendly'. I do not use these terms as pejoratives but merely as correctives to literary approaches which either romanticise the poet as a prophetic and sole begetter of his work and rest satisfied with the poet's subsequent rationalisations and explanations of his text, or which, like New Criticism, Structuralism and Deconstruction, search for the meaning of a text in the text itself as if it were its own explanation. Such approaches are impoverished by their inherent hostility to and ignorance of bibliographical and socio-historical sources of meaning.

We have many contexts within which we read and understand a writer as complex and multifaceted as Yeats. In this book, I have endeavoured to provide another context whose value lies in its fertility, in its power to uncover material buried under the debris of history, and in its ability to harness insights provided by scholars more learned and perceptive than I from different disciplines and theoretical orientations. I have borrowed shamelessly from them and adapted their arguments to my needs. My debts are evident on every page. In putting forward this context, I have argued its claims and merits with a partisan edge and, perhaps, exaggerated them. Nevertheless, by asserting, no matter how forcefully, that the social, political and bibliographical contexts within which Yeats wrote and was received influenced the nature and reception of that work, one is not committed to the grossly simplistic proposition that his work was the product of forces which excluded him and over which he was powerless. The extent to which this book draws on Yeats's letters and biography should dispel any notion that I deny creative agency to the writer or believe that a poem is simply a socially manufactured statement, or that contexts – bibliographical, social, historical – produce the text and are the sole determinants of its meaning. I have stressed this at the expense of other approaches because I think that it has been neglected, to our general detriment, not because I think the others are invalid. If anything, my borrowings testify to their utility.

The following four chapters examine Yeats's work in Irish, British and American periodicals which propagated a distinctive position on Protestant nationalism, Catholic nationalism and unionism, as well as on the cultural and literary underpinnings of the Revival. Each of the periodicals examined – the *Dublin University Review*, the *United Ireland,* the *Boston Pilot*, the *Providence Sunday Journal* and the *Scots/National Observer* – was prestigious and powerful in its own way, and each had strong views on the Irish question which dominated its overall perspective and rendered subservient almost every other consideration. A comparison of Yeats's writings on Ireland in periodicals with such radically opposed stands on this issue makes for an illuminating contrast and raises hitherto unasked questions. In these chapters I have tried to relocate Yeats's work in the 'fabric of tradition' from which it has been extirpated by anthologies and collected editions hoping thereby to recreate the 'aura' that has been denuded in the process and to give the reader a feel for the periodical under discussion. Special attention is paid to the *United Ireland*, because it played the most significant part in the shaping of Yeats's political and literary views, as well as in determining the course and character of the Revival.

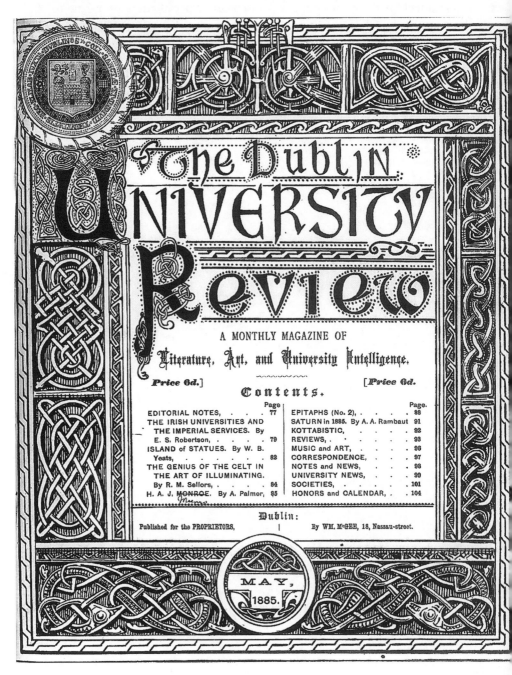

The Dublin UNIVERSITY Review

A MONTHLY MAGAZINE OF

Literature, Art, and University Intelligence.

Price 6d.]   [Price 6d.

Contents.

Dublin:

Published for the PROPRIETORS, | By WM. M'GEE, 18, Nassau-street.

MAY, 1885.

---

1   Cover of *Dublin University Review*, May 1885.

— 1 —

The Dublin University Review: *An Apprenticeship in Protestant Nationalism and Irish Literary Journalism*

I

The *Dublin University Review* (*DUR*), priced at 6d, was started in February 1885 by Charles Hubert Oldham, a graduate of Trinity College, Dublin (TCD), and subsequently Professor of Political Economy at the National University.[1] He was just five years older than Yeats, but their careers had traced very different trajectories. J. B. Yeats had been sliding down the social scale and his son's artistic ambitions had further accelerated this decline; Oldham, on the other hand, had remained firmly within the pale of Protestant gentility opting for a typical Anglo-Irish middle-class career, first at the university and then at the Bar. Contemporaries remember him as a direct and straightforward man who valued practicality above all else. A champion of women's rights and a constitutional nationalist, he opposed the Land League, managed the southern branch of the Irish Protestant Home Rule Association (IPHRA) and sided with Parnell after the split.[2]

Oldham was the *DUR*'s proprietor and managing director for most of its existence and its nominal editor until T. W. Rolleston took over in August 1885. Some members of what later became the Contemporary Club edited the journal collectively. Oldham and Rolleston did most of the work. Help also came from Professor Bury, John I. Beare, Douglas Hyde, George Coffey, Frederick Gregg, Richard Cherry and Dr Fitzgerald. They also wrote articles and adjudicated the print-worthiness of untested writers, most notably W. B. Yeats. Discussions at the club were frequently incorporated into the *DUR*'s contents.[3]

The *DUR* replaced the *Dublin University Magazine* (*DUM*) (1833–77), Dublin's first successful literary periodical, after an eight-year interlude. On a smaller scale, it attempted to emulate its illustrious predecessor by catering principally to a university readership and examining Irish issues from a

Protestant standpoint. As their titles indicate, TCD, the sole college of Dublin University, was the common factor. Both magazines initially published (but later discontinued) the university calendar and society reports. The *DUR*'s first volume featured the college arms on the front cover, was printed at the university press and extensively covered college events. Likewise, the *DUM* contained a frontispiece etching of the college façade (as well as a portrait of Queen Elizabeth, TCD's founder) and followed closely the goings-on at TCD. They shared a close, albeit fraught, relationship with the college and after a few run-ins with the authorities – TCD forbade the Dublin book-sellers to sell the *DUM* and later prohibited the *DUR* from printing the col-lege arms on its cover – the periodicals distanced themselves from the eponymous university. However, as they were dependent on a university read-ership, TCD and its concerns remained important considerations.[4]

Both magazines were monthlies which were initially started, managed, jointly edited and written primarily by coteries of TCD graduates and alumni mainly for a readership with links to TCD. Their founding impulse – an expression of national pride and Anglo-Irish identity – informed their ethos and contents. Their opening editorials proclaimed that in an age of periodi-cals Dublin should compete against the best English productions. They hoped to reinstate Dublin as Ireland's cultural and intellectual capital and put it on a par with London as a seat of learning and culture. Readers were encouraged to support Irish art, literature and industry as evidence of their national spirit. Given these similarities, it is a fitting coincidence that *DUM*'s last proprietor and editor, Kenningale Cook, was also a contributor to the *DUR*.

Both magazines shared a close and mutually beneficial relationship with the greatest (or prospectively the greatest) literary talents of their age: Samuel Ferguson, James Clarence Mangan, Samuel Lover, Charles Lever and William Carleton wrote for the *DUM*; W. B. Yeats and Douglas Hyde wrote for the *DUR*. Though they claimed to be 'literary' productions which were politi-cised by contemporary pressures, their founding motives were unequivocally political: the preservation of Protestant interests against the rising tide of Catholic democracy symbolised in 1833 by Catholic emancipation and the 1832 Reform Act, and in 1885 by the land agitation and the imminence of Home Rule.[5]

The careers of the founders of these magazines, Isaac Butt and Charles Oldham, also followed similar patterns. Both were southern Protestants with distinguished college records; both had lectured there on political economy and then joined the Bar. Subsequently, they founded or managed non-sec-tarian nationalist organisations – the Home Government Association and the IPHRA – which started as pressure groups but later fielded electoral candi-dates. Their political programmes too were similar. For both Butt and

Oldham it was imperative that Protestants reconciled themselves to their diminished status and the landed gentry co-operated with the national effort. Without this, they stressed, the future of their class, and even of their community, would be jeopardised.[6]

Little had changed at Trinity in the half-century separating the founding of the two periodicals. Endowed by Elizabeth I in 1591 as the founding college of the University of Dublin, TCD, in the 1880s, was élitist, staunchly male and Anglican, and catered principally to Protestants. In spite of the Fawcett Act, TCD continued to be dominated by Anglicans, who in 1892 comprised 81% of the student body. Though the percentage of dissenters had increased from 4% to 12% between 1855 and 1892, the number of Catholics had declined from 9.5% to about 7% between 1830 and 1892. TCD's being denounced as dangerous to faith and morals by the Catholic clergy in 1875 may explain this fall.[7] Though it now admitted students without subjecting them to religious tests and had opened fellowships and scholarships to non-Anglicans, it maintained its Ascendancy character and was commonly identified as the bastion of Irish unionism. In the general election of 1885, it was the only parliamentary constituency outside eastern Ulster to return Conservative MPs to parliament, and that too unopposed.[8] Its provost, John Hewitt Jellett, was one of the presidents and founding members of the Irish Loyal and Patriotic Union (ILPU), a small, wealthy, closely-knit and highly influential body established in May 1885 'for the purposes of maintaining the Union' and the 'supremacy of the Imperial Parliament'.[9] Many of the other Fellows were also active unionists. T. E. Webb, Regius Professor of Laws and Public Orator, attacked Gladstone's land settlement scheme and Home Rule in various pamphlets.[10] Edward Dowden – Professor of English and a *DUR* contributor – was an Executive Committee member and vice-chairman of what later became the Irish Unionist Alliance. He frequently spoke from political platforms and commissioned unionist songs from Kipling, Swinburne and other English poets.[11] The most infamous incident of TCD unionism was the mediation of Thomas Maguire – *DUR* contributor, prolific unionist pamphleteer,[12] TCD's first Catholic non-foundation scholar and also its first Catholic Fellow – as intermediary for *The Times* newspaper in the purchase of the 'Pigott' forgeries. The exception was Rev. Joseph Allen Galbraith, cathechist and senior dean. A member of the IPHRA and a leading Protestant nationalist of his day, he revived the term 'Home Rule' after a long period of abeyance.[13]

Though imposing in its presence and authoritarian in its functioning, the college had its rebellious spirits who violated traditional political allegiances, provoked equally perhaps by the college's stifling conservatism as by their own nationalist sympathies. The college disapproved of such 'disloyalty'.

Hyde's applications for teaching posts were sabotaged by Provost Salmon's testimonials, and his application for college rooms were blocked by J. P. Mahaffy, who suspected a nationalist tint in Hyde's Gaelic interests. Mahaffy later imperiously prohibited a meeting of the college Historical Society ('Hist') because 'a man called Pearse' was one of the speakers.[14]

Even though most of the Young Irelanders were TCD men, the college superciliously ignored the social and political processes transforming nine-teenth-century Ireland. Following the Reform Bill, a series of government measures had increasingly democratised and secularised Irish society: Catholic emancipation, the Reform Act, concessions in Catholic education, disestablishment of the Church of Ireland, the Ballot Act, land reforms and, most recently, the extension of franchise. They had also eroded Protestant Ascendancy; power, historically vested in the Protestants, was gradually trans-ferred to the Catholics. The loss of political power and the denuding of their economic and social privileges had by 1885 rendered Protestant ascendancy a simulacrum of its former self; its awareness of this was clear and manifest. Moreover, Home Rule seemed inevitable. At the helm of a strengthened political party in Westminster – 86 members as opposed to 61 in 1880 – Parnell called the shots. Within eight months he toppled two governments, forged alliances with each of them and from each extracted concessions favourable to Ireland; the caretaker Conservative government lifted coercion and passed the Ashbourne Act, which was a major step towards peasant pro-prietorship, and Gladstone agreed to support Home Rule. Each concession further attenuated Protestant Ascendancy and exacerbated their insecurities.

There is a prevalent misconception among scholars that Oldham founded the IPHRA.[15] The northern Protestant, David Briggs, founded the organisa-tion in Belfast in April 1885. Thomas Shillington Junior of Portadown was president; Alfred Webb and Thomas McClelland – both *DUR* contributors – were among the six vice-presidents. A subsidary was later established in Dublin (with Oldham as Hon. Local Secretary) under the auspices and con-trol of the parent body.[16] Representing Protestant efforts to convert their co-religionists to Home Rule, the IPHRA was a unique endeavour in the history of Irish nationalism and a significant exception to the popular gen-eralisation equating Protestantism with unionism. However, it was not a monolithic organisation and the varying agendas and constituencies of the northern and southern branches led to friction and discord.

The Ulster members, numerically greater and more active than their southern counterparts, were mostly Presbyterian tenant farmers and entre-preneurs who supported the agrarian agitation. The intellectual core of the organisation, however, lay in the south, whose members were mostly edu-cated Anglicans, professionals, civil servants, academics and writers (Douglas

Hyde, T. W. Rolleston, Stephen Gwynn and J. A. Galbraith) and even included mavericks like Maud Gonne. Moreover, the southern members opposed the land agitation, partly because of their own connections with the landed gentry and partly because they saw their primary task as converting this influential and wealthy class to Home Rule. They attacked Archbishop Croke's suggestion that nationalists should discontinue paying both landlords' rents and government taxes. Boycotting, the southern IPHRA claimed through its organ *North & South* (to which Yeats was a contributor), was morally justifiable only against a few oppressive landlords.[17] Later, they took issue with William O'Brien's attack on landlords as perpetrators of famines and rackrents, 'foreigners in race and language' and immune to any nationalist appeal. Landlords, argued the *North & South*, despite their faults, were still gifted Irishmen: 'we should strive to retain them and not drive them away'.[18] Their sympathy for the landlords and opposition to the Land League embarrassed nationalists. Rolleston's pamphlet *Boycotting: A Reply* – a response to Samuel Laing's defence of the Land League – attacked the practice as:

> an engine for the wholesale suppression of independent thought, of honest enterprise and industry; for the handicapping of sober, honest, hardworking men all over Ireland down to the level of drunkards and idlers, of those who would rather get twenty-five per cent off their rent by clamour and intimidation rather than treble their profits by toil and thrift. (Loughlin, 355)

This played right into the hands of unionists who circulated the pamphlet in Britain and Ireland as an exposé of nationalist methods by a fellow nationalist.[19]

Though Oldham, Rolleston and other southern IPHRA members were constitutional nationalists, they did not support Parnell, at least not while he was alive. Parnell's Land League affiliations would partly account for this. William Henry Hulbert, an American traveller to Ireland in the late 1880s, noted 'the intellectual revolt against "Parnellism" and its methods, of which his [Rolleston's] attitude and that of his friends here is an unmistakable symptom'.[20] He quotes Rolleston's letter expressing disgust with national politics:

> 'I have been slowly forced,' he wrote, 'to the conclusion that the National League is a body which deserves nothing but reprobation from all who wish well to Ireland. It has plunged this country into a state of moral degradation, from which it will take us at least a generation to recover. It is teaching the people that no law of justice, of candour, of honour, or of humanity can be allowed to interfere with the political ends of the moment. It is, in fact, absolutely divorcing morality from politics. The mendacity of

> some of its leaders is shameless and sickening, and still more sick-
> ening is the complete indifference with which this mendacity is
> regarded in Ireland.' (vol. 2, 292)[21]

Stephen Gwynn's observations reinforce Hulbert's. A member of the southern IPHRA and Dublin's literary circle, he was in a better position than Hulbert to see the capital's Protestant nationalists fighting shy of Parnell:

> Of course, to literary young men, it was the political side that
> made appeal. Rolleston interested us because, being older, he was
> in a position to take a part: and he was strongly Nationalist. Par-
> nell's party was looking for recruits, and men of good brains
> would, we knew, be more than commonly acceptable if they
> came from the Protestant camp. But to accept service under Par-
> nell meant accepting the party pledge, which bound all members
> to speak, vote and act according to the decision of the majority.
> Rolleston and one or two others of his standing – notably
> Charles Hubert Oldham – definitely decided against submitting
> to this sacrifice of their free judgement.[22]

The fundamental difference between the two IPHRA branches, however, lay
in their reasons for supporting Home Rule. For the northern IPHRA, land
reform was the *sine qua non* of their association. The nationalism of the northern members was also motivated by their support for Gladstone, and other
economic and social considerations. Among these was the belief that Irish
dissatisfaction brought about by English indifference threatened economic
growth and the unity of 'the empire of Great Britain and Ireland'. The hostility between the Dissenters and the Anglicans was another factor and the
former felt as victimised as the Catholics for being excluded from high offices
monopolised by 'the ascendancy party'. Such a situation was 'subversive of
true religion'; it created sectarianism and hindered economic progress.[23]

The southern members generally lacked such positive reasons for supporting Home Rule. As Patrick Buckland has argued, southern Protestants
could not afford to be as belligerent and intransigent as their Ulster counterparts in opposing Home Rule.[24] Predominantly Anglicans, few in number
and scattered geographically, they felt their privileges threatened and themselves abandoned by the sympathetic attitude of successive British governments to Catholic demands. Their options were emigration either to the
north, where unionism was more organised, or to England. In either case they
would be uprooted from ancestral lands and cast among a people whom they
considered to be as alien and unsympathetic to their plight as their Catholic
neighbours. They could also stay where they were, hoping that their loyalty
would be rewarded and the Union maintained. On the other hand, they

could join forces with the nationalists. Oldham and other southern Protestant nationalists preferred the latter. Judging by the IPHRA (Dublin) propaganda, their nationalism was of a peculiar southern–Protestant variety largely motivated by a sense of expediency, English betrayal, Catholic ascendancy and Protestant marginalisation rather than revolutionary patriotic fervour.[25] Their leaflets and pamphlets argued that given the inevitability of Home Rule and their own minority status, Protestants' unionism would weaken and isolate them among a predominantly nationalist population. 'The future of Irish Protestantism', one pamphlet asserted, 'depends solely on the position and influence it can secure in Ireland.'[26] By supporting the nationalists, they could better safeguard their influence and interests.

Protestant interests were central also to Oldham's journalistic forays. The *DUR*'s very first issue shows that the periodical was targeted at Protestants. The opening editorial claimed that the *DUR* would function 'as the journal of the educated classes of Ireland and as the organ of the chief Irish university' (February 1885, 2). There was a tremendous overlap between these two groups, as most of the 'educated classes of Ireland' were linked to TCD. The editorial admits as much when it describes TCD as 'the great national seat of learning, the home of much of the rising talent of the country' (1). Another factor linking the two groups was religion: most of the TCD and the intellectual élite of Ireland were Protestants. Targeting the periodical primarily at Protestants, and yet not wishing to appear sectarian, the editors avoided the word 'Protestant' but used a cultural shorthand with a similar import: 'educated opinion of Dublin (twice)', 'cultivated classes of the country (twice)', 'educated classes of Ireland' (1–2). Sixty of the sixty-nine contributors whose biographical details are known were Protestants. Not surprisingly, most of the political articles addressed Protestant concerns.

The *DUR* debated the crisis confronting the community with a view to coaxing it out of its imperial identity into a more Irish one, weaning it from its sense of innate superiority and reconciling it with its diminished status. By encouraging greater participation in the shaping of Ireland's future, the proprietors aimed to bring the community into contact with the Catholic intelligentsia and leadership and gradually convert it to Home Rule. Though they were fast losing their power and privileges, the Protestants still were, for Oldham, Ireland's educated and cultural élite. Instead of relying upon England, he argued, they would be better off capitalising on their advantages, joining the national movement and carving out their own future. United with the nationalists, they would be stronger and better equipped to protect Protestant interests and arrest marginalisation.

In trying to convert southern Protestants to Home Rule, Oldham faced an uphill task. Unlike their northern counterparts, southern Protestants tended to be aristocratic, landed and anglicised. They were also more isolated comprising only ten per cent of the population.[27] The combination of a conservative attitude, a siege mentality, vulnerability and dependence on Westminster for the maintenance of their position added a touch of desperation to their opposition to Home Rule. Oldham would have realised that to even attract their attention he would have to obfuscate, if not deny, both his own nationalist sympathies as well as his periodical's salient political agenda. He would also have to assure southern Protestants that he was of their camp and shared their concerns about the preservation of Protestant Ascendancy.

These constraints determined the journal's initial editorial strategy and necessitated an element of subterfuge. The subterfuge was of two kinds. Instead of a 'nationalist' tone, the journal's opening editorial claimed it would espouse a 'national' tone. This in itself was fairly non-controversial and something that southern unionists could accept, so long as it was restricted to literary/cultural matters and excluded political ones. Anticipating such fears, the editorial assured readers that 'it cannot be too emphatically declared that with the vexed questions of current politics THE REVIEW has nothing whatever to do' (2).

The 'national tone', as clarified by the editorial, entailed asserting national pride, furthering Ireland's claims and reinforcing Irish identity, but doing so in a strictly non-political manner. In another time, or another clime, such an undertaking might have been possible; but in the Ireland of the mid-1880s it was a tall order involving a perpetual balancing act on a fine razor's edge. During a political struggle for national independence which inevitably employed binary oppositions of an essentialist and nativist variety, the distinction between political and national was all too easily blurred. Besides, as events would show, a nationalist rather than a national attitude was what the journal intended to foster.

The second subterfuge involved the periodical's attitude to Protestant ascendancy. As stated earlier, Oldham sympathised with the plight of his coreligionists, especially the landed gentry. However, unlike them he believed that supporting Home Rule was in their best interests and a better safeguard for their position and influence than reliance on the British connection. Also, he did not believe that the Protestants' educational and cultural superiority entitled them to a monopoly of influence and privilege within Ireland. However, it is precisely this belief that the editorial indicates as being seminal to its purposes.

The editorial claimed that the magazine was founded to help the 'cultivated classes of the country' 'direct and develop' Irish opinion (1). By putting their talents at the nation's service, Protestants could vindicate their status as the cultural and intellectual élite, and perhaps regain some lost ground. To thus rehabilitate Protestants at the centre of Irish affairs was the periodical's proclaimed *raison d'être* in its opening editorial. The *DUR*'s precursor had asserted that its title, *The Dublin University Magazine*, indicated its status as the 'monthly advocate of the Protestantism, the intelligence and the respectability of Ireland', for 'unquestioningly the graduates of the University combine all these elements in themselves'.[28] Half a century later, the *DUR* would make a similar though more subdued claim for itself and the Protestantism represented by TCD:

> We assume that Dublin University is, or in the nature of things ought to be, the true centre of culture and educated opinion in Dublin. Many there are who regret that it does not exert a more direct and permeating influence. An influence it undoubtedly has; but it is of a fragmentary character, the effect rather of individual members than of the institution itself. We see no good reason why it should continue to be so. (2)

Oldham's record and political affiliations, as well as the subsequent change in the journal's editorial policy, suggest that this declaration of an *a*political and pro-Protestant policy was the window display meant to lure unionist readers. Notwithstanding its profession to avoid 'the vexed question of current politics', the *DUR* was a political enterprise from its very inception. It drew its gestatory impulse from a political situation and it had a clear political agenda.

The first four editorial notes of its opening issue were directed at TCD readers and focused on college events. In the next number they were even more specific, focusing on the duties of a porter and how parcels should be received for absent students. One fifth of the first few issues were devoted exclusively to 'University News', 'Societies and Clubs', 'Honor Lists' and the 'University Calendar'. Most of the contributors were from TCD – 20 out of 28 in the six issues between March and July 1885 – and most of the books reviewed were written by TCD alumni: 12 out of 17 in the same period. On many occasions, the authors as well as their reviewers were both from TCD.

The list of its contributors makes it quite clear that the magazine attracted the best of Irish talent as well as some of the cream of Dublin's intellectual and cultural circles.[29] Yeats, Hyde, C. F. Bastable (Professor at TCD), Rolleston, Todhunter, Frederick Gregg (a school friend of Yeats) and Katharine Tynan were regular contributors throughout the journal's duration. During the six months of its 'non-political' phase, there were also contributions by Thomas E. Webb (prolific unionist pamphleteer, Regius Professor of Laws and Public Orator at TCD), T. W. Lyster (Assistant Librarian, NLI, and one of Yeats's earliest patrons and advisers),[30] Arthur Rambaut (Assistant Astronomer,

TCD, and later Royal Astronomer of Ireland), J. H. Bernard (Junior Fellow, and later Archbishop of Dublin, Provost of TCD and nominated representative of southern unionists in negotiations with Lloyd George; following the Easter Rising he wrote to *The Times* in his capacity as archbishop advocating martial law in Ireland: 'This is not the time for amnesties and pardons, it is the time for punishment, swift and stern'),[31] Thomas Maguire (*inter alia The Times* intermediary in the purchase of the Pigott forgeries), Arthur Patton (Contemporary Club member, writer of comic songs satirising Irish Catholics, and professional speaker on unionist platforms), Arthur Palmer (Fellow, TCD), Caesar Litton Falkiner (Contemporary Club member, President of the College Philosophical Society, and later literary critic, unionist politician, land commissioner and executive committee member of the Irish Unionist Alliance), G. F. Fitzgerald (Professor, TCD, FRS and eminent academic), William Archer (Librarian, NLI), Edward Dowden (renowned Shakespeare scholar, J. B. Yeats's friend, Professor of English, TCD and active unionist) and Charles Johnston (Contemporary Club member, theosophist, Yeats's boyhood friend and son of William Johnston of Ballykilbeg, one of the most notorious Orangemen of his day). The eminence and social prestige of the *DUR* is evidenced by the fact that many of its contributors can be located in the *DNB*, were well-known public personalities and played a significant role in Irish political and cultural affairs. While some like Hyde, Yeats, Falkiner and Bernard achieved prominence later, others like Davitt, O'Leary, Rolleston, T. W. Russell, O'Grady, W. F. Bailey, Justin McCarthy and the TCD Fellows were already established figures. The fact that their contributions often discussed controversial issues which they could influence added to the *DUR*'s prestige and importance.

Advertisements boasting the custom of 'Her Majesty the Queen and other Royals' indicate that at least initially the readers were expected to be principally loyalists. This impression is reinforced in a later editorial note urging readers to receive the Prince and Princess of Wales at TCD 'with tenfold sincerity, and with all the fervour of true loyalty' (April 1885, 50). A later note described the visit as an 'unqualified success' and lamented its 'unavoidable brevity' (May 1885, 98).

The *DUR*'s first article, a dry, pedantic account of 'New Tendencies of English Political Economy' (3–5), was probably written by Oldham himself. The second article, an obituary on 'The Late Mr P. J. Smyth' (6–8) exemplified the journal's political manoeuvring in the first few issues.[32] Smyth was praised for his 'high and lofty principle, full of poetic enthusiasm' manifested in his struggle 'against fearful odds, for the grand ideal of Irish Nationality' (February 1885, 6). Lest this convey the wrong impression about the obituarist's political sympathies and alarm the more timid readers, a caveat was added to the same sentence: 'we cannot help admiring his unselfish devotion, whatever opinion we may hold as to the possibility or advantage of realising his ideal'. His (Repeal) 'action was brave and noble, however foolish it may have been'. Such seesawing is carried on throughout the article. While the article does mention Smyth's heroic rescue of Mitchell from a Tasmanian prison, his nationalist sympathies are queried, romanticised or neutralised for Protestant consumption. Smyth has all the romance and ardour of the Young Irelanders – remember Davis was a Protestant, and one of TCD's most beloved sons – but also 'exhibited in an eminent degree their most characteristic faults'. Like them, this Don Quixote tilted at windmills: he was 'impractical' and could not 'recognise unalterable facts'. But because he was well intentioned, he, like all true Irishmen, 'denounced land agitation and that "League of Hell" '. His attacks on the Land League are presented as being his most outstanding and 'true' nationalist actions:

> A Nationalist when the cause of Irish nationality seemed most hopeless, who can help admiring his fearless courage, both physical and moral, whatever may be thought of the principles he advocated. His bold and open denunciation of the Land League, at a time when almost every public man in Ireland was quailing before its power, was not the least admirable act in his life. Would that all our public men would speak out their opinions as fearlessly as he did! (7)

As examples of Smyth's 'true' nationalism the article instances his withdrawing support from Home Rule, dissociating himself from nationalists, sitting on the government benches, and committing himself only to the 'restoration of the Irish parliament' (7). For the obituarist, it was the last of these actions that most aptly represented Smyth's brand of nationalism, and, in conjunction with Smyth's oratory, vindicated Disraeli's description of Smyth as a 'second Grattan' (7). Throughout the article the nationalist is presented as a kind of noble savage with all the misguided enthusiasm and idealism of a child needing only guidance and sympathy to set him right. The nationalist bait is dangled before the readers fully decked out in its poetry and romance but minus the sting, rendering it not only benign but also attractive to Protestants in the form of the status quo of 1782. Under the pretext of prohibiting all political discussion, it is only the Catholic nationalist perspective that is effectively excluded from this first issue.

Grattan's parliament, which for the later Yeats represented the Protestant heyday of 'that one Irish century that escaped from darkness and confusion' (*Ex*, 345), featured prominently as an acceptable solution to the current crisis, and was advocated even by supposedly non-political articles. 'Irish Manufactures' (June 1885, 106–8), by Henry Stuart Fagan (Fellow of Pembroke College,

Oxford, member of the IPHRA, and prolific nationalist pamphleteer), urged the patronage of Irish industry above party interests and criticised the subservience to English goods. The nationalist slant of this position was characteristically disguised as Protestant patriotism by a conclusion exhorting TCD to cultivate more of the 'feeling of 1782. . . [for] the good of the country' (June 1885, 106).[33] A few articles, like 'The Genius of the Celt in the Art of Illumination' (May 1885, 84–5), were national yet non-sectarian but these had to delve deep into the past to bypass the 'vexed issue of current politics'. Though the *DUR*'s first six issues adopted a 'national tone' as promised, it always insisted that this expression of national sentiment did not have any political implications. The emphasis was on a Protestant tradition which was pro-Ireland without necessarily being anti-England. However, this was a difficult distinction to maintain and national could very easily blend into nationalist.[34]

The imperial connection figured prominently in loyalist contributions. The *DUR*'s book advertisements indicate that many of the magazine's readers were TCD graduates preparing for the colonial civil service examinations. The nationalist threat to TCD's interests in the Empire is stressed by a TCD graduate in 'The Irish Universities and the Imperial Services' (79–82). After listing alumni who distinguished themselves in the colonies, the article questions the benefits of Home Rule:

> That the connection of the Irish Universities with the Imperial Services has been of great value to the youth of Ireland is sufficiently clear from what I have said above . . . Would it be wise to tamper with a political system which opens such careers to young men of the middle classes? (May 1885, 81–2)

The nationalist perspective was gradually introduced into the review but with enough caveats and reservations to dispel the alarm it might cause readers. A note in the July issue – political discussions were formally admitted only from August – reported on Oldham's address to the 'University Philosophical Society':

> No essay of the present session aroused more general interest or produced a more lively discussion than that read on May 28 by Mr C. H. Oldham (Sch.), BA, on 'The Political Principles of Young Irishmen'. . . for the principles advocated by Mr Oldham were the principles of nationalism. The essayist did not mean by this that he was a supporter of the Irish Parliamentary Party, but he considers that if educated young Irishmen embraced national sentiments, the effect would be to elevate the tone of the movement for self-government, and to advance the cause. We need not be Nationalists, he thinks, but we ought to be national. (158)

It was here that the editors played their cards on the question of nationalism. It would take expert sophistry to explain how 'educated young Irishmen' can espouse the 'principles of nationalism', 'be national', 'embrace national sentiments', advocate 'self-government' and yet not become 'Nationalists'. Unless, of course, what was being advocated was Protestant nationalism and 'educated young Irishmen' was yet another synonym for 'cultivated classes of the country'. 'Nationalist' was a pejorative term conjuring up visions of Catholic rule, land agitation, peasant proprietorship and Protestant marginalisation. It was also generally synonymous with Catholic. Given that Oldham was mainly addressing Protestants, his concerns about elevating 'the tone of the movement for self-government' in order to 'advance the cause' was double-talk for securing increased participation and protection for the Protestant minority. It was to this end that he urged fellow Protestants – or 'educated young Irishmen' – to shed their unionist biases and support Home Rule.

II

Yeats's very first periodical publication was in the *DUR*'s second issue of March 1885. It was a welcome opening especially since it was not until more than a year later (July 1886) that he was published by another periodical (the *Irish Monthly*). He did not have to compete with other poets for editorial favour in this newly established review and, having secured his position, he eventually published 18 pieces of work in its run of 23 issues. Though the review did not pay contributors, it helped establish Yeats as a poet: it introduced him to his earliest publisher – John Walker of Sealy, Bryers and Walker, who published the *DUR* – and to his earliest readers and buyers: many of the subscribers to the privately printed first edition of *Oisin* were members of the Contemporary Club. It also drew attention to his books when he first published in the open market.[35]

The new periodical was committed to encouraging 'the intellectual independence of Irishmen', pressing Ireland's claims and, more significantly for cultural nationalism and Yeats, resisting London's 'centralising tendencies' and cultural monopoly. He had realised very early that literary success would necessitate a struggle against the more established Victorians, that patriotism could prove a useful ally in that struggle and significantly advance his literary fortunes.[36] More importantly, the *DUR* catered to what it called the 'cultivated classes of the country', which, in Yeatsian parlance, translated as 'the book-buying classes of the country'. The readers of this up-market periodical were more likely to buy poetry written by a Protestant than readers of most other Irish periodicals, which were relatively low-brow and Catholic.

Moreover, the *DUR*'s efforts to reinforce Anglo-Irish identity would have strengthened Yeats's own sense of identity when his class was increasingly threatened by Catholic democracy. The periodical provided him with an outlet and a readership which would not look askance at his Protestantism or question his Irishness for that. Given the sharp sectarian divisions within Irish society, it is not a coincidence that, though the literary field was dominated by Catholic periodicals which far outnumbered their Protestant counterparts, Yeats was first published by the latter.

The *DUR* played an important role in the careers of the two leading literary revivalists, Douglas Hyde and W. B. Yeats. It published their early work, encouraged them and introduced them to fellow writers and to each other. On the strength of these associations, which formed the core of the Irish Literary Society membership, Yeats propagated the Revival in England and Ireland. The *Review* also provided them with their earliest audiences, and introduced them to future mentors: O'Leary for Yeats, and Sigerson for Hyde. The importance of Oldham's role in Hyde's life is testified by the latter's diary entry on New Year's Day, 1886: 'The most significant things I did [in 1885] were to join the Mosaic and the new club that Oldham founded' (Daly, 73).

The *DUR*'s bibliographical and historical significance is boosted by its having published some important articles, not only in the careers of these two writers, but also in the literary and political history of that period. Hyde's 'A Plea for the Irish language' (August 1886, 666–76) is an outline draft of 'The Necessity of De-Anglicising Ireland', an address that mobilised literary and political nationalism. It was his earliest statement on the significance of Gaelic to Irish culture and identity, and forms the basis of his subsequent propaganda for the Gaelic League. His later pamphlet *On the Reasons for Keeping Alive the Irish Language* is, as his biographer has pointed out, a condensed version of his *DUR* article.[37] The magazine also published the bulk of Yeats's early work, including *Mosada* (June 1886, 473–83) and *The Island of Statues* (April–July 1885, 56–8, 82–4, 110–12, 136–9). Later, Yeats used the magazine typescript of *Mosada* when he published it in book form. His essay on 'The Poetry of Sir Samuel Ferguson' (November 1886, 923–41), exhorting Irish writers to 'nourish the forces that make for the political liberties of Ireland' (*UP1*, 100), is often viewed as a classic statement of his literary nationalism. Because of its connection with these two writers, the *Review*, by 1921, had achieved the status of a collector's item.[38]

The *Review* also influenced their literary ideas. Justin McCarthy's 'The Irish Language and Literature' (August 1885, 42–6), urging a greater familiarity with 'the splendid stories of legendary Irish history', is a significant and possibly seminal event in the history of the Irish Revival. It had a strong impact on both Hyde and Yeats. Three issues later Hyde published an early version of *Love Songs of Connacht* where he acknowledged his debt to McCarthy. Following Yeats's own admission about adopting Irish subject matter in his twentieth year, critics have seen this article as having partly influenced this change.[39]

Both Yeats and Hyde went on to become key players in the Literary Revival. Their association with the *DUR* has recently prompted a scholar whose views command respect to claim that the magazine pioneered the effort 'to create a national literary culture' (*WBY*, 41). The *DUR*'s opening editorial stated that the periodical would adopt 'a national tone', 'resist the centralising tendencies of the time' and assert the 'intellectual independence of Irishmen' (February 1885, 1). It also promised that its orientation would be 'literary' and not political. As an outlet for Irish 'literary activity', it would prohibit political discussion and focus instead on 'phases and aspects of contemporary art and literature' (2) and 'topics usually dealt with in a literary journal'. This purposeful editorial conveys the impression that the *DUR* was a literary magazine committed especially to encouraging and developing Irish writing with a national aim. This supports Foster's claims about the magazine's literary nationalism and the fact that, 'stimulated by the apparent imminence of Home Rule and a triumphant constitutional nationalism', it had set about creating 'a national literary culture' (*WBY*, 41). The significance of this claim relates to the magazine's status as an early champion of the Revival, and, more importantly, to the actual dating of the Revival itself. It also challenges Yeats's own dating of the Revival to the period following Parnell's death.[40]

There are two aspects of Foster's claim that merit examination: firstly, whether the *DUR* ever was a 'literary' periodical, and secondly, whether it actively and self-consciously worked towards creating 'a national literary culture'. The *DUR* was certainly literary in the broad sense of the word, in that its contents were well written and of a high standard including, but not solely, *belles-lettres*. Its contributors were mainly TCD graduates, and college fellows often submitted articles. The magazine's proof-reading was excellent and typographical errors were rare. Overall, the *DUR* was an extremely attractive 'literary' periodical and would have fulfilled its readers' expectations.[41]

However, in the narrower sense of the word the *DUR* was not what we might call today a 'literary' magazine, as say the *Yellow Book*, *Savoy* and *Bookman* are literary magazines. Despite its initial assertions, it had a predominantly political orientation and purpose, and consistently covered political and social issues more prominently than literature. Even in the first six issues, in which political discussion had officially been proscribed, literature or literary discussion accounted for just 20% of the total copy. Book advertisements, which constituted less than 10% of the advertisements in the review – hairdressing saloons, billiard table manufacturers and ladies' tailors with royal patronage, among others, made up the balance – indicate that the magazine was not popularly perceived as focusing primarily on literature. Besides, the book advertisements – including those by 'Hodges, Figgis and Co., Booksellers and Publishers to the University of Dublin' – catered mainly to candidates for army, navy, home and colonial civil service examinations. The few books for a general readership had titles such as 'Memory and Success' and 'Science and Civilisation'. This is in sharp contrast to the recent publications by novelists and poets one normally sees advertised in late nineteenth-century English literary periodicals such as the *Bookman*.

The *DUR*'s injunction against political debate lasted for six months, after which the magazine became overtly political. The editors claimed that the introduction of political discussion had transformed the review into 'an independent Irish organ for political and social, as well as *merely* literary or scientific discussion'. Hence it could no longer serve '*merely* as an organ for the reporting of Trinity College news' (January 1886, 71; emphasis added). The use of the adverb 'merely' indicates the relative peripherality and insignificance of TCD news and 'literary or scientific discussion' within the magazine's priorities as compared to 'political and social' discussion. Moreover, the common application of 'merely' to 'Trinity College news' and to 'literary and scientific discussion' could also indicate an editorial bracketing of these two topics under a common rubric. This impression is strengthened by the fact that, when the magazine distanced itself from TCD and dropped the college arms from its front cover, it also distanced itself from certain other aspects of its erstwhile character, such as 'literary and scientific discussion'. TCD had served its purpose and so had 'literary and scientific discussion'. When there were pressing political issues on hand, and limited space for discussion, literature was the first to be jettisoned, and in this matter the *DUR*, despite all its claims to the contrary, was no different from its predecessors. Barbara Hayley has shown that it would be inaccurate to categorise most Irish periodicals of this period as literary.[42] With politics being the predominant consideration, and literature viewed as a diversion, 'literary' periodicals in mid-nineteenth-century Ireland either succumbed to the political climate of the time or were drowned in the rhetoric of debate. *Ancient Ireland* (Jan–April 1835), which focused on Irish history and culture, and 'eschewed all politics and polemics', is instanced by Hayley as a representative journal which collapsed in spite of maintaining a national rather than sectarian character. 'The failure of this magazine. . . may indicate not that the intelligentsia was resistant to Ireland's ancient history and language, but rather that they preferred them mixed with a little religion and politics' (Hayley, 37). Other cases in point are the *Dublin Magazine or General Repertory of Philosophy, Belles Lettres and Miscellaneous Information* of 1820 and the *Belfast Magazine and Literary Journal* (February–July

1825). Like the *DUR*, there were other periodicals that hoped to avoid politics and concentrate on developing a national identity. However, they seldom lived up to that promise and inevitably ended up on one side or the other of the sectarian divide, giving more space to politics than to literature. According to Hayley, the Catholic *Dublin Review* and the Protestant *Dublin University Magazine* were successful primarily because they made no claims for objectivity and were openly sectarian.

In examining whether the *DUR* pioneered the effort to 'create a national literary culture', it becomes clear that the magazine played a crucial role in the careers of revivalists such as Yeats and Hyde. At the same time one realises that when these writers were published by the magazine they were mere beginners and known only to a small group. In 1885, with such little capital, it is unlikely that either Hyde or Yeats could have themselves visualised their subsequent roles in literary history. And there is no indication that the editors had either. In Hyde's case, at least, it is quite clear that the magazine did not share his interests. Gaelic received scant coverage in the magazine – two poems, two articles and a book review (all by Hyde), totalling a mere 25 pages (1.5%) – and the editors questioned its utility:

> But we should like to see more definiteness or more common-sense in the aims of *An Chraoibin Aoibinn* and his friends. Do they wish to make Irish the language of our conversation and our newspapers? Impossible, and wholly undesirable. Do they wish to make us a bi-lingual people in the sense that everybody should know two languages? But peasantry and artisans cannot be expected to know two languages except at the expense of both. Would they separate Ireland into an English-speaking country and an Irish-speaking country? But how seriously this would affect the free circulation of thought. . . What is there left except to treat Irish as a classic, and leave it to the Universities? Sufficient endowments will secure their attention to its interests. (June 1886, 547)

On the basis of Hyde's association with the *DUR*'s management, Dunleavy and Dunleavy have speculated that this comment and Hyde's subsequent response (August 1886, 666–76) was an attempt to engineer a controversy and 'stir up debate' (123) at the time of Gladstone's first Home Rule Bill. This is not convincing. When Hyde's reply was printed in August the Bill had already been defeated, Gladstone had resigned and Salisbury had taken a hard line on Irish affairs. If topicality and controversy were hoped for, the reply was printed two months too late. Furthermore, Hyde's managerial role would not have protected him from attack as the Dunleavys seem to imply, at least not in the *DUR*. The Contemporary Club practice of fierce verbal duelling was carried on in the review and members often attacked each other's views in its columns.[43]

Foster's assertion that the *DUR* had consciously attempted to 'create a national literary culture' is further undermined by the fact that the editors themselves were not interested in such an enterprise. Not only did the *DUR's* editors not consider a preference for English over Irish literature important enough to quarrel with in an aggressive way, their own literary tastes, as is borne out by the following statement by Oldham, hardly qualified them to take up an aggressive stand on this issue:

> At least the literary world of England and Ireland is one. And we judge of the great names in this world irrespective of their nationality, placing ourselves in the position of Englishmen, guided by their temper, powerless against the inevitable influence. (June 1885, 109)

This attitude is reflected in the contents of the magazine. Given their claims of literary nationalism, and that political discussions were banned, one would have expected substantial coverage of Irish literature, at least in the first six issues. However, that is anything but the case; Irish literature comprises a mere 16 out of 164 pages (10%). What further damages the editors' (and Foster's) claims is that more space is occupied by classical literature (25 pages, 15%) and TCD news (50 pages, 31%). This trend persists for the magazine's entire duration. Statistical evidence shows that the editors were also not particularly interested in literature nor did they favour the claims of Irish over classical and non-Irish literatures. In the *DUR's* two volumes, Irish and Gaelic literature comprise just 12% and non-Irish literature 28%. Of the total poetry and fiction printed in the magazine, the Irish and Gaelic segment comprises 24%, while the balance is made up of other literatures, with classics and translations once again taking up a sizeable chunk (55%). Of the literary articles in the first two volumes, Irish and Gaelic literature occupy 41%, while English, European and classical literature make up the balance of 59%. Similarly, of the total number of the book reviews printed, 20% cover Irish and Gaelic literature; the balance is made up of classical and translated literature (44%), English literature (7%) and non-literary books (29%). These figures suggest that literature was a low priority and that Irish literature in particular was an even lower priority than classical and translated literature or, for that matter, TCD news. This sufficiently indicates the limits of the editors' interests either in literary nationalism or in the merits of a literary revival. Oldham had helped publish Ellen O'Leary's Fenian poems and was a member of the National Literary Society, while not being particularly active in it; the Young Ireland Society, where literary discussions were inevitably leavened with

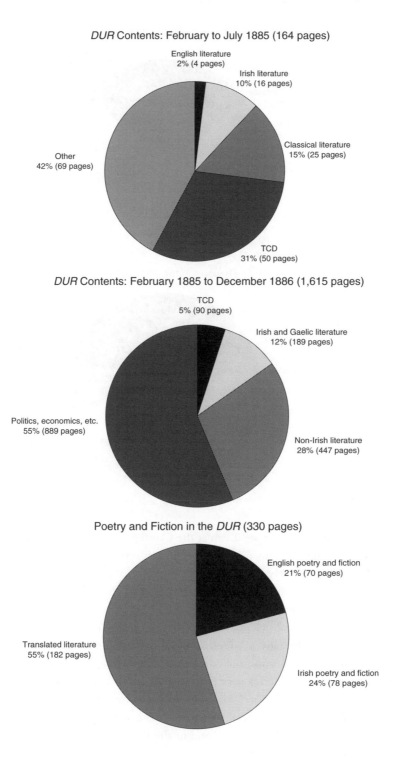

DUR Contents: February to July 1885 (164 pages)

English literature
2% (4 pages)

Irish literature
10% (16 pages)

Classical literature
15% (25 pages)

Other
42% (69 pages)

TCD
31% (50 pages)

DUR Contents: February 1885 to December 1886 (1,615 pages)

TCD
5% (90 pages)

Irish and Gaelic literature
12% (189 pages)

Politics, economics, etc.
55% (889 pages)

Non-Irish literature
28% (447 pages)

Poetry and Fiction in the *DUR* (330 pages)

English poetry and fiction
21% (70 pages)

Translated literature
55% (182 pages)

Irish poetry and fiction
24% (78 pages)

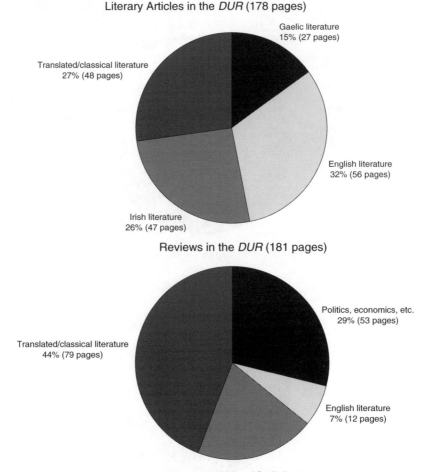

Literary Articles in the *DUR* (178 pages)

Gaelic literature
15% (27 pages)

Translated/classical literature
27% (48 pages)

English literature
32% (56 pages)

Irish literature
26% (47 pages)

Reviews in the *DUR* (181 pages)

Politics, economics, etc.
29% (53 pages)

Translated/classical literature
44% (79 pages)

English literature
7% (12 pages)

Irish and Gaelic literature
20% (37 pages)

politics, was more to his taste. Even at the Contemporary Club, literature was not high on Oldham's agenda and for 'literary rather than political discussion' (Dunleavy, 120) Hyde had to look to other groups. Oldham himself preferred economics and political philosophy, which invariably constituted the subjects chosen by him for discussion both at his club and in his magazine.

The *DUR*'s classical orientation is evident from the title of its literary section, 'Kottabos' – literally, a Greek after-dinner wine – which was also the name of an early Trinity journal containing translations and Latin and Greek compositions. In the *DUR*'s very first issue Kottabos contained one poem in English with three footnotes in Greek, a poem on 'Sir Francis Drake' followed by a Greek translation of the same, then another poem in English followed by a Latin translation, then one in English and another in Latin, then a Latin quotation from Virgil, then a poem in Latin with a note in Latin, and finally a poem in Latin with a footnote in English containing two Latin quotations. Yeats made his debut in the next issue with two poems in similarly august surroundings. While he escaped being translated by a classics-happy rhymester, Fanny Parnell was not so fortunate.

However, Yeats did not escape entirely unscathed. Consciously, or otherwise, he began incorporating classical references into his poems, not always to their advantage as he later realised. Arcadian shepherds in the *Island of Statues* (April–July 1885) display an envious familiarity with Homer and Virgil, their serenades replete with references to Dido, Oenone and Clytemnestra. The genteel setting for 'In a Drawing Room' (January 1886, 75) quite appropriately includes an 'Attic bust', while 'Life' (February 1886, 151) laughs 'upon the lips of Sophocles' (*VP*, 686). Though these poems were not reprinted by Yeats, 'An Epilogue to "The Island of Statues" and "The Seeker"' (October 1885, 230–1) was, but only after strenuous revision which included altering the title and dropping a classical allusion.[44]

The *DUR*'s preference for the classics is consistent with its readers' tastes and background. The 'educated' or 'cultured classes of Ireland' – indeed as of England – considered themselves educated or cultured in direct proportion to their familiarity with classical literature. Irish literature was a poor cousin whose existence one noted but whose provinciality and uncouthness merited snubbing. Further, nineteenth-century Trinity had a very distinguished record in classics boasting some of the best names in the field, such as J. P. Mahaffy, Arthur Palmer, R. V. Tyrrell, R. C. Purser and John Bury. Its disdain for Irish literature was also well known, often provoking Hyde and Yeats's ire. Apparently, ancient Gaelic literature, on which much of the Revival was based, 'was silly or indecent' and 'at bottom abominable'; 'the element of idealism' was negligible and children could not be allowed to read it. Hyde's language 'was not good enough for a patois' and his stories were 'so low – about a dirty wretch who never washed his feet and married the princess So and So'.[45] The *DUR* did not reflect these biases, but neither was it enthusiastic about Irish literature. Doubtless, there was encouragement handed out to aspiring Irish writers, but no more than would be seemly from a 'literary' periodical, intended for the genteel classes, claiming a 'national tone'.

Yeats's *The Island of Statues*, serialised between April and July 1885, was significant both for his contemporaries (AE, Rolleston, Dowden), who rated it highly and wanted it republished, as well as for Yeats, who returned to it at numerous points in his career according it a seminal place in his poetic development.[46] A pastoral set in Arcady, it reflects the influence of his early poetic models, Shelley and Spenser. Naschina asks her suitors to prove their love by procuring 'the flower of joy' from a neighbouring island. Failure entails transformation into a statue by the Enchantress who rules the island.

Kottabistic.

Merchant of Venice, iv. 1.

(*Shakespeare.*)

Οὐκ ἐξ ἀνάγκης ἔλεος, ἀλλ' ἀπ' οὐρανοῦ
στάζει δροσώδους τοι δίκην γάνους κάτω
γλυκὺς βροτοῖσι, καὶ νέμει δίσσην χάριν,
τὸν δόντα γὰρ καὶ τὸν λαβόντ' εὐεργετεῖ·
τοῖς ἐν τέλει βεβῶσι παγκρατὴς πέλει,
ὑψιθρόνῳ τ' ἄνακτι μᾶλλον εὐπρεπὴς
χρυσαυγὲς ἢ στέφος. τὸ μὲν σκῆπτρον κράτη
δηλοῖ βροτεία, σῆμα τῆς τυραννίδος,
γέρας προσάπτον, ᾧπερ ἐμπέφυκ' ἀεὶ
σύνθακος αἰδὼς βασιλέων, μείζων δ' ὅμως
ἔλεος ὑπάρχει τῆσδε τῆς σκηπτουχίας,
ἕδραν γὰρ ἴσχει καρδίας τυραννικὰς,
οὐδ' ἔστ' ἄτεγκτος θεὸς ἔτ' οἰκτιρμοῖς ποτε,
ἀρχήν τε θνητὸς ἐξομοιοῦται θεῷ,
ἐλέου δίκῃ μάλιστα συγκεκραμένου.
Πρὸς ταῦτα, καίπερ χρωμένῳ τοίας δίκης,
Ἑβραῖε, προφάσει, τοῦτο σοί γ' ἐνθύμιον
ἔστω, δίκης ἀρ' εἵνεχ' ὡς σωτηρίας
οὐ μηχανὴ τοῖς ἐνθάδ' οὖν λειφθήσεται·
λιταῖσι δ' ἔλεον εὐχόμεσθα, καὶ λιταῖς
ἔλεον παρασχεῖν τοῖς ταλαιπωρουμένοις
ἡμᾶς διδάσκουσ'· ὧδε δ' εἵρηται λόγοις
τοσαῦθ', ἵν' ὥνπερ λιπαρεῖς τυχεῖν δίκῃ
πεισθεῖσ' ὑπείκῃ, τοὔνομον δ' αἰτημάτων
ἐὰν διώκῃς, χρὴ δικασπόλους ἴσους
τῆς Ἐνετίδος κατ' ἐμπόρου ψῆφον φέρειν.

LAUNCELOT D. DOWDALL.

Σημείωσις. Ἴδε τὰς σημειώσεις τοῦ Ἐμπόρου τῆς Βενετίας ὑπὸ Δ. Βικέλα, ὃ ὁποῖος παρενθέτει σελ. 140 τὴν μετάφρασίν μου εἰς τὴν ἀρχαίαν Ἑλληνικήν.

Sonnet.

(BEAUTY DELINQUENT.)

As searchers thro' rich fields and flowerful lands,
  Yearning, impatient, running to and fro,
  From barren wastes of mountain capt with snow,
O'er summer seas that wanton with warm sands
They flit, to win the hest of Hope's commands,
  To see and feel the dreams of long ago,
  And in the heart to set love's light aglow
With touch of one sweet mouth and clasp of hands.

Ah, lips so sweet, gone dumb for lack of soul,
  Like flowers that with'ring die for lack of sun ;
  How quick the perfumed course of Love is run
When lips alone provide Love's paltry dole :
  Thy poor cold words but deepen man's despair ;
  Thy promise is, as Hope's, both false and fair.

JAMES FOSTER, M.A.

Love and Death.

BEHOLD the flashing waters,
  A cloven, dancing jet,
That from the milk-white marble
  For ever foam and fret ;
Far off in drowsy valleys
  Where the meadow-saffrons blow,
The feet of summer dabble
  In their coiling calm and slow.
The banks are worn for ever
  By a people sadly gay :
A Titan, with loud laughter,
  Made them of fire and clay.
Go ask the springing flowers,
  And the flowing air above,
What are the twin-born waters,
  And they'll answer Death and Love.

With wreaths of withered flowers
  Two lonely spirits wait,
With wreaths of withered flowers,
  'Fore paradise's gate.
They may not pass the portal,
  Poor earth-enkindled pair,
Though sad is many a spirit
  To pass and leave them there
Still staring at their flowers,
  That dull and faded are.
If one should rise beside thee,
  The other is not far.
Go ask the youngest angel,
  She will say with bated breath,
By the door of Mary's garden
  Are the spirits Love and Death.

W. B. Y.

Altiora Spero.

UPON the billowy bosom of the night,
  As babe on mother's breast, my spirit drooped,
  With warfare worn : around me seemed there trooped
An angel-band of spirits, pure and bright,
From God's own mirror imaged to my sight ;
  And as with mystic cadence round they grouped
  One form of radiant firmness o'er me stooped,
And voice of silver softness smote delight.

'Peace!' sang it ; and thereat my spirit leapt
  To the sweet music, and my veins ran fire ;
But its next breath great calm around me swept.
  'Be not afraid, nor let thy spirit tire ;
  Climb on, and ever climb to something higher ;
God's eye will follow where thy feet have stept.'

R. G. P.

Her despotic control, it is prophesied, will only end when her power is challenged by one for whom another will willingly die. While two suitors take to duelling with each other, the third, Almintor, sets off on his quest, chooses the wrong flower and duly stiffens up. He is, however, revived when Naschina defeats the Enchantress after both shepherds have died for her.

The plot itself does not maintain much coherence, and some central questions remain unanswered, such as the reasons behind Arcadia's gloom and fear, and why blood sacrifice should be a prerequisite for Naschina's success. However, the drama does contain the germs of a political allegory which need to be teased out. The very fact that the play is built around two neighbouring islands – Arcady and the Enchanted Island – where one holds the other in some kind of thraldom, invites comparisons with the Irish situation. Spenser's fifth book of the *Faerie Queene* could be a possible influence. Set partly in Ireland, it is a political allegory of Elizabeth's statecraft and dealings with neighbouring countries. Yeats confessedly wrote the *Island of Statues* 'in imitation of Edmund Spenser' (*Auto*, 92) and the names of his shepherds, as Bornstein points out, have a Spenserian ancestry.[47] Yeats was as aware of the allegorical as of the romantic nature of Spenser's writings and during this period he was thinking in an allegorical mode.[48] In the *Island*, the Enchantress, who holds the neighbouring Arcady in some kind of dominion, could be seen as representing England, especially since the source of her power – she is 'far fleeter than the million-footed sea' (*VP*, 670) – parallels England's naval strength. This domination by the neighbouring island could be a possible explanation for the unexplained, excessive and paradoxical Arcadian fear:

> Here, where men know the gracious woodland joys,
> Joy's brother, Fear, dwells ever in each breast –
> Joy's brother, Fear, lurks in each leafy way. (651)

The flower of everlasting joy (Home Rule?), jealously guarded and withheld by the Enchantress, can alone dispel this gloom. However, for those attempting to procure it, the cost of failure is death.

Naschina, who could be seen as representing the spirit of Ireland, or even Irish patriotism, rejects her suitors for lacking the courage to prove their love in any significant way. She laments that elsewhere lovers perform heroic feats, but the 'forest lights / Of green Arcadia do not hide. . . / Such men, such hearts' (651). Her rebuke could be viewed as a demand for patriotic blood sacrifice of the type that Yeats would later dramatise most vividly in poems on the Easter Rising ('O plain as plain can be / There's nothing but our own red blood / Can make a right Rose Tree' [396]).[49] And indeed, blood sacrifice is a prerequisite for Arcadia's liberation. Only when viewed allegorically does this demand for martyrdom make sense. Similarly, an allegorical reading best explains the poem's ending, where Naschina, by being rendered shadowless, is isolated from those she has revived from slumber. Read literally, the ending denies any resolution to the poem's numerous antinomies (nature and art, time and eternity, earthly and ideal). Read allegorically, it signifies the granting of immortality (possibly in popular memory) to Naschina. The granting of immortality to the victor is a stock trope in romantic and folklore literature and Naschina's immortality is a result of her having vanquished the oppressor of her people.

Such a reading undoubtedly necessitates the plugging of numerous gaps, such as the relationship between Arcady, Almintor and Naschina, and between Arcady and the Enchanted Island. Furthermore, the allegory lacks the focus and continuity of *Cathleen ni Houlihan* and is clearly not as successful. While the political parallels, so ready at hand, are perpetually evaded, the poem attempts to remain on the level of a dramatic narrative. Extraneous elements are introduced breaking the continuity and weakening the connections, sometimes even obscuring the central conflict between Naschina and the Enchantress. Nevertheless, it is likely that contemporary readers would have noticed the political allegory; the poem was written and published in a climate dominated by the issue of Home Rule. Neither Yeats himself nor his *DUR* readers could have been oblivious of the allegorical significance of the conflict between two neighbouring islands, even though it is only gestured at and not fully drawn out. During 1885–86 Yeats was writing in an allegorical mode, as is testified by 'The Two Titans' (*DUR*, March 1886, 265–6). Although subtitled 'A Political Poem', it is, as Ellmann correctly assessed, 'strangely unpolitical: Yeats makes one step to the side for every step forward.'[50] The extended allegory of a youth chained to a sibyl on a rock in the middle of an ocean demands interpretation and yet defies it at every step of the way. It remains among Yeats's most obscure productions. Such hesitation was typical of the early Yeats. (His 'Song of the Spanish Insurgents', published in the *North & South* (5.5.87), is yet another example.)[51] It was also consistent with the *DUR*'s editorial policy at that time of disguising, or at least underplaying, their nationalist sympathies. The refusal of *The Island of Statues* and the 'Two Titans' to gesture pointedly to their own allegorical significance parallels the *Review*'s evasion on the national question. That they are not overtly political is in itself politically significant in its context. Things had to be kept sufficiently vague to hint at another meaning without making it too explicit for unionist tastes. This would also help blur the difference between 'national' and 'nationalist'.

III

Oldham's paper to the university Philosophical Society was the prelude to the introduction in the *DUR* of the 'temperate discussion of certain public questions' (July 1885, 133). The 'public questions' was just another euphemism for Protestant concerns, and almost all the articles that followed dealt with this issue. With the August issue of 1885, the *DUR* entered a new phase. The size of the periodical was altered from 22 × 28.5 cm to 14 × 22 cm, the pagination was restarted at zero, the number of advertisements vastly increased, and a new disclaimer inserted in bold type into the inner contents page: **'The Editor disclaims all responsibility for the opinions of contributors.'** Significantly, with the advent of political discussion, the review's earlier subtitle – 'A Monthly Magazine of Literature, Art, and University Intelligence' – was dropped. The transformation from a TCD organ to a political periodical had begun.

Standish O'Grady, an eloquent defender of feudalism and the Irish gentry, opened the discussion with a characteristic, polemical and far from temperate paper entitled 'Irish Conservatism and its Outlooks' (4–15). Despite his ideological differences with Oldham, O'Grady was a good choice. He opposed the Land League and shared Oldham's concerns about declining Protestant fortunes. Currently working on *Toryism and Tory Democracy* (1886), which applied Lord Randolph Churchill's ideas to Ireland, his twelve-page essay in the *DUR* was a compendium of this pamphlet and large passages were later reproduced verbatim. Fiercely anti-democratic –

> this waste, dark, howling mass of colliding interests, mad about the main chance. . . the labourer tied to his toil, or tramping with. . . the Devil at his tail, and tramping perhaps to the polling booth, as an enfranchised citizen, a member of the sovereign people, a ruler in the land. (August 1885, 7)

– and scathingly critical of the landlords, O'Grady yet retained his faith in the latter, 'the best class we have, and so far better than the rest that there is none fit to mention as the next best'.[52] Their status as 'Ireland's rulers' was sanctioned by 'the nature of their position, by inherited right, by defined law' (5). He exhorted the Protestant gentry to take up the leadership they had so shamefully abrogated:

> The grand opportunity was theirs of harnessing, bitting, and bridling this wild, tameless democracy – tameless, but tameable, and in its heart desiring to be tamed – of controlling it, and by methods democratic inevitably, as belonging to these centuries, but aristocratic too, leading forward this people to higher and ever higher stages. It was theirs, and they threw it away. Of what use

> to appeal now by written articles to this class? – still I maintain
> our best and the fittest of all to bear rule, if they but would. (5–6)

That Catholics had 'no capacity for ruling in them' (6) he had no doubt:

> the bare possibility that Ireland will be justly ruled is taken away
> when the lowest and most dependent class becomes sovereign.
> But this class will produce premiers, statesmen, secretaries, &c?
> Yes; as the boiler sends up scum. (8)

With the gentry unlikely and the masses ill-equipped to lead the country,
Ireland's best hope, according to O'Grady, was the Tory party. By providing
industries and employment, they would improve material conditions and
gradually kill Home Rule with kindness. They would also rejuvenate the
gentry, for, once the Viceroy gave a good example, the Ascendancy would
follow suit. O'Grady, a confirmed Tory, and Oldham, a Protestant nationalist,
differed on how Protestant interests could be best protected; however, they
both had these interests as their highest priority and could thus share a
common platform in the *DUR*.

The September issue featured Michael Davitt's response to O'Grady.
Accused by the latter of being the harbinger of 'bottomless anarchy' (14),
Davitt, who subsequently wrote *The Fall of Feudalism*, was supremely qualified to respond in kind. He started by attacking O'Grady's 'landlord party' and
his assertion that the 'territorial proprietors were Ireland's rulers' (94).
O'Grady's support for the Tories, though seemingly altruistic in appearance,
was really a 'scheme for the preservation of the Irish aristocracy' (95). Though
Davitt attacked the Protestants for being West-British and warned them of
further isolation should they continue opposing the national movement, his
was a more temperate article. However, this would have made little difference.
His emphatic assertion –

> The days of the 'sacred rights' of property have given way to those
> of the social rights of labour. The votes and voices of the millions
> will soon control a State that can no longer be governed by priv-
> ilege and caste. These are changes which no class opposition can
> avert – no abuse of the '*canaille* democrats' can withstand. (107–8)

– would have confirmed the gentry's worst fears about the 'socialist' basis of
the nationalist movement and the impending eradication of their class should
Home Rule come to pass. Though Davitt appealed to TCD students to join
the nationalists, he realised the futility of the appeal:

> As you very wisely disclaim, Mr Editor, all responsibility for the
> opinions of contributors to your talented and handsome

REVIEW, I need offer no apology for the intrusion of ideas with
which you are perhaps not in sympathy. (106)

Though Oldham would have no truck with the Land League, his purposes may
have been served by Davitt. While he himself employed more gentle and per-
suasive methods to convert the gentry and ensure Protestant participation in the
national movement, Davitt provided the shock therapy necessary to jolt them
out of their complacent reliance on the British connection into an awareness
that a radical change was necessary if their interests were to be protected.

For the time being, however, readers had to be reassured that the maga-
zine was still Protestant and had not gone over to the Fenians. A poem on
Thomas Davis highlighted the more attractive aspect of Irish nationalism –
Protestant leadership:

> No loftier spirit ever rose to claim
> For man the rights of manhood. Pride had gone,
> Crushed out of sight by anguish; hope alone –
> Nay! Hope and love united – nought could tame.
> Then Davis spoke. Ah, who is there to blame
> If fiercely sometimes rang the trumpet tone
> That roused a nation? Is the people one
> Yet for his bidding? Is the foreign shame
> Ireland's no longer?
>
> (158)

Nationalism is decked out as the Protestant response to national emasculation, as the attempt 'to claim / For man the rights of manhood'. Idealism,
patriotism and leadership are epitomised in Davis, who would have taken
Ireland to her goal but for his untimely death. Having forgotten his message,
his kinsmen have distanced themselves from the national movement and also
from the qualities represented by their favourite son and protector. That
many Protestants saw Davis, despite his nationalism, as the guarantor of their
privileges was highlighted in a famous *DUM* article written by Sir Samuel
Ferguson:

> Mr Davis was by birth a gentleman, and both in feeling and in
> judgement opposed to all designs for destroying the legitimate
> power of the gentry. He would, if he could, have won them to his
> opinion, and through their agency have sought 'to mould, to mul-
> tiply, and to consolidate' the brute mass beneath; but he never lent
> himself to the anarchical project of exterminating, because he
> could not influence them, and of reducing all society to one base
> level of peasants. Had he lived to witness the servile war made on

the Irish gentry since his death, none who knew him can doubt
that he would now be found a generous volunteer in their
camp. . . (February 1847, 194–5)

The sub-text once again is that the 'brute mass beneath' can only be led by
Protestants. By not taking up that leadership, they have ignored their country's need and ensured their own emasculation. Nationalism hence becomes
a masculine response to Protestant enfeeblement.

Despite these assertions of Protestant superiority, fears were not allayed.
Countenancing the Fenian, ex-convict, nationalist fund-raiser and founder of
the Land League was too much for the college authorities and they dismissed
Oldham from his teaching post.[53] Thomas Maguire withdrew his subscription,[54] and readers complained. All this because the journal had opened its
columns to Michael Davitt. Neither the review's assertions of loyalty nor the
fact that O'Grady had fired the first shot with a polemical and virulently anti-
Catholic assertion of Protestant superiority had counted for much.

The League championed what Lyons has aptly called the 'elemental conflict' (*Famine*, 25) between tenant and landlord, native and settler. Though not
a political movement to begin with, it soon became 'the engine which would
draw the national question in its train' (*Famine*, 26). After 1882, however, the
re-formed Irish National League subordinated the demand for land reform
to the demand for Home Rule. This further exacerbated unionist fears that
the national movement was, among other things, a peasant conspiracy against
landlords.[55]

TCD had its own stake in the land issue. Its MP, W. E. H. Lecky, hitherto
one of the most trenchant critics of the Union, became its staunchest sup-
porter because of his opposition to the Land League. As a major beneficiary
of the Ulster plantation of 1609–13, TCD was one of the biggest Irish landlords and its holdings had increased continually over the centuries.[56] Its tenants were mostly wealthy landlords (Lord Chief Justice Lefroy and the Earl of
Leitrim) and middlemen who sublet the land. Even at the height of the various land campaigns, the college had refused to reduce rents, which usually
accounted for half its total income.[57] However, it did suffer acute financial
losses because of non-payments and, during aggravated phases of land agitation – 1850s, early 1860s and mid-1880s – its bank balances dipped into the
red. In 1885, owing largely to Davitt's land campaigns, TCD was to suffer its
biggest ever financial deficit.[58]

The outcry against Davitt's article also indicates the Herculean dimensions
of Oldham's Protestant Home Rule programme. It is to his credit that the
journal did not respond to this furore by an out-and-out declaration of
nationalist allegiance but continued in its policy of gentle persuasion, allow-
ing its more disgruntled unionist readers to have their say. George W. Ruxton,

an industrious pamphleteer,[59] was one such reader, and he began his article, 'The Methods of the Parnellites' (281–93), by expressing dissatisfaction with the journal's editorial policy:

> The Nationalist case has recently, to the general astonishment of all parties, been receiving such extreme representation in the columns of THE DUBLIN UNIVERSITY REVIEW that I venture to hope that a side of the question, which is held by hundreds and thousands of the loyal inhabitants of this country, may now obtain a fair hearing therein. (November 1885, 281)

That Davitt's article would have surprised both unionist and nationalist is no exaggeration given the *DUR*'s professions. However, it was certainly an exaggeration that the nationalist cause had been given 'extreme representation'. Not only was the nationalist argument presented in more temperate tones than the unionist, but it had also received less coverage. Nevertheless, it provoked fears among an already insecure minority of a sell-out to the opposition and resulted in unionists taking a vituperative and antagonistic stand while discussing the political crisis. Ruxton's article was typical. It claimed that the Coercion Act did not interfere with law-abiding citizens, the Catholic clergy sanctioned violence, the nationalists encouraged murder and looting, Parnell lacked human instincts, the National League misappropriated withheld rents to contract Protestant executions and, finally, the independent Irish parliament would grant amnesties to murderers. Negotiating with the nationalists entailed the 'loss of all self-respect and the confidence of the people in Great Britain' and sanctioning 'the means made use of by Nationalists to gain their ends' (281–2). Ruxton hoped that his account of the national movement would 'convince all men, having the lightest regard for right and wrong', that 'no possible good could result from granting independence' (293) to Ireland.

Ruxton and others were perturbed by the *DUR*'s receptivity to nationalist arguments when all did not yet seem lost. Gladstone's son had not yet flown the Hawarden kite and the hope still existed that the Conservatives would not accede to Parnellite demands. Following Gladstone's resignation in June 1885, the Conservatives had formed a caretaker ministry. With elections imminent in November, it would injure the southern unionist cause if a Protestant periodical started vacillating in its political convictions. On the other hand, it would boost the nationalist campaign were the *DUR* to join its ranks at this crucial juncture. To claim the magazine's loyalties, both nationalists and unionists used its pages to argue their cases.

The November issue containing Ruxton's version of the national movement also contained a counter-claim, 'Some Aspects of the National Movement in Ireland' (263–81), by 'A Protestant Nationalist'. This nineteen-page article focused almost exclusively on the land question. Its pro-Land League stand – it included and endorsed the two-page constitution of the Irish National League and criticised existing land laws – as well as its arguments for Home Rule indicate an affiliation with the northern rather than the southern IPHRA. That the examples adduced were mostly from the north – London companies in Derry, Ulster Protestants, etc. – reinforces this impression. Its attitude towards the landlords reflects none of the kid-glove approach of the southern IPHRA: current land laws are the 'true essence of slavery' (275); landlords have perpetrated 'mismanagement, plunder, injustice and jobbery' (266); their wealth derives from exploiting tenants and manipulating national revenues; their titles are based on confiscation; and they have been trained to idleness. They should realise that their interests lie with their fellow countrymen rather than with England; being Ireland's 'natural leaders' (265), they can secure their future by joining the national movement. Should they resist, the article warned, they will be wiped out as a class.

This was too much for TCD and in December the authorities prohibited the *DUR* from using the college arms on its front cover. They also clarified that they neither were associated with the periodical nor approved of its contents.[60] Oldham had begun distancing the review from TCD by discontinuing 'Honor lists' from December 1885. From February 1886 society reports, 'University Intelligence' and 'Kottabos' were discontinued. With the 'steadily increasing sale of the REVIEW' (January 1886, 72) indicating that the periodical had established itself, it was time to take the gloves off and get down to the more serious and worthwhile business of politics.[61]

During 1886, the political landscape kept changing rapidly and Ireland became the cynosure of imperial concerns. In January, the Conservatives were back in government, Parnell held the balance of power and Gladstone had converted to Home Rule. By the end of January, Parnell had toppled the Conservatives and installed Gladstone. The Home Rule Bill, introduced in April, splintered the Liberals, and the Liberal Unionists broke away under Chamberlain. In June, the Bill was defeated and Gladstone resigned. Not surprisingly, the second volume of the *DUR*, commencing in January 1886, took on an overtly political aspect. Eleven out of the thirteen leading articles addressed the current political situation. 'The Conservative Party in Ulster' (15–22), by Perceval Gaussen, a Contemporary Club member and unionist pamphleteer, attacked nationalists for being 'self constituted and loud-spoken reformers' and 'quacks' (January 1886, 16–17). They would prevent improvements that would 'cripple' their 'incomes as professional patriots' and undermine their status as leaders of a discontented people. According to Gaussen, Home Rule could be killed with kindness through efficient and firm policies granting a degree of self-government in local matters subject to imperial unity and the protection of minorities. A similar view was espoused by the Liberal Unionist MP T. W. Russell in 'The Irish Question: From the Stand-point of a Liberal' (104–15), which, while agreeing to grant Ireland some self-government subject to imperial unity, also advocated the passing of a permanent Coercion Act. In July, William F. Bailey[62] argued the case for Federal Autonomy. While recommending Isaac Butt's scheme for local self-government, he stressed the need for imperial unity. However, that was not his chief concern; Protestant Ascendancy was:

> Mr Butt would have restored Grattan's Parliament with certain changes. That is he would have a House of Lords and a House of Commons on the old model, and he looked to the existence of the former as the proper safeguard against hasty or confiscating legislation. (566)

Typically, the Protestant heyday of 1782 was never very far from the contributors' thoughts. Nor was the fear of confiscation under nationalist government, as further evidenced by R. Morice's article, 'Peasant Proprietors in Ireland' (639–50), the next month.

Arguing supposedly for the nationalists, T. W. Rolleston's protest against 'The Archbishop in Politics' (February, 92–103) reflects not only a characteristic Protestant ambivalence but also his inability to take a firm stand.[63] Lest he be accused of bias, Rolleston protests that he 'heartily endorses the political programme of the National League, and believes that boycotting. . . is in many cases justified by the magnitude of the legalised crime against which it is directed' (98–9). This was patently untrue. As discussed earlier (see pp. 51–2), Rolleston was severely critical of the League and would shortly write pamphlets denouncing boycotting and defending landlords. He also claims not to have any 'bigoted feeling of antipathy to the Catholic Church' (98–9). This, after having invoked the Spanish Inquisition and the Huguenot Massacre as other cases of Catholic intolerance. Having begun by asserting that Protestantism is no longer synonymous with unionism, and that most Protestants no longer believe that independence would deprive them of their civil liberties and make the Catholic clergy the '*de facto* and *de jure*' (92) rulers of Ireland, he ends by urging nationalists not to avenge earlier sufferings by persecuting Protestants. Rolleston was evidently rattled by recent events which made Catholic rule seem inevitable. At a loss for a clear response, he wavers between collaboration, appeasement, criticism and supplication.

L. Ginnell, one of the founding members of the Irish Literary Society and, subsequently, a nationalist MP for Westmeath North, sent in a scathing response to Rolleston. It is noteworthy that Ginnell felt it necessary to confess his Catholicism, since it was taken for granted that *DUR* contributors were usually Protestants. He accused Rolleston of having a unionist bias and of having the 'spirit of impartiality without the means of exhibiting it, even when those means are quite accessible' (185). Like W. F. Dennehy in an earlier article (January, 35–47), Ginnell stressed that Protestant patriotism is now of a different order. Instead of chauvinism, it is 'the principle of assimilation' (181) that is called for and 'the National platform [is] the meeting ground' (181). Oldham's 'The Prospects of Irish Nationality' (June, 457–68) discussed the financial provisions of the Home Rule Bill. While urging unionists and Westminster to recognise the fact of Irish nationality, and mildly rebuking Protestants for resisting the national movement, he once again emphasised the need for rehabilitating the gentry into Irish public life.

Sophie Bryant, an expatriate nationalist, educationist and suffragist, examined 'The Truth of National Sentiment' (March, 216–33) as a philosophical problem. Its most interesting feature, however, was her view of the *DUR*'s reputation:

> The present seems to be a fitting time, and the pages of the DUBLIN UNIVERSITY REVIEW a fitting place to enquire into the reasonableness of National Sentiment. (March 1886, 216)

In 1885–86 a political settlement seemed imminent and questions of Ireland's political future inevitably dominated people's thoughts. Bryant's statement suggests that the *DUR* was now perceived to be the appropriate forum for political discussions of a contemporary and topical nature. Following its altered editorial policy, the *DUR* had become *the* forum for an open political discussion (albeit from an essentially Protestant perspective) in accordance with the aims expressed in an earlier editorial.[64]

In the midst of the political debate, the periodical's declining fortunes became apparent. In February 1886 there were twelve advertisement pages, three cover advertisements pages (inside front, inside back and back cover) and two advertisement inserts; in May 1886 there were ten advertisement pages, three cover pages and two inserts, but, of these, two and a half pages were occupied by the proprietors' own advertisements. By September 1886 there were only eight advertisement pages (one and a half of which were the proprietors), three cover pages (again one and a half occupied by the proprietors) and no inserts. When proprietors begin advertising their own wares on any of the cover pages, which are the most expensive, it is a sure sign that advertisers have lost interest in the periodical and that advertising revenues as well as readership have declined. Equally indicative of a decline was the discontinuation in August and November respectively of advertisements for the *DUR*'s Art Supplement and back issues.

With the end in sight, in October 1886 caution and editorial impartiality were dispensed with in matters concerning Trinity College and national politics. 'University Education in Ireland' (799–812) by 'G. C.' urged TCD, for its own future survival, to mend its ways and adopt a conciliatory attitude towards the nationalists. Hugh H. Johnson's 'Rent and Tithes in Wales' (838–41) urged Celts in the UK to resist 'alien and absentee landlords' (838) as well as the equally alien Church of England. Both must be expelled and the Celts must unite against the Sassenach to repel the 'yoke that is as repugnant as it is burdensome' (841). H. S. Fagan's review of 'A Lady Felon's *Letters From Donegal*' (829–37) attacked the book's anti-Catholic prejudice but found hope in the author's love for Ireland: she only needs 'Home Rule to cure her of her misconceptions and to make her as good a Nationalist as the best of us' (833). This was the *DUR*'s first clear admission of its nationalist sympathies. H. S. Fagan, as we have already seen, had in a June 1885 article (see pp. 57–8) urged TCD to cultivate more of the 'feeling of 1782 . . . for the good of the country' (106). His present position represents a more advanced stage of the Protestant nationalism he was preaching the previous year when political, or nationalist, views were excluded from the *DUR*. It is likely, however, that, like Oldham, Fagan's views had not changed in the interim, but that in 1885 they had been altered *mutatis mutandis* to attract unionist readers to the newly founded periodical. His pamphlets of this period are strongly nationalist.[65]

As the *DUR*'s nationalist swansong, John O'Leary's 'Some Guarantees for the Protestant and Unionist Minority' (December 1885, 959–65) was a poor choice. It would have alarmed rather than reassured readers and retarded rather than advanced Oldham's project of converting Protestants to Home Rule. According to his biographer, O'Leary had always 'been implacably opposed to all forms of land agitation by Irish nationalists'.[66] In the *DUR*, however, he adopted a different stand. Published in the magazine's final issue, his article attributed Catholic dislike of Protestants partly to the fact that the latter were mostly landlords. O'Leary's bland solution was 'Take away the cause and you will take away the effect' (December 1886, 962) or, more simply put, 'Give away your lands and you will be loved.' Not only was this simplistic and sanctimonious, it was also hypocritical, as evidenced by O'Leary's hostile opposition to the Tipperary land agitation of 1889–91 which decimated his own rentier income. (This is discussed in more detail in Chapter 3.) Then, his denunciations of manipulative politicians for inciting an honest but misguided tenantry were reminiscent of the *DUR*'s unionist articles.

IV

At a time when the *DUR*'s collapse seemed imminent, O'Leary's article was preceded by a broadside launched against the unionist establishment by his disciple, W. B. Yeats. The review's November issue published the second part of Yeats's essay on the recently deceased poet, Sir Samuel Ferguson.[67] Yeats's first two published articles, written at the age of twenty, highlight his early affinities with Ferguson, an antiquarian, poet, TCD luminary, *DUM* co-founder and Protestant ideologue. Ferguson's views on 'the Protestant wealth and intelligence of the country', their dilemma in the post-O'Connell period and their future role in Ireland were eloquently delineated in his *DUM* essays, most notably 'A Dialogue between the Head and the Heart of an Irish Protestant'.

Though he did not live to see its fruition, Ferguson laid the foundations of an Irish national literature. His views on the importance of literary craftsmanship and the function of a national literature are expressed in letters to fellow unionist poets:

> I think we have amongst us enough of ability to lay the foundations of a school of letters here as will be honourable also to the country. That has been the great aim I have had in view in all my efforts. . . A Dublin School would, I think, restore good taste and good English in our current poetry, now over-run with gaspings, affectation, pet words, and bad prosody. . . The history of this country furnishes plenty of material; its native literature more. But the people – idle, feckless as they are – are a game breed, and won't disappear before the face of any other competitors for existence here; and they must have their history and their humanities *tolites qualites*. I trust in God they will yet recognise as friends the men who revolt against the present teachings given them by those who would make them knaves and cowards.[68]

> We will have to make a literature for this country whatever be the fate of this or that policy. . . It must be lofty, moral and distinctively Irish. . . The Poets will save the people whom the rogues and cowards have corrupted. I shall not live, I daresay, to see the salvation, but I shall die believing in it. (To Savage-Armstrong, 6.3.86. *SSF*, Vol.2, 248.)

> I rely more on the slow but certain effect of a national literature operating among the heads of society and thence downwards than on any instruction or organisation of the people. It has for many years been my great object and ambition to promote a literature of this kind . . .[69]

These letters also anticipate the Arnoldian project of a cultural hegemony that 'sweetens and refines' the lower orders thereby retaining for the upper classes their social and political ascendancy. Ó Dúill points out that, thirty years after the third letter, Ferguson wrote a similar letter claiming that an

Irish national literature 'would cement the Union'. It would divert the masses from a potentially dangerous 'absorption' with Anglo-Irish relations and provide the Ascendancy with what Ó Dúill calls 'a cultural version of killing Home Rule by kindness':

> If the absorption bring nothing but dregs and froth, it will go hard with the cellarer to prevent fermentation and explosion. But all my friends here regard me as abetting dangerous ideas in doing anything to keep alive the national sentiment. They little know its validity and the use that wisdom ought to make of it.[70]

Ferguson's literary output was largely a response to British 'betrayal' over Catholic emancipation and the 1832 Reform Bill.[71] Caught between English indifference and Catholic mistrust, the Protestants, according to Ferguson, could best salvage their position by an imaginative study of Ireland's Gaelic, and therefore pre-sectarian, past. This study would show that underlying the social, political and religious divisions in Irish society was a fundamental unity, a unity ratifying rather than weakening the Act of Union. It would also confer on Protestants an Irish authenticity, endear them to the Catholic masses and underscore their claims to the country's leadership. Though Ferguson granted a 'very high degree of poetic grandeur' to his Gaelic source material, he shared Mahaffy and Atkinson's distaste for it: it contained much that was 'jejune, ugly and barbarous' and confronted cultivated minds with 'obstacles of grotesqueness and exaggeration'.[72] It nevertheless served a purpose and, with a view to thus accommodating the contemporary needs of his co-religionists in an increasingly democratised and nationalistic Ireland, Ferguson set about translating the Irish past and reinterpreting Gaelic legends as arguments for aristocratic, and even Protestant, leadership. His translation of the 'Fair Hills of Ireland', as Tom Dunne points out, transforms the poem from a Jacobite coronach lamenting the Flight of the Earls – an event marking the loss of Gaelic Ireland's remaining leadership – to a Marvell-like ode celebrating the entry into Ireland of her new rulers. Not surprisingly, his work has been described as the 'colonisation of the Gaelic literature in the interests of the Anglo-Irish Ascendancy'.[73]

Like Standish O'Grady after him, Ferguson has often been looked on as a spokesman of the beleaguered Ascendancy. The bulk of his work was published in the *DUR*'s immediate predecessor for a similar Protestant, upper-class and unionist readership, and his views would have been shared by many of the *DUR*'s readers. Yeats, although not quite Ascendancy himself, would later adopt many of its stock attitudes and prejudices. Ferguson, with his traditionalist, paternalistic and pastoral vision of society, resenting the 'field of coal' swamping the 'field of corn'[74] anticipates Yeats's own dream of the noble and the beggarman and his vision of Ireland as a place 'where men plough and sow and reap, not a place where there are great wheels turning and great chimneys vomiting smoke'.[75] Similarly, Ferguson's views on the 'Protestant wealth and intelligence of the country' would be echoed exaggeratedly by Yeats, most famously in his 'great stocks of Europe' address to the Irish Senate in 1925.[76] Though this aristocratic, Protestant chauvinist side of Yeats surfaces only after the turn of the century, it was, according to Conor Cruise O'Brien, not unborn but merely dormant in Yeats's early years. His utterances then were dictated 'not without calculation and not without reference to the given political conjuncture of the moment' ('Passion and Cunning', 208).

It is difficult to judge whether in 1886 these factors spurred Yeats's enthusiasm for Ferguson. Notwithstanding this, the elder spokesman was an ideal subject through which Yeats could advocate some of his most cherished literary tenets. Ferguson's Gaelic translations and poems had made a strong impression on the young poet. Furthermore, Ferguson and Yeats's views on literary nationalism had much in common. Both laboured to create an Irish reading public and a national literature which, though in English, would be characteristically Irish and free of Young Ireland rhetoric; both urged Irish writers to employ Irish themes, especially those culled from mythology and the Gaelic past; and both viewed literature as a way of transcending the political, social and religious divisions in Irish society (witness Yeats's later attempts through the Young Ireland league and the '98 Centenary celebrations).

Yeats's Ferguson essays exemplify his brand of literary nationalism as well as the methods he used in propagating it during the 1880s and '90s. That it 'has not paid to praise things Irish or write on Irish subjects' (*UP1*, 88★) was a major obstacle to his ambitions and a source of considerable anxiety. He lamented that 'the most cultivated of Irish readers'– this, in *DUR* parlance, denoted Protestants and TCD graduates – were 'servile to English notions' and averred that, had Ferguson imitated Tennyson and 'written of Arthur and Guinevere, they would have received him gladly' (89–90). To redress the balance, Yeats praised Ferguson in superlative terms: 'the best Irish book', 'the greatest work' (84★), 'the best Irish poem', 'the noblest woman in Irish romance' (86★), 'the greatest Irish poet' (87★), 'the greatest poet Ireland has produced' (103). At the same time he also criticised contemporary English writers. He pitted Ferguson against both Arnold and Tennyson and gave the Irishman the honours: Tennyson lacks 'the feminine and heroic beauty of "Deirdre"' (95) and Arnold is a mere imitator of the ancients, unlike Ferguson who is '*like* them' (92). Furthermore, Matthew Arnold's dictum, 'literature is a criticism of life', was dismissed as being didactic and utilitarian, key terms in Yeats's later anglophobic critical register. Citing Ferguson as an example, he averred: 'Great poetry does not teach us anything – it changes us' (84★). Using Ferguson as a model, it is strange that Yeats should take up a stand against didacticism, given the transparency of Ferguson's motives in concluding many of his pre-Christian bardic poems either with a pagan character's proleptic vision of Christianity or with a coda of Protestant doctrine.[77] For Ferguson, literature had a direct moral function and many of his works exemplify this belief. His wife endorsed T. W. Lyster's observation that Ferguson's choice of subject from the Irish legends was dictated 'by some moral, or religious, or humane idea, either inherent in the myth or read into it in his imaginative scrutiny'.[78]

More disinterested commentators have eschewed such euphemisms: 'Many of his [Ferguson's] works illustrate a variation upon the "good story" method in which the author chooses from among the old texts subjects conducive to edifying moral or religious interpretation and even fabricates suitable vehicles when he cannot find them to hand.'[79] Malcolm Brown is even more direct:

> Ferguson's task was no longer to disinfect the antiquarian material
> of its Catholicism, for there was no Catholicism in it, but rather to
> suffuse it with the pure tincture of the Thirty-nine Articles.[80]

The didacticism of Ferguson's endings highlight the political dimensions of his versification of Hardiman's translations and his interest in Gaelic legends. Having accused Hardiman of using the legends to exacerbate Irish disaffection with English rule and Protestant ascendancy, Ferguson, in his own translations, uses them to vindicate English rule and Protestant Ascendancy. There are more similarities than differences between Ferguson and Arnold in their views on the uses of culture and didacticism, and it is inappropriate for Yeats to cite Matthew Arnold as a contrast and then to criticise him for his didacticism. Though his references to Tennyson and Arnold are extraneous to his ostensible purpose of reviewing Ferguson's achievement within an Irish context, they serve a purpose. Given the bias in Irish reading tastes that Yeats was doing his utmost to counter, his constant invoking of the Victorian poets only to compare them unfavourably with Irish writers had its advantages.

Yeats, in his *Fireside* article, asserted that England's neglect of Ferguson was motivated by a racial bias and chauvinism which prompted a rejection of all things Irish. He reinforced his accusation by invoking biblical parallels and bracketing England with the Egyptians and Ireland with the conquered Jews: 'Anti-Irish feeling ran too high. "Can any good thing come out of Galilee", they thought' (85★). Beneath this literary snobbery, Yeats claimed, lay the more sinister political agenda of collaboration in the English domination of Ireland by suppressing nationalist literature:

> Sir Samuel Ferguson himself, declares the true cause of this want
> of recognition in English critical centres in a letter published the

> other day in the *Irish Monthly*. He sought to lay the foundation of
> a literature for Ireland that should be in every way characteristic
> and national, hence the critics were against him. (85–86★)

Yeats's article was published on 9 October 1886; Ferguson's letter, that Yeats refers to above, was published earlier that month in the October issue of the *Irish Monthly*.[81] Only a few days separated Yeats's perusal of Ferguson's letter and the publication of his own *Irish Fireside* article, which probably had been submitted well in advance of its actual publication.[82] Yeats, therefore, would have had to act with some alacrity to include the reference and alter the typescript of an article already under the printer's gaze. He obviously felt Ferguson's letter worth this effort and his use of it certainly lent his review a political slant which catered to what he otherwise bemoaned as being the Irishman's propensity for sensationalism.[83]

However, Yeats's synopsis of Ferguson's letter is very misleading. Written in July 1884 by Ferguson to the editor of the *Irish Monthly*, the letter was only published in an obituary:

> My dear Sir – Let me thank you for your obliging letter, enclosing Mr de Vere's note, which reached me while on vacation in the country. I have also heard from Judge O'Hagan, who tells me you contemplate the insertion of a second notice of my poems. It is very grateful to me to find appreciation among my own countrymen. It has hitherto been almost totally denied me in the great centres of criticism in England. Possibly de Vere divines the true cause. My business is, regardless of such discouragements, to do what I can in the formation of a characteristic school of letters for my own country. For the sympathy and encouragement you give me, accept my warmest thanks and believe me. . .

Ferguson does not himself explain the motives underlying English indifference, but merely refers the reader to Aubrey de Vere's note. Neither de Vere's note nor the editor's letter accompanied the publication of Ferguson's letter in the *Irish Monthly*. However, in his letter to Mary Ferguson and in numerous essays on her husband's poetry, de Vere's explanations for his compatriot's lack of recognition in England – a different style, a novel subject, 'embarrassing. . . Gaelic names', 'mediocrity in high places', the indolence of readers and the degeneration of literary tastes – contrast sharply with Yeats's assertions.[84] In spite of these obstacles, according to de Vere, and 'the latent antagonisms of national tastes' (de Vere, 125), Ferguson's poetry 'can hardly fail sooner or later to conquer that difficulty which the most accomplished Englishmen often find in understanding poetry which worthily illustrates the highest Irish themes. . . and their award will be, "The author of these poems

added another string to the great English harp – the Gaelic string"' (124–5).
Judge O'Hagan, whom Ferguson mentions in his letter, gave very similar reasons to de Vere's in his two anonymous reviews of Ferguson's poetry.[85] This is
not surprising, since both O'Hagan, as a judge, and de Vere, as a writer, looked
to England for their patronage. De Vere, unlike Ferguson, was a Catholic but
he was also a staunch Tory and nowhere in his critical writings does one
encounter anti-English sentiment. In fact, it is quite the reverse. Ferguson's
poem on de Vere puts the case for both in a proper perspective:

> De Vere possessed the art
> To touch, nor wound, the generous English heart.
> With words of strength and clearness to express
> The power of purity and manliness.[86]

Yeats's assertion apropos of Ferguson's letter is unfounded and his claims
about the reasons for the Irish poet's lack of success in England do not derive
from his professed sources. They have clearly been foisted onto Ferguson by
Yeats in order to strengthen, and even perhaps sensationalise, the nationalist
argument against English literature. This would not be the only instance of
Yeats fabricating evidence to support his cause. He would later assert that
Blake was an Irishman and even a member of the Golden Dawn – in effect,
a prototype of Yeats himself.

Ferguson was a poor choice to illustrate Ireland's suffering under England's
cultural and political stranglehold. According to the obituary composed by his
friend, J. P. Mahaffy, which Yeats cited in his *DUR* article while attacking the
TCD don:

> there was never a more loyal or orderly British citizen [than Fer-
> guson], or one who felt more deeply the mistakes that are made,
> and the crimes that are committed, under the guise of demand-
> ing justice for his country. He never lent his poetic talent to
> increase the volume of Irish discontent.[87]

Ferguson would have made a prime target for the charge of 'West Britonism'
that Yeats levelled against Dowden and other anglophiles. Instead, Yeats
ignored this aspect of Ferguson's character and fallaciously represented him
as an Irish nationalist. He averred that the Irish critics' anglophilia, best exemplified by Dowden, had cost Ferguson his rightful place:

> If Sir Samuel Ferguson had written to the glory of that, from a
> moral point of view, more than dubious achievement, British
> civilisation, the critics, probably including Professor Dowden,
> would have taken care of his reputation. (89)

Ferguson had in fact written copiously 'to the glory of that. . . dubious achievement' and his feelings about the Empire are reflected in 'The Widow's Cloak', an offering of gratitude on the receipt of his knighthood:

> Victoria's sheltering mantle is over India spread;
> Who dare to touch the garment's hem, look out for men in red:
> Look out for gun and tumbril a-crash through mound and hedge
> For shot and shell and Sheffield shear – Steel, point and edge![88]

Unmindful of such aberrations, Yeats classified Ferguson with Homer, and asserted that he was made in 'the purifying flame of National sentiment' (*UP1*, 103). He cited Ferguson's elegy on Thomas Davis as proof of his patriotism and concluded, 'Irish singers. . . must, whether they will or no, nourish the forces that make for the political liberties of Ireland' (100). Could it be possible that Yeats was unaware that Ferguson had just the previous year publicly denied harbouring nationalist sympathies?[89] Even if he was, Yeats could not claim ignorance of Ferguson's essay accompanying the elegy on Davis which Yeats had adduced as evidence of Ferguson's nationalism. There Ferguson had stated quite categorically that his admiration for Davis was owing more to the latter's Protestant gentility than to his political convictions. Davis's radicalism was, he alleged, misconstrued and despite appearances his real sympathies lay 'with the true friends of the people', namely his fellow Protestants. For he:

> was by birth a gentleman, and both in feeling and in judgement
> opposed to all designs for destroying the legitimate power of the
> gentry. . . Had he lived to witness the servile war made on the
> Irish gentry since his death, none who knew him can doubt that
> he would now be found a generous volunteer in their
> camp. . .[90]

The elegy, which Yeats cited as an indication of Ferguson's 'national feeling', is a better indication of the strength of his sectarian feeling; and the 'unwavering nature of his patriotism' is similarly applicable only to his class interests. When Yeats hailed Ferguson as 'the greatest Irish poet' the reasons he gave were that his poems 'embody more completely than in any other man's writings, the Irish character' (*UP1*, 87). They were 'the refutation of the calumnies of England and those amongst us who are false to their country' (104). Yeats omitted all mention of Ferguson's Orange poems, which relentlessly caricatured Irish Catholics and substantiated rather than refuted 'the calumnies of England'. A few verses of 'An Irish Garland' – an antiphonal chorus of Protestant gentleman and Catholic jackasses – indicate how far Ferguson was from Yeats's idealised version:

Gentlemen:	Jackasses:
Ye Gentlemen of Ireland	Ye jackasses of Ireland,
In country and in town,	In stable, shed, and lane,
Whose honor'd flag in ninety-eight	Whose ears, though cropp'd in ninety-
Put foul rebellion down;	eight,
That glorious standard raise again	Now flout our skies again;
To face the Tricolor,	Pick up your hairy standarts,
Where it waves on their graves	Come, take a roll and fling,
Who put it down before –	And brey, while ye may,
Oh, face it as your fathers did,	While your dust is on your wing,
'Twill shame your skies no more.	'Ee-eeh, ee-eeh, ee-eeh, ee-eeh, ee-aw!
	Down, down with State and King!'[91]

Clearly 'the most Irish of poets' (*UP1*, 363) was just as capable of penning political doggerel as the greenest of nationalist versifiers.

While 'nationalising' Ferguson, Yeats made a series of strongly worded assertions: literature must be national; Irish writers must 'nourish the forces that make for the political liberties of Ireland' (100); and the 'professorial classes. . . in Ireland, at least, appear at no time to have thought of the affairs of their country till they first feared for their emoluments'. These could not have edified or entertained the 'shoddy society of "West Britonism"' (104) that constituted both the object of Yeats's attack and the readership of the *DUR*. Nor would the fact that he had, in successive paragraphs, attacked Edward Dowden – Professor of English – and J. P. Mahaffy – Professor of Ancient History and later Provost of TCD – for being 'academic', anti-Irish and 'servile to English notions' (89). According to Yeats, both Mahaffy and Dowden were motivated by expediency: they had praised 'what it is conformable to praise' (88) and were 'entangled' in what he was later to describe as:

> the subtle net of bribery which England has spread among us by Courts, by Colleges, by Government offices, by a social routine, and they [the English] fold and unfold their nets before us that they may make us like themselves. . .[92]

Yeats's debut as a critic in the *DUR* vindicates his description of himself as 'an old-fashioned brass cannon full of shot', uncertain 'as to my capacity to shoot straight' (*Auto*, 116). Though this referred to him as a seventeen-year-old, it seems applicable in this instance five years later where his aggression as well as the underlying nervousness are evident. His disquietude is understandable: lacking TCD credentials, he may have felt disadvantaged writing on a literary topic for a relatively erudite and élite readership. Besides, this was only his second article, prepared at short notice on a topic that was not quite familiar territory. As in later life when he 'ruffled in a manly pose / For all his timid heart' (*VP*, 489), on this occasion too his nervousness manifested itself through bravado and belligerence.

Yeats's attacks on TCD, West Britonism and literary unionism, so prominent in his *DUR* article, are conspicuously absent in his *Fireside* review published a month earlier. To account for this difference, one must consider the influence of the *DUR* and its readers on Yeats's polemic. As with the *Island of Statues*, the inflexion of Yeats's nationalist tone was largely influenced by the magazine's current editorial policy. It was only when its end was near that the *DUR* declared its support for the nationalists. In such a situation, Yeats's own inchoate nationalism took on a more aggressive note. Moreover, his antagonism towards TCD and West Britonism were spurred by the *DUR*'s recent publications and by the fact that in the review he was confronting his literary adversaries head-on.

Yeats's Ferguson essays are important because they exhibit in a stark fashion stock Yeatsian strategies which the later and practised propagandist would dress in a more sophisticated garb of rhetoric. These also exemplify a propensity towards attacking the Victorian poets while advancing the claims of Irish literature. Furthermore, Yeats, as Thomas Kinsella points out, takes Ferguson's poetic excellence for granted.[93] He also uses a selectively sanitised version of his subject as a symbol of a literary martyr done to death by English cunning and Irish indifference. Even early on in his career, Yeats was not averse to misleading readers, logrolling or deliberately falsifying facts when it served his own purposes. Neither was he above appealing to patriotic sentiment rather than literary judgement, something which he later chastised the Young Irelanders and nationalist newspapers for doing. Literature was made to cohabit the sacred space with patriotism and one could not love the country without loving the literature. True patriotism can only exist in those for whom 'heroic deeds are possible and heroic poetry credible' (*UP1*, 104).

As literary criticism in the *DUR*, Yeats's essay was an aberration. Though the periodical had encouraged Irish art and literature, the tone was always one of gentle chiding. A letter lamenting the lack of interest in Irish culture would recommend that public halls be decorated with Celtic art. An Irish sculptor's anonymity would be attributed to the preference for things English and European rather than Irish. Or, at the very most, a book review would cavil about a writer's choice of English and not Irish subject matter, but not with any seriousness or political overtones.[94] Besides, as we have already seen (see p. 64), the *DUR*'s editors freely confessed their willingness to be guided by English literary tastes. Anomalous as it was in the *DUR*'s genteel literary cosmopolitanism, Yeats's article provoked the inevitable backlash.

A complaint was printed in the *DUR*'s last issue, not under 'Correspondence' but 'Notes of the Month'. The first note, announcing the termination of the *Review*, attributed its demise to the untenability in Ireland of an open forum for political discussion:

> Wise after the event, however, we may say confidently that any attempt to found in Ireland an organ of political discussion which shall be open to writers of every shade of politics, must, under present conditions, fail. . . There is let us hope, an ample field of patriotic labour on which they can meet simply as Irishmen, but only on condition that they suppress, for the time being, their views upon the political destinies of Ireland. (December 1886, 1046)

In a similar vein, the second note lamented the inability of patriotic Irishmen to sink their political differences in the cause of non-political projects like education and industry. The third note, containing the complaint against Yeats's article, was prefaced with an editorial comment linking the complaint to the previous two notes, and reinforcing the point about political considerations colouring every aspect of Irish life.

> Sir, – In common with most Irish lovers of poetry, I was glad to notice, in the November number of your REVIEW, an enthusiastic paper by Mr W. B. Yeats, on 'The Poetry of Sir Samuel Ferguson.' To some, however, the value of his comments, and the pleasure occasioned by his genuine appreciation of his subject, was spoiled by the rather petulant intrusion of political polemics in almost every page of Mr Yeats' article.
>
> May I be allowed to deprecate – not as a partisan dissenting from Mr Yeats's political sentiments, but simply as one interested in literature - the tone which the writer has seen fit to adopt. Let me quote, before proceeding, as an example of what I object to, the concluding passage of the paper: –
>
> 'I do not appeal to the professorial classes, who, in Ireland at least, appear at no time to have thought of the affairs of their country till they first feared for their emoluments – nor do I appeal to the shoddy society of "West Britonism," but to those young men clustered here and there throughout the land, whom the emotion of Patriotism has lifted into that world of selfless passion in which heroic deeds are possible and heroic poetry credible.'
>
> Apart from the sneers, wholly out of place in a literary criticism, at West Britonism and the alleged political apathy of the professorial classes, it seems to me not only absurd but highly injurious to Irish literature to narrow its study to a peculiarly

limited section of Irishmen. Whatever our political opinions, we
are all prepared to be Nationalists in literature, and to admire
genius and poetic gifts independently of the side on which they
are enlisted; and it cannot but be regretted that pleasure in the
writings of a man of such wide sympathies and broad tolerance
as Sir S. Ferguson should be thus denied by the intolerance of his
critic, to a large number of his cultured fellow-countrymen.

> I am,

> Faithfully yours,
> A NATIONALIST IN LITERATURE
> Nov. 6th, 1886.

The complainant claims not to oppose Yeats's political views but he rejects
Yeats's locating of Irish literature at the very nub of cultural politics, and
denies that West Britonism is hostile to Irish literature. He attempts to pull
literature back into the realm of gentility and good taste from the arena of
political differences and hostilities which, according to Yeats's article, govern
its reception in Ireland. By qualifying his nationalism and restricting it to
literature, the complainant begs all kinds of questions in cultural politics. He
also ignores the whole thrust of Yeats's argument, which is that being a
nationalist in literature entails being a nationalist in politics; 'genuine' Irish
writers must 'nourish the forces that make for the political liberties of
Ireland' (100).

Yeats's tendency to balance literary evaluation with political considerations
becomes more pronounced with time, as we shall see. However, that the complainant found Yeats's conclusion particularly offensive suggests that he himself may be among those indicted in 'the shoddy society of West Britonism'.
His attempt to define literature as a genteel, apolitical category is itself a political statement. From this follow his other objections to Yeats's aggressive literary nationalism. Clearly, political considerations, albeit of a different kind,
have played as important a part in his own views as in those he found so
objectionable.

That this letter was printed in the *DUR*'s final issue, not under 'Correspondence' but under 'Notes of the Month', where it was buttressed by other
instances of the politicisation of seemingly apolitical issues, is in itself significant. Its significance is underlined by the editors' view that the letter represented an attitude that had brought about the *DUR*'s demise. In responding
to the complainant, they distanced themselves from Yeats's views, but
reinforced his argument about political considerations governing the reception
of literature. They suggested that the complainant's claim – that a division
between literature and politics can be maintained – evades politically sensitive
issues, and disagreed with his assertion that 'we are all nationalists in literature'.

While granting that their correspondent was an exception and hoping that he would convert others, they concluded by warning him that 'he cannot work long in this direction without the real state of affairs becoming clear'. This note of pessimism and regret which rounded off the *DUR*'s last editorial comment was a response not only to 'A Nationalist in Literature' but also to its own failure at establishing an open forum for political discussion.

Though Oldham was committed to converting Protestants to Home Rule, he had given the unionist and nationalist perspectives almost equal coverage. (The magazine's 23 issues contained 20 unionist and 19 nationalist articles.) That open and not sectarian political discussion had brought about the *DUR*'s demise was clear not only to Oldham and his team but also to the new management who revived the periodical in February 1887.[95] There were other social and political factors as well. Converting the landed gentry to Home Rule was a Herculean task and had proved insurmountable for many more seasoned and established public figures than Oldham. The number of Protestant nationalists in Dublin whom he could rely on was very small and they had come forward at the very beginning. It was unlikely that their number would increase significantly after the founding of the magazine. Furthermore, the failure of Gladstone's 1886 Home Rule Bill and the Tory election victory that followed it ensured that Home Rule was shelved, at least for the duration of the Salisbury ministry. This made the issue appear a distant, if not a bad, prospect, and discouraged Protestant unionists from switching political allegiances. Even the southern IPHRA activities suffered a decline after 1886 as they found Protestants more resistant than ever to the idea of Home Rule. Finally, instances of Protestant nationalists being 'boycotted' by unionist co-religionists raised spectres of ostracism, harassment and blighted career and business prospects.[96]

Yeats's first skirmish with literary journalism would have alerted the young novice to the harsher realities of Irish political and literary attitudes. The periodical's fortunes would have made it clear that political allegiances suffused and dominated Irish perspectives making people extremely sensitive to the political overtones and underpinnings of even supposedly non-political activities. Literature, far from being exempt from this gaze, was itself a political gesture rooted in a politically charged environment. Success often depended on non-literary criteria and to succeed a writer would have to accommodate his audience's predispositions, especially where political issues were involved. Being politically committed secured one the support and hearing of a large number of people, whereas neutrality was, from a reader's perspective, both boring and inherently dubious. For the writer, it was also impractical. Literature, devoid of political leavening, would not retain an Irish audience for very long.

Playing the unionist card did have its advantages, as Yeats would have noticed from the *DUR*'s initial strategy. Protestants were 'better educated. . . & have a better instinct for excellence' (*CL1*, 455) than most Catholics, Yeats later claimed. However, he also would have realised that hectoring them from a nationalist platform was not the best way of aligning them to his purposes. When he next had an opportunity of propagating Irish literature before a Protestant audience – see, for example, his letter of 27.2.95 in the *Dublin Daily Express* (*CL1*, 440–5) containing his list of thirty best Irish books – he carefully modulated his politics to suit those of his readers and 'avowedly excluded all books of strong political feeling' (*CL1*, 453). Shedding a nationalist vocabulary in deference to their unionist biases, as well as modulating a sales pitch to suit their tastes and prejudices would be more effective in winning them over to national literature, if not nationalist politics, the former being his chief concern. And, finally, judging from his varying and controlled political expressions in the *Island of Statues* and the Ferguson essay, Yeats had apparently learnt the art of toeing the editorial line and modulating his work to suit the management's political agenda. This would become more evident in his later association with the advanced nationalist periodical, the *United Ireland*, and the equally advanced unionist monthly, the *Scots Observer*, managed by W. E. Henley.

APPENDIX I

DUR Contributors (select list)

Contemporary Club Members:

W. F. Bailey	John I. Beare	John Bury	George Coffey
John Eyre	C. L. Falkiner	Perceval Gaussen	T. W. Lyster
T. W. Russell	Alfred Webb	Frederick Gregg	W. M. Crook
J. F. Taylor	Arthur Patton	C. H. Oldham	Dr Fitzgerald
T. W. Rolleston	W. B. Yeats	Roman I. Lipmann	Richard Cherry
Douglas Hyde	John O'Leary		

Yeats Circle: were connected to Yeats at some point in his life:

W. F. Bailey	George Coffey	Edward Dowden	Sophie Bryant
John Eyre	C. L. Falkiner	John McGrath	W. M. Crook
T. W. Lyster	John Boyle O'Reilly	T. W. Russell	Edwin Ellis
Frederick Gregg	Charles Johnston	John F. Taylor	A. C. Hillier
Douglas Hyde	T. W. Rolleston	John O'Leary	Fr. M. Russell
Roman I. Lipmann	John Todhunter	Katherine Tynan	

TCD Staff:

C. F. Bastable	John Bury	John I. Beare	J. H. Bernard
Edward Dowden	G. F. Fitzgerald	Thomas Maguire	Arthur Palmer
Arthur Rambaut	T. E. Webb		

Well Known or Active Unionists:

P. Bagenal	J. H. Bernard	C. R. Chichester	Edward Dowden
C. L. Falkiner	Perceval Gaussen	Thomas Maguire	T. W. Russell
Arthur Patton			

Well Known or Active Nationalists:

John O'Leary	Sophie Bryant	George Coffey	T. W. Rolleston
Michael Davitt	John Eyre	L. Ginnell	Justin McCarthy
Alfred Webb	W. M. Crook	Douglas Hyde	C. H Oldham
H. S. Fagan	John Boyle O'Reilly		

Members of Parliament:

Michael Davitt	L. Ginnell	Alfred Webb	Justin McCarthy

Eminent People in Dublin Society:

W. F. Barrett	John Bury	J. H. Bernard	Sophie Bryant
George Coffey	Edward Dowden	Thomas Drew	G. F. Fitzgerald
T. W. Lyster	W. B. Pearsall	Alfred Webb	W. F. Bailey
C. L. Falkiner	John O'Leary	Michael Davitt	Justin McCarthy
William Archer			

— 2 —

Yeats and the United Ireland:
Catholic Nationalism and Populist Culture

I

The *DUR* did not have a large readership, nor was it devoted primarily to literature. Yet it was a prestigious periodical and while writing for it Yeats had interacted with Ireland's political and literary élites. He had also received a favourable mention in the leading nationalist weekly, *United Ireland* (*UI*).[1] In 1887, the year following the *DUR*'s demise, his name would have become even more familiar to Irish readers as he published at least twelve articles and poems in Irish magazines.[2] However, these were not of the same stature as the *DUR*.[3] Nor had he yet established a foothold in the English periodical market; the *Leisure Hour*, the only English magazine to publish his work that year, was another 'family Journal of instruction and recreation'. Published by the Religious Tract Society, it advertised itself as 'an effort to employ the Press in the service of morality and truth, by the production of a healthy literature written in a Christian spirit.'[4]

In April 1887, the constitutionally impractical J. B. Yeats moved his family once again to London in search of greener pastures. It did not improve his finances and was a setback to his son, who was plucked out of a relatively sheltered environment and cast into the deep end of Grub Street. The immediate results were disastrous. London life made Yeats miserable: it necessitated long walks instead of buses, 'experiments in cheap dinning', and the embarrassment of constant borrowings and late repayments. He also found the city 'just as dull and dirty as my memory of it' (*CL1*, 15, 11). Professionally, the outcome was even grimmer. In the previous two months (February–March 1887) Yeats was published five times (twice in *Irish Fireside*; once in *Irish Monthly*; twice in *North & South*) and had placed another article in the *Gael* before leaving for London.[5] In his four months (April–August 1887) in the

94

metropolis not a single item by him appeared in any of the English periodicals and even hack work was difficult to come by. His article on 'Popular Ballad Poetry of Ireland', though commissioned in May 1887, was not published
until November 1889. Even his Irish publications suffered a diminution and
only two reviews appeared under his name.

Not surprisingly, he took the opportunity of spending an extended summer
holiday with his relatives in Ireland: it eased the strain on J. B. Yeats's finances
and allowed Yeats to improve his own. This soon paid dividends. In five months
(11 August 1887 to 28 January 1888) six pieces were published in the Irish
press.[6] More importantly, he received the most important break of his career,
one that would influence the rest of his life and thought and launch him into
national politics and literature. When the *UI* commissioned the 22-year-old
Yeats to review W. S. Blunt's *Love Sonnets of Proteus* they forged a partnership
which, with the help of a few accidents in history, would culminate in the Irish
Literary Revival and Yeats's undisputed status as Ireland's leading poet.

II

The history of the *United Ireland* has all the elements of a popular thriller and
more: a heroic struggle against a more powerful adversary, defiance in the
teeth of oppression, midnight escapes, smuggling, imprisonment, revolution,
patriotism, persecution, break-ins and a doomed love-affair. This is a bit
unusual for a weekly newspaper, but the *UI* was never intended to be a mere
newspaper, was never run like any ordinary newspaper, and yet achieved more
than perhaps any newspaper had or has done ever since.[7] Parnell's ownership
of the *UI* and its unswerving loyalty to him add the finishing touches of
melodrama to the five-act Irish thriller (in which the weekly played a significant part) featuring the agrarian agitation, a battle against coercion, parliamentary obstructionism, the O'Shea affair and the Irish Literary Revival.
Indeed, the melodrama and the cloak and dagger of spy thrillers surrounds
the *UI*'s very founding. The newspaper that hounded Tory and Liberal governments alike and contributed significantly towards the resignation of at least
one Chief Secretary was purchased from a blackmailer and British spy. In June
1881, Parnell, using Land League funds, bought two political weeklies (*Irishman* and *Flag of Ireland*) and one monthly periodical (*Shamrock*) for £3,000
from Richard Pigott. Though subsidised by American Fenians to advocate
Fenianism, these journals had been used by Pigott, at the behest of his English paymasters, to denounce both agrarian agitation and constitutional
nationalism.[8] He later used Parnell's letters to perpetrate one of the century's
most notorious forgeries. While the *Flag of Ireland* was renamed *United Ireland*,

the *Irishman*, despite Parnell's opposition, was continued by O'Brien, under the direct supervision of Dr Sigerson – a man 'utterly incapable of ever writing a line in encouragement of crime' – until it died a natural death in 1885.[9] Its circulation had been falling and, according to O'Brien, 'it was a hopeless concern'. Discontinuing it, he felt, would alienate the extreme nationalists who saw it as their mouthpiece. Continuing it, on the other hand, cost merely 30 shillings a week. Land League funds were used to purchase the newspaper and Parnell covered its running expenses. It was only after 1884 that it started recording profits and repaid the £3,000 to the League. While Parnell and Patrick Eagan were the principal shareholders, O'Brien, Justin McCarthy, J. G. Biggar, Richard Lalor and Dr Kenny also held small shares.

Even after the founding of the *UI* in 1881, the nationalists were poorly represented in the Irish press. In the following year, out of 107 Irish newspapers with clear political leanings, only 16 were nationalist and all of these were weeklies.[10] Of the 15 national newspapers (i.e. those published in Dublin and circulated throughout Ireland) 5 supported Home Rule (*Irish Citizen and Industrial Advocate*; *Nation*; *Weekly News*; *Irishman*; *UI*); 3 were Liberal (*Evening Telegraph*, *Freeman's Journal*, *Weekly Freeman*); 3 were Liberal/Conservative (*Irish Times*, *Evening Irish Times*, *Weekly Irish Times*) and 4 were Conservative (*Daily Express*, *Dublin Morning Mail*, *Dublin Evening Mail*, *Dublin Weekly Mail*).

In 1881, though chairman of the Irish Parliamentary Party, Parnell's control over the Home Rule MPs was tenuous. His position was further undermined by the fact that, unlike the different sections of the party, he lacked the unqualified support of a single national newspaper. Moreover, his hold over the extremist faction, who were suspicious of his moderate leanings, was wearing thin and a split seemed eminently possible after the second reading of the 1881 Land Bill.[11] Through the *UI*, which would advocate advanced nationalist views in extreme language and function as an organ of the Land League, he hoped to appease the radicals in his own party as well as the Irish-Americans who controlled the purse strings, thereby leaving him free to carry out his own agenda. Furthermore, the newspaper could also be used to put across Parnell's own moderate views to a left-wing readership inherited from Pigott. The appearance of radicalism for less than radical purposes entailed taking on the militant's vocabulary to mask a constitutional purpose.

William O'Brien was invited to become the *UI*'s first editor. Twenty-nine years old, he was an established reporter with the *Freeman's Journal* and his articles (especially the series 'Christmas on the Galtees', December 1887 to January 1888) had established his reputation as a champion of tenant rights. His militant writing style, his standing among tenant farmers and his popularity among all shades of Home Rule MPs, not to mention his loyalty to and admiration for Parnell, were his main qualifications. As per his agreement with Parnell, O'Brien had complete control over the contents of the paper and his own rhetorical excesses were to be allowed free rein. Parnell wanted the weekly run on 'straightforward and advanced lines. It will, of course, always be my [Parnell's] duty to conciliate all sections of opinion comprised in the movement . . .' (W. O'Brien, 307). For the first few years, the entire paper was written almost solely by O'Brien and until the Parnellite split (referred to hereafter as 'the split'), he retained direct control over its functioning without any interference from Parnell.[12]

O'Brien's characteristically martial description of the *UI* as 'an insurrection in print', 'from crest to spur a fighting organ' (W. O'Brien, 315) is quite accurate: its very first issue reportedly had the Chief Secretary crying out in despair, 'Who on earth is this new madman?'[13] Shortly thereafter, his daughter, Florence Arnold-Foster, noted in her diary apropos of the *Freeman's Journal*, the leading nationalist newspaper: 'As the organ of the Land League it will soon be outdone by the *United Ireland*.'[14] The newspaper incited Irish policemen and soldiers to abandon their posts, published the Plan of Campaign in two successive issues, and urged Catholic jurymen to reveal the names of their Protestant co-jurors who returned guilty verdicts so that 'the white light of public opinion and the hot fire of public odium' may influence the most 'besotted and bloodthirsty juror . . . [and] moderate his eagerness for conviction' (4.12.86, 5). In its extremity of language, vituperative tone and inflammatory opinions, the *UI* mocked the laws of libel, sedition and public order. No means seemed too audacious or indecent, no position or personage above insult and abuse. The distinction between polite and coarse language, professional and scurrilous journalism, decency and indecency were irrelevant. Neither was the paper beyond casting unfounded personal aspersions on the Viceroy and the Chief Secretary.[15] A landlord's agent was his 'bum-bailiff' (27.9.90, 5); land-grabbers were a 'species of reptile' (*PSC*, vol. 3, 254); Arthur Balfour, in addition to being called 'Bloody Balfour', was also the 'cowardly little cur' (16.2.89; cartoon); Tory MPs were a 'pack of well-dressed cads' (30.3.89, 5); the Prime Minister was 'a snivelling hypocrite' and a visiting member of the royal family was 'His Serene Humbug the . . . Duckling of Teck'.[16] The newspaper even had its own primer: 'A is an Ass on the Viceregal throne / B is old Buckshot – boys! give him a groan. . .' (J.V. O'Brien, 17). Even by the standards of late-Victorian journalism, this was excessive. What with the ever-increasing libel suits, Parnell and the other Home Rule MPs wisely withdrew from the *UI*'s directorship to avoid personal bankruptcy.[17] The combative weekly always faced such challenges head-on and its acting editor, M. M. Bodkin claimed that until the split, the paper was often charged with libel but never really punished.[18] Its legal advisers ensured that it always stayed within a hair's breadth of infringement. Hence, its cleverly masked appeals inciting violence and public disorder and its reporting of clearly inflammatory speeches:

> Metaphorically speaking, whenever you see a Radical head, hit it
> . . . wherever a vote can help to kick a Radical, kick him.

> I tell you and I wish the Government reporter was here to listen to it, that if our people had power to meet them, man to man and rifle to rifle, I for one would cut short my speechmaking this very moment and the next speeches that the destroyers of your homes would hear would be the speeches out of the mouth of your guns. (J. V. O'Brien, 24, 41)

Florence Arnold-Foster, the daughter the Chief Secretary of Ireland, referred to the *UI* as the 'ablest' and 'cleverest of all the rebel papers' (Arnold-Foster, 248) and the majority of clippings in her press journal were from this paper. Her feelings on reading the weekly may perhaps convey the effect it had on its readers:

> On coming in I performed my unpleasant duty of reading the rebel papers. *United Ireland* is going ahead in every respect, and I believe its circulation is already very large. It is certainly the ablest of the whole set . . .
>
> I always come away from my study of these papers with my fist metaphorically clenched and feeling a Saxon to the backbone; the amount of lying, the misrepresentation, the gratuitous insolence they contrive to compress into a small compass is sickening, and yet at the same time there is a fervour of nationalism, an enthusiasm of hatred, a spirit of genial camaraderie of Irishmen of which I can quite understand the attraction. If ever there is civil war between England and Ireland, the *United Ireland* may fairly claim credit for a large share of the responsibility. (262)

In the course of the Parnell Commission hearing, the Attorney-General complained that agrarian outrages and murders were described by the *UI* as legitimate warfare between landlord and tenant.[19] These 'incidents' were reported in their fullest detail 'without one single word of comment against them':

> An endeavour to tar and half drown a bailiff was called 'Bathing a bailiff.' An account of moonlighting and persons approaching a place and being shot at was called 'An escape', and week by week the details of the outrages were put down, stating what had happened, and so far as I know, my Lords, neither by any expression

3   Cartoon from *United Ireland*, 23 July 1887.

of opinion in the paper, nor by any reference to any of those outrages in any articles, was there the slightest syllable which would
lead people to suppose that the publishers, the writers, and the
proprietors of *UI* disapproved of them, and side by side with them
speeches were reported which were practically inciting to the
same conduct. (*PSC*, vol. 1, 70)

To prove his point he read out six of the twenty inflammatory articles
adduced as evidence.[20] Even the dead were not exempt from boycotting:

I may also refer your Lordships to the case of a man, Mr Fenton,
who had to travel more than 30 miles to obtain wood for his
father's coffin – and that fact is noticed apparently with satisfaction in *UI* of the 31st of December [1881]: 'In the agrarian conflict dead men are not exempt from the penalties inflicted upon
offences against neighbourly union and combination. One of the
last funerals boycotted was that of an old man buried at Millstreet,
county Cork, on Sunday.' (*PSC*, vol. 4, 269)

The paper also published 'O'Donovan Rossa's Warning to Landlords', an
unmasked threat that the Clan-na-Gael kept records 'of every landlord who
exercises the power of eviction in Ireland, and for every such death sentence
executed on a tenant a death sentence will be recorded by the Irish race
against the murderer's house, and the Irish race all over the world will give
encouragement to the avenging angel' (*PSC*, vol. 2, 725). He concluded by
asking readers to provide details of evicting landlords. Similar threats were
made against tenants paying rents to boycotted landlords. Arnold-Foster
noted in her diary:

one thing is certain, murder is not discouraged by the present
leaders of the agitation – witness their organ *United Ireland* in
which every fresh cruelty committed against an unhappy man –
whether landlord or bailiff – or farmer, is entered under the heading – 'Incidents of the Campaign' or 'Spirit of the Country'.
(Arnold-Foster, 318–9)

The particulars of the following case, which is typical, appeared under the
general heading of 'The Spirit of the Country':

'A Midnight warning' – A telegram of Thursday says: – A party
of armed, disguised men last night visited the house of a farmer
named Michael Walsh at Berring, 23 miles from Cork, and cau-
tioned him repeatedly not to pay his rent or they would take his
life. He said he would pay his rent and would not be intimidated

by them. One of the party then fired and wounded him, it is believed, mortally. The tenants were about to pay their rents to Mr Sanders, of Charleville, who is an agent. It is stated they are afraid now to pay. (*PSC*, vol. 1, 789)

The paper welcomed news of any colonial unrest. It repeatedly expressed solidarity with Indians, Zulus, Egyptians, the Blacks in America (the Irish unionists were 'the Anti-Irish Ku-Klux Klan' [23.1.86, 4]), and the Mahdi in Sudan:

> We wish the Mahdi every success. For us he is no False Prophet, but a Hot Gospeller from heaven, that, we trust, may be vouch-safed to every suffering people. Go on, sweet Mahdi and put every infidel Giaour in Khartoum to the edge of the sword . . . With the slaughter of its garrison, no man can tell what complications the future has in store for the Gladstone Govern-ment. (J.V. O'Brien, 24)[21]

Such extravagance begged for attention and the *UI* was described in parlia-ment as 'a direct incentive to outrage' (*UI*, 21.3.85, 1). At the Chief Secre-tary's Lodge in Dublin the impression was no different:

> The boy shot down and maimed for life simply because his father was a bailiff – the woman insulted in her home and her husband half beaten to death on the road, screaming for help to the neigh-bours, but with no one to come to their rescue because, as the woman told Major Neild, 'she and her husband were bad land Leaguers' – the landlord, who in former days had done all he could for the people as their friend, now living in complete iso-lation and obliged to go about armed, and under police protec-tion – every where sullen hostility, and deadly fear and suspicion.
>
> All this seemed just the practical illustration and explanation of the teaching of the *United Ireland*. (Arnold-Foster, 315)

The Dublin Metropolitan Police Superintendent, John Mallon, suggested that O'Brien be arrested for 'treasonable and seditious writings' (Warwick-Haller, 55). Lord Spencer, the Lord Lieutenant, in a letter to Gladstone, described the weekly as being 'violent and abusive beyond all precedent' (Warwick-Haller, 73). For the Attorney-General, the *UI*, the *Irish World*, the *Boston Pilot* and the *Chicago Citizen* 'incited to sedition, to the commission of crimes, and to outrages' (*PSC*, vol. 1, 70). That the newspaper was unique in Ireland in this regard is indicated by the fact that the other periodicals mentioned in the above list are all American Fenian journals. The Parnell Commission reports discuss this aspect of the *UI* at great length.

Cartoon from *United Ireland*, 10 May 1890.

The paper was not formally and permanently suppressed, because the government, having clamped down on agrarian crime, feared that suppression might 'intensify' the paper's nuisance value giving it 'a fictitious importance in the eyes of the more ignorant classes'.[22] After a slow start, its sales in 1882 had reached 30,000 copies. By 1885 they were 90,000; the following year they crossed the 100,000 mark and, when the paper published a portrait of Gladstone, sales soared to 125,000. Between 1885 and 1890 the paper's readership itself was probably well over half-a-million. This was a tremendous achievement. The *Irish Times*, established in 1859 and similarly priced at 1d, had advertised a sale of 35,000 copies in 1887. The *Weekly Irish Times* had sales figures of 40,000. In 1889, the *Armagh Standard* sold around 18,000, the *Union* 10,000, *Sligo Independent* 6,000 and the *Carlow Independent* 2,000.[23] Chief Secretary Foster did indirectly try to suppress the paper by jailing everybody connected with it – O'Brien, four successive editors, the rest of the editorial staff, mechanics, press setters, news vendors and delivery boys – but replacements were always found and the paper kept getting published. So ineffectual were these attempts at suppression that, in 1881–82, when the entire *UI* staff was jailed, O'Brien still managed to smuggle out the copy for the next issue using press clippings smuggled in to him. To avoid a whole edition being seized, editions were published simultaneously from different cities: Dublin, London, Liverpool, Glasgow and even Paris! In the case of the last, the consignment was smuggled into Ireland in all kinds of containers, including flour barrels and the petticoats of the Ladies Land League.[24] Such daredevilry further enhanced the *UI*'s popular appeal.

Ireland had never experienced anything even remotely like the *UI*. In comparison, the other national papers seemed tame. The self-professed conservatism of the *Freeman's Journal* is a good example:

> We are no advocate of extreme or visionary doctrines in connection with the distribution of land or of anything else. We are opposed to all violence and all illegality. We have never encouraged those who dream of a separation of Ireland from England ... We did not identify ourselves with all the proceedings of the Land League nor have we approved of the No Rent manifesto. (J.V. O'Brien, 21–2)

However, according to Florence Arnold-Foster, with the success of the *UI* eating into its own sales, the *Freeman's Journal* was compelled to take on a more radical aspect.

> *Apropos* of the *Freeman* and its apparently lurking desire to see a fair trial given to the Act [Land Act], notwithstanding Mr Parnell, I was told that its spasmodic but violent Parnellism is caused to a

5   Cartoon from *United Ireland*, 14 January 1888.

great extent by dread of successful competition on the part of their paper *United Ireland* [*sic*].

This has already a very large circulation, and if the *Freeman* should flag its extreme anti-Government doctrines there would be every possibility of the *United Ireland* taking its place as the popular daily paper; at present it comes out weekly. (Arnold-Foster, 251)

By 1883–84, after the compromise of the Kilmainham treaty with Gladstone, when prominent Irish politicians kept a low profile, the *UI* occupied centre stage. Conor Cruise O'Brien observes that during this period 'the people seem to have turned for leadership and incitement not to the parliamentary party, but to William O'Brien's newspaper, *United Ireland*'.[25] Its missionary zeal and recklessness had given it a patriot's prestige.

The *UI* consisted of two pages of advertisements and six closely printed pages (16.5 × 22 inches) of news with seven 20.5-inch columns to a page. The font and type depended on the importance of the news item. A penny weekly, it was issued on a Saturday and printed on a Wednesday. Its sensational A4-size cartoons, inflammatory language and provocative editorials were the main selling points. It also published the relevant sections of all legislation pertaining to Ireland and speeches made by nationalist politicians. The cartoons, which were displayed in the newsagents' windows, comprised of crude caricatures and equally crude deifications. Unionists – English and Irish – were portrayed as diabolical and cowardly; their facial expressions were limited to hatred, anger, cunning or fear. Nationalists, on the other hand, were dignified and heroic with expressions of composure and saintliness. Though funny and effective in their way, they were blatantly inflammatory; in fact, most of them depicted scenes of physical injury.[26]

Unlike the other newspapers, the *UI* gave extensive coverage – about one-and-a half pages – to the Land League, even reporting the activities of the suppressed branches. It was also exceptional in eschewing regular features such as a cultural and literary section, English and international news, etc. Barring the occasional book review, which invariably was of a political nature, the newspaper contained nothing that was not political and of direct relevance to the national movement.

The paper had a tremendous impact on rural and urban Ireland. Its own battle against coercion and British rule had lent it credibility and established its nationalist credentials. It was therefore with some authority that it sought to guide its readers' opinions on the overwhelming questions of the day. The readers, however, looked to the paper as a repository not only of nationalism but also of various other kinds of knowledge, and they wrote in with their queries as to a national confessional. These questions ranged from the dates

CAUGHT IN THE ACT.

LORD R—L—PH CH—H—L.—Please, Mr. Policeman, 'twasn't I. I did nothing at all. I wouldn't for the world.

Cartoon, *United Ireland*, 28 August 1886.

of the Dublin Horse Show, to a crash course in patriotic literature, Gaelic or typing; from the suggested treatment of a sick farm animal or relative, to the appropriateness of accepting a government job in straitened circumstances; from a list of Irish traitors, to whether it had been empirically proved that Irishmen were taller and stronger than Scotsmen and Englishmen (the editorial answer was in the affirmative). The editors were believed to be infallible in both spiritual and temporal matters and they treated readers and their queries as a schoolmaster would a backward pupil.

Though the paper did maintain a politically correct non-sectarian aspect, claiming that it did not matter at which altar Irishmen prayed so long as they were united by their nationalism, it did have a clear Catholic bias. As the nationalist/unionist divide largely corresponded to the religious divide in Irish society, the paper addressed itself primarily to Catholics, and occasionally political animosity towards unionists manifested itself as religious bigotry towards Protestants:

> To their mind it [papal infallibility] is a monstrous assumption. The Catholic Church itself is a monstrous mass of falsehood and superstition. We Irish Catholics are degraded and priest-ridden slaves . . . The POPE is called in by the people of the superior race and religion as a kind of bogey to frighten us poor foolish Catholics into abject submission to Coercion. (19.5.88, 4)

Not only does the above extract polarise the readership between 'us' Catholics and 'them' Protestants, it also implies that anti-Catholicism is part of the unionist creed. From being a political philosophy, unionism is transformed into religious bigotry. The opposite of nationalist, therefore, is not merely unionist, but also Protestant. Whatever its factual basis, such views further alienated the small minority of Protestant nationalists. Moreover, the yoking together of 'race and religion' with the common adjective, 'superior', immediately put all Protestants, Irish or English, into the coercionist quarters. A later article saw the 'astonishing' difference between northern and southern Irish poetry as indicative of racial differences. Southerners were 'the spiritual race, the race of high poetic genius, of deep and tender sentiment, of grace and beauty and generous chivalry, but the race of many weaknesses', northerners, were 'the gross, material, brutal, dull but strenuous and powerful conquerors'. The vulgarity and crudity of the latter's poetry bespoke a 'remarkably low intellectual and moral state. One deduces from them the idea of a narrow, grasping, bloodthirsty, but brave and self-reliant race, imperfectly developed intellectually, but apparently incapable of much development in that way' (7.11.91, 5). Regional characteristics were equated with religious and racial characteristics, and southern, Catholic and Celtic chauvinism combined against a forced grouping of northern and Protestant. Northern Catholics were evidently of no consequence. The paper covered the activities of the IPHRA, carried its advertisements, published its letters and reported its speeches as examples of right-thinking Protestantism.

Though the *UI* fought tooth and nail against coercion, censorship and suppression, it exercised its own form of coercion, censorship and suppression. When readers raised awkward questions they were informed that the 'best and most patriotic course' would be to remain silent. 'Let us not encumber our hopes of National emancipation with questions which can be settled hereafter more satisfactorily in College-green than at St. Stephen's' (17.4.86, 6). Another such letter, though complimented by the editor, was rejected because 'the time is not favourable to its publication. You must remember what our enemies are looking for now' (9.7.87, 1). Later, Yeats was pulled up for daring to criticise the Irish Library scheme in an English publication, even though the *UI* editor agreed with his views.[27] The paper's policy of silencing internal dissent and opposition also extended to the literary domain. A poem was rejected for publication because it preached forgiveness, which, the contributor was told, 'is good for individuals but not for nations' (14.5.87, 1). To stop the caricature of Irishmen on the stage and music hall, the paper suggested that 'theatrical authorities simply be required to cut out those insulting and degrading parts' (17.1.85, 5). Sometimes, such bullying took on insidious overtones and impinged on the personal freedom of its victims. Those whose names were published as land-grabbers or collaborators were lucky if they escaped bodily injury before making amends through contrite and grovelling apologies to the paper and a 'voluntary' payment of £5 to the local Land League branch. Often, when the paper got the name wrong, there were frenzied letters of protest from the victimised nationalist. District Inspector Crane testified that *UI* notices of boycotting and ostracism often led to the person named being attacked or murdered and he cited examples.[28] The power wielded by the paper over common lives and opinions mitigates the scepticism that naturally arises over the authenticity or sincerity of the following letter:

> Dear Sir – I can't express what pain I felt on learning that my horse had disgraced himself by working for the police. Till this misfortune came upon him, there was nothing against the animal's character that could cause me to suspect he could give the least offence to the country, or in any way become associated with the dirty set in Meelin who are working for the Government and the peelers. I was from home the day it happened. If I had been at home my poor horse, believe me, would have a clean character today. I am sure your League will accept this expression of regret, coming from

me, who am no sycophant, that I would set myself against my neighbours to please anybody; but of a family that never took sides against my country. Yours truly, William Sullivan. (8.2.90, 6)

As an organ of the Land League, the paper used its resources to coerce people into joining its organisation. It published the names of those who did join with all the veiled and sinister threats this implied for those who did not join, as is made clear in its 'editorial hint' responding to a report from a local Land League branch:

> we call on all landowners in our parish who have not yet joined our branch to do so before this day fortnight, and if they do not, we call on our secretary to publish their names in the next issue of *UI*.

> We cannot do that; but we can publish those who have joined; it will do as well. ED. *UI*.' (8.10.81, 7)

That this threat was not an idle one was proved by the fact that, three days after the *UI* published a report in a later issue demanding that people in a particular district be asked to produce their National League membership cards, that district was raided by League members and its inhabitants were asked about their League membership.[29] On another occasion, the weekly published a resolution demanding that those who have not joined the League by 1 June be 'considered as great enemies' and that 'their names be posted up in a conspicuous place' (*PSC*, vol. 3, 225). In his evidence, O'Brien agreed that there have been 'thousands of resolutions boycotting persons or naming them reported in *United Ireland*' (*PSC*, vol. 3, 221).

When T. W. Rolleston protested against the paper's intention to expose Protestant jurymen returning guilty verdicts, he highlighted the paper's tendency to persecute 'all dissentient opinion which lay within the limits of its power'. He also wondered whether the 'assurances we [Protestants] have received, that our liberties will be respected by our Catholic fellow-citizens in a free Ireland, mean anything more than that we shall be let alone, if in our civic and political actions we take care never to run counter to the dominant spirit of the time and place' (11.12.86, 6). In responding, the paper pleaded its standard excuse that unsettled times demanded harsh measures but remained unapologetic about the core issue. Instead, it averred: 'he who is not with us is against us, and must expect to be dealt with accordingly. That is not liberty; but it is the way of winning it . . .'

Though Bodkin states that the paper 'disdained advertisements' (Bodkin, 149), the truth casts light on the seamier side of the paper's character. In spite of its large sale, the *UI*, like any other paper, depended on advertisements for revenue. These were procured through a typical *UI* tactic. When the paper was started, O'Brien circulated among all the Land League branches Parnell's letter recommending the *UI* and soliciting help. Along with that he also circulated his own letter outlining the kind of assistance he required. The third clause is relevant:

> (As to branches in cities and towns.) We intend to publish in our advertising columns weekly, under the head of 'The Trade Directory of the People', a list of traders in all the cities and country towns of Ireland who seek the patronage of the people . . . Traders will thus be sure of having their names constantly under the eyes of the people to whom they must look to for business. In order that 'The Trade Directory of the People' may become so full as to include the name of every trader desirous of popular support, and so form a link in the chain of popular organisation, we propose to insert such names and addresses as are now forwarded by the secretaries of the local branches at extremely modest prices for long periods; but, as our advertising space will be limited, we must reserve the power of charging higher rates for names subsequently received. (*PSC*, vol. 1, 70)

Advertising in the *UI* became proof of one's nationalism. Not only was this a subtle form of protection money extorted from Irish traders, but it was also a means of intimidating those who did not support the League or its militant newspaper. The 'modest rates' referred to were anything but modest and were, in fact, the highest charged by any Irish newspaper.[30]

In his memoirs, while O'Brien skirts the issue of the coercion exerted by his own paper, he argues that, in a country where the 'British Constitution was forced upon us at the point of a bayonet' (W. O'Brien, 316) and where 'the elements of anything like constitutional warfare were thrown to the winds by those whose special function it was to guard them' (315), the Irish were compelled to turn these weapons to their own advantage and exploit the Constitution and the law to its fullest possible extent. Boycotting, a seemingly voluntary act, violated no laws. Neither did strong language, which according to O'Brien was the only means of securing a hearing for moderation.

O'Brien was more candid about the *UI*'s literary merits: it neither had nor aspired to any: 'The writings of *United Ireland* purported only to be to literature what a bugle-charge in the midst of the battle is to music' (O'Brien, 360). Parnell's own lack of interest in the subject was shored up by the view that 'Literature has no chance against the *Freeman*' (W. O'Brien, 400), something O'Brien could easily vouchsafe, having earned his spurs with that journal where his own facility with military metaphors, strong language and sensationalism had contributed to his success. To his mother's criticism of the prosaic and distinctly unliterary quality of the new movement as compared to the earlier one of Davis and the Young Irelanders, he had retorted that theirs was 'a movement that was not rich in literature' and that 'Ireland had had more than enough of drawing-room knights and their fopperies' (W. O'Brien, 56). Literature was something frivolous, a mere spectacle lacking substance, a sham. It was also unmanly, foppish and namby-pamby. As compared to the blood and gore of battle, it was mere 'rose water', best left to a Florence Nightingale for bathing soldiers' wounds. In itself, literature had no place in O'Brien's *UI* and even scheduled reviews were often edged out at the last moment by political news.[31] Unlike Parnell, O'Brien had a literary disposition and went on to write numerous novels. However, the national struggle remained his favoured deity and literary pursuits were indulgences that could only be allowed after the battle was won; while it waged, the muses served as handmaidens to the national cause.

Patriotism was the *sine qua non* in literature and technique merely a 'secondary attribute' (23.6.88, 6). Technique and sincerity were viewed as being opposed to each other and the general rule for composition was, 'the less time the better'. A book was found to be especially praiseworthy because it contained 'simple, well-expressed pathos and patriotic feeling' (23.4.87, 1) and its author was a farmer who wrote only for relaxation. The weekly column of political verse, which for many years was penned by O'Brien, was little more than crudely versified political propaganda in the form of either lampoons or paeans. The following are typical:

'Prayer of the Irish Peasants'

O God, our souls are sick of want and poverty,
Our hearts are broken with our children's hungry cries!
(12.1.89, 4)

'What the People Say'

AH, poor Willie! ah, poor fellow! as ye sit within your cell
Do you hear the people praying, them you loved so true and well?
(9.2.89, 4)

The readers' poetic contributions show the widespread acceptance of the paper's own view of literature, literary technique and literary subject matter. Published poems often had titles like 'For Thee, O Erin Fair' (14.5.87, 1), 'Sacrifice, The Price of Freedom' (22.6.89, 4), 'A Meeting of the League' (22.4.90, 4), and were often addressed to Parnell, Gladstone and O'Brien ('Brave Irish Heart – the Truest and the Best' [16.2.89, 1]). The following is a good example:

'My Native Land'

My Native Land ! My Native Land !
There's magic in the words
That sweeps the fond heart's subtlest strings
And strikes its sweetest chords.

(16.7.87; 4)

Such 'subtlest' and 'sweetest' gushings of patriotism were what the paper generally demanded from literature. Rhyming verse which was simple, sentimental and patriotic was considered a high literary achievement because it
served the national cause.

Viewing literature as a means to a political end, the *UI* dismissed its claims
for independent consideration. Its reviews – really, thinly disguised propaganda – generally focused on political tracts and pamphlets.[32] Strong language, sensationalism, didacticism and invectives directed at unionists which
characterised the paper's political coverage also suffused its book reviews, both
literary and non-literary. A review of P. G. Smyth's *King and Viking* opened
with the following explanation:

> As its name indicates, it deals with the period when the Scandi-
> navian invader was unsuccessfully trying the tactics of Balfour for
> the robbery and extirpation of a people whom he despised and
> failed to comprehend. (9.2.89, 1)

The author's politics and his work's didactic potential determined a
review's tone and content. To be praised in the *UI*, the book had to be patriotic, as the few literary works that were reviewed were discussed purely in
terms of their political merits. A good example is the paper's views on Emily
Thompson Skeffington, who had 'a more than average share of political
instinct' and whose novel *Moy O'Brien* was 'one which we would like to see
in every Irish home, so high is its tone, so broad and tolerant its patriotism,
and so far-sighted its prescience in its political forecastings'. Its other merits
were a 'preface with some appropriate references to current politics' and the
fact that its author was 'an Irishwoman [not] of English descent, but Irish *pur
sang*; and she is proud to trace her descent from the great house of the
O'NEILLs . . . [from whom] she inherits all the patriotism of that great race'
(18.8.88, 3).[33] If there was a didactic or propagandistic element to the work
which served the national cause, and if space permitted, the book was assured
of a puffing up, which, in a paper with a half-million readership, could boost
sales and reputations significantly:

> To speakers and writers on the national question at the present
> time, the 'Literary Remains' of our gallant forefathers of '98 give

TRIUMPH OF LAW AND ORDER IN GWEEDORE.

(BY OUR SPECIAL ARTIST IN FALCARRAGH)

7   Cartoon from *United Ireland*, 27 April 1889.

an inexhaustible supply of apt illustration and ready retort in scorching epigrams upon the notorious enemies of Ireland. Every member of the National League branches in England and Scotland ought to have at his hand a copy of this inestimable little book. Apart from political controversy, for which it is most useful, the collection includes a great number of caustic ditties – some of them rough, but yet pointed – which cannot fail to amuse, and at the same time to inspirit and instruct a receptive audience. We wish our space would permit us to say all we feel as to the value of [Dr Madden's] 'The Literary Remains of the United Irishmen' whose memory shall live for ever in Irish hearts. (11.6.87, 2)[34]

If a nationalist writer was attacked for any reason by the unionist press, the *UI* immediately made amends. It championed the book, even if it had already been reviewed favourably in the past,[35] defended the writer and denounced unionist bigotry. On the other hand, the very fact that a book had been written by a unionist was enough reason to slate it in characteristically violent fashion. Though the paper did not physically threaten unionist writers, it did subject them to ridicule and scorn, Edward Dowden and Standish O'Grady being the principal targets.[36] One column in every issue was devoted to attacking and abusing unionist publications. Andrew Dunlop, the Irish correspondent for the English *Daily News*, was among its many victims. While it normally addressed its unionist rivals with sobriquets – the *Liarish Times* for the *Irish Times* – and heaped them with ridicule and insult, it also threatened and intimidated individual reporters and editors:

> The Irish public will sooner or later have to bestir themselves to stamp out the lying brood of correspondents who live upon the infamous traffic with the English news agencies and the London papers . . . The evil has only to be resolutely grappled with to be put down, and we hereby give public warning that the news agencies, rather lies agencies, will not be tolerated any longer in their present system of secret service to the Government. The men who send these telegrams are known. We have on hand the materials to publish a full list of them, with full particulars of their political and newspaper connections. On the turf, jockeys who misconduct themselves are warned off every racecourse . . . The Irish public, if they are put to it, will make the one occupation as hazardous as the other.[37]

Dunlop points out that such threats and 'gutter journalism', typical of *UI*, were eschewed by its nationalist contemporaries.

While discussing Irish literature the *UI* invariably attacked English literature. Hence Irish periodicals were superior to their 'trashy' English counterparts 'which have the vapidity of stale newspapers without the robust interest
of good fiction'. Similarly, Irish poetry too was of 'an immeasurably higher
sphere than those of the namby-pamby versifiers whose wooden measures
bore the English magazine reader to death' (10.10.85, 5). This remained
unchanged after the split. Katharine Tynan regularly extolled the virtues of
nationalist politicians by casting them in a biblical mould. At the very height
of the Union of Hearts, she had composed a one-column paean on Gladstone,
'In Time of Expectation', full of the most banal, pathetic expressions and hack-
neyed clichés including 'You shall be our Moses – your face is like to his'
(29.5.86, 4). Later, in an article on William O'Brien in the *Catholic World*, she
invoked the prophet Ezekiel to best describe 'the passionate fervour and devotion – one had almost said saintliness – which mark him out pre-eminently as
a Christian soldier' (November 1888, 151–61). Her sycophancy was rewarded
and her own virtues extolled in turn when the *UI* reviewed *The Pursuit of
Diarmuid and Grainne*. She had outdone Swinburne, Rossetti (to whom the
poems were dedicated) and even Tennyson. One of her poems ('The Dead
Mother') was of 'surpassing excellence' and 'among the very best the age has
produced' (13.8.87, 5). Her name would be remembered for ever alongside the
best poets of the century. If this were not enough, the characters in her title
poem were held to have surpassed those of Tennyson's 'Arthur' in chivalry,
purity, bravery, sweetness and wholesomeness. Implied in this hyperbole was a
comparison between not only the two poets but also their respective countries, their national mythologies and their people.

Before and after the split, Tennyson and Swinburne were the *UI*'s stock
targets, because both had opposed the first Home Rule Bill. Since their literary merits were beyond question, or at least beyond the powers of *UI* to
challenge, it was their morals that were attacked. Both were held to be
'modern', by which pejorative the paper meant anything that was not worthy of being called Irish. Hence, Swinburne's 'passionate pulses' and 'lasciv-
ious languors' were inferior to the 'high thoughts' and 'pure music' of
Tynan's poetry; Tennyson's 'delicate, courtly . . . modern grace' had paled
before her 'wild music.' Irishness in this context constituted a primitive,
pristine and almost pre-lapsarian state of purity unstained by passion, virility untarnished by desire, and rusticity untouched by urban decadence.
Other un- or anti-Irish literary traits were 'affectation of outré style' and
'transcendentalism in thought or treatment' (24.12.88, 1); their Irish counterparts were sincerity, earthiness, spontaneity and truth. *Fin de siècle* was
another pejorative and was used synonymously with modern or 'un-Irish',
especially in connection with English writers.[38] While Ireland was the land

of saints and scholars, England was 'the Modern Babylon'; Irish literature
was pure and robust, while English literature was 'trashy' and 'pernicious'
(28.1.87, 1). English influence was a 'blight', a word evoking the horrors of
the numerous potato blights – the last being in the early 1880s – that had
decimated the peasantry, virtually stamped out Gaelic and forced millions
to emigrate. Modernism had bred corruption, impotence and effeteness in
English writers. 'Swinburnian phrases' made one unnatural and inane, while
Tennyson rendered one effeminate.[39] While reviewing John Boyle
O'Reilly's poems the paper always stressed his Celtic masculinity and his
Fenian past as being his strongest literary attributes.[40] His proven patriotism, along with the sincerity and political didacticism of his work, had made
literary technique superfluous; it would detract from the natural spontaneity of his patriotic effusions. It was the effeminate poets of 'the transcen-
dental school' (2.7.87, 6) who needed technique and effort to compensate
their lacking the vigour, martial spirit and patriotism of a Boyle O'Reilly.
Such a view of literary Irishness was informed by racial stereotypes in a way
that the latter often substituted for the former. In 'The Prose and Verse of
John Boyle O'Reilly' his physical strength and masculinity are given as
much importance as his literary merits:

> Mr John Boyle O'Reilly is a man of a physical strength that it
> would be scarcely unfair to describe as gigantic. Although he is
> not more than common tall, he has the breadth and the thews of
> a Viking of the days when Olaf Tryggveson dwelt by the Liffey in
> Dublin town and wooed and won the fair daughter of an Irish
> royal house. He excels in all manly arts and accomplishments in a
> way that we are almost afraid to chronicle, so like a hero of
> romance the list would make him seem. Who among amateurs can
> ride better, row better, walk better, above all, who can box better?
> If such a man is red-hot in his enthusiasm for the brawn and
> biceps of a famous pugilist, it is not with the sham enthusiasm of
> the dandies of old Rome who pinched the muscles of gladiators
> with slim, feminine fingers. In the society of the physically strong,
> of the physically skilful, Boyle O'Reilly is among his peers, and if
> he finds a man stronger or more skilful than himself it is scarcely
> wonderful if he accords him his highest admiration. (30.6.88, 6)

O'Reilly's physical strength and stature have as their literary equivalents a
masculine style and elevated philosophy. His ruggedness brings a primitive
simplicity, earthiness and purity into his writing. His moral sincerity has as
its equivalent a literary spontaneity that is not diluted by artificial considerations of technique and style. His excellence in 'all manly arts' includes a

facility with literature to the extent that it is manly and not decadent or *fin de siècle*. And he is romantic. This view of literary Irishness remained unaltered after the split, based as it was on racial stereotypes cutting across party affiliations.

III

It was the *DUR*'s 'national tone' that first directed the *UI*'s attention to Yeats. The nationalist weekly had already noted in the *DUR*'s opening number the 'distinct though subdued flavour' (14.2.85, 5) of national sentiment. Though the paper did not esteem TCD – an 'all too sterile and provincialised University' – and did not find and did not expect to find this national flavour 'very strongly marked in . . . [its] dust-of-ages-obscured atmosphere', it commended the 'well-favoured and well-written' monthly's aspiration 'to assert the intellectual independence of Irishmen'. Its next mention of the *DUR* was again occasioned by non-literary factors. By then, political discussion had been admitted into the review causing consternation among the TCD fellows and, consequently, joy in the *UI*:

> We must own to an admiring interest in the *Dublin University Review*. It promises to be an important focus of higher thought in Ireland, and it is a most cheering omen that higher thought in Ireland, even when concentrated within the frigid walls of Trinity College, cannot apparently choose but take a National tinge. If it be true (as we believe it undoubtedly is) that Dr Maguire, F.T.C.D., had his name erased from the list of subscribers because Mr Davitt was admitted to its pages (or for any other cause), so much the worse for his wretched Cawtholic [*sic*] sycophancy and worse taste. The *Review* looks like thriving without his sixpence. (10.10.85, 5)

In typical fashion, the following note favourably compared the *DUR* with English monthlies. Its poetry, however, 'weakened' by the influence of Matthew Arnold's scepticism, lacked 'the burning soul of belief which informs every verse of Davis with a certain apostolic fervour'. Exception was made of Yeats ('An Epilogue to "The Island of Statues" and "The Seeker"') and Todhunter's poetry, which were 'not without suggestions of gifts' higher 'than those of the namby-pamby [English] versifiers'.

Given this dislike of TCD, and that J. P. Mahaffy in particular was a stock target,[41] the *UI* had expectedly attacked this 'cowardly assailant' (11.9.86, 5) and 'learned pig from the sty of *Epicurus*' for his 'West-British' and 'anti-Home Rule' obituary of Sir Samuel Ferguson. The weekly refused to concede that

Ferguson was 'a loyal and orderly British citizen' who 'never lent his poetic talents to increase the volume of Irish discontent' as Mahaffy had averred. Instead, it depicted him as a thorough nationalist who blessed the freedom struggle, stirred Irish discontent and exulted 'in the shout of Irish chiefs "swooping on the Saxon quarry"'. In the next two months, Yeats published two essays on Ferguson in the *Irish Fireside* and the *DUR*, which, replete with nationalist rhetoric and unionist bashing, matched the *UI* blow for blow in denouncing Mahaffy, nationalising Ferguson and attacking English literature. It is possible that these essays impressed the *UI*, for, a month or so after the second piece, Yeats was given the Blunt commission.

W. S. Blunt had been a *cause célèbre* and headline news in the *UI* for some time before Yeats's article. After championing Egyptian and Indian nationalism, he had now turned to Ireland. In a stage-managed affair designed to attract national attention and challenge the government, Blunt courted arrest by addressing a proscribed meeting of the National League in Woodford, County Galway. While inviting Blunt to the Woodford meeting, O'Brien informed him that the 'chances are that it will be "proclaimed". . . If you could come in time to attend that meeting, it would be a great advantage to us, and I need scarcely say that your wife's co-operation would lay us under an additional obligation.' In his diary, Blunt observes:

> It was in the expectation, therefore, of great doings that we arrived on the morning of Saturday, the 15th, at Dublin, knowing that a crisis had occurred, and that something in the way of a fight with the Government must have been arranged by our friends, in which we might hope to take a part.[42]

The meeting was interrupted, Blunt and his wife were jostled before being arrested, and Blunt was sentenced to two months' imprisonment. With characteristic distortion, exaggeration and sensationalism, the *UI*'s screaming headlines capitalised on the farce: 'GOVERNMENT BY BRUTE FORCE: THE WOODFORD MEETING DISPERSED: ASSAULT UPON MR. BLUNT: English Ladies and Gentlemen Ill Used: THE PEOPLE BLUDGEONED', 'The Lying Proclamation', 'Scandalous Travesty of Law', 'At the Platform', 'The Murderous Order', 'A Gallant Struggle', 'A Brave and Devoted Wife', 'Mr Blunt Arrested and Lodged in Jail', 'Balfour's Thugs', 'Hand to Hand Fights', 'A Woman Almost Murdered', 'Revolt of a Policeman', 'Lady Blunt Injured', 'A Noble Woman' (29.10.87, 2). Blunt was portrayed as a never-say-die romantic revolutionary, a 'true knight-errant' 'knowing no fear, thinking no thought but what was pure and noble, going about the world pitying human suffering and redressing human wrong'. One issue carried his portrait and numerous others sang his praises. He had earned the admiration and gratitude of the Irish people and redeemed the English race. In 'recognition of his services to Irish freedom' (17.12.87, 6) the 'New Irish Avatar' and 'champion of liberty' (7.1.88, 5), was toasted throughout the British Isles and speeches made in his honour were reported by the newspaper. It was claimed that *en route* to court he received addresses of 'welcome and sympathy' at station platforms by 'large and enthusiastic crowds of people' and all the town shops downed their shutters in protest against the 'Chimpanzee antics' of the law courts. In jail, he was serenaded from boats outside his prison window.[43] In the three issues before Yeats's essay, Blunt was given about 320 column inches, i.e. an average of over five columns per issue. Commissioning the article was yet another political gimmick and was meant to be of no literary import whatsoever. The book supposedly under review, *The Love Sonnets of Proteus*, was already out of print.

Yeats clearly knew what was expected of him. Not one to look a gift horse in the mouth, especially not one that contains half-a-million readers, he toed the editorial line and his essay is an accurate reflection of the *UI*'s critical idiom. The title, 'The Prose and Poetry of Wilfred Blunt' (28.1.88, 6), was a misnomer which should have read 'The Life and Adventures of Wilfred Blunt', for the man rather than his writings was the essay's focus. The dramatic opening sentence, which is also a compendium of the essay's thematics and aesthetics, is a good example:

> Mr Wilfred Blunt has asked for pen and paper that he may edit a volume of his poems – believed to be the Love Sonnets of Proteus (1880), now out of print – a book as daring and unconventional as his own life of adventure; not with the self-conscious originality of so many modern books, but with the barbaric sincerity of one who has not time for conventions. (*UP1*, 124)

Taking for granted that the reader is familiar with Blunt's incarcerated status, the first line adds another dimension to his romantic character: in the finest traditions of Irish revolutionaries, Blunt too is a poet. Deprived of the sword of liberty, he has picked up a pen to serve the cause in another way. This ratifies the *UI*'s view of literature as an activity of leisure, something to occupy oneself with in one's spare time when more productive work is not possible. Yeats's description of Blunt's poetry also ratifies the *UI*'s nationalist aesthetic. Blunt's writings are not fanciful or namby-pamby; neither are they conventional or self-consciously original, which in the *UI*'s vocabulary indicates artificiality produced by a concern with technique, labour and thought as opposed to spontaneity, inspiration and impulse. Finally, his work is not 'modern', that ultimate hold-all of literary and moral heresies. Instead it is suffused with the author's revolutionary spirit: it is daring, masculine and sincere.

MR. BLUNT'S APPEAL.

THE SENTENCE CONFIRMED.

Judgment Delivered in the Language of Passion.

Removal to Galway Jail.

The People Brutally Bludgeoned.

At Portumna, on Saturday, the Recorder of Galway, Mr. Rice Henn, Q.C., confirmed the sentence of two months' imprisonment, passed upon Mr. Wilfrid Blunt, by the Coercion Court at Woodford, for resisting the police on October 23rd.

The Judgment.

Mr. Henn, in delivering judgment, said—The law as to unlawful assemblies is clear and indisputable. The Executive Government has not only an inherent right, but it has a duty cast upon it which it dare not neglect, to forbid, and, if necessary, to disperse by force all public meetings which, be their purpose lawful or unlawful, it has sufficient reason to believe are likely to produce danger to the peace and tranquility of the neighbourhood. Nay, more, the law as to such meetings is so jealous and imperative that it says magistrates are criminally negligent in not putting down such meetings, and they are liable to prosecution for their neglect. Now as

mithed a still greater outrage. He publicly burnt the Lord Lieutenant's proclamation—an act which was nothing less than an act of insurrection. Mr. Blunt spoke there, but he did not protest against Mr. O'Brien's speech, and having heard it, he is as guilty as if it had been spoken by himself. Nor did he protest against this outrageous and deadly insult to the Queen's deputy. He is as guilty as if he handed the match to O'Brien with which to light the paper. The gifted advocate in a burst of eloquence, which was worthy of a better cause, spoke of freedom—the freedom so dear to England—and he asks me if I am going to deprive this English gentleman of his precious birthright—his right to hold meetings which will tend to create harmony between his countrymen and ours. Well, I will ask The MacDermot will he tell me what freedom is. No. Then I will tell him, and I will tell it in the words of one whose youth was the admiration of my own boyhood, and whose manhood and whose age has won the admiration and reverence of all classes of his countrymen—the most profound jurist of our time, a truly pure and upright statesman, the Roundell Palmer of his earlier career, the great and good Earl Selborne of to-day; and how does he define it? He tells us that supremacy of the law is of the very essence of freedom. I have taken down his words as he uttered them; and one of his distinguished successors, the present Lord Chancellor of England—(I have taken down his words also)—has recently declared that respect for the law—while it is the law—is the very foundation of civil society. This, then, is the freedom which is the birthright of every Englishman, and it is the basis on which the greatness of his great country rests—reverence for law. And why? Because obedience to the law as Englishmen have been taught from generation to generation—is what Scripture says it is—the law of God. I cannot, therefore, and I will not believe that a gentleman who has had so little respect for the law, while it is the law, and has so widely departed from the principles of freedom, would in reality if he had been allowed to hold his meeting have achieved it for good. Now, I have no doubt what-soever that had he held it it would have proceeded on the lines of the meeting of the 16th. Hara than is a gentleman moving in the front

At the Station,

As the Galway platform was reached the cheering was deafening, and it was found that inside and outside the terminus several thousand people had congregated. Notwithstanding the precautions to keep the platform clear, it was very soon thronged by crowds who scaled the walls on each side of the railway track. A carriage was in attendance to convey the prisoner to the jail, but on the arrival of the train the man who was in charge of the carriage drove off, after a posse of police had marched the prisoner towards it, and what made the thing more laughable was that the mounted escort followed the empty carriage. Cheers were given for Gladstone, Parnell and William O'Brien; groans were given for Salisbury and Balfour; and "God Save Ireland" was sung on the platform by a number of young men, who crowded around the police escort. After a delay of about forty minutes a long two-horse car was obtained, which was driven by a police-constable when no other person could be got to drive. A start was then made, after the prisoner had taken his seat. But just as the horses emerged through the railway gate they were frightened back by the crowd outside. An order was given then to the police to charge, and they did so (says the Express reporter) in an earnest and determined style, with sword and baton, causing the mob to fly in all directions. A number of persons received scalp wounds on their heads, and five of them had their heads dressed at Dr. Grealy's Medical Hall. The car on which the prisoner sat was driven by a circuitous route to the jail, thus deceiving the crowd, who had run ahead by the shortest route, followed at a rapid pace by the constabulary on foot, who made a free use of their batons on all who showed the slightest disposition to obstruct the carrying out of the law. The different passages leading to the jail were blocked by the police to prevent the crowd following the vehicle, and those who had the hardihood to venture across the bridge leading to the jail paid dearly for their foolishness.

An Address by Mr. Blunt.

In reply to an address presented to Mr. Blunt by the people of Portumna before the judgment

'Mr Blunt's Appeal', *United Ireland*, 14 January 1888.

Like Proteus, Blunt is a man of many parts, but, like John Boyle O'Reilly, he is first and foremost a man:

> But here . . . are the poems of one who is man first, not even poet or thinker or artist first – scarcely artist at all unhappily. He writes always like a man of action – like one who is intent on living his life out.
>
> They are so frank and personal – these sonnets – that the reader thinks more of the writer than the writing.
>
> Many of his best poems are not love poems at all, but lookings forward into that manhood to be spent in battle . . .
>
> As in the writings of all strong natures, whether men of thought or men of action – of men of action more than any, perhaps – there is much melancholy, very different from the ignoble, self-pitying wretchedness – with a whimper in it – of feeble natures. (124–5)

Yeats's essay, which is really a catalogue of Blunt's masculine attributes, focuses more on his adventures than on his literary work. It is the *man*, as opposed to the poet, that he continually emphasises. Complying with the *UI*'s priorities, he also emphasises Blunt's anti-imperialist struggles, particularly against English imperialism in Egypt and India. In the former, England is shown to have propped up 'the Turk . . . filled his wallet and sent him on his way with a blessing to tyrannise and brutalise' (127). While presenting Blunt as a champion of liberty, Yeats outdoes even the *UI*. Where the newspaper estimated that Blunt had spent £3,000 for Arabi's defence when the latter was faced with certain execution, Yeats put the figure at £5,000.[44] A comparison with the *UI*'s literary reviews discussed earlier will indicate how completely Yeats has moulded himself to fit in with the paper's methods and its literary and political agenda.

The artistic and intellectual compromises necessitated by his Blunt essay were playing on Yeats's mind when he wrote despondently to Tynan a fortnight later:

> I am trying to get some sort of regular work to do however, it is necessary, and better any way than writing <u>articles about things</u> <u>that do not interest one – are not in ones line of development</u> – not that I am not very glad to do the Folklore book or any thing that comes to my hand. The hope of regular work may come to nothing. . . . To me the hope of regular work is a great thing for it would mean more peace of mind than I have had lately but Papa sees all kinds of injury to me in it. It makes him quite sad. perhaps the loss of mental liberty entailed in routine is always harmful. On

the other hand it would save me from the <u>insincerity of writing</u> <u>on all kinds of subjects, of writing on other men's truth</u>. And I am anxious to look about me and become passive for a while too . . .

I am very anxious about this search for regular work. Neither I nor papa know well how to set about it . . . (*CL1*, 47–8, 50; underlining added)

Yeats nowhere mentions the Blunt article in his letters. However, the underlined sections probably refer to it, because Yeats's previous article was a review of Tynan's poetry seven months earlier and it is unlikely he was referring to that, certainly not while writing to Tynan herself. Moreover, since Tynan's *Shamrocks* was largely influenced by Yeats's own advice on technique and the necessity of Irish subject matter, his review of her book could hardly be described as 'writing on other men's truth' or 'articles about things that do not interest one – are not in one's line of development'. That at this time he was neither interested in nor moved by Blunt's poetry was something that he confessed to later.[45] The reference to 'other men's truth' once again points to the Blunt essay, where Yeats perforce had to modulate his work to toe the *UI*'s editorial line. In other periodicals he was not as constrained by external pressures as he was in the *UI*, and in his *Irish Fireside* review, for instance, he dwelt at some length on the technical and literary niceties of Tynan's poetry and bypassed her politics altogether. Compromising with the *UI* had troubled him and he voiced his preference for 'regular work' such as transcribing or librarianship. Straining his already poor eyesight and coping with a soul-wrecking and stifling monotony was preferable to a troubled conscience and self-accusations of insincerity. Earning money through poetry seemed light years away.

Yeats's debts to Tynan's father and to O'Leary possibly influenced his decision to write the Blunt review. However, despite ardently espousing the *UI*'s literary and political agenda, he did not receive payment for at least two months. In his letter of 12 February quoted above, he complained: '"United Ireland" has not paid me, bad luck to it, when it does I meen to pay my debts. They must wait until then' (*CL1*, 51). Between 4 and 7 March Yeats wrote to the paper requesting payment.[46] By 14 March it was still pending, even though the *UI* on 10 March carried the following note in 'The Editor's Room': '**W.B.Y.** – Please excuse delay. The matter shall be seen to immediately' (1). £2 finally arrived on 22.3.88 enabling him to pay off his debts and assist in the family's relocation from South Kensington to Bedford Park.[47]

In 1888 Yeats was small-fry for the *UI* and it could afford to shelve his claims for a while. Besides, its literary editor and columnist, Edward Leamy, had possibly detected a rival in Yeats. Leamy was himself a poet, dramatist and folklorist with an interest in fairy stories. Yeats's *Fairy and Folk Tales*, when briefly noticed in the paper, was accorded no praise for itself but presented as being the harbinger of a greater event, 'a hopeful sign if it is to be taken as the herald of more to come' (5.1.89, 6). That greater event was to be Leamy's own *Irish Fairy Tales*, which was nominated by the *UI* as the 'Christmas Book for Ireland' (14.12.89, 5), reviewed in glowing terms on page 5 – unprecedented prior to the split – and described as marking 'an era in Irish literature'. On 16.2.89 the paper announced in its 'Editor's Room' (1) that it had received Yeats's '"The Wanderings of Oisin" &c' but regretted being unable to review it owing to the pressure of political news. The next week there was still no review, even though that issue did carry a literary column. Instead, there was a similar apology as the last week's and an article entitled 'The Wanderings of some Boycotted Barley' (23.2.89, 3). To add further insult to injury an article on Sir Samuel Ferguson contained a few snide comments which seemed to be directed at Yeats. While commenting on the splendour of Irish legends, the article, probably Leamy's, lamented that had Ferguson concentrated not on Irish rhapsodies but on Irish legends 'a great work would have been greatly done, and an acquaintance of mine need never have attempted an over-daring task' (6). Having assented with a civil leer, the paper, when it reviewed *Oisin* four issues later, damned it with faint praise. Clubbed with Mrs Piatt's *The Witch in the Glass*, *Oisin* was found to pale in comparison with the other 'collection of more finished work' (23.3.89, 6). The rest of the review alternated between praise and undermining of the praise with stronger criticism. While admitting that Yeats's treatment of the Oisin legend 'relieves the mind from any sense of triteness', the paper also complained that the theme had become 'over-worked':

> One would really think, so many have been the essays in prose
> and verse on this particular and misty point in Ireland's history,
> that there were never in actual life any individuals or incidents
> worthy of a twang of a harp or the thought of a poetical brain.

Leamy's rivalry may have accounted partly for Yeats's indifferent reception, but then *Oisin* was hardly grist for the *UI*'s propaganda mill: it did not meet its requirements nor was it directly serviceable to the national cause. Besides, Yeats's own political credentials, though adequate to get him a polite mention in this advanced nationalist weekly, were not unequivocally nationalist. His being a Protestant could not have helped either.

Yeats needed the *UI* much more than it needed him and he could not be too insistent on payment or prompt reviewing if he wanted further commissions. His letters reveal that the *UI* was the only Irish newspaper he read regularly, that it was a talking point even among the Irish community in Bedford Park and that it was important to him for its political as well as for its limited literary coverage. Even while in London, he followed closely its goings-on and continually requested Tynan and O'Leary for copies, which, when they arrived, were 'very welcome'.[48] Having established himself in the London literary marketplace by 1903, he could disdain Irish reviews, but not until then. In the 1880s and 90s the *UI* was very high on Yeats's list of newspapers that were sent review copies of his books. He courted its favour and sent Tynan twice to the newspaper's offices to inquire about and speed up the delayed *Oisin* review.[49] Writing to D. J. O'Donoghue, the *UI*'s London-based literary correspondent, he ingratiated himself by stressing his Irish and nationalist credentials.[50] Despite possible reservations, he could not afford to pass up any opportunity of aligning himself with Ireland's largest selling weekly.

Yeats's situation at this time was more uncomfortable than we with hindsight might suppose. While the paper's politically governed view of literature would have jarred, Yeats, as a Protestant, would have also been sensitive to the paper's Catholic chauvinism (as manifested, for example, in the article on northern Irish poetry discussed earlier, see pp. 107-8), and to the fact that it was consciously catering to a Catholic audience and its prejudices. He was acutely conscious of such prejudices, as seen in his feeble attempts to placate Fr Matthew Russell, the editor of the *Irish Monthly*, about Carleton's early anti-Catholicism. These were of little avail and the Catholic monthly later attacked him for *Representative Irish Tales*'s insensitivity towards Catholics.[51]

Nevertheless, this did not hinder him from adopting the paper's politics and affecting its literary aesthetic and style in the Blunt essay and in his contributions to other nationalist periodicals. His work for the American *Boston Pilot* – a periodical which, according to the Parnell Commission, 'incited to sedition, to the commission of crimes, and to outrages' (*PSC*, vol. 1, 70) – and the *Providence Sunday Journal* are instances where the *UI*'s training in propaganda, nationalist aesthetics and moulding his own position to that of the editor's politics were put to good use. Both journals had strong Irish interests: the former was edited by the epitome of masculinity, John Boyle O'Reilly, and catered principally to an expatriate, nationalist, Catholic community, while the latter had a more general readership and was edited by Alfred M. Williams, an American reporter with an enduring interest in Ireland.[52]

It is a significant indication of Yeats's own critical malleability that the *UI* style is more pronounced in his articles for O'Reilly than in those for Williams. Out of the fourteen literary articles written for the *Boston Pilot*, a more nationalist paper than the *Providence Sunday Journal*, five open with an attack on England, six others contain political criticism of England and six contain criticism of English literature. On the other hand, out of the seven *Providence Sunday Journal* articles, two contain political attacks on England and one contains criticism of English literature; none opens with an attack on England. The *Boston Pilot* audience would probably have been suspicious of

Yeats's Protestantism and this would explain his increased reliance on the *UI* style of literary journalism. It would also explain why in his *Boston Pilot* and not in his *Providence Sunday Journal* articles he felt it so necessary to go out of his way and repeatedly stress that he was a nationalist. He is constantly dropping references to 'the English garrison' (22, 23) and the mistaken 'loyal minority' (55).[53]

Like the *UI*'s, Yeats's literary reviews are dominated by a political overview: 'To the greater poets everything they see has its relation to the national life . . . nothing is an isolated artistic moment' (78). Allingham's *Laurence Bloomfield*, though criticised in some respects, is found to be 'a good poem in its way' because it is full of 'much sound knowledge of the land question' (78) and because it had Gladstone's approval. On the other hand, O'Grady is criticised, as he was in the *UI* a year earlier and for the same reasons: in *Red Hugh's Captivity* he 'writes many pages to glorify extremely murderous [*sic*] Sir John Perrot' (34). (It was only later, when Yeats was more confident of his nationalist standing, that he included O'Grady into the pantheon of Irish writers.) In another instance (11), he traces a connection between his subject of discussion, a cobbler-cum-poet named Pat Gogarty, and the Parnell Commission through the medium of the Clondalkin branch of the National League. While writing about Maud Gonne, he attacks the calumnies and anti-Irish propaganda disseminated by the 'magnificent *Times*' (61). There are also references to 'Saxons', 'Sassenachs', the English conquest and the extirpation of Gaelic.[54]

In keeping with the *UI* practice, his American reviews do not focus exclusively on literary texts. They also include reviews of three tracts on Irish political prisoners. The one by the MP and ex-Cabinet Minister, Shaw Lefevre, though 'chockful of facts and figures somewhat Dryasdustically' is yet found to be 'good work', 'useful' and 'valuable as an admission from the English Radical standpoint of iniquitous treatment of political prisoners by England, both in the past and the present' (16). The lengthy quotations from some unpublished letters by a Fenian which he has 'but skimmed through' and is intending to deal with at greater length later is characteristic of the *UI*'s style of reviewing:

> 'Believe me', he writes (this was in 1847), 'the old leaven of Orangeism and anti-Irishism will start up from their graves . . . England is England still; the Saxon is unchanged – as indomitable as the hyena. Britain is strong, Ireland is prostrate, fallen, nearly annihilated.' 'If the country does not rise', he writes, 'we will be trampled into the unblessed graves of those who have already sunk victims of hunger and disease', and if on the other hand they shake off this 'vile torpor of slavery and contented beggary' and take to arms, still he has small hope, but then at any rate

they will be 'going like their fathers of old . . . to die nobly rather than live as paupers, whining and cringing slaves'; and he adds, 'should such things happen may I share this glorious privilege.' (34).

Yeats's Fenian rhetoric and his approval of 'such unwatered treason' would not have gone unappreciated by his readers or by his editor, Boyle O'Reilly. It would have also established his political credentials with them.[55]

Besides the political slant given to the reviews, the Fenian rhetoric and his nationalist self-projection, Yeats also adopts the *UI*'s literary aesthetic. His *Boston Pilot* essays repeatedly insist that Irish literature should be political, should draw its themes from history and politics and instil nationalism.[56] Only then will it 'move some Irish hearts and make them beat true to manhood and to Ireland' (65), this has always been the way: 'Every movement of Irish nationality has had its singers' (42). For Yeats, as for the *UI*, nationalism is the *sine qua non* for masculinity as well as for Irish literature. About Allingham, Lover and Lever he complains, 'Political doctrine was not demanded of them, merely nationalism' (78) and he is incredulous that they have not complied. He repeatedly adverts to Allingham's 'non nationalism' as 'a sad business' (78), claiming that 'it is the most central notion I have' of him (77). Had he 'remained in touch with the people' (30) – and these do not include unionists – his work would have improved because he would have imbibed their nationalism and his 'political sympathies would certainly have widened' (30). This deficiency has 'limited his vision, has driven away from his poetry much beauty and power – has thinned his blood'. His other literary shortcomings – 'impulse and momentum' (30) – would also have been compensated by nationalist beliefs. Nationalism gives depth and conviction; its absence begets 'shallowness' and 'cynicism' (78). Most importantly, and here Yeats is letting his guard down, nationalist writers 'have more influence in Ireland' (78).

Not only is nationalism made the primary ingredient of literary talent, and the determining factor in literary success, it is also synonymous with 'Irish feeling':

> Whenever an Irish writer has strayed away from Irish themes and Irish feeling, in almost all cases he has done no more than make alms for oblivion. *There is no great literature without nationality, no great nationality without literature.* (30; emphasis added)

His oft-quoted and oft-repeated statement (in italics) is neither merely literary nationalism nor a romantic commonplace as has often been thought. Read in its context, it is a demand that literature be politically serviceable. The dictum may be O'Leary's but its application is the *UI*'s. When Yeats speaks of 'nationality' and 'Irish feeling', he is not referring merely to patriotism. In a later *UI* review, in which he reiterated the 'alms for oblivion' theme, he attacked George Savage-Armstrong for his unionist beliefs and claimed that his poetry had 'suffered the inevitable penalty' accruing out of a 'false philosophy of life' (*UP1*, 229): 'he must choose between expressing in noble forms the life and passion of this nation, or being the beater of the air all his days.'The linking of Savage-Armstrong's unionism with his not reflecting 'the life and passions of the nation' as a cause-and-effect relationship indicates quite clearly that 'life and passions' could only be of the nationalist variety. This reductive and self-serving view of Irishness and Irish feeling, and its use as a scourge to whip political opponents, dissidents and marginal figures, is very much part of the *UI*'s standard practice and something Yeats himself was not averse to exploiting.

In these essays, nationalism is presented as a kind of literary panacea that can remedy even the most serious handicaps: it can widen a limited vision, complete incompleteness, transform ugliness into beauty, debility into power, effeteness into passion, shallowness into depth, cynicism into conviction and, last but not least, oblivion into influence. If nationalism can do all this, why bother with technique; it pales into insignificance and is really of little use. For Yeats the literary nationalist, as for the *UI*, technique is not merely a 'secondary attribute', it is the most un-Irish of things, it is 'cosmopolitan':

> I have strayed from [Todhunter's] 'The Children of Lir' and 'The Sons of Turann.' Nothing could be less like *Helena* than these 'Children', *Helena* essentially belonging to what is called poetical poetry, everything seen through the spectacles of books, 'The Children of Lir' almost too simple, almost too unelaborate. One is cosmopolitan, the other ethnic, falling on the cosmopolitan ear with an outlandish ring. One is written throughout in blank verse – most artificial if most monumental of forms – the other in strangely unstudied, fluid and barbaric measures. (*LNI*, 80)

> But in all [Todhunter's poems], whether epopee or ballad, is the same charm of sincerity, of Celtic sincerity. There is no trying for effect, no rhetoric, no personal ambition, no posing . . . All this simplicity and directness comes from great sympathy with his own creations. They fill him with so much pity and interest . . . that he has not time to hang purple draperies or embroideries, or consider his own attitude to the world. In this we believe he is a Celt, or at any rate of a type more commonly found in Ireland than in England. The Saxon is not sympathetic or self-abnegating; he has conquered the world by quite different powers . . . But these poems are altogether different with their simplicity and tenderness. They rise from the same source with the courtesy of the

Irish peasant; and because there is no egotism in them there is no
gloom. (89)

It is often pleasant to turn to the latter; to turn, when bewildered
by the gigantic, to men who have nothing extravagant, exuber-
ant, mystical; to turn from the inspired to the accomplished. (102)

The first quotation creates an opposition between poetry that is indifferent
to technique and that which is governed by it. This opposition is then sub-
sumed under the wider rubric of ethnic and cosmopolitan. The second quotation substitutes ethnic and cosmopolitan with Celtic and Saxon as defining
categories, listing additional features for each. The third quotation provides an
alternative set of categories under which it lists some further characteristics.
The cumulative register reads as follows:

Celtic / Ethnic/ Technically indifferent / Inspired	Saxon / Cosmopolitan/ Technical / Accomplished
simple	elaborate
unstudied	bookish
unskilled	skilled
sincere	insincere
spontaneous	affected
primitive	pretentious
humble	ambitious
direct	complex
self-abnegatory	selfish
natural	artificial
sympathetic	aggressive
patriotic	egotistical
tender	gloomy
exuberant	lifeless
young	old
mystical	practical

Like the characteristics, the categories are linked to each other within their own
logic. 'Celtic' entails 'Inspiration', which in turn necessitates 'Technically indifferent'. So also 'unskilledness' entails 'simplicity', 'naturalness' and 'spontaneity'.
Racial stereotypes adumbrate literary stereotypes and both reinforce each
other. Though Yeats's catalogue of racial qualities resembles the *UI*'s, it was not
necessarily derived from that paper, nor was such essentialisation the *UI*'s preserve. As Terence Brown points out, it was the product of the rise of romanticism and nationalism in the late eighteenth and early nineteenth centuries: 'In

this new philosophic context what had once been regarded as mere barbarism could be esteemed in Romantic terms as uncorrupted innocence and in nationalist terms as racial characteristics.'[57] The difference here is that these nationalist and racial characteristics are extended to the literary realm, where they function as critical concepts and arbiters of literariness and literary merit. The *UI*, being the most widely read and most influential Irish weekly, would have contributed significantly to strengthening and disseminating this view of literary Irishness. It would have also sanctioned it as the politically correct view. Many years later, Yeats would scorn such political correctness and assert his own class, ethnic and religious chauvinism. He would also add other categories of difference to this list, ones that stemmed naturally from the others, but now he would place himself on the opposite side, along with 'Form' and against 'Form-lessness', with the manor and against the marketplace, with tragedy and against comedy, with Protestants and against Catholics:

> The sense of form, whether that of Parnell or Grattan or Davis, of form in active life, has always been Protestant in Ireland. O'Connell, the one great Catholic figure, was formless. The power of self-conquest, of elevation has been Protestant, and more or less a thing of class. All the tragedians were Protestant – O'Connell was a comedian. He had the gifts of the market place, of the clown at the fair. (*Mem*, 212)

By 1909 Yeats could afford to be contemptuous of what he called the 'rabble' and the 'Leaders of the Crowd', but in the 1880s and '90s it was with precisely the 'rabble' and the 'Leaders of the Crowd' that he sought to ingratiate himself.

Another similarity between the *UI*'s aesthetic and Yeats's American essays is the pejorative use of 'cosmopolitan' and the privileging of a narrow provin-cialism.[58] As seen in the above quotations, 'cosmopolitan' can be made very easily into a synonym of 'English' and hence an antonym of 'patriotic'. It too is un-Irish:'but I wish he [Todhunter] would devote his imagination to some national purpose. Cosmopolitan literature is, at best, but a poor bubble, though a big one. Creative work has always a fatherland' (*LNI*, 12). Later, Yeats would stress the necessity of technique and of learning it from English writers, but by then he was more assured and could speak his mind. At this early stage, to admit as much would be to risk accusations of 'West Briton-ism' and un-Irishness, things Yeats himself bandied about freely. Hence, any form of contact with English literature was branded anti-national, debasing and literary suicide:

> Mr Justin McCarthy, in an article last week, said that Irishmen leave little impression on contemporary literature – they are absorbed into journalism and politics. This is true, unhappily,

though he did not mention all the things that absorb us. Cosmopolitanism is one of the worst. We are not content to dig our
own potato patch in peace. We peer over the wall at our neigh-
bour's instead of making our own garden green and beautiful. (32)

They both [John Francis O'Donnell and Miss Wynne], however,
belong to the same school of Irish writers. Both have read much
English literature, and have taken from it, rather than from their
own minds and the traditions of their own country, the manner
and matter of their poetry. (47)

Besides the obvious patriotic reason – imitating England is unpatriotic –Yeats
also attacked cosmopolitanism for providing bad models. Such attacks draw
on the same stock of racial and literary stereotypes that inform his view of
Irish literature and literary technique. English literature is old, decayed,
impoverished and effete. It will soon be 'broken, crumbled into dust and
. . . blown away in pieces by the wind' (89) like the man in the Irish folk-
tale. Its 'dramatic fervour has perhaps ebbed out of her' (9) and its 'themes of
verse and prose are used up' (67). Her 'poets must scrape up the crumbs of
an almost finished banquet, but Ireland has still full tables' (60).

A few years later, he would dismiss as 'absurd' (*UP1*, 352) Dowden's
charge that he encouraged people to shun English literature. And many years
after that he himself would admit that he owed his soul to Shakespeare,
Spenser and Blake.[59] But now, he claimed, English literature 'is not writ in
my bond. With Irish literature and Irish thought alone have I to do' (*LNI*,
53). Writers were praised for being 'ardently Irish' (20) or criticised for not
being 'more Irish' (55). He asserted that Dr Todhunter's book of Irish poems
'concerns us more than all the others' (60) written by Rhymers' Club members. He defended this parochialism by averring that, if 'we do not take care
of our own singers, who will?' These bad pennies that he had knowingly cast
before the Irish public, thinking that they were like 'soft wax' and malleable
to his manipulations, came back to him at frequent intervals. In 1894 when
he attacked the *UI* for its 'adamantine indifference' to international critical
standards, he was treated to the same defence he made of Todhunter's Irish
poems. Though he would iterate and reiterate that criticism should be as
international as possible, his own criticism during this period had helped
foster and celebrate a parochialism that was to haunt him for many years
thereafter. Following the *UI*, Yeats too urged readers to support Irish literature as fervently as they would support Irish nationalism. Literature would
be united 'to the great passion of patriotism' and the otherwise apathetic
Irish audience 'will do for the love of Ireland what they would not do for
the love of literature' (65). Having desired as much, and cast his appeal not

to the readers' aesthetic sensibilities but to their political sentiments, he was in no position to rail against the eunuchs that 'ran through Hell' ('On those that Hated', *VP*, 294) and condemned Synge's *Playboy*; they were partly begotten by Yeats himself. What jars most in these instances is not so much the opinions themselves but an awareness that he is writing against his natural grain, mouthing opinions he does not believe and aligning himself with the kind of vulgarity and shallow criticism that he was so contemptuous of later. As he himself admitted, he 'knew better than he wrote' (*LNI*, xviii), was conscious of the 'unrealities and half-truths propaganda had involved me in', realised that 'I was a propagandist' and hated himself for that.

— 3 —

Yeats Among the Imperialists: Celticism and the Aesthetics of Yeatsian Unionism

I

After a productive stay in Ireland over the summer and autumn of 1887, Yeats returned to London in January 1888. Shortly thereafter, he was again beweeping his outcast(e) state, and with good reason. Regular work was difficult to come by and his letters testify to the anxiety this caused him.[1] Articles and poems were rejected at a rate he was probably unaccustomed to in Ireland but which was quite normal for a newcomer in the proliferating but already overcrowded periodical marketplace. He sometimes had to wait over nine months before learning whether commissioned articles were accepted or not. Some of those that were accepted remained unpublished for over two-and-a-half years.[2] The pile of rejected manuscripts kept increasing, prompting the lament that he had 'built up a useless city in my sleep' (*CL1*, 92). Though O'Leary's contacts in the United States published two articles in the *Providence Sunday Journal*,[3] the respite was short-lived and Yeats was forced to do work that he would later regret or deny.

Two months after Yeats's return from Ireland, his family moved to Bedford Park. His father was not faring well and money was difficult to come by. At this time, he was offered the chance of penning a literary gossip column for the unionist *Manchester Courier*, and in his *Memoirs* he claimed to have declined the offer, much to his father's relief. Gossip-mongering was no job for a gentleman, as Wilde gently reminded him, and besides, the paper's politics were not quite right. Actually, Yeats was in no position to refuse and had undertaken the commission despite his reservations over the social and political compromises involved.[4] Under similar compulsions artistic principles were compromised and illustrations versified for a purveyor of low-brow popular literature and Protestant morality.[5] Though he would later claim that he 'kept the Muses' sterner laws' ('The Grey Rock', *VP*, 273) and never sold his talent for money, the reality was quite different. As an Irishman in England and a newcomer to Grub Street, Yeats was very much on the margins. Though confident of his talent, he needed exposure and money, and that sometimes came at a price.

It was shortly after moving to Bedford Park that he met W. E. Henley, who lived within walking distance at Chiswick. Henley was already a respected figure in English journalism and letters: he had edited two magazines (*London*, February 1877 to April 1879, and *The Magazine of Art*, 1882 to 1886), written the famous 'Invictus', collaborated in four plays with R. L. Stevenson, and recently published *A Book of Verse*. He was then a freelance journalist and would shortly take up the editorship of the *Scots Observer* (*SO*).[6] A sixpenny weekly, the *Observer* boasted access to the 'Wealthy and Cultured Classes'. Though its sales never exceeded 2,000 copies, it had a readership of around 10,000, largely because of its popularity in gentlemen's clubs. It had a high literary reputation owing to Henley's ability to attract the best talent, and by contemporary accounts it was the best written and most quoted journal of its day. According to C. Lewis Hind, 'no young writing man of the period was content till he had an article accepted by Henley.' The *SO* also had a high profile owing to Henley's editorship, for, as Hind observed, 'it may be said that literary London was divided into those who hated and those who adored Henley'. The *SO*, according to Max Beerbohm, 'was rowdy, venomous, and insincere. There was libel in every line of it. It roared with the lambs and bleated with the lions. It was a disgrace to journalism and a glory to literature.' Arnold Bennett gave it the 'sobriquet of the "National Snobserver" for its cynical, contemptuous, self-assertive style, that affects an exaggerated culture and superiority and finds nothing to praise'. Despite its acknowledged quality and its notoriety, it cost its chief financier, Robert Fitzroy Bell, £4,000 annually.[7]

Yeats frequented Henley's weekly literary gatherings at Chiswick. He soon became a member of the Henley regatta and a regular contributor to his journals. Henley was Yeats's 'chief employer' (*Mem*, 37), 'our leader and our confidant' (*Auto*, 127), and Yeats 'admired him beyond words' (124).

II

By the mid-1880s Henley had acquired a formidable reputation as a man of letters and talent spotter. His activities spanned the literary spectrum – lexicography, journalism, literary and art criticism, essays, poetry, plays and periodical and book editing – and Kipling aptly described him as 'more different varieties of man than most'.[8] An individualistic, outspoken, self-confident and erudite brand of criticism had become synonymous with Henleyism, as had generosity, a commanding presence, courage and literary perspicacity. Contributors to his journals comprised the *crème de la crème* of Victorian literary journalism: Henry James, C. B. Fry, Wilfred Blunt, Charles Dilke, Alice Meynell, George Steevens, T. E. Brown, Cosmo Monkhouse, Alfred Austin, George Saintsbury, William Archer, Andrew Lang, Austin Dobson, J. M. Barrie, Charles Whibley, Kenneth Grahame, Charles Swinburne and Edmund Gosse. Rodin, Millet, Whistler and R. A. M. (Bob) Stevenson (who acquired fame as an art critic and conversationalist) were some of Henley's finds. He was also among the first British editors to champion the early careers of, among others, Robert Louis Stevenson, Rudyard Kipling, H. G. Wells, Stephen Crane, Henrik Ibsen, Verlaine, Mallarmé and Joseph Conrad. Not surprisingly, Henley was one of the most influential figures of his generation during the 1890s: his imprimatur was prestigious, valuable and widely accepted; writers courted and revered him and his close circle adopted his prejudices, mannerisms and idiom. He was generous to his protégés, took pride in their success and supported them to the utmost. When he was described by one of his acolytes in the *Bookman* as being 'beyond question the most formidable presence in English letters today', it was not an aberration or a hyperbole. Kenneth Grahame admitted that Henley was 'was the first Editor who gave me a full and free and frank show, who took all I had and asked me for more: I should be a pig if I ever forgot him.' For Ford Madox Hueffer, 'Henley was a very great man' and 'nearly all that is vital, actual and alive in English work of today is due to the influence of Henley and his friends'. Wells dedicated *The Time Machine* to Henley; Kipling, who preferred to take a pay-cut and write for Henley, described him 'as kind, generous, and a jewel of an editor, with the gift of fetching the very best of his cattle';[9] Meredith attributed to him his reputation in the late 1890s and hailed him as 'one of the main supports of good literature in our time'; and Conrad, another migrant like Yeats, saw Henley as 'a distinguished authority', the last word in literary judgement casting 'about the spell of his individuality, the beneficent white magic of his masterful temperament working for the truth, vigour, for the right expression and the right thought in literature'. As Todd Willey demonstrates, Henley was the 'immediate object of Conrad's most ingratiating attentions'. He freely admitted to tailoring *The Nigger of the Narcissus* to suit Henley's tastes, and, on its being accepted for serialisation in the *New Review*, he wrote euphorically to Garnett, 'Now I have conquered Henley I ain't 'fraid of the divvle himself.' Obtaining Henley's critical approbation was his primary consideration, and having 'the good fortune to please that remarkable man' was, for Conrad, the 'most gratifying recollection of my writer's life'.[10]

In Henley one half of Victorianism meets its apotheosis and the other half
its nemesis. He saw himself as the bard of the Empire and much of his own
poetry was geared towards fostering imperial ideology. His anthology, *Lyra
Heroica*, was, as he told Tennyson while requesting permission to reprint 'The
Charge of the Light Brigade' and 'The Siege of Lucknow', 'for boys, designed
. . . to bring into particular relief the dignity of patriotism, the beauty of battle, the heroic quality of death'.[11] As the 'Chosen daughter of the Lord, /
Spouse-in-Chief of the ancient Sword', England demanded imperial might
and conquest:

> They call you proud and hard
> England, my England:
> You with worlds to watch and ward,
> England, my own!
> You whose mailed hand keeps the keys
> Of such teeming destinies
> You could know nor dread nor ease
> Were the Song on your bugles blown,
> England,
> Round the Pit on your bugles blown![12]

While eminently Victorian in this regard, Henley was eminently 'anti-
Victorian' in other matters. Claiming that Grundyism had rendered 'the theory and practice of British art' subject 'to the influence of the British
schoolgirl', he took it upon himself to outrage Victorian prudery. Sex, he
declared, was 'the great subject, the leaven of imaginative art'. As editor, he
issued in a 'Special Literary Supplement' (*NO*, 14.11.91, 673–5) Hardy's 'Saturday Night in Arcady' – the seduction scene from *Tess of the D'Urbervilles* –
after the *Graphic*, the novel's original serialiser, had refused it on moral
grounds. Similarly, he highlighted the sexual motifs in Swinburne's poetry as
well as the riotous and not-so-respectable aspect of R. L. Stevenson following the publication of a sanitised biography. He defended Byron's profligacy
and promiscuity in Fielding's *Joseph Andrews*, claiming of the latter that 'fornication is a detail as it is in life'. While co-editing a dictionary of *Slang and
its Analogues* he wrote excitedly to Charles Whibley of the discovery of a new,
'*new*, mind you', synonym denoting the female genitalia. This, after he had
already sent his co-editor 'a first list of 300 equivalents for the same delectable vocable'.[13]

It is in social Darwinism that Henley's politics and aesthetics merge. His
'Song of the Sword' celebrates conflict and extermination as 'God's gift
returning / In fury to God!' Apostrophising the weapon as this 'Angel of
Destiny', 'Prince and evangelist', 'War-Thing, the Comrade, / Father of

honour / And giver of kingship', Henley finally proclaims: 'I am the Will of God: / I am the Sword'. He commands others to follow his example:

> Thrust through the fatuous,
> Thrust through the fungous brood
> Spawned in my shadow
> And gross with my gift!
>
> . . .
>
> Sifting the nations,
> The slag from the metal,
> The waste and the weak
> From the fit and the strong;
> Fighting the brute,
> The abysmal Fecundity;
> Checking the gross,
> Multitudinous blunders,
> The groping, the purblind
> Excesses in service,
> Of the Womb universal,
> The absolute Drudge . . .[14]

In both literature and politics, Henley championed the cult of masculinity, strength and virility and opposed anything that smacked of sentimentality, effeminacy and weakness. Politically, this translated as an espousal of imperialism, authority and oligarchy, and a rejection of democracy, socialism, suffragism, the Salvation Army and the Liberal and Labour parties. Its literary equivalents were an espousal of realism and high art and a debunking of the mass reading public and New Journalism. His opposition to democracy manifested itself as an aversion to popular culture, and his faith in an oligarchic form of government was paralleled by his avowal of a high-brow literature written in a style reflecting high breeding and an aristocratic disdain for common tastes. 'Average opinion', he declared, was beneath contempt and 'the sweet phrase "popular culture" was the sorriest contradiction in terms'.[15] The 'Great Democratic Joke' (New Review, February 1895, 161) had emasculated novelists and politicians, producing in their stead writers of penny dreadfuls and democratically elected demagogues. It was the intellectual's responsibility in both art and politics to militate against the mob's degrading influence which reduces everything to its own base level. To immunise himself, the artist must ignore the existence of the 'many-headed monster':

> it is enough for him if he pleases himself and his friends. If once
> he listen to the voice of the great public, or yield to the tinkling

of its shillings, he is a traitor to his art, and henceforth a stranger to literature. (*NO*, 11.4.91, 528)

Society was to be governed in both art and politics by a cultured aristocracy of enlightened élites. For the Commander of the Regatta, he and his boys formed the core of this group. As for the rest, 'the vast majority of adult men are mere grown-up children, physically mature, but intellectually under-developed' (*New Review*, May 1895, 508); women, needless to say, did not count. Social work by either socialists, suffragettes or the School Board was dismissed as pure 'sentimentalism':

> Much has been done by the School Board in the cause of culture; so much that the cultured Domestic Servant – or rather she who but for culture might have been a contented scullion, is now resolved to be nothing but a discontented operative, a tailoress with views and an empty stomach, a 'hand' who recognises no rule but that of hunger and opportunity. That, so far as we can judge, is the net result of the democratic message: to wit, that Jill, like Jack, is a good deal better, and more apt for culture, and more useful than her mistress . . . (*SO*, 4.1.90, 173)

Educating the working classes or improving their living conditions obstructs nature and gives the weakest

> chances of life they never had before, and of which they have made such use that one has but to look upon our populations in street, workshop and factory to see that the puny and low-class Briton is rapidly outnumbering the larger and finer types. (*SO*, 6.12.90, 65)

In spite of his very definite political and literary views, Henley was beyond group allegiance and his bugbears often cut across party lines. For instance, though a Tory in politics and a realist in literature, he was averse to Lord Randolph Churchill and 'Henrietta James'. The former, a cheap demagogue lacking principle, catered to the ignorance and prejudices of the populace. This made him distinctly unmanly. Of James, it was conceded that, though his style was 'never *bourgeois*', 'the vulgar is as far out of his reach as the heroic'. He was not 'skilled to quicken the blood nor to marshal men of spirit and of war' (*NO*, 23.5.91, 11).[16] Though a self-confessed political jingo, Henley was sensitive to developments in continental literature and championed Rodin, Verlaine, Mallarmé and Ibsen. His artistic cosmopolitanism and anti-populism along with his privileging of art over morality would have rendered him a natural ally of the *Yellow Book* aesthetes. However, they were too effeminate for his tastes and he did not scruple to attack Wilde's *The Picture of Dorian Gray* and Richard Le Gallienne's *Quest for the Golden Girl* on moral grounds; the latter being a 'mightily offensive . . . farrago of underclothing, fornication, lickerishness, and "purity"' (*New Review*, March 1897, 441–6).[17] Similarly, while Pater was acknowledged by the Henley circle as the 'high priest of aestheticism' and praised for his artistic principles which set him apart from other writers, he was also described as 'the culmination of literary foppery' and criticised for his 'waywardness, his preciosity, his lack of virility' (*NO*, 2.5.91, 608–9) and for his effeminising influence on the Aesthetes and Decadents.[18]

The political implications of such effeminacy were analysed in 'The Matter With Us'. Sentimentality had emasculated the all-conquering and ever-victorious Anglo-Saxons. Supporting Home Rule for Ireland or the freedom of colonised people were symptoms of 'the craven fear of being great' (*SO*, 4.1.90, 177) that rendered its victims

> incapable of playing any longer the part their fathers played as the representatives of a ruling race . . . They may attempt to disguise their condition by prating of sympathy with the subject races; they may try to deceive themselves and their fellows by impassioned appeals to justice; they may even, as some have done, renounce their fathers and all their works; but the fact remains: they are effete – and they know it. (176)

Manliness lay in 'carrying order and good government to the dark places of the earth.' It also lay in accepting hard facts. Primary among them is that the 'Nigger' – a pejorative even in the 1880s – is a thief, a liar and a compulsive beggar. He is 'human certainly, but of a humanity which is half-way to the baboon'. 'What he wants, like the big child that he is, is firm, kindly control' (*NO*, 10.10.91, 526):

> The black will not become a civilised being according to our standard, even the humblest we can make. On the contrary he will, Nature having so provided, continue to be what he has been for countless centuries in his native Africa. Under compulsion which sets him a task, gives him rules of life, and keeps him to them by nose-bag and whip, he may be made a good servant. No Southerner denies his merits in that character and under those conditions . . . As for allowing the blacks to have any share in the government of the States, the South learnt what that meant in the days after the war. The whites have stopped it by force and by stratagem, by hanging, shooting, whipping, and manipulating the ballot box . . . The application of all this to Ireland and Indian

Native Congresses is – as Mr Kipling might say – another story.
A story which men of sense can tell for themselves. (*NO*, 17.1.91,
214–15)

The 'sentimental demagogues' demanding equality 'between the English
colonist and the man who was but the other day his slave' are asked to study
the history of the black republics:

> The Haytian negro, like his brother of Jamaica or Trinidad, is one
> of the most degraded creatures in existence . . . Scarcely removed,
> as his configuration shows, from the highest type of gorilla, he is
> swayed by animalism and rum. His inherent immorality is such
> that . . . [in] whole neighbourhoods in the Southern States . . .
> there is not a single negro couple, whether legally married or
> not, who are faithful to each other beyond a few weeks. (*SO*,
> 20.7.89, 243)

Over Ireland, the *SO* was aggressively unionist and the overwhelming
majority of its articles and notes dealt with the Irish question. Judging by the
amount of space devoted to Ireland – in most cases more than half the copy –
the journal's nomenclature seems somewhat inappropriate in both parts: it
focused extensively on Irish affairs and scarcely on Scottish, and it was more of
a vehement partisan than a detached observer. Henley was particularly zealous
in the matter of Ireland. Before the paper went to press, he filled whatever
empty spaces remained by penning doggerels and lampoons, the overwhelming majority of which were on Irish politicians and Gladstonians:

> Lofty ladies, Liberal ladies,
> If you must be on the side
> Of the Coffeys and Joe Bradys,
> Show a little proper pride.
> Tis of all sad sights the saddest
> To behold you flocking round
> Where the Pedant and the Faddist
> And the Ass alone are found.
> (*SO*, 16.3.89, 456)[19]

The first six notes on the first page of the *SO*'s inaugural number as well
as many of its leading articles were devoted to Ireland. Its arguments against
Home Rule were dressed in the same pseudo-scientific garb as its Darwin-
ian justification of imperialism. Like other colonised people, the Irishman 'is
fit not to govern, but only to be governed. In the racial evolution of history
it is the Fittest, not the Unfittest, that ultimately survive, however much the

of so many Churchmen and of so many Dissenters that they left him rather than cease to be patriotic according to their lights. Here and there, more particularly in the north of England, some of Sydney Smith's Wild Curates may preach a jumble of Home Rule and the Old Testament; one stumbles occasionally on a Rector or even a Dean who has discovered that it will be safe to give Ireland a Parliament of her own because Mr. Parnell is a Protestant and an Episcopalian, and who is convinced that if Mr. Gladstone ever does return to power he will be sure of the hat of at least a Colonial Bishop; but the Church as a Church, and Nonconformity as Nonconformity, have on both sides of the Tweed declared against the ex-Miraculous One. There is not a single dignitary—nor a single clergyman of any persuasion who in virtue either of eloquence or of character is more influential than any dignitary—but has pronounced against Home Rule, and still more emphatically against its Prophet-in-chief. There may be sullen acquiescence on the part of certain —not all—of the Disestablishment chiefs in that alliance between Liberalism and Home Rule in favour of which Mr. Gladstone has declared; but has Principal Cairns, or Dr. Rainy, or Dr. Hutton, been known to advocate Home Rule or champion a Gladstone candidate at a public meeting? Hence it is that such aid as Mr. Gladstone obtains from either church or chapel is 'horridly tabernacular.' There are Gladstonian pulpiteers who rave about the 'backslidings' and 'short-comings' of Mr. Chamberlain and Lord Hartington, illogical sentimentalists to the solution of the problem of saving 'misery's sons and daughters and the multi-tude that are ready to perish.' He sees the superficial resemblances between Socialism and Christianity, and, like many fanatics in Germany and a few crack-brained egotists in London, would, if he could, make out a theory of Christian Socialism. But, like other weak-kneed politicians of the time, he has come to believe that whatever savours of rebellion against the existing order of things is right: that in fact whatever is is wrong. So he finds himself the apologist of Home Rule as the reconciler of Socialism and Christianity, the preacher of anarchy *minus* the police-constable. This variety of the Gladstonian pulpiteer is more disinterested than the other: but his case as a political lunatic is even more hopeless. Not till Home Rule disappear will he find himself clothed and in his right mind.

A KEENING.

ERIN, me counthry, where, thin, is thy Bard?
   Tanner,—bould Tanner!—got a month with hard,
For shpittin' on a peeler! Och, bad scran to um!
Sure, when he saw they'd brought the ould Black Van
   to um,
The cratur kicked and scratched and sat down solid!
They took um by the coat-tails, so they did,
And dhragged um to that same convaynience squalid,
And while we wailed, the pathriot there they hid!
And yet no pote in po'thry tells the tale
How Tanner—Erin's Tanner!—faced the jail!

Unfittest may desire the contrary' (*SO*, 13.7.89, 203). The Union would effect the genetic improvement Irishmen so desperately needed: 'This is the Irishman's only chance of rising to a higher civilisation in course of time' (*SO*, 16.3.89, 454). The journal supported the Coercion Act – 'it is a pity that Ireland has not had a little more of it, and had it a little sooner' (*SO*, 7.9.89, 426) – but demanded that it employ 'more nosebag':

> If Irishmen would be governed on the system which Mrs Esmond Warrington of Castlewood, Va., thought, very justly, to be adapted to the needs of coach-horses and negroes, we know nobody better fitted for the place of coachman or overseer than Mr Balfour. The excellent lady, it will be remembered, considered that her four- and two-legged cattle required a judicious mixture of whip and nosebag . . . But the Western Irish are no more fit to be let alone than the population of the Ganges valley. They are dependent, weak in will, and pauperised in soul already. (*NO*, 1.8.91 261)

Rejecting palliative Gladstonian legislation, the *Observer* modestly proposed a 'final solution' to the Irish question:

> there can be no doubt that if finality be the thing, the complete extinction of the Irish variety of the *genus* Celt is the surest way of ending the business. Nor are we strangers to the extinction of inferior races [instances the Maories and the American Indians], which in our hands has undoubtedly been a great means of extending the pale of what is called civilisation . . . It is not wonderful if the wearied Saxon have sometimes heaved a sigh over the strange partiality of Nature which dooms the noble savage of other continents but protects that other kind of wild man he grows at home. And as all men know, time was when we tried to settle the Irish question by making up for Nature's deficiency in this respect. The 'Plantations' were nothing more nor less than the extrusion and virtual extinction of the 'mere Irish', and the substitution of men of a different fibre in their place. More: the settlement of the Irish question by this means was, so far as it was actually carried out, perfectly successful, whereof the proof is obvious in the north of Ireland even unto this day. Is it, then, a wise thing to refuse to return to a form of Irish policy of which it can truly be said that it is the only one which has come well out of the test of experience and time? (*SO*, 10.5.90, 691–2)

The arguments against Home Rule – 'the most corrupt political influence ever developed by man' (SO, 14.9.89, 450) – were not new, but perhaps the vehemence with which they were argued put the journal in a class apart from its Tory rivals.[20] The Irishman in the SO was generally an object of ridicule and invective. The 'natural turbulence and instability of the Irish character, indeed, is as sempiternal as the stars' (SO, 20.7.89, 234), the SO observed, and was grateful that 'Irish emigration is sparing our colonies' (SO, 19.10.89, 596). Verse lampoons and prose satires made merry with stereotypical Irish attributes and these invariably had political overtones. The SO had repeatedly attacked the Edinburgh City Council for bestowing the freedom of the city on Parnell. To highlight the folly of granting respectability to Irish politicians, the weekly published a satire entitled 'The Freedom of Edinburgh to Follow'. At a prestigious gathering, the narrator is taken aback when he hears an Irish accent in the background. He wonders whether its owner is a common burglar with an eye on the cutlery. The Irishman is then caught stealing a handkerchief and is recognised by others as a prominent Home Rule MP. He is also recognised by the narrator as being a former waiter at the Dash Dash Club. He is shown to be obsequious, servile and entertaining, yet surly, stubborn, mendacious and foolish when confronted. While claiming to not recognise the narrator as someone whom he has served, the MP addresses the narrator by his name, which he ought not to have known. Even now, though no longer a waiter, he still behaves like one and returns the handkerchief, holding it 'before him in his two hands, just as a waiter walks when he is carrying plates'. 'As we parted I felt for a sixpence in my waistcoat pocket, and Daniel, I think, watched my hand with only affected indifference. Then I remembered that he was in Parliament now, shook his hand warmly instead, and walked home reflecting' (SO, 13.7.89, 208). All the stock Irish attributes are present: childlike, dishonest, simplistic, menial, obsequious, funny, stubborn, mendacious, unintelligent and undignified. In other words, the ideal foil for the English gent and the perfect excuse for the civilising mission.

Though barely restrained in other matters, with regard to Ireland the journal threw decorum to the winds. Irish MPs were 'swashbucklers', 'miserable', 'mean', 'unprincipled', 'beggars', 'dangerous as a plague', 'incendiaries' and 'the party of bargees'. The journal lamented that hemlock 'does not flourish in Ireland' (SO, 29.12.88, 147) for the use of its politicians. Parnell and William O'Brien were singled out for special treatment. The former, a 'Hibernian sturdy beggar who has whines for the strong and violent robbery for the weak' (SO, 20.4.89, 609), was 'confessedly, the deadly foe of Britain'. The weekly averred that 'it cannot, nor must it ever, be forgotten . . . that it has been the work of his life to bring disunion upon the Empire; and that, so far as we know, it is only with being that he will relinquish his design' (*SO*, 9.3.89, 433). On his death, the weekly reminded its readers that he was 'the most deadly and dangerous enemy that Britain had' (*NO*, 10.10.91, 527) and to 'regret the death of Mr Parnell would be an act of treason' (520). When the Special Commission absolved Parnell of involvement in the Phoenix Park murders, the *Observer* published Kipling's attack in italics. '*Cleared*', as it was called, had been rejected by *The Times* as well as by the *Fortnightly Review*, which found it dangerously libellous, and to publish it Henley had to have it literally retrieved from Kipling's bin:

> Hold up those hands of innocence – go, scare your sheep together,
> The blundering, tripping tups that bleat behind the old bell-wether . . .
> My soul! I'd sooner lie in jail for murder plain and straight,
> Pure crime I'd done with my own hand for money, lust, or hate,
> Than take a seat in Parliament by fellow-felons cheered,
> While one of those 'not provens' proved me cleared as you are cleared.

The last line summarised the *Observer*'s perspective on the Parnell Commission findings: 'We are not ruled by murderers, but only – by their friends' (*NO*, 8.3.90, 424).[21]

However, it was O'Brien and the *United Ireland* rather than his chief and the journal's proprietor that were the *Observer*'s stock Irish targets. The attacks on the militant nationalist weekly started in the *SO*'s second issue and carried on uninterrupted in almost every issue thereafter. Its articles and cartoons were described as 'mendacious', 'flapdoodle', 'inflammatory', 'vile', 'disgraceful' and 'dangerous as a plague'. Its journalists were producers of 'filthy calumnies' who encouraged 'bad manners and bad taste' and exemplified 'what the "Liberty of the press" means according to Hibernian ideas'. Entire articles were devoted to quoting extracts from the *United Ireland*, 'the organ of what may be described as Undistrouserment', a reference to O'Brien's refusal to wear prison attire and the fracas that ensued.[22] Not surprisingly, O'Brien's prison antics were fodder for Henley's political doggerels, as the following representative example indicates:

> 'Study for an Historical Picture'
> He stood, his linen fluttering in the wind,
> Scorning the Saxon with a constant mind;
>
> And in the prospect of his many boons
> He half-forgot his ravished pantaloons.
> (*SO*, 9.2.89, 318–19)

His speeches were reported as objects of mirth and ridicule, 'far above comic singing':

The O'Brien of our days is much too shrewd to aim at dignity
or manliness. In Mr W. O'Brien a new figure, the comic patriot,
has made his *début* on the political stage. Irish patriots have been
ridiculous enough before; but Mr W. O'Brien is the first of them
who has sought and found a leadership by deliberately rendering
himself a laughing-stock unto men ...The only people who need
regret the advent of the new (or farcical) patriot are the keepers
of music halls . . .

Lest the comedy of his speech escape notice, it was followed by the following 'Paraphrase':

> Go on, Ingenious Torturer, go on!
> Govan has spoken, and your day is gone.
>
> Shave, limp and lily-fingered Ruffian, shave
> Me martyred counthry even to the grave.
>
> Know, though ye clip her whiskers night and day,
> Ye cannot take the roots of um away.
>
> And so, ye Thief, howe'er ye rack and screw,
> Her Emerald Freedom still she will renew.
>
> Thrimble then, Tyrant, thrimble and despair!
> There is no killing liberty or hair.
> (*SO*, 2.2.89, 289–90, 292)[23]

The journal's preoccupation with Ireland is truly remarkable. The subject
was interpolated into an article at the slightest opportunity. That Ireland did
not figure in the Queen's speech 'means that Ireland has had no history, and
that it has been governed' (29.12.88, 145). Similarly a decrease in the naval
budget would 'afford the Nationalists of Ireland every facility for making that
country a hornet's nest of hostile cruisers on the outbreak of the next great
war in which they are engaged' (*SO*, 19.1.89, 229). Even while discussing
Swinburne's claims to the Laureateship it was felt necessary to 'recall the fact
that the poet of *Songs before Sunrise* happens to be a strong Unionist' (*SO*,
9.3.89, 429). To such an extent was this carried out that even some letters to
the editor on non-Irish topics alluded to Ireland in a derogatory way. When
William Archer wrote remonstrating about a misunderstanding of his views
on Ibsen, he followed the anti-Irish tone of the journal:

> If you go on at this rate, we shall have you proving, one fine day,
> that Home Rule is the only possible solution of the Irish diffi-
> culty, and scoffing at Mr Gladstone for his stiff-necked Unionism
> . . . Had you been an Irish instead of Scots *Observer* I could have

take out the mummies of their ancestors, to elect half of a Committee. The Road Trustees, with propriety, disappear, and there is wisdom in leaving licensing at present in the hands of the Justices, and thereby saving the Bills from the fatal attentions of the various Temperance sects. But it is distinctly unfortunate that advantage has not been taken of the reconstruction of the Parochial Board to invest it also with the charge of Education. This would do not a little to raise the status of the Parochial Board, and give it a better class of members than it is likely to possess even after its reconstitution, without at the same time casting on it more work than it could successfully deal with. The expense of a register would also be saved. As things now stand, there will have to be three registers —not merely two, with all deference to Mr. Haldane : the Parliamentary, without women and with the service franchise ; the county, with women and with or without the service franchise, according as its holders pay or do not pay county rates; and the School Board, with women and without the service franchise. So that here, as in other matters, the proposed changes will by no means operate in the direction of economy. It is indeed well that there are to be no aldermen—or even bailies —on the Council, but one fails to see what reasonable objection, even in this democratic age, could be stated against the Sheriff of the County being *ex officio* member of the Council. His business training and legal knowledge would be of great service : while his presence on it would enable the control of the Police to be handed over to the Council, and so permit of the unfortunate Commissioners of Supply being put out of pain.

But noting and regretting this failure of the Bills to do enough, there is another point of view from which in fairness one should also regard them, and that is the standpoint of the Government. Ministers, being sensible men, wished to introduce measures likely to pass, and they have done so. And they have done more. They have introduced measures which will form a substantial and satisfactory basis for future legislation. When the new machinery has got fairly started, more work can be given it to do. In short, though too little in the way of unification is attempted at present, lines are laid down on which unification will surely and safely proceed. The whole licensing question, for example, will probably have to be dealt with very soon. Educational legislation also is admittedly required. And so it may not be long before the omissions in the present Bills are more than supplied.

THEN AND NOW.

Extract from Sir C. Russell's speech before Special Commission.— 'The Times,' *April 4th, 1889.*

'My Lord, I should like to add to this account that of one other person. I take this account, and call this witness from the columns of *The Times.* It is the testimony of a man now lost to the country; a man held in the highest

Extract from leading article in 'United Ireland' *(edited by Mr. W. O'Brien), Feb. 9th, 1884.*

'SPEED THE MAHDI.'

'All hail again to this most excellent Moslem. The more we hear of him the better we like him.

 * * * *

We trust that our next news may be that Gordon, who is advancing

esteem and admiration for his generous impulses of humanity—I mean the late General Gordon.'

loaded with specie from Khartoum, has met the same fate as Baker.'

Extract from leading article in 'United Ireland,' *Jan. 26th, 1884.*

'This Mahdi is doing excellent service. The whole horde of Egypto-British task-masters and usurers are being hunted out of the Soudan ; and, if happily Khartoum and the other strong places fall into the Prophet's hands, Cairo will be seriously threatened, and the grip of the British on Moslem races all over the world will be in danger. We, therefore, wish this excellent Mahdi every success. . . . Go on, sweet Mahdi, and put every infidel Giaour in Khartoum to the edge of the sword. Hast read of Drogheda, most puissant Mussulman ? '

Extract from 'Daily News' *summary of the Report of the Proceedings before the Special Commission, April 4th, 1889.*

'And he' [Sir Charles Russell] read out Gordon's description of Kerry, as contained in that great man's letter, published in *The Times.* All this is old, it may be said. It is old, and it is unredressed—scenes of wretchedness such as those over the recital of which Sir Charles Russell could hardly restrain his emotion, are still occurring in Ireland at this very hour.'

Extract from article entitled 'Week's Work,' *in* 'United Ireland' *of September 13th, 1884.*

'England's Lord Wolseley and his army are gathering for a march to the rescue of Gordon in Khartoum, through a thousand miles or so of burning desert, and now that they are ready to start, there comes the ugly intelligence that Gordon and Khartoum have fallen long ago into the lap of the Mahdi. The intelligence, we regret to say, awaits confirmation.'

Extract from Leading Article in 'United Ireland,' *February 14th, 1885.*

'A TERRIBLE CALAMITY.'

'All Ireland is in mourning, public manifestations of sorrow are universal, and gloom sits on every face, and crape on every arm ; for Khartoum has fallen, and General Gordon has been slain. We cannot express the poignant emotion which the receipt of the news of the English disaster caused in this country. Never since the fall of Limerick has so terrible a misfortune befallen Ireland. Immediately on hearing the sad intelligence we caused a special messenger to be despatched to Dublin Castle to offer Lord Spencer our sincere condolences ; and His Excellency was graciously pleased to remark that he fully understood the sincerity of our sorrow. . . . If recruits are needed, thousands of loyal Irish youth will at once fly to the standard of St. George; and if further reinforcements be still required, there are hundreds of thousands of our race in America who only pant for the moment when they can employ themselves in assisting the oppressor who expelled them from their homes. Courage, then, England dear! "Smash the Mahdi," by all means. Ireland, as well as India, is interested in the operation ; and if further woes should betide your arms, you can then turn for consolation and succour to the nations you have robbed and scourged and strangled and bayonetted. God save the Queen ! '

> understood your course of action, which is not unlike the con-
> duct of Sir Lucifer O'Tiger towards Captain Absolute in *The
> Rivals*, Act IV, Scene 3. (*SO*, 13.7.89, 213)

The editorial response in a similar vein used Hibernicism as a synonym for chicanery or deceit.

With such treatment being handed out to Irish MPs, the nationalist press and everything to do with Ireland, it is only to be expected that most Irish writers reviewed in the journal were slated principally because they were Irish:

> Mrs Houston's *Bunch of Shamrocks* is a shilling doleful, of which
> the scene is laid mainly in Ireland, and of which the depressing
> effect is in no way mitigated by the final jangle of wedding bells.
> The chief characters, by their merciless twaddling, would arouse
> a desire for their destruction in the breast of the meekest reader.
> (*SO*, 29.12.88, 165)

> She achieved (or had thrust upon her) a wide reputation for prac-
> tical philanthropy and impracticable Nationalism. She was
> belauded by Home Rule leaders (in the redundant and pictur-
> esque language we all know), and idolised by a 'bhould pisantry'
> ... She was brought up in the Anglican Church, but she was con-
> verted (or 'perverted') to Roman Catholicism in 1858, like many
> more Anglicans about that time. (Review of Sister M. Francis
> Clare Cusack's *The Nun of Kenmare: An Autobiography*) (*SO*,
> 16.2.89, 362)[24]

In Henley's journal, Irish writers were generally attacked regardless of whether their works were nationalist or apolitical. If, on the other hand, the book or the author supported the Union, they were usually well received. Standish O'Grady was praised for being 'Homer-like in the bardic accuracy' with which in *Red Hugh's Captivity* he describes 'an epoch of Irish history, which is marked by the establishment of the Tudor ascendancy in the island, and the subjugation to the Queen of the petty dynasts and feudal magnates whose internecine conflicts had deluged the country in blood for centuries' (*SO*, 13.4.89, 587). Similarly, *The Two Chiefs of Dunboy* by J. A. Froude – the historian of 'Protestant heroism and Catholic villainy' (*Ireland*, 103) – was praised for its 'views on Irish History, Irish patriots and patriotism, and the proper way of dealing with them' (*SO*, 18.5.89, 725).

Given Henley's belief in the chest-thumping variety of manliness and what W. S. Blunt called 'the deification of brute courage and strength',[25] it is not surprising that his journal was utterly contemptuous of folklore and the supernatural. Studies of folklore were merely 'scientific defences of Mumbo Jumbo' (SO, 5.10.89, 543), superstition, especially in the case of Irish peasants, was ridiculed, and the Folklore Congress, for which Yeats had been nominated as Ireland's representative by the *United Ireland*, was attacked in an article entitled 'Fairies in Congress' (NO, 10.10.91, 524). 'Mystical, magical books . . . no man can read with intelligence' (SO, 13.4.89, 584), a belief in ghosts was childish, and supernatural visions and communions were dismissed as delusions.[26] Celtic fairy tales, in which Yeats had begun to specialise, were found to be common, mundane and over-rated. Celticism itself was found to be a fraudulent marketing strategy. 'Celtic' was a 'vague adjective introduced of late into the language of criticism to which no meaning may attach save a suggestion of undiscriminating praise or blame' (NO, 7.2.91, 298). The 'Celtomaniac's' refusal to allocate a precise meaning to the word was yet another indication of his 'revolt against the despotism of fact'. More irritatingly still, he selects 'such samples of art, literature, and politics as satisfy his ideal, and he labels them Celtic'. The weekly refused to 'take this jargon seriously'. 'Not being Celts and professing no admiration for the Dockers, New Tipperary, or General Booth, we find in it nothing but a flow of words.' It denounced the Celtic crusade which Yeats was then leading in the English and Irish periodicals, and remarked of Joseph Jacob's *Celtic Fairy Tales*:

> But so much have we heard of late of the Celtic spirit, of that imaginative temperament which lurks beneath the name of Jones, that the folk-lore of the Celts might be expected to possess a unique charm of its own. The present volume confirms the opinion we have ever maintained that the Celtic genius is a pleasant invention. There is scarce a story in the book which might not have been – and indeed has not been – written by a vile Teuton. The humour – which consists in an inability to reason, and whose best expression is the Irish bull – is characteristic, but it does not amount to much. Mr Grant Allen, and those with him have always pursued the deductive method. They have created a something – vague as electricity – which they term the Celtic spirit, and they proceed to label Celtic all men and all things which please their wayward fancy. And so they set the most fraudulent artificer of wall-paperings high above the supreme masters of the Teutonic race. Alas for Rembrandt and Shakespeare! If the Celtomaniacs would but discover the quality of the Celtic mind from examples of its offspring, first determining what in the world they mean by Celtic, they might avoid many errors and much ridicule. (NO, 2.2.92, 173)

THE SCOTS OBSERVER

A Record and Review

| Vol. II. | SEPTEMBER 28, 1889 | No. 45 |

NOTES

SPEAKING at Stockton-on-Tees, Lord Londonderry said excellent things of the Irish policy of the Government. During his tenure of the dignified office from which he has been obliged to retire his lips have been sealed, with the result, of course, that rumours of the most absurd kinds have been set agoing by Home Rule journalists and gutter politicians. When, for instance, the announcement of his resignation was made, it was at once asserted that Lord Londonderry had seen the futility of maintaining the law, and would soon be a follower of Mr. O'Brien. Last week's speech, if it does nothing else, will effectually prove that these, like so many other Irish 'statements of fact,' were, to use John Bright's word, 'lies.' But Lord Londonderry's words do more than this: they prove that he has come back from his three years of Dublin impressed more thoroughly than ever with the paramount necessity of continuing to govern Ireland with a strong hand. He holds that 'the real solution of the Irish difficulty will be found in the steady pursuance of a policy which would achieve the result of eradicating sedition and crime and leaving Ireland a law-fearing and consequently a law-abiding country.' Lord Londonderry further in the course of his speech defended the resident magistrates from some of the saner attacks which have been made on a 'fearless and impartial' body.

SPEAKING at Belfast, Lord Dufferin observed that while 'to do credit to Ireland and to prove himself not unworthy of the native strain from which I am descended' had been 'the constant object' of his ambition, in India he had been subject to 'a more special anxiety': namely, 'not to emulate, for that would be impossible,' but at least to follow in the footsteps of those illustrious Ulstermen to whom India owes so much,' and to whom, in the terrible times of the Mutiny, England herself was so 'greatly indebted.' He quoted the Lawrences, the Nicholsons, the Gillespies, the Montgomerys, 'and many another North of Ireland hero'; he noted the fact that 'both Ireland as a whole and Ulster as a province have imported a vast amount of ability, industry, and valour' into the Indian services; he went on to tell over the roll of distinguished Indo-Irishmen; he reminded his hearers that Lord Connemara rules in Madras, while Sir Frederick Roberts comes from Waterford, Sir George White from Antrim, and Sir David Barbour from Belfast; and he declared it to be his conviction that 'the British Empire could never get on without Irishmen.' Lord Dufferin is loyalty itself, and his claims for his country were such as every reasonable Briton would hasten to substantiate and to applaud. But his words, in spite of the fact that a special significance attaches to them, were translated into an argument for Separation, and he himself was solemnly saluted as the first Home Rule Viceroy. It is plain that Mr. Gladstone's heirs and successors to the kingdom of misrepresentation are more promising than those of Alexander of Macedon.

THE seditious priest is growing as plentiful in Ireland as the treasonable attorney or the rebellious pig-jobber. Father M'Fadden at Falcarragh and Father O'Dwyer at Fermoy have been sequestered from the opportunity of excelling in the way they most affect; and of late it has been found necessary to remove the Rev. T. Moran and the Rev. Patrick Byrne from the chaplaincy of Clonmel Gaol for supplying certain prisoners (Dr. Tanner among them) with sandwiches and tobacco. The dismissal of the Derry chaplain is already ancient history; but it is interesting to remark that his Vicar-Capitular has refused to appoint another in his room, that the clergy of his deanery have passed a resolution applauding his refusal to submit to examination 'in reference to the conveyance of letters for Mr. Conybeare for publication in the press,' and that Mr. Conybeare himself (whose sentence expires on the fourth of October, but who will probably be returned to the Camborne Radicals and the brass band attached thereto some few days sooner) has expressed his conviction (by letter) that the charges against Father Doherty are 'unfounded and unproved,' and that 'the brutality of Balfour is only equalled by his stupidity.' Of course it matters little or nothing what the member for Camborne utters or keeps to himself; but the resurgence at this moment of the Fighting Clergyman bodes ill for immediate peacefulness. On the other hand, it is by some regarded as a sign that the Parnellites have played out their hand to this particular card, and from that point of view the circumstance is cheering enough.

WITH these exceptions there has been little doing in the Separatist parts of Ireland. Mr. Stansfeld and Lady Sandhurst have received the freedom of the City of Dublin; but, nobody taking it upon him to object, or indeed to visit the circumstance with any sort of notice, they have returned to London, with Mr. Carvell Williams and the rest, as wise no doubt as when they crossed from Holyhead, but not, it may be suspected, any wiser. Then Mr. Healy has pointed out that he knew from the first that the Irish Secretary was playing them false, and said so; but as at this time nobody is given to minding Mr. Healy—at least to the extent of being interested in anything he may or may not know, still less in anything he may or may not say—his remarks have fallen as it were *in vacuo*, and may be repeated with an effect of novelty as soon as he thinks proper. Lastly, it may be noted that Mr. Redmond has been sentenced to three months' imprisonment for performances in the intimidation line, and that his parting words to Mr. Balfour were that he and his might 'go to the devil and shake themselves.' Meanwhile an appeal has been lodged, and the hero, like so many of his kind, is still at large.

T

The very use of 'Celtic' by Irish writers was enough to provoke the periodical's spleen and such was its antipathy on this issue that it even refused to consider the Irish as racial kinsmen: 'It is customary to speak of the Irish as Celtic: the majority of them is rather of some prehistoric race – Basque or Finnish – which is much further removed from Celtic than Celtic is from Saxon or Norman' (*SO*, 26.10.89, 623).

While attacking the whole Celtic movement of the 1890s, the journal undercut the very foundation on which the movement rested: history and mythology. Ireland was found to have no history and hence no claim to nationhood. The former deficiency was not due to any lack of historians,

> but, simply, that Irish history there is none. Records of the squabbles of Geraldines and Desmonds do not make the history of Ireland any more than a chronicle of raids of the Clan Chattan would be a history of Scotland . . . the inhabitants of Ireland were a 'race of cattle rearers and dealers; their kings and dynasts were merely glorified graziers, who had more stock than their clansmen' . . . and from that date [the incident of Brian Boroimhe] to this the chronicles of 'Ireland, a nation' have not been even chronicles of small beer. (*SO*, 28.12.89, 149)

The only substitute they have are 'the anecdotes of the landowners and peasants' – 'a domestic diary' – and it is this that makes 'the Separatist contention dishonest or absurd'. Voters were urged to remember that 'Ireland has no more history – has no more right to call herself a nation – than Little Pedlington.' On another occasion, the *SO* recommended W. G. Wood-Martin's *History of Sligo County and Town* to anyone who 'wishes to get some definite idea of the inexpressibly dreary history of Ireland'. It was 'deadly dull reading' because 'Irish history is barren of events':

> One long raging quarrel fills it from first to last, except when at intervals the English were sweeping over the land with fire and sword. And as the general history, so the local. (19.4.90, 611)

III

In May 1890, Katharine Tynan sent Henley a nationalist poem, probably 'The Wild Geese'. Considering that she had already published two poems in the *SO* – the first on a beloved and absent 'Blackbird' and the other on the death of a lover (1.6.89, 46, and 7.12.89, 99) – her present contribution reflected an acute naïveté about the politics of periodical publication. She was gently chastised by Yeats: 'You should not have sent the poem to the Scots Observer it was too political – Irish exiles are out of their range I think' (*CL1*, 217). The penny finally dropped and her next contribution showed that she clearly understood what was expected of her. Entitled 'Soothsaying', it carried the epigraph, '*If your petticoat comes down your sweetheart's thinking on you.*' It began:

> As I came down the stair,
> Blithely, without ever a care,
> Singing 'Lasses, love me',
> Fell my petticoat so gay,
> Round about my feet it lay:
> Some one's thinking of me.
>   (*SO*, 16.8.90, 331)

Clearly, Tynan was quite happy to play the Irish Biddy to Henley's manly unionist reader. But what about Yeats? Was he willing to play Paudeen? Henley's virulent racism would have surely bothered him. If so, why did he linger on? How did he survive in this atmosphere which was hardly conducive to an Irish nationalist? Further, if 'Irish exiles' were 'out of their range', what was Yeats doing there? Was he not himself an Irish exile? Or had he quite consciously modified his work so that it did not fit that category? He was not above this. Six months earlier he had announced to Tynan that his planned history of Irish literature was going to 'be *systimatically* political or national' (*CL1*, 201; emphasis added). To suit his purposes, he could just as 'systimatically' be apolitical or anational. But what had he to gain from being so? Why did Yeats court Henley?

In the late 1880s, when William Morris was Yeats's 'chief of men', he was also the butt of many of Henley's attacks and lampoons. During that same period, Yeats claimed to be in all things pre-Raphaelite. The Pre-Raphaelites too, according to Yeats's own testimony, were among Henley's many strident aversions. Similarly, neither Pater nor Blake nor Villiers de L'Isle-Adam commanded much respect from Henley. (The latter's play was contemptuously dismissed in a review entitled 'A Crank Axel'.)[27] Henley was allergic to the word 'Celtic', scorned Irish folklore, mysticism and magic, and opposed Irish literary nationalism. And manly realism was not quite Yeats's style. Neither, for that matter, were zealous jingoism, imperialism and unionism. In 1888 he had begun writing for the *United Ireland* and was already identifying himself with the nationalist faction in Irish politics; his poetics, too, as articulated in his Ferguson essays, were staunchly nationalistic. On the other hand, Henley's political and literary prejudices were an open secret in the mid-1880s. An advertisement of the *SO*, which mentions Yeats as among its contributors, announces that, 'Politically, it supports the Constitutional Principles essential to the maintenance of Imperial unity' (15.6.89, 3).[28] Though Yeats began attending Henley's soirées some time between March and August of 1888, it was not until the following March that he was published by Henley. He thought Henley's poetry 'cobwebby' and disliked most of it; 'his prose [was] violent and laboured' (*Mem*, 38); he 'disagreed with him about everything' (*Auto*, 124) and 'scarcely shared an opinion of his' (*Mem*, 38). Furthermore, in his letters Yeats gives the impression that he did not enjoy the regatta gatherings where the discussion was often boring – the thickness of steaks in different parts of the world – and sometimes shocking, probably Henley's discovery of another 'delectable vocable' supplementing his 'first list of 300 equivalents' for the female genitalia. On one occasion Yeats found the conversation so distasteful that he resolved to walk out and never return. However, he reconsidered his position and did nothing.[29] Why then did Yeats court Henley?

Quite apart from Yeats's attendance at the regatta, it is quite clear that Yeats was trying to ingratiate himself with Henley. While writing to him in 1891 about the *NO*'s reviewing Jack Yeats's paintings and his own *John Sherman and Dhoya*, Yeats concluded his letter by complimenting Henley on a recent poem. He passed on AE's praise of that poem and then seconded it. However, the actual composition of the letter is revealing and I reproduce John Kelly's typescript of the last paragraph. Passages within square brackets are those Yeats wrote and then cancelled:

> My visionary by the by showed me your 'God in the garden' poem & called [it your very best poem] it one of your best things. He is a reader of your verse & in all ways one of the few true students of poetry I know. [I did not quite think your God in the garden your best] I think with him about your 'God in a garden.' Its verse has a fine ringing sound. Yours very sincery. . . (*CL2*, 633)

In a letter to John Quinn, Yeats said that the need 'to escape this family drifting, innocent, & helpless' (*CL1*, 520) drew him to dominating men like Henley. Certainly, Henley and J. B. Yeats were antithetical characters and in this oedipal conflict Yeats found in Henley a surrogate father-figure who had in abundance the will, energy and resolution that his father lacked. Furthermore, Henley, a typical anti-Victorian Victorian, 'was quite plainly not upon the side of our parents' (*Auto*, 127). His commanding presence, individuality, 'complete confidence and self-possession' (*Auto*, 124) were extremely attractive qualities. Besides, Yeats also found some of Henley's political ideas appealing, such as his 'aristocratic attitudes, his hatred of the crowd' (*Mem*, 39), and particularly those pertaining to a 'tyranny' of a cultural élite like that 'of Cosimo de' Medici' (*Auto*, 126).

Yeats's achievements since returning to London in January 1888 had been quite ordinary. Though he had not given in wholesale to the demands of popular taste and his compromises had been limited, they had enabled him to carry on with writing and had subsidised his more serious work, which could now find an outlet through Henley's journal. Henley offered a resolution to the dilemma between producing saleable work and establishing a foothold among the literary élite. Writing for Henley's magazines alongside the low-brow periodicals, Yeats could hedge his chances of success with those of survival. While money from the *Observer* was very welcome and came at a higher rate than that from Irish editors – Henley paid a guinea for a poem as well as for a column of prose as opposed to a pound paid by most other editors[30] – Yeats's association with Henley also brought other benefits which, though not immediately quantifiable, would in the long run yield financial dividends.

In the literary London of the late 1880s and the 1890s, Henley was among the more powerful 'symbolic bankers' and the only one to whom Yeats had access in 1888. As editor of *London* and the *Magazine of Art*, he had garnered a considerable store of cultural capital, prestige and authority. Having already championed Whistler, Rodin, R. L. Stevenson and other successful artists, his imprimatur was not only a widely accepted certificate of merit, but, if his proven perspicacity was any indication, then it was also an augury of success. To sponsor his candidature in the world of high art, to underwrite his career and to endorse his talent, Yeats needed one such banker to invest in his cause. In his personal writings, Yeats repeatedly expresses his admiration and respect for Henley's judgement and his deep desire to secure Henley's approbation:

> we listened to him, and often obeyed him . . . (*Auto*, 124)

> he made us feel always our importance, and no man among us could do good work, or show the promise of it, and lack his praise . . . Henley got the best out of us all, because he had made us accept him as our judge and we knew that his judgement could neither sleep, nor be softened, nor changed, nor turned aside. (128)

> I was ready, as were all those others, to test myself and all I did by the man's sincere vision . . . when I heard that he had said to somebody, 'I do not know if Yeats is going up or going down', I doubted myself. His hold was perhaps that he was never deceived about his taste, that he wished one well and could not flatter. (*Mem*, 38)

He re-wrote my poems as he re-wrote the early verse of Kipling,
and though I do not think I ever permanently accepted his actual
words I always knew that he had found a fault. (*Mem*, 38)

Yeats well knew that Henley's affiliation and imprimatur would improve
his literary prospects as it had those of other writers who had drawn their first
cheques on Henley's bank. As a young clerk in the Bank of England, Kenneth Grahame had proposed to Matthews and Lane that they publish 'a quite
small selection of articles that I have had in the *National Observer* and *St James's
Gazette*'. He reinforced the viability of his proposal by adding that it had the
support of his mentor, W. E. Henley, according to whom 'a "blend" of these
short articles with verse would perhaps make a "feature" that might take'.
When Grahame was reviewed by the *Critic* – described by the *Academy* as 'the
first literary journal in America' – the periodical claimed never to have heard
of him before, but added, 'the fact that he is one of Henley's assistants on *The
National Observer* prepossesses one in his favour'.[31] Much later, when Grahame
was an established name, an *Academy* profile remarked on Henley's part in his
success:

> It may be that when the history of the *Scots* and *National Observer*
> is written – and it would make, with selections, a most agreeable
> and invigorating book – we shall be told to what extent Mr Hen-
> ley supplied not only a haven for young writers, but also an
> impulse and momentum. We shall then know whether Mr Gra-
> hame wrote his stirring essay on Orion – the Hunter – from
> within or without, whether it was his own idea to continue the
> diverting narrative of the childhood of Harold and Edward, Char-
> lotte and Selina. As the cause of wit in others Mr Henley holds a
> very high position. (no. 1135 [n/s], 4 Dec 1897, 493)

Yeats was aware that with Henley's endorsement his other work would
become more marketable. He used Henley's favourable review of *Oisin* in
publicising the book with Irish periodicals in 1889 and, three years later,
mentioned it to T. Fisher Unwin while trying to flog off the remaining
copies.[32] Later, while trying to publish, and then promote, the *Celtic Twilight*
and the *Secret Rose* – a collection of 45 poems and essays, of which 17 were
first published in the *Observer* – Yeats made it a point to mention the Henley
connection to Ernest Rhys and Charles Elkin Mathews: '"The Secret Rose"
... will be a tolerably portly volume of Irish stories many of them reprinted
from the National Observer & certainly my best prose book' (*CL1*, 467).[33]
Similarly, while seeking a meeting with Mallarmé in 1894 Yeats mentioned
in his letter that 'Mr Henley is a friend of mine & that I [like yourself] am a
contributor to the National Observer' (*CL1*, 381). Besides marketing his

work and networking with literary élites, Yeats also used Henley's certification to enhance his own reputation among his peers.[34]

Henley's group offered, as McDonald points out, 'distinction, in the double sense of prestige and difference'. McDonald and Willey have drawn on Bourdieu's theories of 'co-optation' – a ratification of one's self-image through the perception of one's peers – to explain Henley's appeal for Conrad. This is equally applicable to Yeats. Bourdieu convincingly argues that writers, like scientists and other specialists, write 'not only for a public, but for a public of equals who are also competitors'.

> Few people depend as much as artists and intellectuals do for their self-image upon the image others, and particularly other writers and artists, have of them. 'There are', writes Jean-Paul Sartre, 'qualities that we acquire only through the judgements of others.' This is especially so for the quality of a writer, artist or scientist, which is so difficult to define because it exists only in, and through, co-optation, understood as the circular relations of reciprocal recognition among peers. (Bourdieu, 1993, 116)[35]

Membership of Henley's regatta, through which he first met R. A. M. Stevenson, Oscar Wilde, Kenneth Grahame and George Wyndham, gave Yeats admittance to an élite and distinguished company of artists which bolstered his own sense of artistic identity and pride. He enjoyed the privilege of being part of a prominent and outspoken literary élite whose onslaughts 'had created such a terror among innocent sentimental writers and all flatterers of public tastes' (*Mem*, 39).

Despite the fact that many of Yeats's strongest affinities were Henley's aversions, and vice versa, Yeats had much to gain from Henley. But what had Henley to gain from Yeats? Aesthetically and politically they were more antagonists than allies. Yeats's heroes – Pater, Morris, Blake and the Pre-Raphaelites – were Henley's aversions, and Yeats's associates – Arthur Symons, Oscar Wilde, Richard Le Gallienne and William Sharp – were Henley's pet hates. Henley was dismissive of folklore, magic, mysticism and fairy tales and Yeats was clearly not a manly realist of the chest-thumping, tell-it-as-it-is variety. Yeats's political beliefs were anathema to Henley and vice versa. Henley savagely attacked William O'Brien, Parnell and the *United Ireland* while Yeats glorified the Fenian tradition, lauded Irish martyrs and patriots, attacked unionists and curried favour with O'Brien's *United Ireland*. Why then did Henley publish Yeats? There is no clear answer. While some of Yeats's articles, especially one enumerating the differences between Scottish and Irish fairies, may suggest that Henley published Yeats as a kind of private joke among his regatta, there is enough evidence to dismiss such a possibility. To begin with, Yeats is mentioned in the *SO* advertisements as a signing contributor, which would be taking the joke too far. On the other hand, if Henley did respect Yeats's literary talent, it seems strange that there is no mention of Yeats in any of Henley's extant letters, and there are some two-and-a-half thousand of them.[36] Kipling, on the other hand, is conspicuously present in many of them, and of Henley's many finds it was Kipling of whom he was most proud.[37] A writer's political beliefs, especially if he was going to be a regular contributor, were of supreme importance to Henley. While interviewing William Archer for the *Magazine of Art*, he bluntly asked him about his politics and whether, 'In one word, are you a Conservative?'[38] Yeats was a regular contributor to the *Observer* as well as to the *New Review*, and Henley, given that he closely followed the goings-on in the *United Ireland*, must have been aware of Yeats's nationalist activities.

Yeats frequented Henley's gatherings (how was he invited?) as a junior member of a regatta of which Henley was the commodore, and it is possible that Henley took the younger writer under his wing simply because Yeats admired and respected him and because he was the object of Yeats's ingratiating attentions. Furthermore, Henley was quite capable of recognising talent even if it did not conform to his own tastes, as we have seen in the case of Henry James (see p. 137). W. E. Gladstone – whom Henley had nicknamed 'Pantaloon' and regularly attacked – and W. S. Blunt – a champion of colonised people all over the world – are other instances of writers whose politics were antagonistic to Henley but who were published in his periodicals because of their renown. Both, however, were compelled to conform to Henley's editorial line: Gladstone wrote on aesthetics and Blunt on Arabian equine bloodlines.[39]

Another reason why Henley may have published Yeats is suggested by Yeats's 'Scots and Irish Fairies', his very first contribution to the *SO*, and by Henley's review of *The Wanderings of Oisin and Other Poems* in the following issue.[40] Though Yeats did not quite play Paudeen, he certainly donned the garb of the stereotypical Celt revolting against the despotism of fact. His first contribution contrasted Scottish and Irish peasants' attitudes towards fairies and their effects on these ethereal creatures:

> The two different ways of looking at things uncanny have influenced in each country the whole world of sprites and goblins. For their gay and graceful doings you must go to Ireland; for their deeds of terror to Scotland. (*SO*, 2.3.89, 411)

The article concluded with an expression of mock hostility and a childish accusation directed at the *SO* readers:

> You – you will make no terms with the spirits of fire and earth and air and water. You have made the Darkness your enemy. We – we exchange civilities with the world beyond.

Evidently, Henley was quite prepared to brook Irish hostility so long as it was restricted to 'sprites and goblins'. And perhaps he was equally prepared to publish Yeats so long as he portrayed the Irishman's supposed impracticality and his dreamy, fanciful, childlike nature. These characteristics were perfect foils to the Saxon's hard grasp on fact and a justification for the genetic and other improvements English rule would gradually effect in Ireland. They reiterated, in milder language and with only the slightest of blurring around the edges, Henley's contrast between the manly Saxon conqueror and the childlike Irish native. Moreover, by bypassing the freedom struggle in Ireland, such writing could convey the impression that the nationalists were not typical of the country as a whole and were merely a fanatical fringe. Declan Kiberd's observation about Yeats's peasants who 'do not grow up not because they do not want to but because their adult creator . . . prefers to keep them and his readers ignorant of a world based on . . . social injustice' is particularly apposite in the context of Yeats's contributions to the *Observer*. This, Kiberd points out, 'has the unintended effect of infantalizing the native culture':

> Within British writing, there had long been a link between children's fiction and the colonial enterprise, which led to an identification of the new world with the infantile state of man . . . All through the nineteenth century, the Irish had been treated in the English media as childlike – 'broths of boys' veering between smiles and tears, quick to anger and quick to forget – unlike the stable Anglo-Saxon. In the words of historian Perry Curtis: 'Irishmen thus shared with virtually all the non-white peoples of the empire the label childish, and the remedy for unruly children in most Victorian households was a proper licking.'[41]

Henley's review of *Oisin* reinforces this impression of the Irish as infantile and effeminate. His critical overview is typically Arnoldian and he focuses almost exclusively on the poem's barbarous, exotic and feminine aspects: its 'wildness', fluidity, liquid imagery, wantonness, escapism, mystery and fantasy.[42] He praises *Oisin* for its faraway atmosphere:

> . . . you are carried away into rainbow-coloured lands of fantasy, there is a blowing of magic horns, a lovely enchantress is speaking in silken phrases, the swords of heroes are ringing in onsets, and the work-a-day world is for a time forgot. (*SO*, 9.3.89, 446)

Yeats is praised for his 'handling of various lyric measures' and his 'flowing and daintily turned couplets'. His verses have 'the wilding charm, the wayward grace touched with elfishness, characteristic of true Irish song'. They 'echo the rustling of leaves and the lapse of streams . . . that catch and convey the beauty and mystery of the flying clouds, and the shimmering plain of ocean, and the dewy forest aisles, with their shifting arabesques of shade and sunlight' (446–7). The lines in his poem seem 'to flow at their own sweet will, wanton as the robe of Nora' (446) and 'the style admirably befits a tale of faery, the dreamy, haunting cadences enhancing the impression of glamour and weirdness like a tune blown on the horns of elf-land' (447).

According to Henley, along with its 'wild and graceful fancy', *Oisin* also has 'lines in which the tones of war and hunting and heroic comradeship ring out bravely'. Though he states that Yeats 'can stir the blood as well as beguile and lull with sensuous dreams', he stresses the latter rather than the former. Given Henley's usual preference for manliness and martial imagery, it seems odd that he should underplay the poem's martial aspect and highlight its feminine and escapist tendencies. It seems odd until one makes the connection between his poetics and politics. Just as the imperialist is authoritarian, strong-willed, realistic and manly, so is the native effeminate, sentimental, impractical and fanciful, and must be judged by the appropriate standards. The aesthetics of imperialism cannot be applied to native art. Moreover, the poem's martial aspects, when read in a nationalist context, would be anathema to Henley, and these therefore are undermined in his review. 'The principal poem', he claims, 'founded on a wild Irish legend . . . tells how Oisin . . . met a damsel of faery, for love of whom he forsook kin and country' (647). Wishing perhaps that all Irish nationalists would do likewise and consign their heroics to dreamland, Henley casts a cold eye on Oisin's resolve to return 'to the Fenians' and 'chaunt / The war-songs that roused them of old'; on his desire to see them 'rise, making clouds with their breath, / Innumerable, singing, exultant'; and on his hope that 'the clay underneath them shall pant, / And demons be broken in pieces, and trampled beneath them in death' (*VP*, 61). He concludes by predicting a bright future for Yeats and welcoming a poet 'who can speak out with the right heroic accent, and kindle the blood with tales of the (*strictly historical*) deeds that were done in the brave old days "When the Fenians made foray at morning with Bran, Sgeolan, Lomair" ' (emphasis added).

By thus ignoring the poem's political import and by consigning to myth its martial spirit, Henley renders the poem unionist-friendly. By focusing so exclusively on the softer, more feminine and stereotypically 'Celtic' aspects of the poem, he also perhaps indicates what he expects of Yeats as a contributor. In Yeats's case, this was not quite necessary; his first contribution on Scots and Irish fairies shows that he had sussed out Henley quite well. One of the reasons Henley may have published Yeats is that he presented the acceptable aspect of Irish life and culture: its dreamy, childlike, sentimental, non-threatening and apolitical aspect.

Registered as a Newspaper.]   [Price 6d.   By Post 6½d.

THE

SCOTS

OBSERVER

A Record and Review

No. 25.

CONTENTS : MAY 11, 1889.

EDINBURGH: 9 THISTLE STREET.

LONDON: 142 FLEET STREET, E.C.

12   Cover, *Scots Observer*, 11 May 1889.

Yeats's other contributions to the *Observer* bear out this impression. Following Henley's review, Yeats's very next article, entitled 'Irish Wonders', reviewed David McAnally's book of that name. Harsh though it may be, one can imagine the mirth provoked among the regatta by the title, to them a contradiction in terms, as well as by the contents of the review:

> ... Celtic fairies are much like common men and women. Often the fairy-seer [one who sees fairies] meets with them on some lonely road, and joins in their dance ...

> 'They have', said one old peasant to the writer, 'the most beautiful parlours and drawing rooms.'

> There is probably not a village in Ireland where a fairy-seer or two may not be found. (*SO*, 23.3.89, 530; *UP1*, 139–40)

Yeats's next contribution, 'Village Ghosts' (*SO*, 11.5.89, 692–3), also dealt with peasant superstition. 'Columkille and Rosses' (*SO*, 5.10.89, 549–51) is representative of the prose Yeats published in Henley's *Observer*.

> 'Columkille' and Rosses were, are, and ever shall be, please Heaven! places of unearthly resort. I have lived near by them and in them, time after time, and, with the sweet child-verses ringing in my ears, have gathered any crumbs of fairy lore I could find therein, looking for some trace of the old king on his journey. (549)

> Columkille and Rosses are choke-full of ghosts. By bog, road, rath, hill-side, sea-border they gather in all shapes: headless women, men in armour, shadow hares, fire-tongued hounds, whistling seals, and so on. A whistling seal sank a ship the other day. (550)

> My friend, 'the sweet Harp-String' – (I give no more than his Irish name for fear of gaugers) – the best of all our folk-tale hunters – seems to have the science of unpacking the stubbornest heart, but then he supplies them with grain from his own fields. Besides, he is descended from a noted Gaelic magician who raised the 'doul' in Great Eliza's century, and he has a kind of prescriptive right to hear tell of all kind of other-world creatures. They are almost relations of his, if all folk say concerning the parentage of magicians be true. (551)

None of this is to suggest that Yeats did not believe in fairies and that he was merely pretending in order to conform to Henley's stereotype, but merely that he was conforming quite deliberately to Henley's political prejudices. While discussing his apprenticeship with Henley, Yeats rather naïvely claimed that, in order to 'avoid unacceptable opinions, I wrote nothing but ghost or fairy sto-ries' (*Auto*, 129). Such stories clearly avoided an embarrassing, not to say poten-tially disastrous, ideological clash with his editor, one that some of his contributions to the *United Ireland* or the *Boston Pilot* would have undoubtedly provoked. However, these stories were not as neutral as Yeats would like to believe. By emphasising the context of publication I have tried to indicate how such work by Yeats served to aesthetically rationalise imperial ideology. More-over it also ratified popular perceptions in the readership of a journal that was utterly scornful of superstition, folklore, mysticism and the supernatural and that had always portrayed the Irish as being ignorant, childlike people whose cultural, genetic and evolutionary development had been halted prematurely.

In this matter, his poetic contributions were similar to his prose. Lullabies and poems such as 'A Cradle Song' (*SO*, 19.4.90, 606; *VP*, 118) and 'A Fairy Song' (*NO*, 12.9.91, 432; *VP*, 115–6) reinforce the notion of Celt as child-like and superstitious. Many of Yeats's other *Observer* poems depict a renun-ciation similar to Henley's Oisin who 'forsook kin and country' for the love of 'a damsel of faery'. In 'Fergus and the Druid' (*NO*, 21.5.92, 15–16; *VP*, 102–3) the 'king of the proud Red Branch kings' abdicates kingship and governance for 'dreamy wisdom', claiming 'A wild and foolish labourer is a king / To do and do and do and never dream' (*VP*, 103). The famous 'Lake Isle of Innisfree' (*NO*, 13.12.90, 96; *VP*, 117) dwells on the calm brought about by a retreat into rusticity and nature away from the travails of daily life. Similarly, in the 'Fairy Host' (*NO*, 7.10.93, 540; *VP*, 140), which anglicises all Irish names, Niam riding on the wind calls out to mortals below:

> 'away, come away.'
> And brood no more where the fire is bright
> Filling thy heart with a mortal dream,
> For breasts are heaving and eyes a-gleam;
> Away, come away, to the dim twilight.
>
> (*VP*, 140)

The narrator's comment endorses and ornaments the invitation:

> The host is rushing 'twixt night and day,
> And where is there hope or deed as fair?
> Coulte tossing his burning hair
> And Niam calling 'away, come away.'
>
> (*VP*, 141)

Other poems, which also clearly depict an Irish context, advocate a renunci-ation of worldly involvement and struggle for either love ('The White Birds', *NO*, 7.5.92, 641; *VP*, 121–2) or 'the mystic brotherhood':

> Outworn heart in a time outworn,
> Come clear of the nets of wrong and right;
> Laugh, heart, again in the grey twilight,
> Sigh, heart, again in the dew of the morn.
>
> Thy mother Eri is always young,
> Dew ever shining and twilight grey,
> Though hope fall from thee or love decay
> Burning in fires of a slanderous tongue.
> ('The Celtic Twilight', NO, 29.7.93, 279; VP, 147–8)

In the context of the *Observer*, where any and every mention of Ireland was suffused with a strong political charge, the escapism of these poems takes on overtones of political pacifism. While it is true that much of Yeats's early poetry dramatises the dangers inherent in a fascination with fairyland, it is also true that, out of the 16 poems he published in the *Observer*, only 'The Man who Dreamed of Fairyland' fits this description. Most of them, *à la* Goldsmith, seem to suggest that politics do not impinge on the condition of human existence, that:

> In every government, though terrors reign,
> Though tyrant kings, or tyrant laws restrain,
> How small, of all that human hearts endure,
> That part which laws or kings can cause or cure.[43]

'The Peace of the Rose' (NO, 13.2.92, 328; VP, 112–13) advances the view that national struggles are inconsequential in the larger framework of human relationships, destiny and the after-life. The renunciation of war for a beautiful woman by the Archangel Michael, the commander of God's legions, is seen as an example for mortals below:

> And all folk, seeing him bow down
> And white stars tell your praise,
> Would come at last to God's great town,
> Led on by gentle ways;
>
> And God would bid man's warfare cease,
> Saying all things were well,
> And softly make a rosy peace
> A peace of Heaven with Hell.

In an environment suffused with Irish politics, one can well imagine how the *Observer* readers would have interpreted 'Heaven and Hell' in the year of Gladstone's second Home Rule Bill.

At this point, it is worth noting the remarkably different portrayal of Ireland and Irish characters in the 'Death of Cuchulain', which Yeats published in the *United Ireland* around the same time that he published the above-quoted poems in the *Observer*. From beginning to end, the poem is steeped in masculinity. It opens with a swineherd, Aleel, casting 'aside his draggled hair' and informing Queen Emer of the return of her husband, Cuchulain, victorious after a campaign:

> Not any god alive nor mortal dead,
> Has slain so mighty armies, so great kings,
> Nor the gold that now Cuchulain brings.
>
> (*VP*, 106)

When she hears that Cuchulain has returned with a beautiful woman for whom he made 'an army cease to be', she has Aleel whipped with leather thongs and informs her son, Finmole, that he has to kill a man. Hitherto con-signed to being a mere cattleherd, Finmole welcomes this opportunity to prove his mettle. She orders him to go to the Red Branch camp and tell his name and lineage only to the man who defeats him in combat and who is bound with a similar oath. In the fight that ensues, neither son nor father recognise each other, until, when defeated and at death's door, Finmole is commanded by Cuchulain:

> 'Speak before your breath is done.'
> 'I am Finmole, mighty Cuchulain's son.'
> 'I put you from your pain, I can no more.'
>
> (*VP*, 110)

Seeing Cuchulain consumed with grief, and fearing for their safety, Conchubar, the Red Branch King, orders the Druids to 'Chaunt in his ear delusions magical' or else he will arise from his brooding, 'and raving slay us all' (*VP*, 110–1). They do their bidding and the poem closes with the image of a demented Cuchulain battling with the sea.

Cuchulain and Finmole embody qualities (courage, passion, strength of character, vigour, daring and romance) that are conspicuously absent in the poems Yeats wrote for Henley. Even the poem's leading female character, Emer, has more blood than any of the male characters in Yeats's *Observer* poems. For Yeats, Cuchulain's end typified tragic intensity, the hero making his mask in defeat, a theme he was to develop further in a cycle of five plays. In 1904, he described Cuchulain's character in *On Baile's Strand* as being:

> a shadow of something a little proud, barren & restless as if out of
> sheer strength of heart or from accident he had put affection away
> . . . He is a little hard, & leaves the people about him a little
> repelled – perhaps this young mans affection is what he had most

need of . . . Without this thought the play had not had any deep
tragedy . . . The touch of something hard, repellent yet alluring,
self assertive yet self immolating is not all but it must be there.
(*CL3*, 527)

The 'Death of Cuchulain' would have suited Henley ideally, and not only
because of his preference for manly literature, grand passion, heroism and
bloodshed. Henley, for Yeats, also embodied a Shakespearean tragic intensity,
pride, restlessness, presence, self-assertion and strength of character.[44] Moreover, between 1890 and 1892 Yeats had published the bulk of his poetry in
the *Observer* even though he was simultaneously also writing regularly for the
United Ireland. When Yeats published the Cuchulain poem in the *United Ireland* in June 1892, he had already been writing for Henley's periodicals for
three years and had published 23 pieces of work, the majority of which were
poems. In the *United Ireland*, on the other hand, by June 1892 Yeats had published 13 pieces of work, only one of which was a poem. It would seem more
natural therefore for him to send the 'Death of Cuchulain' to Henley rather
than Leamy, the *UI*'s editor. Why didn't he? The poem's Irish subject matter
could not be a reason because he published plenty of Irish poems in the
Observer. A possible answer could be that Yeats felt, and felt rightly, that the
poem would go down well with the *UI*'s nationalist readership, that it would
fulfil all the prerequisites of literary Irishness as defined by him and the paper,
and that it would strengthen his own position in the paper and in nationalist Ireland. However, at the same time one can also see that he may not have
thought the poem suitable for the *Observer* because it did not conform either
to Henley's political programme or to his preferred image of the Celt that
Yeats's own work had ratified.

According to Edward Said, Yeats's use of Irish place names represents a 'cartographic impulse' and a desire to artistically reappropriate one's colonised
homeland. This desire 'radically distinguishes the imagination of anti-impe-
rialism . . . Because of the presence of the colonising outsider, the land is
recoverable at first only through the imagination':

> To the imagination of anti-imperialism, *our* space at home in the
> peripheries has been usurped and put to use by outsiders for *their*
> purposes. It is therefore necessary to seek out, to map, to invent,
> or to discover, a third nature, which is not pristine and prehistor-
> ical ('Romantic Ireland's dead and gone' says Yeats) but one that
> derives historically and abductively from the deprivations of the
> present. This impulse then is what we might call *cartographic*, and
> among its most striking examples are Yeats's early poems collected
> in 'The Rose' . . .[45]

Thirteen of the 23 poems that make up 'The Rose' section in *VP* (100–39) were first published in Henley's *Observer*. Many of them do contain Irish place names: Eire, Innisfree, Dromahair, Lissadell, Scanavin, Lugnagall, Kerry, Knocknarea, Clooth-na-bare. However, if one reads them in their original context, Said's claim that they enact an imaginative reappropriation of a lost homeland becomes somewhat dubious. In the *Observer* Yeats's use of Irish place names lends the poems a primitive, exotic, faraway atmosphere. These characteristics are integral to Arnold's understanding of Celticism in the arts, which, as John V. Kelleher has persuasively argued, informed much of the literature produced during the Revival.[46] Kelleher also demonstrates how Arnoldian Celticism – with 'sentiment as its main basis, with love of beauty, charm, and spirituality for its excellence, ineffectuality and self-will for its defect' – is a poorly disguised justification for English rule in Ireland. Given the fact that Henley was a zealous unionist and that Yeats was at pains to conform to his Arnoldian prejudices, Yeats's use of Irish place names in the *Observer* is not an expression of an anti-imperialist writer's 'cartographic impulse'. It is rather a reinscribing of Arnoldian notions of Celticism and through that of Henley's own notions of Ireland's place in the UK. The argument that Said's views are valid because these poems soon appeared in collections where the *Observer* context was powerless to affect their meanings is a naïve and dangerous form of collaboration in authorial attempts to control meaning through republication, something which, as we have seen, Yeats did quite successfully with 'September 1913' (see pp. 25–7). Surely, if Said and others are seeking to establish a connection between Yeats's statements and his political beliefs, what is important is the context in which those statements were made, not the context in which they were subsequently anthologised, collected and encountered. The context of first publication is not the sole determinant of meaning, but it certainly illuminates what was intended and understood by Yeats and by his first readers.

In the context of the poems' first publications, Said's claim is untenable. But there are other problems with it as well which are not central to my argument. Within Irish and Gaelic literature the Gaelic writers focused on history and the Anglo-Irish on landscape. The latter's absorption with the landscape had nothing to do with reappropriation but with avoiding a contentious subject (history) while yet staking a claim to Irishness and roots. Moreover, topographical poetry is a sub-genre of Gaelic poetry and not a literary development following colonisation. Finally, topographical poetry which names places is also an important part of the English tradition of regionalism of which Hardy's 'Wessex' poems are an example.

The extent to which scholarship can be undermined by an ignorance of a text's context of publication is further evidenced by Said's quotation from

'September 1913'. The dualism the poem embodies is not between 'outsiders' and natives but between Protestants and Catholics, which are not the same thing in the context of the *Irish Times*. For Said to act on the assumption that Protestant/outsider and Catholic/native are interchangeable terms is to undermine his own thesis about Yeats as a poet of decolonisation existing on the threshold between nativism and 'liberation' after having sounded the nationalist note. It also ignores the fact that the poem was addressed to Protestants, who resented being called outsiders. Moreover, to see the poem's refrain as indicating the loss of one's homeland to 'outsiders' is patently wrong. For Yeats, as we have seen, romantic Ireland existed in the eighteenth century, and for the greater part of that period it was still under direct British rule.

IV

In his *Autobiographies* and *Memoirs*, and even in some of his letters, Yeats takes pride in his association with Henley, but it sometimes embarrassed him with his Irish friends. Though he told Tynan that he only read the *Observer* when he had something published in it, his letters mention issues not featuring his work.[47] Besides, if he was attending Henley's weekly gatherings, it does seem improbable that he did not read the magazine. His *Autobiographies* (129) give the impression that he was quite familiar with its contents. Yeats's letters also exhibit a sheepishness about Henley's jingoism and anti-Irish sentiments. When the prospect arose of reviewing Ellen O'Leary's poems, he wrote apologetically to her brother on 21 January 1891:

> I fear I cannot do anything with 'National Observer' in the matter
> as Henley I think looks after all the verse himself. If you send him
> a copy I will write to him about it but cannot foretell result. He
> is an unpersuadable kind of man. (*CL1*, 241)

The primary difficulty at this stage was getting Henley to accept the book for review. If that was done, the second hurdle was getting Henley to consent to not reviewing it himself. If both obstacles were removed Yeats seemed to be quite willing to write the article. As things transpired, Henley did not prove 'unpersuadable'; he agreed to accept the book and to let Yeats review it. (This aberration is explained by his letters to Whibley, where he often complains about being too tied down by editorial work to do much writing himself, and about being desperately short of reviews.) Now that both obstacles were removed, one would imagine that Yeats would have got down to the job. But then we have this letter to O'Leary five months later:

> I am rather in a difficulty about Miss O'Leary's poems. I find it
> almost impossible to review it for so ultra-Tory a paper as the
> *National Observer* . . . When I consented to Henley's suggestion
> that I should review it for him I had no idea how difficult it
> would be. If I were a Tory it would be easy enough, or if I could
> descend to writing as a Tory who did not let his politics quite kill
> his literary sympathies. A few saving clauses would make all well,
> but they are just what I cannot put in. (*CL1*, 250)

What was this sudden 'difficulty' of which there was no mention in the
earlier letter? The *Observer's* politics had not changed: it was still as Tory as it
had been in January 1889 when Henley began his editorship or in January
1891 when Yeats first wrote to O'Leary about the review. Moreover, Yeats had
long known about the nationalistic quality of Ellen O'Leary's verse. He had
seen her poems published in the *Dublin University Review* (for example,
August 1886, 681), and seen them reviewed in the same periodical by Charles
Gavan Duffy (December 1886, 1011–21). Besides, Yeats himself had been
praising her poetry precisely for its nationalism ever since he first spoke of it
in print almost two years earlier and had reviewed the book in question in
April 1891, two months before the second letter.[48] Though he thought her
poetry simple, moving and ennobled by its nationalism, he also thought it
'unequal' (*UP1*, 258), unsophisticated and technically crude. However, it was-
n't his reluctance to criticise it publicly that prevented him from reviewing it
for Henley. The artistic sincerity demanded by John O'Leary permitted criticism. Moreover, a few months later Yeats's preface to a selection of her poetry
did advert to its defects.[49] The problem was not that he could not criticise
Ellen O'Leary's poems in the *Observer* but that he could not bring himself to
praise them there, not even to the limited extent demanded by his allegiance
to O'Leary and perhaps to his own conviction. This reluctance had two
aspects. Yeats took pride in the high literary standards and outspoken élitism
of Henley's group which had 'created such a terror among innocent sentimental writers and all flatterers of public taste' (*Mem*, 39). Ellen O'Leary certainly belonged to the category of 'innocent sentimental writers' and, though
Yeats aligned himself in Ireland with the 'flatterers of public taste', he could
not afford to do so with Henley. There was too much at stake. He could not
possibly praise Ellen O'Leary's poems for the literary merits (which he
thought they lacked) without seeming to align himself with 'popular culture',
that 'sorriest contradiction in terms'. To praise them for non-literary and 'sentimental' reasons would be to compromise the high literary standards and
artistic purity that Henley demanded. Either would jeopardise the 'distinction' – prestige and difference – accruing from membership of Henley's
group. It would also jeopardise his professional reputation and standing in the

eyes of his peers upon whom he, like other artists, depended for his self-image. The second aspect of Yeats's reluctance pertains to Henley's role as his 'symbolic banker'. Yeats respected Henley's literary acumen. He also needed Henley's backing and was anxious to win his critical approbation. To secure Henley's 'sponsorship' into the literary world, he played along with Henley's prejudices, and even catered to them. He also desisted from saying anything that might be seen as opposing or dissenting from Henley's views: 'certainly I did not dare, and I think none of us dared, to speak our admiration for book or picture he condemned' (*Auto*, 128). The only way that Yeats could retain Henley's admiration, safeguard his professional standing and at the same time not betray his relationship with O'Leary was by not reviewing the poems.

In his *Memoirs* Yeats gives the impression that he did not mind Henley's attitude towards Ireland because he was privy to certain information that redeemed Henley's outward bias:

> I remember his saying, 'It is not that I do not think Ireland fit for self-government, it is as fit as any other country' – Ireland's unfit-ness was the stock argument made [in] his time – 'but we have to think of the Empire. Do persuade those young men that this great thing has to go on.' There was comfort in such an attitude of mind, and he could admire as I could the folklore and folksong that Hyde had begun to discover, and he was about to write of Parnell, 'He has been eighteen years before the country and we knew nothing of his character but that he was haughty', and describe, if my memory does not deceive me, Parnell's hatred of the British Empire as 'noble.' He wanted to found a paper in Ire-land and try his chances there. I was drawn to him also, I doubt not, by his aristocratic attitudes, his hatred of the crowds . . . (*Mem*, 38–9)

A similar claim is made in *Autobiographies*:

> Once he said to me in the height of his Imperial propaganda, 'Tell those young men in Ireland that this great thing must go on. They say Ireland is not fit for self-government, but that is nonsense. It is as fit as any other European country, but we cannot grant it.' And then he spoke of his desire to found and edit a Dublin news-paper. It would have expounded the Gaelic propaganda then beginning, though Dr Hyde had, as yet, no League, our old stories, our modern literature – everything that did not demand any shred or patch of government. He dreamed of a tyranny, but it was that of Cosimo de' Medici. (*Auto*, 126)

Yeats's memory does indeed deceive him. His claims – that Henley admired Parnell, that he was interested in folklore, that he wished to promote the Irish Literary Revival and that he believed Ireland fit for self-government – are gainsaid by every page of the *Observer*. The written comments that he attributes to Henley about Parnell cannot be found in his weekly. On the other hand, what does come across very clearly is the journal's violent antipathy towards, and even hatred of, the Irish chief. He was regularly and severely attacked in the leaders of almost every issue from the *Observer's* founding till the time of his death and a large number of Henley's lampoons satirised Parnell. In the issue following his death, Parnell's hatred of the Empire was not described as being 'noble' but as being 'able', 'desperate, unscrupulous' (*NO*, 10.10.91, 63). As for his character, 'his political gift was of uncommon excellence, and as a leader and manipulator of men his equal is yet to find'. He was a 'ready and undaunted liar', 'bold', 'prescient', 'unscrupulous', 'dispassionately and carefully relentless', 'ruthless' and 'shameless' (527).

Since Yeats draws on private conversations to give a different account of Henley's attitude towards Parnell, it is perhaps worth mentioning that the accounts given by Henley's close associates ratify the impression conveyed by the *Observer* and conflict starkly with Yeats's. The following is a description of a meeting of the regatta and the celebrations that ensued 'in circumstances of altogether peculiar exhilaration':

> These, however, were but minor and decorative elements in the songs of joy which filled our hearts. For we had read – I believe in that morning's newspaper – the report of the divorce case in which Mr Parnell was the unsuccessful – and silent – respondent. The fatuous conduct and inept Report of the Special Commission had been a bitter disappointment to all of us, and the revelation of the shifty and mendacious habits of Parnell's private life, which as we well knew would cause profound astonishment and disappointment to his Liberal allies, were to us a source of such amusement and delight as we had not hoped that the course of politics would ever afford us. The festivity of our party reached and maintained the highest possible degree, and 'Kitty O'Shea' was toasted with frantic acclamation. Henley was the life and soul of the party ... (Herbert Stephen, *London Mercury*, 391–2)

Stephen goes on to narrate how he was honoured by being asked to write the leading article – a satirical attack on Parnell's relationship with Mrs O'Shea and his use of aliases – in the *NO's* very first issue. Henley eventually wrote a large part of it himself because Stephen's article was not cutting enough. But even that 'did not exhaust our hilarity', because Henley then went on to compose the lampoon (see p. 278, n. 19) on 'The Statesman and the Fire Escape'.

Given the overwhelming evidence indicating Henley's aversion to Parnell, Yeats's claim does not appear credible. Similarly, Yeats's other claims about Henley's views on Ireland, his interest in folklore and his desire to promote the Revival are contradicted by the *Observer's* contents. In fact, it is surprising that Yeats should think that Henley wished to support the Revival given that Henley had, quite characteristically, rejected Yeats's article on the 'Revival of Irish Literature'. And what's more, the rejection would not have surprised Yeats:

> Dear Mr Henley,
>   I enclose article on 'Revival of Irish Literature.' The subject was thorney & I fear I may not in making it suitable for my own purposes have made it suitable for you. (*CL1*, 521)

If in 1894 Yeats thought the subject too 'thorney' and unsuitable for Henley, what made him change his mind so drastically in 1922? While writing his *Autobiographies*, why should Yeats pick up on remarks that Henley may have made to him in private but which were totally belied by his public conduct? Yeats's account of Henley tries to convey the impression that Henley was sympathetic to Ireland, that he was not as anti-Irish and as unreconstructed an imperialist as people think, that there was much in Henley that Yeats would have found agreeable, and that they shared an interest in folklore and Irish literature. However, the impression that it does convey is that Yeats is trying to justify his association with Henley because he is uncomfortable with the thought that people might wonder why he associated with Henley and why he was writing for as virulently anti-Irish a weekly as the *Observer*. The association would appear even more startling when one considers that Yeats had aligned himself not only with the Fenians and the Irish nationalists but also with those trying to 'answer that ceaseless stream of calumny England has sent forth against us' (*UP1*, 213):

> England has indeed, as Mitchel phrased it, gained the ear of the world, and knows right well how to tell foreign nations what tale of Ireland pleases her best. By the mouths of her magnificent *Times* . . . she repeats to the admiring nations a ceaseless tale of English patience and Irish insubordination. (*LNI*, 61)

In the passage quoted from *Memoirs* (p. 167), Yeats perplexingly claims that he took 'comfort in such an attitude of mind' as Henley's. The corresponding passage in the *Autobiographies* also quoted above offers some explanation. The rule of the cultural élite, as symbolised by de' Medici — c.f. the discussion of 'The Gift' in the Introduction — translated into Irish terms for an embittered

Ronsard's 'Sonnet pour Hélenè' [literal translation]

When you are quite old, at evening, by candlelight,
Sitting by the fire, unwinding and knitting,
Will sing my lines, and find it wonderful:
Ronsard celebrated me when I was young.
Then you will have no servant telling you such news,
Already half-asleep under (her) work,
Who at the mention of my name wakes up,
Blessing your name with immortal praise.
I will be under the earth and, boneless ghost,
Among the myrtle shades will take my rest:
You will be an old one squatting by the hearth,
Missing my love and regretting your proud disdain.
Live, if you believe me, don't wait until tomorrow:
Pluck today the roses of life.

Henley's 'When You Are Old'

When you are old, and I am passed
    away —
Passed, and your face, your golden face,
    is grey —
I think, whate'er the end, this dream of
    mine
Comforting you, a friendly star will
    shine
Down the dim slope where still you
    stumble and stray.

So may it be: that so dead Yesterday
No sad-eyed ghost but generous and
    gay,
May serve you memories like almighty
    wine,
When you are old!

Dear Heart, it shall be so. Under the
    sway
Of death the past's enormous disarray
Lies hushed and dark. Yet though there
    come no sigh,
Live on well pleased; immortal and
    divine
Love shall still tend you, as God's angels
    may,
When you are old.

Yeats's 'When You Are Old'

When you are old and grey and full of
    sleep,
And nodding by the fire, take down
    this book,
And slowly read, and dream of the soft
    look
Your eyes had once, and of their shad-
    ows deep;

How many loved your moments of
    glad grace,
And loved your beauty with love false
    or true,
But one man loved the pilgrim soul in
    you,
And loved the sorrows of your chang-
    ing face;

And bending down beside the glowing
    bars,
Murmur, a little sadly, how Love fled
And paced upon the mountains over-
    head
And hid his face among a crowd of
    stars.

Yeats in 1922 (which is when the passage was written) as the rule of the Ascendancy currently marginalised by the Catholic masses. There would be 'no League', no enforced Gaelic and no Catholic government. Yeats's mention of Parnell and his haughtiness is followed by an expression of admiration for Henley's aristocratic demeanour and disdain for the populace. If one calls to mind Yeats's myth of Parnell and the use to which he put it,[50] one comes across a figure very similar to Henley in his contempt for the middle classes and the mob, his aristocratic demeanour, his self-possession and confidence, his intransigence in the face of opposition, his formidable and awesome reputation, and the fear with which he was looked on by his underlings. Yeats's would later match Henley's avant-garde aesthetics and reactionary politics. Henley's views on oligarchy, social hierarchy, genetics and the position of the intelligentsia anticipate, and perhaps may have influenced, Yeats's later views on eugenics and the 'caste system that has saved Indian intellect' (*Ex*, 424) as delineated in *On a Boiler*.

There are other similarities as well. Curious though it may seem, it is likely that the penner of jingoistic war songs may have influenced one of Yeats's famous early lyrics (see facing page). It has been suggested that Yeats's poem was derived from Pierre Ronsard's sixteenth-century lyric 'Quand vous serez bien vieille'. There are two problems with this speculation. Firstly, Yeats had little French, and secondly, most of his interest in French poetry was restricted to the nineteenth-century Symbolists, Verlaine and Mallarmé, whom he read through Arthur Symons. Henley, on the other hand, was knowledgeable about French literature and fluent in the language; much of his correspondence with Rodin is in French. Not surprisingly, Henley is closer than Yeats to Ronsard. In both Ronsard and Henley, the lover foresees a time when he is dead. In Yeats's version, the lover is not dead but estranged from his beloved. Ronsard, and Henley to a lesser extent, end by advising the beloved to make the most of whatever time she has left. However, the maidservant from whom, in Ronsard's sonnet, the beloved no longer derives solace, has been eliminated in Henley's version, as she has been in Yeats's. Both Henley and Yeats also eliminate the bitterness of Ronsard's lover, his reproaching of his beloved for not requiting his love, and his harsh reminder of her own impending old age and mortality ('old one squatting by the hearth', 'boneless ghost', 'under the earth'). In their versions, the lover reiterates his love and hopes that his poems will lend comfort and solace to the beloved in her old age. Though Yeats and Ronsard both envisage the beloved sitting by the fire, examination shows that Yeats's lyric has more affinities with Henley's version, which seems a closer and more probable source for Yeats both in content and in mood. The similarities are too obvious to be missed: the opening line, the iambic pentameter, common words (grey, dream, star, slopes, mountains), and the theme of ageing and the recovery of youth through memory and the text of the poem. While Henley's beloved 'stumble[s] and stray[s]', Yeats's beloved has a 'pilgrim soul'. So also the 'sigh' in Henley has been replaced by a 'murmur' in Yeats.

Henley's poem was published in 1888 as part of a larger collection whose first edition was quickly exhausted. Kennedy Williamson points out that the poems were well received by the critics and that 'When You Are Old' attracted attention.[51] Yeats's poem was completed by 21 October 1891 and published in September the following year in the *Countess Kathleen and Various Legends and Lyrics*.[52] In the period between its composition and publication – 21 October 1891 to September 1892 – Yeats contributed six pieces to Henley's *NO*, all of which were poetry, and all of which were published in the *Countess Kathleen*. One wonders therefore why Yeats did not publish 'When You Are Old' with Henley. A possible answer is that perhaps it was too close to home. In a letter to Tynan written shortly after Henley's collection was published, Yeats mentioned that Miss Sigerson is 'greatly enthusiastic about Henley's little book which would be really a wonderful affair if it was not so cobwebby – I have not read the Hospital part yet' (*CL1*, 91). It is possible that Yeats, given his own taste, would have deliberately avoided the gory realism of the 'Hospital' poems, dealing with Henley's stay at the Old Infirmary in Edinburgh where his foot was amputated, and would have started reading the collection from the 'Lyrics and Rondeaus', which would be more to his liking.

In his accounts of Henley, Yeats adverts repeatedly to the generosity and affection Henley showered on his boys – he 'all but loved us as himself' (*Mem*, 38) – to explain why he felt compelled to accept the revisions Henley made to his work:

> Henley often revised my lyrics, crossing out a line or a stanza and writing in one of his own, and I was comforted by my belief that he also rewrote Kipling, then in the first flood of popularity . . . I was not compelled to full conformity, for verse is plainly stubborn; *and in prose, that I might avoid unacceptable opinions, I wrote nothing but ghost or fairy stories* . . . But if he had changed every 'has' into 'hath' I would have let him, for had not we sunned ourselves in his generosity? (*Auto*, 129; underlining and italics added)[53]

There appears to be a slight contradiction between the first admission and the second sentence (underlined). If Henley revised Yeats's lyrics, in what way were they not compelled to 'full conformity'? Perhaps he means that he was not compelled to conform ideologically, as Henley's revisions to his poetry were only of a stylistic or technical nature, and that, while such revisions are possible, ideological ones are not. This seems a likely explanation because in the latter part of the second sentence (italicised) Yeats speaks of deliberately restricting himself to 'ghost or fairy stories' in order to avoid 'unacceptable opinions' in his prose. As we have seen, Yeats did not confine merely his prose to 'ghost or fairy' themes; his poetry too was governed by the same imperative and dictated by a like prudence. In *Memoirs* Yeats claims that it was during his apprenticeship with Henley that he 'came to feel that the necessity of excluding all opinion was my first discipline in creative prose' (*Mem*, 39). Here, but more so in the earlier quoted passage from *Autobiographies*, Yeats suggests that by restricting himself to innocuous themes that allowed for the excluding of all opinion he was able to preserve his artistic and intellectual integrity and remain true to Ireland. That his work did not antagonise Henley or that it did not contain opinions that were 'unacceptable' to Henley does not mean, as I have demonstrated, that his work was in any way value-free, neutral, or true to the Irish cause, especially in the context of the *Observer*. Moreover, Yeats's integrity was compromised even in matters that were close to his heart and which elsewhere or in another context would have provoked him to take a stand opposite to that which he adopted while writing for Henley. There is enough evidence indicating that he consciously modified his work to align it with Henley's political views. His essay on William Carleton reflects what he calls his 'first discipline in creative prose'. In this particular case such 'discipline' entailed not merely the exclusion of all 'unacceptable opinions' but also the inclusion of acceptable ones, acceptable, that is, from the *Observer's* perspective.

From January 1888 to March 1890 Yeats had been reading Carleton intensively, and between September 1888 and March 1891 the fruits of this labour were realised in three anthologies – *Fairy and Folk Tales of the Irish Peasantry*, *Stories from Carleton (SC)*, *Representative Irish Tales (RIT)* – and one *SO* article. The individual histories of commission, completion and publication of the last three texts[54] are deeply intertwined and perhaps, when tabulated, will seem less complicated:

	SC	*SO*	*RIT*
Commissioned	*c.* 14.11.88	*c.* 21.4.89	6.8.89
Completed	mid–late July '89	–	16.3.90
Published	Aug. '89	19.10.89	March '91
Length (approx)	2,300 words★	1,600 words	1,900 words★[55]

★ of Yeats's Introduction to the Carleton section.

After completing *Fairy and Folk Tales* in August 1888, Yeats concentrated on the Introduction to *Stories from Carleton* until he completed it in July 1889. He then used this as a master text for the *SO* article and, later, for the Introduction to the Carleton section in *Representative Irish Tales*.[56] As *Stories from Carleton* was an anthology of only Carleton's stories, Yeats's Introduction there was longer than both the *SO* article – a review of Carleton's recently published novel, *The Red-Haired Man's Wife* – and the Carleton section of Yeats's Introduction to *Representative Irish Tales*. Given that both the *SO* review and the Introduction to *Representative Irish Tales* were based on the longer Introduction to *Stories from Carleton*, they were bound to contain omissions and changes, but closer inspection reveals that there is an underlying policy determining what is to be excluded and what new material added. The changes made for the *SO* article, especially when compared to those made for *Representative Irish Tales*, are particularly interesting as they shed light on the influence Henley exerted on Yeats's work and Yeats's willingness to revise his work to appease not only Henley's political prejudices but also those of other targeted audiences.

The biographical details of Carleton's life which constituted more than half of the Introduction to *Stories from Carleton* were excluded from the *SO* article published just three months after the former was completed. The fact that this material was reinstated in very large measure in the Introduction to *Representative Irish Tales*, which is only a bit longer than the *SO* article, indicates that its absence in the latter was not determined by considerations of space. On examination, it becomes clear that material from the Introduction to *Stories from Carleton* was not merely excluded, it was censored from the *SO*, because of the 'unacceptable opinions' contained in the biographical details of that Introduction.[57] Moreover, a comparison of Yeats's biographical account of Carleton with Yeats's source, Carleton's *Autobiography* published in the 1843 edition of *Traits and Stories of the Irish Peasantry*, shows that Yeats has doctored information for his purposes.

In the Introductions to *Stories from Carleton* and *Representative Irish Tales*, but not in the *SO*, Yeats situates Carleton in the context of a living and vibrant Gaelic culture characterised by Gaelic songs, sports and language. Carleton's father had knowledge of Gaelic charms (*) and his mother of old Gaelic songs (*). One of these songs was called 'The Red-Haired Man's Wife' (*), which Carleton subsequently used as the title of the novel Yeats was reviewing for the *SO*. The reason that Yeats does not mention this interesting fact about the novel's genesis in the *SO* review, even though it would seem central to his purpose there, is because it is linked to details that would undoubtedly affront Henley's unionism:

> She [Carleton's mother] had a great store of old Gaelic songs and tunes. Many an air, sung under all Irish roof-trees, has gone into the grave with her. The words she sang were Gaelic. Once they asked her to sing the air, 'The Red-haired Man's Wife', to English

words. 'I will sing for you', she answered, 'but the English words
and the air are like a quarrelling man and wife. The Irish melts
into the tune: the English does not.'[58]

Yeats was perhaps being 'systematically' national in paying lip-service to
Gaelic culture and its revival through organisations such as the GAA. His reference to the demise of Gaelic, his privileging it over English, along with his
reference to Mrs Carleton's suggestion of the incompatibility of the two lan-
guages and the foreignness of English, have a strong emotional and nationalist charge within the context of Anglo-Irish relations. Not surprisingly, they
have been omitted in the *SO* article. At this stage, when the Gaelic League
had not yet been founded and at a time when the Language Revival posed
no threat to him, either as a Protestant or as a writer in English, Yeats could
affect sympathy with the demise of Gaelic before Irish audiences. However,
his response to Hyde's de-anglicising address in 1892, by which time the
threat had taken real form, strikes a less enthusiastic note for Gaelic and a
more enthusiastic one for translations:

> When we remember the majesty of Cuchullin and the beauty of
> sorrowing Deirdre we should not forget that it is that majesty and
> that beauty which are immortal, and not the perishing tongue
> that first told of them. (*CL1*, 340)

The nationalist charge of Yeats's Introductions to *Stories from Carleton* and
Representative Irish Tales is maintained by a continuing emphasis on the demise
of Gaelic Ireland. For instance, in both Introductions he links Carleton's date
of birth to the 1798 Rising: 'On Shrove-Tuesday, in the year 1798, when
pitch-caps were well in fashion, was born to these two a son, whom they called
William Carleton' (*P&I*, 23) (★). In his *Autobiography*, Carleton states that his
date of birth is 1794.[59] By shifting this date forward by four years Yeats makes
it coincidental with the year of the Rising. This facilitates the reference to the
pitch-cap, a linen or paper cap fastened with burning pitch on the head of
Irish revolutionaries that lacerated the scalp on removal. The variation of this
detail in *Representative Irish Tales* provides an insight into Yeats's use of nationalist iconography in literary criticism directed at Irish readers: 'William Carleton was born on Shrove Tuesday, in the year 1798 when the pike was trying
to answer the pitch cap' (*P&I*, 46). A year later, in a letter to the *United Ireland*
(14.5.92), Yeats drew on similar symbols while explaining the connection
between nationalist sentiments and the reading of Irish literature:

> In the old days when Davis sang there was no need to teach it,
> for then Apollo struck his lyre with a pike-head, but now he has
> flung both pike-head and lyre into the sea. (*CL1*, 299)

This curious mixture of Greek mythology, Gaelic iconography, nationalist (even martial) rhetoric and literary propaganda is absent in the *SO* review. So also is the expression of regret (in good Fenian fashion) for the abandoning of armed resistance. In the *SO*, as we shall see, he condemns the use of force.

Yeats's mention of the 'hedge schoolmasters' (*) in his Introductions is similar in its ideological drift to his use of Gaelic culture and the pitch-cap:

> At this time Ireland was plentifully stored with hedge school-
> masters. Government had done its best to crush out education,
> and only succeeded in doing what like policy had done for the
> priestcraft – surrounding it with a halo. (*P&I*, 24)

Yeats locates Carleton firmly within this context of cultural colonisation and extirpation by pointing out that 'the boy Carleton sat under three hedge schoolmasters in succession' (*P&I*, 24). In the Introduction to *Representative Irish Tales* the context of colonial oppression is made even more explicit, as the hedge schoolmasters are said to be 'bred by government in its endeavour to put down Catholic education' (*P&I*, 46).

In addition to these biographical references, there are other 'unacceptable' details about Carleton that are omitted from the *SO* article and substituted by more 'acceptable' opinions. They all relate to the land question. Carleton, as Yeats points out, was the historian of rural Ireland and his own peasant background fuelled his lifelong preoccupation with the land question: 'almost everything he wrote deals with it' (*SO*, 609). The *SO* had very definite views on this matter. From its very first word (quite literally), it had vehemently opposed land agitation and criticised the Plan of Campaign. In its inaugural number, the first six notes on the first page as well as some of its leading articles focused on the land issue. For the *SO*, the New Irish Tenants League – 'Based upon a lie, framed for the accomplishment of a fraud, and winding up with an appeal for Money' – was just another 'Irish Sham' (27.7.89, 261). The 'alleged injustice and oppression' of the peasants were dismissed as being 'utterly unreal' (19.1.89, 235). Peasant resistance was mocked, the withholding of rent was excoriated, agitators were called 'thieving, robbing, murdering scoundrels' (14.9.89, 454) while the raising of rents and evictions for non-payment were celebrated.[60] 'Wherever a landlord has shown firmness', the *SO* declared, 'and wherever the law has been allowed to take its course, the result has been most satisfactory' (18.5.89, 706). It urged the reintroduction of the Irish Crimes Act and the implementation of the Coercion Act with greater severity.

The *SO* understood the centrality of the land issue both for the Home Rule struggle in Ireland and the maintenance of the social status quo in Britain. It warned the government that, if it succumbed to the 'old story of the Law of the League endeavouring to override the Law of the Land' (8.12.88, 62), the whole social edifice would crumble and 'we shall never again be in a position to demand any of these things [repayment of debts and protection of private property] as a right' (20.4.89, 597). While it urged the speedy resolution of this issue through land purchase Bills as a prerequisite for order in Ireland and the maintenance of imperial unity, it also staunchly opposed land agitation and the tactics adopted by the Land League:

> If a man under no circumstance has the right to be paid for the occupation of his own land by a tenant who has contracted to pay for it, then those who defend the Olphert tenants are justi-fied . . . If it be a rule of right conduct that a landlord should indefinitely prolong the occupation of tenants who cannot, and say that they cannot, live upon their holdings, and if it be equally his duty to refuse the right of occupation to solvent men who can and will take their places, then those who are in favour of stereotyping pauperism in Donegal may be right . . . If it be a wise and patriotic thing to urge an ignorant peasantry to take the law into their own hands, and to brutally bludgeon and mutilate the officers of the law for carrying out the elementary duties for which they are appointed, then the abettors of the tar-throwing, stone-heaving sisters of Donegal may conceivably be wise and patriotic men. (20.4.89, 597)

Yeats's Carleton review was published on 19 October 1889, two months after the commencement of the agitation in Tipperary and the founding of 'New Tipperary'.[61] The Tipperary campaign had been closely followed by the *SO* in consecutive numbers from 7.9.89 onwards. Their position there was the same as on the earlier land campaigns in other parts of Ireland, but had grown more vituperative with time. Once again the strengthening of the Coercion Act was urged to curb the 'village ruffians' and the 'Parnellite MPs' who have loosed 'a reign of terror in Tipperary' (*SO*, 7.9.89, 421). In the issue immediately preceding Yeats's Carleton review there was another attack on the Tipperary campaign and Parnell's role in it. The Carleton issue contained the usual number of attacks on things Irish: nationalists were opposed to 'civilisation, liberty and order' (19.10.89, 596), 'which are so hateful to the Irish politician' intent on bringing about 'the curse of Irish misrule':

> Perjury, bribery, intimidation, and violence; the stealing of docu-ments, the corruption of witnesses and jurymen; every act which can stamp a party or a people as unfit to exercise the most rudi-mentary privileges of free citizens – these are the poisonous growths which have sprung up in rank abundance . . . From top

to bottom the conspiracy is Irish: the murderers were Irish, the murdered man was Irish, the methods by which murder is to be sustained by perjury and shielded by intimidation are Irish through and through. (596)

This was followed by 'The Lessons of the Elections' (598), which focused primarily on Ireland. Yeats's 'William Carleton' (608) was followed by an essay entitled 'Irish Land Tenure' (610).

Yeats's ideas on the land question derived compositely from his father's experiences and John O'Leary's views. J. B. Yeats inherited a substantially mortgaged estate which, rarely visited, was further mortgaged by him to a point beyond redemption. He finally sold the remainder under the provisions of the Ashbourne Act in 1886 thereby completing his withdrawal from the land-owning classes. Given Yeats's own class snobbery, and the fact that he liked to think of himself as belonging to the Ascendancy, he must have resented this forced demotion in the social order. Writing to Tynan in March 1889 he said that he sympathised with the national idea but not with 'any secondary land movement' (*CL1*, 154). This was the classic John O'Leary position. With vested interests of his own to protect, O'Leary had bitterly opposed the land agitation, in private conversations as well as in letters to the press, ever since his return to Ireland.[62] The Tipperary agitation was a severe blow to his finances, as his entire income was derived by renting his properties in that town.[63] New Tipperary, according to O'Leary, was 'a patent fiction' and 'indefensible morally'. His arguments, relying on the moral right to property, and his denunciation of the instigation and coercion of a misguided but honest tenantry by manipulative politicians like William O'Brien and John Dillon, echo those of Tory ideologues. There 'has never been, in the whole history of Irish agitation', he alliterated, 'anything so reckless, ruthless and utterly ruinous as this Tipperary affair from beginning to end'. No good could come of it, either for the tenants or for the cause of Irish nationalism. O'Leary received little sympathy from his town folk, who saw him 'not as an Irish patriot but as a "hard landlord"' (Bourke, 198). Even in times of general hardship, he had insisted on his rent as a moral duty and, as a result, for most of 1886 a branch of the local Land League was occupied exclusively in alleviating the distress caused by his intransigence.

Yeats's first mention of the land issue in *Stories from Carleton* is with reference to Carleton's 'Wildgoose Lodge', a tale named after a house that was burnt down along with its eight inhabitants by Ribbonmen. Though Yeats says that Carleton warned people against secret societies, his account of 'Wildgoose Lodge' sympathises more with the hanged leader than with his eight victims:

A quarter of a mile from the priest's house was Wildgoose Lodge, where, six months before, a family of eight persons had been burnt to ashes by a Ribbon Society. The ringleader still swung on a gibbet opposite his mother's door, and as she came in and out it was her custom to look up and say, 'God have mercy on the sowl of my poor martyr.' The peasants when they passed by would often look up too, and murmur, 'Poor Paddy.' (*P&I*, 25)

By instancing the arson as merely one more fact in a catalogue of other bland facts such as the geographical distance of the Lodge from the priest's house, a lot of the horror and savagery of the deed is glossed over. On the other hand, the punishment is depicted in all its savage and gruesome details and is sentimentalised by the invocation of the bereaved mother and by the attitude of the town's peasants. Not surprisingly, there is no mention of either 'Wild-goose Lodge' or Ribbon societies in the *SO*.

Carleton's attitude is quite different, as is also his account of this incident. He describes the arson as 'another black national crime', an 'inhuman and hellish tragedy' which 'clung to me through my sleep with such vivid horror that sleep was anything but a relief to me' (Carleton, 114–5). The massacred family are reported as being 'decent and very civil', 'a very moral and pious family' (115). Before being burnt alive

they received a nocturnal visit; their door was smashed in, and the house was filled with ruffians, who beat and maltreated them with such brutality, that one of them recovered from the injuries he had received with great difficulty. (115–6)

Carleton also takes a rather different view of Devaun:

The meeting of that woeful night was summoned by Devaun, who made the chapel – the House of God – the scene in which the blind and wretched dupes were sworn to execute, without hesitation or inquiry, that which *at a proper time* should be made known to them. Whisky had been subscribed for, and the greater number of them had been primed with it. On the very altar of God, every preparation for the projected crime was made; on the very altar of God, the ignorant dupes were sworn to perpetrate what, with the exception of those who were in the secret, they knew nothing of. (116–7)

He makes his position towards Devaun quite clear by undercutting any sympathy that the mother's sorrow might provoke among readers: 'It was quite clear that the affection of the mother prevented her from assenting to the belief that her son could be guilty of such a crime' (118).

In the Introduction to *Stories from Carleton* as well as in the *SO* review Yeats criticises the propagandistic element in Carleton's writings, but there is a difference in the criticisms made. In *Stories from Carleton*, which is written for an Irish audience, he claims that *Valentine M'Clutchy* 'is full of wonderful dialogues, but continually the intensity of the purpose lowers the art into caricature' (*P&I*, 27). In the *SO*, he employs stronger language and his criticism is more direct and less vague: 'In *Fardarougha* there is none of the fierce political feeling that degraded some of Carleton's later novels into caricature' (*SO*, 608).[64] In itself, and especially in the context of nationalist aesthetics, 'intensity of the purpose' is not necessarily a bad thing morally, and its artistic fallouts are to some extent mitigated by the novel's being 'full of wonderful dialogues'. On the other hand, 'fierce political feeling', especially with reference to Carleton's most nationalist and anti-Protestant novel, is a damning criticism, especially to an *SO* audience.[65] So also, 'lowers the art into caricature' (*Stories from Carleton*) is much milder than the *SO*'s 'degraded some of Carleton's later novels into caricature'. That Carleton's later and more political novels are still art is something conceded by Yeats in *Stories from Carleton* but denied by him in the *SO* review.

A similar manoeuvre is evident when Yeats deals with Carleton's prophecies. While in both *Stories from Carleton* and the *Observer* review the prophecies are shown to have been fulfilled, the outcome is presented in contrasting ways:

> Most of the prophecies he made about the land question have been fulfilled. He foretold that the people would wake up some day and appeal to first principles. They are doing so with a vengeance. Many of the improvements also that he recommended have been carried out. (*P&I*, 26)

> The great thing about Carleton was that he always remained a peasant, hating and loving with his class. On one point he was ever consistent, was always a peasant moralist; that is the land question. Almost every story he wrote deals with it; and in *The Red-Haired Man's Wife*, written just before his death in 1870, he makes a curious prophecy. Then Fenianism was everywhere; but this, he said, was not the movement to be dreaded, but a new one that was coming – a land war that would prove the greatest movement Ireland had seen. He says this several times in different parts of the book. A few years later a now famous agitator called on an old Fenian (since dead) and asked him, Would the people take up a land cry? 'I am only afraid', was the answer, 'they would go the gates of hell for it', and the event has shown how far he was right. (*SO*, 608; *UP1*, 145–6)

In *Stories from Carleton* the land agitation is seen as something the people adopt after a long period of darkness and somnolence when they belatedly wake up to the clear light of day and come to their senses. Their methods, appealing to 'first principles' – 'fundamental truths or law as the basis for reasoning or action' (*OED*) – have resulted in 'improvements'. The prophecy is seen as being not only accurate but also a good one. By contrast, the *SO* presents a very gloomy picture where Carleton, a veritable Jeremiah, plays the prophet of doom. Fenianism is dreadful enough but worse is still to come in the form of the land agitation, which will be the greatest dread of all. The results will be in keeping with the methods and will damn the agitators to hell. The anecdote was supplied to Yeats by O'Leary and reflects the latter's hostility towards the land war. Hence, the anecdote is included in an article for unionist consumption but left out of a book intended for a nationalist readership. The 'famous agitator' was Parnell and the old Fenian was Kickham:

> And he . . . asked Kickham, novelist and Fenian leader, if he
> thought the people would take up a land agitation, and Kickham
> answered, 'I am only afraid they would go to the Gates of Hell for
> it'; and O'Leary's comment was, 'And so they have.' (*Auto*, 238)

In the *SO* review, Yeats presents the land agitation as something to be dreaded, not just by the Protestant unionists but also by its supposed beneficiaries, the peasants themselves, and adduces the testimony of Carleton: the historian of rural Ireland, satirist of Protestant proselytisation and, most importantly, one who 'always remained a peasant, hating and loving with his class'. Once again the implication is that the peasants are being manipulated by self-serving politicians into a position that will leave them worse off than before. However, before one jumps to conclusions about Yeats being a unionist (literary or otherwise), it is advisable to view these utterances in their contexts of publication, to contrast them with others that he had made elsewhere on the same issue, and take cognisance of the fact that at this stage Yeats, a young ambitious writer, would have had to make opportunistic choices and concessions in his dealings with periodicals in order to establish himself. He also would have been susceptible to compromises and the dictation of a strong, dominant personality like Henley from whom he had much to gain. Rather than as examples of Yeats's political beliefs, these instances are perhaps better understood as examples of Yeats's political malleability, or what Joyce called Yeats's 'treacherous instinct of adaptability'.[66]

Yeats concluded the Introduction to *Representative Irish Tales* with a prediction of his own about the revival of Irish literature:

> We are preparing likely enough for a new Irish literary move-
> ment – like that of '48 – that will show itself at the first lull in

> this storm of politics. Carleton scarcely understood the true ten-
> dency of any thing he did. His pages served now one cause, now
> another, according to some interest or passion of the moment . . .
> (P&I, 36–7)

Carleton was himself a consummate master of the art of modulating his work
to suit the preferences of his editor and publisher. Robert Lee Wolff points
out that 'his dominant position in the Irish book trade' was partly owing to
his shifting 'his point of view opportunistically to suit the prejudices of his
employers'. He instances the fact that the anti-Catholic stories, written for the
proselytising clergyman Caesar Otway's *Christian Examiner*, were toned down
and modified when Carleton republished them in book format. Vivien
Mercier attributes this change to the fact that Carleton was now publishing
with James Duffy, 'a Catholic from County Monaghan with a hedge-school
education resembling Carleton's'.[67]

Yeats's prediction about the Revival will be discussed in the following
chapter, but it is worth pointing out here a curious detail about responses to
Yeats's conclusion in *Representative Irish Tales* which follows closely after the
above quote:

> Most things are changed now – politics are different, life is dif-
> ferent. Irish literature is and will be, however, the same in one
> thing for many a long day – in its nationality, its resolve to cele-
> brate it in verse and prose all within the four seas of Ireland. And
> why should it do otherwise?

Compared to many of Yeats's other utterances in the *United Ireland* and the
Boston Pilot, the literary nationalism of the above passage is fairly mild.
Nevertheless, it was yet construed as being extreme by one of the most
respected English periodicals; in a note inscribed in John Quinn's copy of
Representative Irish Tales, Yeats mentioned that 'this book was reviewed by the
Saturday Review under the idea that it was written by a barbarous super-
republican American' (*Bibl*, 214). Keeping in mind this over-sensitivity to
Irish nationalism in the English media, and also the fact that he was writing
for Henley and was dependent on an English readership for his book sales
and royalties, one begins to understand his desire to avoid any association
between himself and Irish nationalism whilst writing for English periodicals.

Besides the changes already discussed, there is one striking addition to the
SO article. Notwithstanding the fact that most of Yeats's review is spent discussing Carleton as a novelist and very little space (about one-seventh of the
essay) is given to the *Red-Haired Man's Wife*, he does include one small detail
about the novel's original publication:

it was published a few years ago – (do the publishers know this?) – in the *Carlow College Magazine*, under the editorship of that Father Kavanagh who was killed by the fall of an image while celebrating mass, after a series of incidents that made the awe struck peasantry see in his death an event unearthly and tremendous. It is at last re-issued in a flaring red cover. (*SO*, 608; *UP1*, 142)

This is exactly the kind of thing that would interest Yeats, not out of any bias or scorn for superstition, but because he was genuinely interested in folklore and peasant beliefs. However, in the context of Henley's journal, it would have served another function, especially when it was a preface to a review of an Irish novel. A similar incident was reported by the magazine in its second issue:

Donegal is in a ferment over a series of miracles – chiefly of a therapeutic description – that are taking place all over the county. The blind are reported to be receiving their sight, and cripples to be casting their crutches to the winds in the most reckless fashion. The wonder-worker is not an aged statesman, but a young Catholic priest bearing the suggestive name of Larkin. (*SO*, 1.12.88, 35)

That the Irish, like other colonised people, were credulous, simplistic overgrown children who had to be shown the way to a higher stage of civilisation was the standard justification for the maintenance of the Union. Yeats's work in Henley's magazines, focusing as it did almost exclusively on folklore, fairy tales and ghost stories, would have reinforced this belief. The company who sang to sweeten Ireland's wrong was temporarily disbanded and the dictates of the Ferguson essay 'systimatically' forgotten.

— 4 —

Bred out of the Contagion of the Throng:
The Fall of Parnell and the Irish Literary Revival

I

The split in the Irish Parliamentary Party marks a turning point in the *United Ireland (UI)*. In the issue of 6.12.90 — the last day of the meeting in Committee Room 15 — Matthias Bodkin, the acting editor, denounced Parnell on O'Brien's instructions. Parnell subsequently stormed the newspaper's offices and expelled Bodkin. The issue of 13 December was destroyed and that of 20 December, under Edmund Leamy's editorship, came out strongly Parnellite.

Following the split, Parnell's political strategy changed in two important ways. Since Gladstone had dictated his expulsion from the party leadership, his faction calling itself the Independent Irish Party made a virtue out of necessity and stressed the importance of independence: English alliances were untrustworthy and Irishmen could only attain freedom through their own efforts. Parnell also adopted a hostile attitude towards England. His famous appeal to the hillside men followed naturally.[1] *UI* articles such as 'Mr John Dillon and Clerical Intimidation', 'Independence in Irish Politics' and 'The New Gladstonian Irishmen' (8.8.91, 5) reflected this Parnellite policy. As a logical corollary, the paper also stressed the necessity of independence in all occupations: religious, intellectual and social.

A spate of violent and polemical anti-English articles followed. The *UI* scoffed at an independence brokered by the Liberals and averred that, like Davis, it scorned 'the notion of assimilating our morals, manners, or passions to those of any other people on the face of God's earth; least of all would we wish to change the faithful, pure, natural, affectionate Irishman into that animal, John Bull' (7.2.91, 5). The Union of Hearts had been rent asunder and hell hath no fury like the paper scorned. The Sassenachs were now portrayed as bloodthirsty 'wolves . . . with famished and cruel jaws' who had patiently tracked down their natural prey, 'watching him with sleepless glittering eyes and gleaming teeth' (20.12.90, 5). Article after article warned 'our brothers in arms all over the world' against English perfidy: 'The history of our loyalty to English leaders is a history of desertion and defeat' (3.1.91, 3). While, earlier, the paper's poison ink had been reserved for the unionists, it now stained the whole English nation. The paper also made a concerted effort to woo the Fenians, especially after Parnell's death. Among other things, it published leaders by 'A Physical Force Man' (10.10.91, 5; 19.12.91, 5), organised a subscription for the Fenian leader James Stephens and presented him a house amid great fanfare.[2] It also started a new column, 'Among the Gaels', focusing on Gaelic Athletic Association (GAA) activities.

Shortly after the split, the newspaper's revenues decreased sharply. In August 1891, Bodkin, now editor of the anti-Parnellite *National Press*, predicted the *UI*'s demise claiming that its circulation had dropped to 5,000.[3] Though this cannot be taken entirely at face value, it does contain an element of truth. Advertisements in the paper were at an unprecedented low and, but for Parnell's death, which, ironically, gave the paper a new lease of life – the advertisements increased sharply for the 'funeral' issue – it would have certainly collapsed by the year's end. The decrease in advertisements and circulation was inevitable. The majority of the Land League branches had defected to the anti-Parnellites, the Catholic clergy had been denouncing Parnell and the *UI* from the pulpits, and electoral defeats (North Kilkenny, North Sligo and Carlow) followed in quick succession.

The paper was also having trouble finding suitable news items, especially for its cover and leaders pages. Political coverage was too embarrassing and the defection of the majority of the Land League meant that the paper's weekly report on the branches' activities occupied less space. Page 3, which normally covered the week's news, now carried a new column entitled 'Profitable Pig Keeping', which continued for a few weeks and then metamorphosed into 'Profitable Duck Keeping' and then to 'Profitable Rabbit Farming'. Later, the page was devoted entirely to athletics, ostensibly to advocate the 'development of the Athletic superiority of Irishmen' (11.5.95, 4). Gradually literary reviews and articles replaced the page 5 leaders and dominated the front page. Page 6, which was earlier devoted to Land League reports, now increasingly began to cover international news, something unprecedented in the paper. Readers were now told about 'The Chillian Revolution', 'The Outrages on Christians in China' and 'Troubles in the East' (12.9.91, 6). For twelve issues between 5.5.94 and 21.7.94 a full column on the cover page discussed Indian politics. Novels were serialised and new columns started. However, filling up page 1 with headline news that did not reflect badly on the Parnellites remained a problem and the newspaper resorted to some desperate measures. For three consecutive weeks the *UI* carried cover page articles on a French Count's Indian experiences (2.33 columns), an Irishman's rescue of a Russian aristocrat's grand-daughter and Robert Emmet's speech from the dock.[4] The extent of the newspaper's difficulties is also indicated by the fact that at one point Carleton and R. L. Stevenson were serialised simultaneously on the cover and leaders page respectively. For four months (26.1.95 to 20.4.95), Carleton occupied more than half of page 1.

The *UI*, hitherto a stark political weekly, eventually became Dublin's most literary paper and a major player in the Revival. It is therefore worth examining this transformation and how it came about. For the first four issues after the split (20.12.90 to 10.1.91), the *UI* was chock-full of political news, recriminations, accusations of betrayal, the North Kilkenny election propaganda and the election results and analysis. Literature was as peripheral as ever, and it seemed as if the split's effect on the paper's management and political agenda had left the literary policy changed. During this period, there was absolutely no indication whatsoever that the paper would experience a shortage of politically serviceable news in the future or alter its attitude towards literature. The defeat in Kilkenny changed all that. The shortage of news flattering the Parnellite cause and the paper's sudden interest in literature and international news between 17.1.91 and 21.3.91 was a sign of things to come. It was during this period that four new columns were started ('The Farm', 'Among the Gaels', 'North & South' and 'Beyond the Seas'), the last three on the cover page.

The North Sligo election effected another swing and for five issues between 28.3.91 and 25.4.91 political coverage and election propaganda dominated the newspaper, edging out non-political topics almost completely. With the defeat of the Parnellite candidate, political events were again too embarrassing to be given the same kind of extensive coverage. As a result, the paper rediscovered its literary enthusiasm for the next five issues (2.5.91 to 30.5.91). The fact that the paper's literary coverage had depended so entirely on the political fortunes of the Parnellites leads one to believe that, had Parnell won these elections, particularly Kilkenny, the *UI* would have remained as indifferent towards literature and the concept of a Literary Revival as it had always been. This is not to say that the Revival would not have occurred but that it would have been significantly retarded and of an altogether different character without the backing that it eventually received from the paper.

For the next five issues (6.6.91 to 4.7.91), propaganda for the Carlow election dominated the *UI* to the exclusion of everything else, but by now the writing was on the wall. Though literary coverage had been suspended, it was evidently only a temporary measure till the dearth of political news made itself felt again. What with the three Parnellite defeats and the drastically reduced revenues, this lack of cover-page news and the desperate attempts to fill in the gaps had put the paper on the brink of closure. With Parnell's death, literary articles, serialised novels and international news were dropped unceremoniously and the explosive headlines returned to the front page.

While the advertisements did not decrease for another year-and-a-half, suitable news items for pages 1 and 5 did. The emotional appeal of Parnell's death could not be flogged for ever. Until the Cork election results (14.11.92), political coverage filled the newspaper. In the number (21.11.91) immediately following the defeat of John Redmond, the leader of the Independent Party, international news returned to the cover page. From the next issue (28.11.91) onwards, literary reviews dominated page 5. So acute was the shortage of politically serviceable news that, on the eve of the Waterford contest (19.12.91) between Davitt and Redmond, '"Michael Davitt in Parliament" By a Physical Force Man' competed for cover-page prominence with a three-column review of 'John Boyle O'Reilly as a Poet of Humanity'. In the following issue (2.1.92), election results and coverage once again edged out literary articles on pages 1 and 5, but by the next week normalcy had returned and so had literary and international news.

The *UI*'s enhanced literary and international coverage was not a matter of choice but of necessity, caused by the shortage of newsworthy items from a Parnellite perspective. Before the split, literary articles and reviews annually averaged about 12 columns. (In 1888 they amounted to about 12 columns; in the 15 issues prior to the split [30.8.90 to 2.12.90] they amounted to four columns, which roughly corresponds to an average of 12 columns annually.) However, in the 15 issues after the split (20.12.90 to 28.3.90) literary articles and reviews amounted to 21 columns. In the four years before the split (4.12.86 to 6.12.90) international coverage averaged one column per year; in the first five years after the split (till 7.12.95) it averaged about 12 columns per year.[5] By 2 April 1892, political news worth reporting for a Parnellite paper had become so scarce that the *UI* announced its lack of interest in the subject: 'Politics just now are in the doldrums. There is no progress to report ...' (5). The next week it started on a new policy of engineering debates to fill up the cover and leaders pages, a feature that would prove more endurable than travel items like 'A Bird's Eye View of Boston' (2.4.92, 5) or occasional pieces of the kind that the paper had depended on hitherto. Beginning with 'The Irish Intellectual Capital: Where is it?' (9.4.92 to 9.7.92), the paper orchestrated debates on 'Irish Nationalists and Trinity College' (16.4.92 to 30.7.92), 'A Satisfactory Constitution for Ireland' (3.9.92 to 28.1.93), the dating of the 'Irish Literary Revival' (21.4.94 to 19.5.94), 'The *Irishman* and Mr Davitt' (28.7.94 to 22.9.94) and even on the political situation in India

(16.6.94 to 21.7.94). These debates started on the leaders page but rapidly shifted to the cover, where they remained for a while. However, they were always interrupted by the intermittent and sporadic outbursts of politically newsworthy items and Parnell's death anniversary. Not just the debates, but international news, athletics, literary coverage and Revival propaganda were altogether excluded on such occasions to make room for politics.[6] To all effects and purposes, the *UI* was still primarily a political newspaper and the Parnellites' premier media organ. However, so long as the weekly news did not advance its cause, it was forced to resort to other means, including front-page gossip columns,[7] to fill up its pages and stay afloat.

II

The shortage of politically serviceable news items resulted in the *UI* gradually shifting its attention from politics to literature. However, even though they were relatively downplayed, Parnellite politics and the Parnellite agenda determined the paper's literary policy. In tandem with Parnell's call to the 'hillside men', the *UI*'s literary articles struck a Fenian note wherever possible. As in the past, though not as frequently, book reviews were given a political slant but with a different political agenda. Hence when introducing Patrick O'Brien's 'The Emerald Isle', the reviewer emphasised that the poem 'is conceived in a martial spirit', that it 'is an assertion of the rights of Irishmen to achieve liberty by arms' and that the author 'was inclined to believe that Ireland could never gain her just rights by constitutional means' (31.1.91, 6). However, it was mostly only a slant, not an exclusive preoccupation with the book's political merits. The paper also published Fenian poems advocating violent uprisings. The following is a particularly good example:

> The Old Pike' by 'Ned of the Hill'
>
> The ash-shaft may be rotten –
> Its steel shall shine again;
> (Of treachery to Ireland
> *That* never bore a stain),
> It drank at Ross and Wexford
> Of Saxon blood its fill,
> And charged with Father Murphey
> The day on Oulart Hill.
>   . . .
> Once more the fates decided
> Our country should remain

A slave to faithless Albion
And drag a weary chain.
But take you, son, this rebel pike –
Be grief or joy your fate,
Bear with it to the Sassanach
My heritage of hate.

(2.5.91, 1)

During the Irish–Liberal alliance the *UI*'s political versifiers had directed their ire at the unionists and crowned the nationalists with their paeans. The nationality of their heroes or villains was not significant. Now, the paper attacked the whole English nation, advocated unremitting hostility towards it and used literature as a means to this end:

> I am one of those who believe that a vigorous Irish Nationality, though based largely on pure love of country, cannot be altogether divorced from a feeling of hate for English tyranny ... and I hold that the keeping these wrongs, the 'treasured wrongs' of centuries, in our hearts is one of the surest means of preventing us ever being false to our country or selling our birthright for a mere mess of pottage. Their repetition, even in a mild way, on the stage would make the possibility of forgetting them, humanly speaking, out of the question. (14.4.94, 1)

The paper also attacked the anti-Parnellite press with equal hostility. Politically motivated reviews of the earlier kind were rare. However, in the case of the few anti-Parnellite writers – the Literary Revival being essentially a Parnellite affair – political hostilities influenced literary evaluations. Before the split Katharine Tynan had been a favourite with the newspaper and was always reviewed in extravagant terms. However, after the split, with the paper becoming more conscious of its literary role, Tynan fell out of favour. Her reviews and poems were still published by the *UI* but her own books met with marked disapproval. However, when the anti-Parnellite *National Press* attacked her biography of Mother Xaveria, *A Nun: Her Friends and her Order*, the *UI* immediately rallied round:

> Miss Tynan is a Parnellite; but even that fact could not sufficiently explain to me why any Irishman should so very ungallantly and so very coarsely attack the most distinguished Irish literary lady of our generation. (19.9.91, 1)

To make further amends it printed a glowing review from the *Athenaeum* which it claimed had better literary credentials than Tynan's revilers.[8] However, on the rare occasion, the *UI* too was as guilty as its anti-Parnellite rivals.

While attacking Edna Lyall's *Doreen* the paper averred that her 'being a great admirer of Mr Gladstone' was responsible for her novel's 'perfect travesty of Irish politics' (24.11.94, 1).

Towards the unionists, however, the *UI*'s attitude changed enormously. For three consecutive years (1892–94) immediately after the split, O'Grady's books were nominated as the *UI*'s 'Christmas Book for Boys'.[9] He was a true Irishman 'of whose literary ability every Irishman worthy of the name should be proud' (7.5.92, 1). The *UI* took it as a sign of literary prosperity that his books were available on Irish bookstalls and that he could be praised in a nationalist newspaper despite his unionist views. The weekly's attitude towards unionist newspapers underwent a similar transformation. After the split not only did it discontinue its attacks and threats, but it also established a kind of *entente cordiale* with the unionist media. It urged them to promote Irish literature and reprinted many of their articles, including those critical of the *UI*. It also preached tolerance and fairness.[10] The unionist media in turn congratulated the weekly for its 'improved tone' and remarked on its sudden transformation:

> Not long ago, for example, nothing said, done, or written by any Irishman of Conservative political opinions was ever greeted by the so-called patriotic organs with anything but ridicule and contumely. The only form of patriotism, the only form of Irish effort in any direction recognised in those quarters was something calculated directly or indirectly to play into and assist the Home Rule movement . . . In other words, we notice now in these quarters an appreciation of literature as literature, and a desire to foster good work done in that line, let the politics of the writer be what they may. (23.4.92, 1; reprinted from *Dublin Daily Express*)[11]

This rapprochement with unionists was dictated by political rather than literary considerations. After the split, the Parnellites had made a concerted effort to woo unionist votes and urged a form of tactical voting against the clerically dominated anti-Parnellites.[12]

The most significant difference in the *UI*'s literary coverage lay in its attitude towards literature. Not only was literature now considered to be on a par with politics in the national struggle, but it was also thought to be the more important player. Within six months of the split the paper proclaimed that 'political liberty alone will not make Ireland a nation' (30.5.91, 1), something that would have perplexed O'Brien's *UI*, believing as it did that Home Rule was the panacea for all of Ireland's woes. Averring that 'much of what is noblest in Irish National Sentiment had its origin in the literature of Ireland' and that it is from this very source that 'both Nationality and Manhood'

(4.6.92, 5) draw their sustenance, the paper proclaimed literature to be the surest safeguard for the nation's dignity and independence. It was 'above and beyond politics' (4.6.92, 5) in its scope. Within six months the tables had turned and now politics was the poor handmaiden. In comparison with literature, its influence 'would be small in creating the sturdy *Irishism* amongst our people which will be the ultimate guardian of our national liberties'. So long as Ireland had a thriving national literature she 'need never fear coercion acts or . . . for the matter of that, Home Rule Bills' (9.4.92, 5). Both had been rendered superfluous, for the mantle would now be borne by literature. Literature, it was claimed, would not by itself bring Ireland freedom but it would make her worthy of it.

Despite the compulsions underlying the *UI*'s literary coverage rendering it a substitute for serviceable political news, its post-split literary character underwent a sea-change. This had a significant impact on the development of Irish literature and on the Irish Literary Revival. Earlier a book was mentioned only if it had any political import; its being praised or criticised depended entirely on whether its writer was a nationalist or a unionist, and, if the former, the level of praise was commensurate with the book's propagandistic value. After the split, political considerations did impinge on the paper's literary perspective but not as stridently. No longer a poor handmaiden, but a player in its own right, literature was allowed to develop in ways that were not ostensibly political. The direct political relevance of a work hardly figured as a critical yardstick and reviews were no longer thinly disguised political propaganda. The *UI*'s annual four-page literature supplement exemplifies this difference. Before the split, it was entitled *A Campaign Christmas* and its stories and poems were blatantly propagandistic and full of references to the Plan of Campaign, the Land League, boycotting, eviction, rack-renting landlords, land grabbers and jury packing. Their constant theme was that of a unified people, solidly behind the nationalist politicians, stoutly opposing the government and succeeding in the end. After the split, the supplement's political nomenclature was dropped as was its propagandistic objective; the contents were now mainly literary and non-political.

The paper's attitude towards Ireland's lack of a literature is another area where the difference between the pre- and post-split *UI* is very evident. Before the split this lack was regretted but it was felt that the time was not ripe for literature to come into its own, and that to want otherwise would be irresponsible. Literature could not feed starving peasants or fight an alien rule that was draining the life blood of Ireland. 'We must have butter to our bread before we can lay money aside to buy books' (10.4.86, 7). There was no fear, however, that such neglect would dry Ireland's vast reservoirs of poetic talent. Her literary 'genius' is 'coterminous with the existence of the Irish race itself. It is like the soul, an imperishable essence.' All it needed to bloom gloriously was to be 'warmed by the sun of freedom' whose first rays were already visible:

> The clouds which have so long overhung our isle are lifting; the flush of dawn is beginning to brighten our horizon; the perfumed breeze of liberty is sighing faintly over the sea. Its inspiration must fire our poets, a fostering home legislation must retain at home the intellectual forces which an alien and unnatural policy has hitherto driven forth to enrich and adorn the brows of the strangers. (13.4.89, 3)

A year before the split the paper was confident that an Irish 'renaissance ... [would] take place both in Irish art and letters under the sun of a new-born National life' (14.12.89, 5) and not till then. After the split, however, article after article, with titles such as 'Has Ireland Become Songless?' (10.10.91, 1–2), bemoaned the lack of an Irish literature, the dearth of writers and the apathy of booksellers, publishers and editors.[13] Most of all they bemoaned the indifference towards Irish literature and the anglophilic tastes of readers and critics. Not merely did they bemoan, they also exhorted these various cogs in the literary chain to bestir themselves and remedy a national shame. The Scots and the English, it was claimed, are indisputably duller and yet have a thriving literature; Irish writers, on the other hand, would not figure even amongst the 'second rate literary men of the day'. The situation, though, was not irredeemable:

> There is nothing plainer under the sun than that Ireland could build up a literature of her own, if the cultivated classes of the country and the young fellows of talent had spirit and energy and self-sacrifice enough to 'face the situation.' (14.2.91, 5)

Earlier, self-sacrifice, spirit and energy were associated with the political struggle, never with literature. Now, the paper anxiously awaited the day when Ireland's literature would 'after her faith, be her greatest glory' (24.6.93, 4) and 'a beauty and a possession for the entire world' (21.2.93, 1).

Eight months before the split, the paper justified Ireland's literary unproductivity by blaming the political situation. An alien rule had made Ireland too 'depressing' a place. Furthermore, its 'artificial state of "civilisation"' leaving no room for intellectual or emotional stimulation demanded that a man imbibe only that modicum of literature required for a good job. Consequently, an 'entirely literary' (5.4.90, 1) book was doomed and literature became a profession open only to the rich or reckless. In England, the article went on to argue, Irish littérateurs suffered no such handicap. The same issue (6) also published an extract from Justin McCarthy's article in *The Times* reiterating the same arguments. According to him, Irish intellect was, quite justifiably, absorbed by politics. Citing the example of Fichte, who had disbanded his lectures during Napoleon's invasion, McCarthy defended Irish artists and intellectuals for similarly going into hibernation. When Ireland became independent, he asserted, they would return and Irish art and intellect would flourish once again. Nine months later, i.e. one month after the split, the *UI*'s view had changed completely. Now it was not the political situation but artists, readers, critics, booksellers, newspaper editors and publishers that were blamed for the lamentable barrenness of the Irish literary landscape:

> How long is the rich field to lie fallow, the rig-furrows only of which were marked by the plough-shares of Ferguson and Davis? Is the bleeding process to go on forever? Or is Irish fame not worth the fight for it? Is it nothing to an Irish Poet! 'One is much', says Heine,' when one is a poet, and especially when one is a great German lyrical poet.' Why should not 'one be much' under similar circumstances in Ireland? The fact is, in modern literature Ireland is the poorest province we know of. (24.1.91, 5)

Here the paper roundly dismisses its own erstwhile attitude towards the status of a poet. Before the split, he was a mere rhymester who versified political propaganda in the weekly column of lampoons and paeans. At best, he was a bugler exhorting a regiment in battle. In either case, he was a mere underling. Now, the paper distances itself from this perspective and instead bestows on the poet a high status which is absolute, unconditional and independent of the political situation. Further, the confidence in the never-ending and perennially fresh reservoir of Irish literary talent is missing; instead there is a fear that Irish talent awaiting fertilisation may dry up and go to seed, thereby exacerbating the existing literary famine. A year earlier, Ireland's literary sterility was viewed with equanimity in the confidence that a dose of political independence would revive its potency. Now, however, the same situation is seen as dire, life-threatening and in need of immediate attention. This, a subsequent article asserted, is 'our darkest hour' (11.6.92, 1). The earlier argument that the time was out of joint was dismissed out of hand:

> Any time during the last twenty years that enthusiastic men have endeavoured to form such [National literary] societies, they have been met on all sides by the objection that the time was not yet ripe for such a movement, and that, above all, political affairs were critical. 'Let us wait', said the objectors, 'for quieter times.' Alas! We have been waiting for quieter times all our lives. Well, but we are much mistaken if [we] ... have not made up [our] minds that the

> waiting policy is a huge mistake, and that the day is now, and the
> hour. (18.6.92, 5)

Made on the eve of a general election, the above assertion is that much more emphatic a rejection of the earlier position. Also, quite startling is the schizo-phrenic cleavage that the paper makes between them, 'the objectors', and us, the enthusiasts, given that in the pre-split period the *UI* had sided with the objectors rather than the enthusiasts in opposing the idea of a literary revival for precisely the reasons mentioned. This was not the only occasion that the paper would betray such symptoms with regard to its former self and, Dr Jekyll-like, disown Mr Hyde. Three months after the above article, while reviewing Irish newspapers, it remarked that the *UI* 'after a hideous period of dull vulgarity before the great split of December, '90 . . . has become, under its present editors, the most literary paper in Dublin. That is, it is the most inti-mately concerned with literature' (10.9.92, 2). It is no coincidence that, on the two occasions the paper displays this schizophrenia, it does so with refer-ence to the split and on both occasions uses literature to highlight the differ-ence. This assumes importance when discussing the beginnings of the Revival.

The pre-split articles discussed earlier (13.4.89, 3, and 5.4.90, 1) alluded to the success of Irish writers settled in England. While the second article did not regret this phenomenon, the first regretted the loss to Ireland, blamed it on 'alien rule' and concluded with the confidence that the loss was only tem-porary. There was no cause for concern, as expatriate writers would return home once Ireland was free. As always, Home Rule would resolve everything. This simplistic approach precluded the possibility that these writers may have become anglicised, lost their 'Celtic strain' and, worse still, that they may be serving imperial interests. However, it was only literature, and for the old *UI* lending one's horse to the British garrison in Ireland was of more immedi-ate concern. Within a month of the split, the sea change in the newspaper's attitude is all too evident. While reviewing Francis O'Donnell's poems, the *UI* ranked him above the Young Irelanders. Nevertheless, this was not a mat-ter of pride but of regret because O'Donnell had migrated to England and catered to an English audience. As a result, his Irishness had been eroded by 'Cockney influences and Cockney ways' (24.1.91, 5): his sensibilities were English, his nature poems described an English landscape and his Irish work, though full of Irish, Catholic and national sentiments, was quite artificial and paled in comparison. After a violent diatribe against the hegemony of Eng-lish tastes in Ireland, the article lamented that O'Donnell had not adorned the Irish Valhalla. In a later article the paper urged literary émigrés to return, claiming that, though England had benefited them financially in the short term, it was at the expense of their future literary reputations.[14] And not merely their literary reputations, but also their individual and national pride:

Celtic genius will never find a home in Ireland, but will fly to the Thames, and wearing a rose in its breast where it should have worn a shamrock, it will twist its face to suit the requirements of Mr Bull, and limp about the pavements of London with the chains of Cockney fashion on its limbs, and the rust of Cockney flunkeyism in its soul. (7.2.91, 5)

The metonymic and pejorative use of 'Cockney' for 'English' here and in the above quotation (24.1.95, 5) indicates the newspaper's bitterness over literary anglicisation, which is presented as a kind of humiliating self-debasement. Even the consolation afforded by Messrs Arnold, Renan and co. that the Celtic strain had ennobled, spiritualised and strengthened the whole body of English literature did not mitigate the *UI*'s bitterness and sense of loss. 'Why should the Celtic genius of Ireland', it exclaimed, 'go to perfect and glorify English literature when it might have a literature of its own? Did we come to the world merely to wreathe laurels around the brows of our conquerors? . . . are we willing to remain mere literary hewers of wood and drawers of water?' (14.2.91, 5). 'We have made quite enough Shakespeares and Burkes and Byrons and Charlotte Brontes for "*English* Literature". Our idea now is to make them for *Irish* literature' (14.4.94, 1). Indeed, such consolations only strengthened the paper's determination, prompting it to declare that it would use all its resources and influence to fight this subservience.[15]

The *UI* certainly lived up to its promise. It was aware that the success of its endeavour depended not merely on the writers but also on critics, publishers, newspaper editors, booksellers and finally readers. The paper closely monitored the publication of Irish books, reviewed them enthusiastically and at length, and often noticed them even before they were published.[16] The reviews played unashamedly on their readers' emotional sensibilities. Apropos of the *Patriot Parliament*, readers were told that 'the man will "hang his head for shame" who gave not to the first edition of this volume of *our* Library the hospitality of his heart and of his home' (23.9.93, 4; emphasis added). The use of the possessive pronoun is indicative of the paper's deep identification with the whole Revival enterprise. Buying an Irish book was made tantamount to striking a blow for freedom. The National Library Scheme was presented as being 'part of a noble National design, of a lofty National endeavour. Every purchaser of the book, every man who induces another to purchase it, contributes to the effective carrying out of that endeavour.' Publishers were rebuked for their apathy and, in a tactic reminiscent of the older *UI*, booksellers had their names publicised for not stocking Irish books. Perhaps most significant of all was the paper's demand, as a prerequisite for an Irish literature, for 'that serious, deep, broad, profound criticism which is one of the greatest formative influences in a literature, and which is such a large and important element in the culture and education of the people' (14.2.91, 5). This was something Yeats had been urging ever since his Ferguson essay in 1886 when he attacked Dowden for having failed Irish writers. Independence was once again the key word, but with regard not only to English influence – and here the *UI* was breaking fresh ground – but also patriotic considerations. Patriotism, the paper asserted, must not be allowed to influence literary criticism and evaluation.[17] However, it was itself often guilty of transgression.

The *UI* exploited every opportunity to encourage writers to create an Irish literature along Irish lines. This involved: writing primarily for an Irish audience, using Irish themes, having Irish locales and publishing in Ireland. Numerous articles advised writers on the best way of achieving a national literature, possible themes, pitfalls and techniques.[18] The pre-split attacks on English writers and literature remained integral to literary reviewing, but with a slight difference. The attacks now were more virulent and the paper found it inexcusable that Irish people should continue to read this 'low and cheap literature' instead of boycotting 'the nasty stuff', especially since they now had a wholesome and soul-enriching alternative in Irish literature, 'the best books the world has ever known' (15.8.91, 1).

Integral also to the *UI*'s literary nationalism was its unabashed parochialism. In a speech reported by the *UI*, Charles Gavan Duffy had averred that literature would teach Irishmen 'to understand their own country' (24.6.93, 1, 4) and 'render her more essentially our own'. It would also dispel the ignorance that 'relaxes our grasp on our country'. While proclaiming (à la Foucault) that '*Knowledge is power*', the paper enthusiastically endorsed Duffy's view as 'the *raison d'être* of the new Irish movement'. In its efforts to de-anglicise Irish literature, the paper advocated a narrow parochialism and xenophobia quite similar to its pre-split attitude except that it was now directed towards building a national literature. '*We do not work on our own material*' (14.2.91, 5), the paper insisted, and therefore we have no literature, implying thereby that writing on non-Irish topics by Irishmen was not Irish. (Yeats too would dismiss the claims of Swift, Burke, and Goldsmith for similar reasons before *UI* readers.)[19] Irish writers did not know their subject. The subject, of course, was Ireland and knowing Ireland entailed knowing its topography, history and people. To be an Irish writer was not merely a matter of talent or inspiration. 'It is a matter of knowledge, of information, of experience.' Since this itself would take a lifetime to achieve, and since English influence corrupted, the paper averred: 'He only is safe, indeed, who stays at home' (24.1.91, 5).

> In art, eclecticism means loss of character, and character is everything in art . . . And national character can only be acquired by

remaining at home, saturating ourselves so thoroughly in the
spirit of our land until it oozes from our pens and pencils in every
slightest word, in every slightest touch. Our lives should be one
long sacrifice for this one thing – national character. Foreign
travel should be eschewed, we should turn our eyes from Paris
and Rome and fix them on our own fields; *we should strive to
remain ignorant, making our lives mole-like, burrowing only in our own
parish soil.* (11.4.91, 1; emphasis added)

The only desirable type of character, according to this extract, is national
character and this is essentially opposed to cosmopolitanism, which deracinates and loosens one's hold over the motherland. All other interests should
be subservient to developing this trait, which must inform everything one
writes. The writer's life ambition should be to become as Irish as possible and
this necessarily entails a studied ignorance of everything non-Irish. The
paper's own view of what characterised Irish literature was fairly narrow and
constricting. A book was considered 'Irish' if it was published in Ireland, written in an 'Irish' style and if it dealt with Irish topics. Once it fulfilled any of
these criteria, it was praised in patriotic and hyperbolic terms. P. J. McCall's
Irish Nóiníns, much to Yeats's irritation, was hailed as 'a distinctly and distinctively Irish production' with an 'intensely Irish atmosphere and its firm,
almost defiant, Irish point of view'. 'It has grown naturally out of the Irish
soil, and in the Irish air it will flourish and live.' It was above all 'Irish – kindly
Irish of the Irish, and neither Saxon nor Italian':

It was conceived in Ireland, written in Ireland, printed and published in Ireland; and one feels in reading it that the author meant
it for his own people . . . You feel instinctively on reading it that
it has gone out into the world ready to stand or fall by the judgement of Irish people, and equally ready, if necessary, to maintain
an adamantine indifference to the judgement of all the rest of the
world.

And I hold that this is the only logical or honourable position for an Irish book to take up if we are to have a really national
literature. (10.11.94, 1)

It may seem surprising today, but the repetition of 'Irish' and 'Ireland' was
meant to exhort, not jar. The de-anglicising project and the Parnellite focus
on independence meant that Irishness could not be over-emphasised. However, in a country as divided as Ireland, any view of Irishness was bound to
be exclusive and excluding. Given the paper's own macho and political perspective on literary Irishness, the female voice was eminently vulnerable to
the charge of being un-Irish as was that of a different political ideology or

ethnic, racial, or religious background. What exactly constituted Irishness, Irish style, etc., never was and never could be defined and this suited the newspaper quite well. It meant that the *UI* became the sole judge in this matter. For example, it decided that there were some subjects, though it did not mention which, that were 'necessarily most foreign to the Irish instinct and intellect' (25.7.91, 1), and that the genre of landscape poetry was as un-Irish as 'transcendentalism' (by which it meant modernism and non-realism) and '*fin de siècle*' literature.[20] Shortly after the split, Stephen Gwynn wrote in to protest against the paper having monopolised Irishness and reduced it to three arbitrary categories, namely style, locale and subject.[21] He argued that such narrow definitions would exclude Shakespeare, Byron, Shelley and Browning from Englishness because they often wrote on foreign subjects in foreign places. There was no editorial response.

The paper's literary perspective was governed by political considerations in as much as its political agenda influenced its literary policy, and literature's enhanced importance derived from its potential service to the national cause. These considerations were essentially Parnellite. After the split, the paper's efforts to create a distinctively Irish literature derived from its insistence on independence in all spheres of life. 'We do not see why it should not be possible to establish a standard of patriotism in Irish art and literature as well as in Irish politics' (14.2.91, 5). Since political patriotism entailed shrugging off a dependence on English politicians, the paper insisted that, if its readers wished 'to be not only patriotic but also consistent', they would have to rid their literature of 'those insidious Anglicising effects' (28.2.91, 1) and 'do away with all such poisonous pabulum' (28.3.91, 1). When told that London and not Dublin was Ireland's intellectual capital, the paper remonstrated acerbically: 'We have had quite enough London centralisation without making London the centre of an attempt one of whose great objects will be to *break down the system*' (30.7.92, 5; emphasis added). The Parnellite agenda underpinning the paper's interest in the Revival was not directly stressed but it dominated its overall attitude towards literature: its whole de-anglicising endeavour, as well as the emphasis on independence, Irish subject matter and themes, had a strong Parnellite subtext. A year after it began championing the Revival, the paper clarified the principles governing its literary interests:

> Twelve months ago we wrote in these columns an article which attracted attention on both sides of the Channel, and on both sides of the Atlantic, that *a mere Parliament* alone would not make Ireland the nation we longed to see her. We held that *all true and thinking Nationalists* are striving not alone for independence in politics, but for independence in literature and in art. Indeed, we went so far as to say that without these we could never become

the independent people we hoped one day to be. We stand by these principles . . . It is in fact conceivable that *a native legislature of a certain character* might not work towards this sentiment at all; it is possible, indeed, that it might work in the very opposite direction . . . If we wish to become a self-respecting, self-relying, *and really independent nation*, we must have minds of our own. We must be ourselves. We must stop the Anglicising process, which, without any doubt in the world, is going on today at a pace that to *genuine Nationalists* is alarming. (9.4.92, 5; emphasis added)

Parnell's rejecting the Liberal alliance, even if it meant rejecting the possibility of Home Rule, had been a significant factor leading to the split. The Parnellites had suffered heavy defeats in the polls and, with a general election in which a Liberal victory was likely just a few months away, it seemed inevitable that Home Rule would be an anti-Parnellite–Liberal affair. This would explain the *UI*'s scepticism towards 'a mere Parliament' and a 'native legislature of a certain character' as well as its desire to divert 'all true and thinking Nationalists' (read Parnellites) away from a politics which was subservient (not to mention successful), to a literature that would make Ireland a 'really independent nation'. With its party having been routed in the political sphere, the paper had turned its attention to literature and culture with the clear intention of stamping them with the Parnellite brand. The ends were still political, and 'real', 'genuine' or simply 'Parnellite' independence in literature was an attempt to further the Parnellite cause by other means.

The *UI* had championed the Revival and therefore its views were influential. Its view that literature should be subservient to Parnellite politics was supported by some prominent Revivalists, such as Dr Anthony McBride and John Augustus O'Shea. McBride had written a polemical letter to the paper arguing that the 'Irish literary revival, or any other Irish revival . . . is part expression [*sic*] of the great national desire of the Irish people, it is part and parcel – when properly guided – of the Irish movement for freedom'. Claiming that the attempt to separate the two was essentially a plot hatched by the Irish Whigs in the London-based Irish Literary Society (ILS), he adverted to O'Connell and Parnell's alliance with the Whigs and argued that the advent of anglicised Irishmen 'with their concomitant "Whiggish ideas and English-cum-Irish brogue"' had brought about the failure of every Irish movement. In what was probably an allusion to Yeats, he claimed that 'Anglicised Irishmen' had personal motives in desiring the separation of politics from literature:

'Litterateurs, their lives, their works, their promise', were not supreme and are not supreme questions for Ireland; they are only

a factor in the working out of the main and supreme problem of
National Independence. (5.5.94, 1)

McBride's use of political examples to prove a point about a literary society
indicates how deeply intermeshed the two seemingly disparate issues were.
His ire had been provoked by the suspicion that the ILS had been taken over
by the anti-Parnellites and was toeing the Liberal line. His position as treas-
urer of the Irish National Alliance meant that his views would carry weight
with the *UI*. They did, and his letter was published on the cover page. The
allegation was serious enough to merit a prompt reply by W. P. Ryan, published again on the cover page (12.5.94), claiming that McBride's fears were
unfounded and that the ILS and its committee were principally Parnellites.
As examples he adduced the names of Barry O'Brien, Yeats, Lionel Johnson
and Mark Ryan. Not only was the literary enterprise riven with the political rivalries that characterised national politics, it was also equally volatile.

Largely, literature still served a political function, whether it was preparing
the people intellectually, spiritually and culturally for political liberty or providing an effective future safeguard for that liberty when it finally arrived. The
difference between the *UI* before and after the split was that earlier the paper
had considered literature an insignificant player in the freedom struggle; now
it was held to be as important if not more than the political manoeuvrings
in Westminster or in the Clan na Gael in America. For Irish writers, this
altered perspective made the *UI* an oasis in the otherwise unwelcoming and
barren landscape of Irish journalism. Not surprisingly, they flocked to its
shores, even if it meant adopting its political principles and its sometimes not-
wholly-appealing literary agenda.

III

The *UI* played a major role in conceptualising, organising and propagating
the Irish Literary Revival. Its decision to do so was taken consciously almost
immediately after the split when the paper increased its literary coverage:

The Irish Intellectual Capital: Where is it?

It is *here* – in Dublin. When eighteen months ago, the conductors
of this journal decided, in the interests of Irish literature . . . to
devote as much of its space as its political and other obligations
would permit to certain intellectual interests so long neglected
by our newspapers and public men, they hoped that, perhaps, in
the not distant future some good might in consequence come to
Ireland. Their endeavours have been rewarded . . . today, after only

a year and a half's exhortations, we are face to face with a movement which, for the future of Irish literature and art, promises to
rival the efforts of Young Ireland. Eighteen months ago there was
no man so poor as to do Irish national intellectual life reverence;
today – why, today, good sirs, it promises to stand against the
world! (4.6.92, 1)

Though the literary impetus was provided by the Parnellite débâcle at the
polls when political coverage was proving too embarrassing, what made it
stick was the fact that the literary agenda coincided with and ratified the Parnellite stance on independence. That Leamy and McGrath – both literary
men – controlled the paper's overall policy and literary sections, respectively,
also cemented the *UI*'s relationship with the Revival. However, this last factor should not be overestimated, for even in the pre-split period the paper had
its share of literary personalities – William O'Brien, the editor, and Justin
McCarthy, one of the *UI*'s directors and shareholders – but that did not then
affect its literary perspective.

The *UI*'s efforts to create a national literature and resist literary anglicisation were not restricted to its own columns or correspondents. Within two
months of the split, it boasted that its efforts in bringing about an 'Irish Literary *Renaissance*' (28.2.91, 1) had encouraged other papers. It engineered
debates on literary topics attracting national attention. These debates drew
numerous letters and the attention of nationalist as well as unionist newspapers, which conducted their own parallel discussions which the *UI* subsequently reprinted. Newspaper editors across the political spectrum were
urged to support the Revival as a sign of their patriotism and, when they rallied to the task, they did so citing the *UI* as an example. Although a new
entrant in the literary field, the *UI* took up a proprietorial attitude towards
the Revival. It noted its progress with satisfaction, urged other newspapers to
support it and commended them when they complied.[22] It referred to its role
in this matter as a 'mission' (24.11.94, 5) and indeed it set about fulfilling it
with missionary zeal. Recognising the tremendous power it wielded over
public opinion, it noted that a newspaper's *raison d'être* lay in not merely supplying an existing demand but in creating it.

Irish people are notoriously the least inclined of any to show
what they want in literature, and even if the reverse were the case
some enterprise is still essential. A newspaper is generally started
not in order to cope with a loudly-expressed demand, but to
practically create it – except in very rare instances. (14.5.92, 5)

It conceded that Dr Shaw's unionist *Evening Mail* was Dublin's best-written
paper, but it appropriated for itself the status of the 'most literary paper in

Dublin. That is, it is the most intimately concerned with literature' (10.9.92, 2). Both claims, namely that it was Dublin's most literary paper and that the Revival was its baby, are corroborated by the increased coverage of literature in the paper and by its numerous exhortations to writers, readers and publishers after December 1890. They are also corroborated by the contemporary opinions of other newspapers and readers. The *Chicago Citizen* noted in its issue of 28 February 1891 that the '*UI* has followed up its plea for Irish nationality of the true type with a stirring appeal for the resuscitation of Irish literature' (28.3.91, 1). The unionist media too commended the *UI*'s efforts at de-anglicising Irishmen and promoting Irish literature. Based on the *UI*'s 'improved, and we will add, more cultured tone', the *Dublin Daily Express* of 16 April 1892 expressed a hope, that 'in the future an Anglo-Irish school of literature may again strike root and bear fruit' (23.4.92, 1). Readers too commended the paper's new-found literary zeal.[23]

The argument as to when exactly the Revival began has engaged scholars, commentators and even the participants of that event from the early part of the last century right up to the present day and there seems to be little agreement among them. While T. W. Rolleston located it in the poetry of the Young Irelanders, particularly Mangan and Ferguson, A. E. Boyd dated it to the publication of Standish O'Grady's *History of Ireland* (1878).[24] The earliest debate about the dating of the Revival is perhaps that between W. P. Ryan and John McGrath in the *UI*'s columns. This debate is interesting because it anticipates arguments propounded by later theorists and clarifies many subsequent misconceptions.

In 1894, when W. P. Ryan's book, the *Irish Literary Revival*, was published, the paper was grateful for 'some kindly references to the assistance rendered to the new movement by *UI*' (14.4.94, 1). However, Ryan had located the beginnings of the Revival in the early 1880s, as Roy Foster has more recently done, and in the Southwark Irish Literary Club. The *UI* would have none of it. It argued that the present interest in Irish literature 'is not to be traced to any society' any more than it is to the early eighties or the forties when 'the people had been surfeited with politics' (21.4.94, 1). Anticipating Yeats's later assertion, the *UI* argued that the Parnellite split had marked the turning point, 'the end of one epoch and the beginning of another'. Prior to that, 'anywhere that literature lifted a head, it is hardly an exaggeration to say, that head was struck ... *In November 1890, there was as much indication of an Irish Literary Revival as there is at the present moment of a revival of Irish Paganism*' (emphasis added).[25] What changed attitudes were 'the times and the events' capitalised upon by the enterprise and dedication of the *UI*. While conceding that the Southwark and other literary clubs did do good work, the *UI* argued that these efforts would not have counted for much 'had it not been that the tide was taken at the flood – largely through the prompt action of this journal, as Mr Ryan justly says'.

In his article 'The Fall of Parnell', published in 1976, John Kelly surveyed the debate on the origins of the Revival (T. W. Rolleston, A. E. Boyd, F. Mac-Manus, AE, Yeats) and summarised the broad arguments.[26] Though he did not take cognisance of the *UI* debate, he quite rightly pointed out that 'the critics involved have not sufficiently defined what they mean by a literary "movement," or, more specifically, what they understand the Irish literary "revival" to have been' (2). His definition of the terms 'Revival' and 'movement' are succinct and apposite. Rather than geographic proximity – according to AE, a literary movement was 'five or six people who live in the same town and hate each other cordially' (2) – or the publication of particular books of literary or historical significance, Kelly argues that 'the term "movement" implies a community of interests, a certain coherence of outlook, a sense of shared purpose not merely among the writers involved but also among their readers. The publication of individual books may in time produce such a cumulative effect but this will be very gradual.' His views on the Irish Revival are particularly germane to this discussion and worth quoting at length:

> But the interest in Irish literature in the early nineties was not such a gradual process: it happened suddenly. Contemporaries were astonished at the speed with which cultural self-awareness grew in Ireland at this time and already in 1893 Dublin critics were conscious that Irish literature had taken a new aspect, that there was an interest in books and ideas such as had not been known since the Young Ireland movement in the forties. Nor was the phrase 'Irish literary revival' one coined with the benefit of hindsight: it was already in use by 1892. (2–3)

Though Kelly instances the issue of 4 June 1892 as the first use of the phrase 'Irish literary revival' or 'Irish Literary Renaissance', it was, as we have seen, used by the *United Ireland* more than a year earlier in its issue of 28.2.91, 1 (see p. 201). The *UI*'s concerted efforts at literary propaganda typify the self-consciousness, 'the community of interests, a certain coherence of outlook [and] a sense of shared purpose' which are the prerequisites for an event such as a literary revival. And the radical sea change in the weekly's literary attitude circa 1891 supports Kelly's contention about the suddenness of the event and about the Revival having taken place after Parnell's fall.

In his *Autobiographies* Yeats claimed the credit for diverting Ireland's mind towards literature and culture after Parnell's death:

> A couple of years before the death of Parnell, I had wound up my introduction to those selections from the Irish novelists with the

prophecy of an intellectual movement at the first lull in politics, and now I wished to fulfil my prophesy. I did not put it in that way, for I preferred to think that the sudden emotion that now came to me, the sudden certainty that Ireland was to be like soft wax for years to come, was a moment of supernatural insight. How could I tell, how can I tell even now? (199).

The introduction of the mystical element – 'supernatural insight', 'prophecy' – makes it appear as if it was Yeats, and Yeats alone, whose heightened receptivity to supernatural frequency waves had facilitated this special divination, and that there was no other more mundane way of knowing that literature would blossom at the 'first lull in politics'. Whether this premonition was arrived at through some psychic experience or by simply reading the *UI*, which Yeats did regularly, is not the point. What is, is the fact that this 'insight' was not Yeats's monopoly but a view that was aired repeatedly in the columns of that paper before the split. The other significant point to be noted is that the change in opinion about literature and its role comes not with the death of Parnell in October 1891 as Yeats seems to think, but with Parnell's fall in December 1890 as has already been seen. Though Yeats was always 'on the watch for any sign of a new start' (*CL1*, 174), he was not quite on the ball on this occasion, despite his claims some years later.

Yeats's most recent biographer, Roy Foster, has taken issue in two important ways with his subject's reading of this period. He argues that Yeats's view of the ' "lull" in politics [following Parnell's fall] should not be taken as read'. It shouldn't. 'Vacuum theories notwithstanding, politics went on happening.' Agrarian agitation, parliamentary manoeuvrings and local government reforms did not come to a grinding halt with Parnell's death. Neither did the demand for Home Rule.[27] Foster is also suspicious, and rightly so, of the Yeatsian theory postulating the diversion of political torrents into cultural channels.[28] He skilfully illuminates Yeats's own reasons for downplaying the political gains of this period and for shifting the spotlight onto literature and, consequently, onto himself: his distaste for Catholic democracy and his fear that the literary movement would be swamped and overshadowed by the Gaelic one. To these ossified misconceptions, Foster's revisionism imparts a much-needed debunking.

Foster's second point follows from his first. He argues that the Revival 'had begun several years before [Parnell's death] as a function of constitutional nationalism's success, not its failure' (*WBY*, 115). The 'effort ['to create a national literary culture'] was being made from 1885' and the agenda then 'was not about creating an alternative to politics; it concerned what to do when politics had delivered Home Rule' (41). This, however, is not as convincing. His instancing the *Dublin University Review* as one such pre-split pioneer of the Revival is not accurate, as I have attempted to show. Neither is his dating of the Revival to 1885 or his claim about the 'agenda'. The last is more applicable to the post-split than the pre-split period. This is clearly evidenced by the all too visible difference in the *UI*'s literary coverage and attitude towards literature before and after the split. As I have pointed out, this difference was commented on by the *UI* itself on at least two occasions.[29] The *UI* was undoubtedly merely one of the many Irish newspapers but there are sound reasons for using it as a yardstick of post- and pre-split attitudes towards literature. Prior to the split it was the most widely-read and influential of all Irish newspapers, whether nationalist or unionist. And after the split, by contemporary accounts as well as by the testimony of other newspapers, it was in the forefront of literature.[30] Further, it must also be remembered that the Irish Literary Revival was essentially a Parnellite affair and the *UI* was the Parnellites' flagship media organ.

Though Foster shows that Yeats is not central to the political and cultural events of the period, he yet takes too Yeats-centred a view of the Revival. He ignores the fact that other factors besides Yeats could have played a significant role in the revival of Irish literature after the split. To assert that Yeats was wrong about the Revival taking place after the split because he was wrong about politics coming to a halt after the split, and wrong also about his own centrality to the Revival enterprise, is to throw out the baby with the bath-water. Admittedly, after the split political activity did make substantial gains, and Yeats had his own motives in rewriting Irish history around himself and in grossly exaggerating his own role in the Revival. But this does not in any way controvert Yeats's view, the view of his contemporaries and the evidence of newspapers and periodicals that it was only after the split that literature came into its own, that there is a tremendous difference in the pre- and post-split attitude to literature and that the latter eventually led to the Literary Revival. This evidence is overwhelming and a casual comparison of a few of the *UI* issues before and after the split would dispel any notions about the Revival having taken place before 1891. John Kelly had pointed this out more than two decades ago in his Ph.D. thesis as well as in an article ('Fall of Parnell') that Foster has often cited.

After the split, Parnell had begun flirting with the physical force side of Irish politics, had proclaimed 'that I am not a mere parliamentarian' and had announced his intention to resort to extra-constitutional methods if 'I can no longer hope to obtain our constitution by constitutional means' (*Parnell*, 539). For Parnellites, these statements, along with the three consecutive electoral defeats, represented – at least in the immediate term – the failure of constitutional nationalism. And consequently, *pace* Foster, the *UI* did manifestly shift its emphasis to literature as an alternative to politics. This is not to say that

there was a lull in Irish politics or that politics – parliamentary, local or agrarian – stopped happening but merely that from the Parnellite perspective what
was happening was not very encouraging or newsworthy. (We have already
seen that the Parnellite weekly was having difficulties filling its pages after a
string of electoral defeats. See pp. 185–8.) The coinciding of two curious
statements highlights this fact. In April 1892, a few months before the general election, in an article entitled 'The Sober Saxon', the *UI*'s Newcastle-
upon-Tyne correspondent reported that 'politics are in the doldrums. There
is no progress to report, and the country in general has clean forgotten what
the most august assembly the world has ever seen (that is the courtesy title,
isn't it?) was doing last week' (2.4.92, 5). Three issues later a *UI* reader (Frank
MacDonagh) wrote to say that he was pleasantly surprised that 'in these days
of political turmoil' the weekly had increased its literary coverage so significantly, especially since 'in *quieter* times it did little to stimulate the public interest in Irish literature' (30.4.92, 1; emphasis added). Clearly, there was a lot
happening, but not from the *UI*'s perspective. It was still the media mouthpiece of a political party with no intention of becoming an Irish precursor
of the *TLS*. Its enhanced literary coverage was necessitated by a series of con-
tinuous political setbacks. In this sense, it was the failure of constitutional
nationalism for Parnellites that, indirectly, led to the *UI*'s increased emphasis
on literature and eventually to the Irish Literary Revival.

If my argument about the dating of the Revival is correct, it necessitates
a whole new view of this very important event in Irish cultural history.
1885, which for Foster marks the origins of the Revival, also marks the
renewal of the 1882 Coercion Bill, a measure undertaken by the Liberals
with the knowledge that it would undermine their Irish prospects in the
general election, which was only a few months away.[31] In 1885 Ireland was
still considered to be disturbed and in turmoil, and with good reason. For
each year between 1885 and 1887, i.e. till the Union of Hearts had begun
taking root, agrarian violence was more pronounced than it had been in
1883 and 1884.[32] Throughout the 1880s, agricultural revenues had been
falling and by 1886 the agrarian storm clouds were once again looking
ominous and threatening. Evictions followed non-payment of rent and the
Commons' refusal to countenance Parnell's Tenants' Relief Bill made the
situation even more critical.[33] The 'Plan of Campaign', launched in the *UI*
in October 1886, caught the Irish imagination. It was ruthlessly suppressed
by Balfour's 'perpetual' Crimes Act and his consistent use of coercion over
the next three years, but not before it had roused popular passions. Locating the Revival within this milieu implies that literature was not only
allowed to co-habit the same space as politics, but that it also flourished
alongside it. (Books such as T. S. Cleary's *Lays of the Irish Land War*, which

grew out of an immediate political situation and which were typical of Irish literature in the 1880s, come to mind.) Further, it would also imply that the bases of the Revival were populist, grass roots, subaltern and Catholic. In effect it would be to democratise and secularise a phenomenon that was principally Protestant, upper class and élitist.

IV

Before the split Yeats had shown little interest in Parnell. Foster astutely points out that 'Four Years' (1887–91) in Yeats's *Autobiographies*, presenting Parnell's death as a watershed mark, is in fact a later historical construction disguising Yeats's own indifference to the politician during his lifetime.

> Parnell figured little in WBY's universe: his idea of a heroic leader was William Morris. It was the first two years that counted, from early 1887 to the beginning of 1889. And the climax is not the public upheaval of a politician's death, but a more personal apotheosis: the publication of WBY's first book. (*WBY*, 59)

Yeats's very first reference to Parnell in print was in October 1889 while reviewing Carleton's the *Red-Haired Man's Wife* for the *Scots Observer*. As we have seen, while writing for Henley, Yeats consciously adjusted his pitch to blend with the *Scots Observer*'s unionist trumpeting and his reference to Parnell reflects the periodical's opposition to land agitation and Home Rule. The linking of the two through the New Departure is described as 'the movement to be dreaded' (*UP1*, 145), and Parnell, 'a now famous agitator' (145–6), is the person who has led the movement and the Irish peasantry to 'the gates of hell' (146). Yeats's view of Parnell here is quite antithetical to his subsequent mythologisation of the politician as one from the pantheon of heroic, aristocratic and haughty Protestants 'born into that ancient sect / But thrown upon this filthy modern tide / And by its formless spawning fury wrecked' ('The Statues', *VP*, 611).

Foster dates Yeats's commitment to the Parnellites to 4 December 1890.[34] The date is important because it marks Yeats's first-ever mention of Parnell in his letters. The wranglings in Committee Room 15 were still in progress on 4 December 1890 when he wrote O'Leary a short letter. The split took place two days after this letter but on 3 December the Standing Committee of the Irish Hierarchy had asked Irish Catholics to reject Parnell. However, too much importance should not be attached to this event, for the letter and the incidental remarks on Parnell were occasioned by something more mundane: the request for a photograph.

My dear Mr O Leary

I send that photograph. I hope you will let me have one of yours if you have one to spare. This Parnell business is most exciting. Hope he will hold on, as it is he has driven up into dust & vacuum no end of insincerities. The whole matter of Irish politics will be the better of it.

Yours very truly
W.B. Yeats

(*CL1*, 237)

Yeats generally modulated his writings to conform with the political perspectives of his intended audience, both public and private.[35] O'Leary had publicly announced his Parnellite allegiance early in December.[36] For a Fenian, wary of clerical domination, constitutional politics and English alliances, the matter was settled when the Church denounced Parnell and the anti-Parnellites sided with Gladstone. That Davitt, Dillon and O'Brien – the architects of 'New Tipperary' – were in the opposite camp made the matter a *fait accompli*. Yeats could not possibly send the photograph without an accompanying letter and the previous day's events provide fodder for this as well as for reaffirming his own radical credentials before his mentor. Significantly, a letter sent on the same day to Tynan, an ardent Parnellite, does not mention either Parnell or current politics. This must be taken into account while evaluating the significance of Yeats's letter to O'Leary. To read the letter as indicating Yeats's Parnellite allegiance is premature. It ignores the fact that Yeats is writing to O'Leary, whose political sympathies are well known and whose approval and support are important to Yeats. It also ignores Yeats's own guardedness on political issues, his tendency to hold his cards as close to his chest as possible and to play his hand as late as possible, especially on matters that are potentially divisive. This is not to say that Yeats did not feel a genuine affinity for Parnell at this moment, but that a statement like 'This Parnell business is most exciting' indicates that it is the excitement and affinity a cinema-goer would feel for a character in a film nearing its denouement. One cannot imagine it coming from a *UI* reader, Tynan or anybody with a genuine stake in the matter. The fact that his letters, as Cruise O'Brien points out, do not show any trace of grief, either at Parnell's fall or even at his death, reinforces the impression that during this period Yeats was indifferent to Parnell.[37] Even Yeats's being a Protestant cannot account for his emotional distance from the circumambient partisan frenzy. Oldham, who championed southern Protestant nationalism, was brim-full of political fervour. His letter of 20.12.90 to Hyde in Canada is a passionate account of current events. Written just a fortnight after Yeats's letter to O'Leary, it provides sound grounds for comparison. 'The dividing line runs through all one's acquaintances', Oldham remarks. 'Everyone feels under a fierce unavoidable pressure *to take sides.*' If he were in Ireland, Oldham assures Hyde, he too would feel the pressure and, 'like *all the purely national* elements among the Irish people', he would support Parnell. 'All purely national Ireland', claims Oldham, looks upon Parnell 'as the only hope of an independent party for Ireland in our generation'. 'He must win . . . if his health does not break down' (Dunleavy and Dunleavy, 152). Compared to this, Yeats's letter is apathetic and bloodless. He was clearly under no pressure to either make a choice or prove his credentials. (That comes much later.) That he was in England and therefore somewhat distanced from the events would still not explain his detached tone. Oldham's letter highlights the difference between someone who is 'firmly and publicly in the Parnellite camp' (*WBY*, 113) and someone like Yeats who is yet undecided.

Yeats's next mention of Parnell is again, significantly, to O'Leary in a letter written more than a month after the split. In the interim, at the Kilkenny North by-election in December, Parnell had issued his famous appeal to the hillside men. The battle lines were drawn, with Parnell and the Fenians facing the combination of Catholic nationalism and the clergy. In good Irish fashion, the Fenians fought bravely but lost hugely to the strenuous efforts of the priests who, as the Bishop of Ossory boasted to Archbishop Walsh, 'worked night and day and strained every energy to win and it is to them that is really due the victory that crowns our banners'.[38] This context, as well as O'Leary's political allegiances, must be borne in mind when reading Yeats's letter of 21 January 1891. Once again, the Parnell comment figures incidentally and only at the end of a long letter which is dominated by news of Yeats's Blake edition, other work on hand and his inability to review Ellen O'Leary's poems for Henley's *Observer.*

> It seems as though Parnell's chances had greatly improved these latter weeks. His last two speeches were wonderfully good. I wish I was over in Ireland to see & hear how things are going. The Hartlepool victory should help him by showing that his action has not injured the cause over here as much as people say. My father is bitterly opposed to Parnell on the ground chiefly now, of his attacks on his followers. To me, if all other reasons were absent, it would seem plain that a combination of priests with the 'sullivan gang' is not likely to have on its side in political matters divine justice. The whole business will do this good any way. The Liberals will have now to pass a good measure if any measure at all – at least so I read the matter.
>
> Daily News this morning has a long article on Hydes book which I have not yet seen. I shall ask Scots Observer for it.
> Yours very sncely
W.B. Yeats

(CL1, 242)

Once again the perspective remains that of an interested by-stander who regrets not having ring-side seats rather than that of a committed participant who is worried by the Kilkenny débâcle and the Liberal victory in Hartlepool. (One can imagine Oldham tearing his hair out in frustration.) To read the Hartlepool result as Yeats does indicates that the 'cause' referred to is not the Parnellite cause but the cause of Home Rule, even if brokered by the Liberals, something the Parnellites and *UI* rejected vociferously. The 'sullivan gang' had indeed behaved badly and Tim Healy's sexual allusions – if Parnell is the master, 'Who is to be the mistress of the party?', and Parnell has put O'Shea into Galway for 'the price of his wife' (*Parnell*, 528, 540) – would have invoked the standard O'Leary rebuke of there being certain things a man must not do to save his country. In condemning this combination of ungallant behaviour and clerical interference to a Fenian of the old school whose troops had just been routed in Kilkenny by the same combination, Yeats was offering moral consolation, not his own views which normally ignored considerations of 'divine justice'. This becomes plain in the following comment ('The whole business . . . matter.') about the possible benefits accruing from the situation. To see the anticipated Home Rule measure as a gain extorted from the Liberals and as a 'good' resulting from the split indicates a more earthly and practical perspective, albeit an anti-Parnellite one. It also either contradicts the sop about 'divine justice', or, in a more Yeatsian fashion, tries to have it both ways: divine justice in heaven, and a Liberal measure of Home Rule in Ireland. In either case, it is not a Parnellite perspective on Home Rule. That perspective, when it does appear in Yeats's writings for the first time six months later, does so clearly and emphatically.

On 21 January 1891, when Yeats wrote that letter to O'Leary, he had not yet felt it prudent or necessary to commit himself one way or the other. Hence his objective evaluation, free of party loyalties and manifestos, of the potential gains arising out of the current political situation. That his letter to O'Leary cannot be construed as a declaration or even an indication of his Parnellite allegiance is made evident by examining his diametrically opposed professions about Gladstonian Home Rule and the 'Union of Hearts' once he does commit himself. In July 1891, while writing on Todhunter's plays, Yeats indulged in the usual criticism of English literature, belittling of the Saxon race and hyperbolic praise of Irish writing. The Irish were a young, imaginative, heroic, poetic, idealistic and noble race while the English were just the opposite; Todhunter's *The Poison Flower* had 'improve[d] on Hawthorne'; English drama was essentially an Irish creation. He then lamented, 'We have never been fairly tested' (*UP1*, 193), and wondered if a poetic drama on an Irish theme written for and performed before Irish audiences would be successful. He concluded:

Surely, they would not find the mere fact of its being poetry the very great difficulty English audiences seem to find it. We have had the only popular ballad literature of recent days. Does that not prove the poetic capacities of our uneducated masses? *Or has English influence and 'the union of hearts' made us as prosaic as our neighbours?* (*UP1*, 193–4; emphasis added)

The italicised statement and his comments to O'Leary show the difference between a perspective or statement that is essentially Parnellite and one that is not. In the second letter, the 'union of hearts' is accorded value and its influence is seen to be potentially 'good'. Here it is denigrated and its influence is seen as being detrimental. Before the split, the emphasis was primarily on Home Rule: it would reverse anglicisation and the Irish would become Celtic again. One followed the other; they were not thought to be concomitant and interdependent processes. After the split, they were, at least for Parnellites. Independence in politics entailed independence in all other spheres of life: 'If we wish to become a self-respecting, self-relying and really independent nation, we must have minds of our own' (9.4.92, 5). Hence, when the post-split *UI* attacked anglicisation, it was attacking the English connection in all its manifestations, particularly the anti-Parnellite–Liberal alliance.[39] For Yeats to have derided English influence in a Parnellite newspaper was in itself a significant political statement. To link it with the 'union of hearts' as he did is a clear expression of Parnellite allegiance. Its implications are no longer restricted to fears of cultural anglicisation but extend to the political domain as well. By invoking the political alliance, Yeats's statement translates the cultural implications of anglicisation into political ones. Being prosaic culturally is one thing, but, in political terms, especially when it is linked to a dependence, it takes on connotations of emasculation, servility and cowardice.

Yeats's very next *UI* article two months later again attacked the English connection in distinctly Parnellite fashion. While describing 'A Reckless Century' he recalled a period when the 'infamous invaders' left Irishmen with no choice but to make 'amends for a life without dignity by a death without fear' (*UP1*, 201). The gentry, though decadent were also passionate, and only a 'little conviction would have made them good rebels' (200). 'Their swords were strong, at any rate, though they were not turned often enough, or persistently enough, towards the enemies of their country' (202). It was only the poor who harboured any 'sense of national duty' or 'patriotic hope'. It was they who

attacked the Parliament House and made the members swear truth to Ireland one after another, and then, to show their contempt of England, set an old woman with a pipe in her mouth upon the throne of the Viceroy. (201)

The Fenian rhetoric, the laments against misdirected passion and lost opportunity, the portrayal of the English as conquerors and the equating of 'national duty' with swearing allegiance to Ireland instead of England and with showing contempt for the English monarchy foreshadows the *Sinn Fein*. It is also of a piece with the *UI*'s Parnellite propaganda, which, as John Kelly observes, laid the basis of the *Sinn Fein*'s ideology.[40]

The question that now arises is why did Yeats wait till July 1891 before committing himself to the Parnellites. Prior to the split, the Yeatses' attitude to Parnellite politics bordered on indifference and distaste. Like his son, J. B. Yeats paired people with their opposites. Butt and Parnell were one such pair. For Yeats Sr., Butt was warm, generous, sincere, reliable and incapable of hate while Parnell, was a cold, cruel, conniving and untrustworthy usurper – he was good at 'doing business' – whose outstanding quality was 'an immense, unrelenting, inexorable hatred'.[41] There were personal reasons underpinning these judgements. The Butts were close family friends; Yeats *père* admired and respected Isaac Butt and his brand of gentlemanly Protestant nationalism. Further, Butt's daughter, Rosa, was the unrequited love of his life. Parnell's Land League, on the other hand, had threatened and significantly reduced J. B. Yeats's rentier income thereby alienating this erstwhile land-owning family from their rightful place in upper-class Protestant society.

There is nothing in Yeats's writings before December 1890 that would make his subsequent Parnellite affiliation seem a foregone conclusion. His letters do not mention Parnell at all. In fact, they contain very few political references and most of them are to prospective anti-Parnellites. These are anything but derogatory. William O'Brien, 'who has a message to deliver', is excluded from the 'tittering jeering emptiness' of most journalists who 'have all made what Dante calls the Great Refusal' (*CL1*, 91). And Yeats, on a visit to the House of Commons, is 'Altogather . . . delighted with Healy' whose 'good earth power' and 'rugged passionate speech [was] the most human thing I heard' (*CL1*, 13–14).

Even after the split, there is nothing to suggest that Yeats had a greater affinity for either the Parnellites or the anti-Parnellites. His later writings make it clear that he was intrinsically opposed not to the principle of the split but to the vulgarity and frenzy it provoked on both sides, showing 'how base at moments of excitement are minds without culture': 'There were reasons to justify a man's joining either party, but there were none to justify, *on one side or on the other*, lying accusations forgetful of past service, a frenzy of detraction' (*VP*, 818; emphasis added). His essay on Parnell repeats the point about Parnellites and anti-Parnellites being carved from the same block: 'They were all tolerant men of the world, except the peasant-born Irish members; toleration is most often found beside ornamental waters, upon smooth lawns, amid conversations that have no object but pleasure. But all were caught in that public insincerity' (*E&I*, 488). In spite of Lady Gregory's classifying Davitt as a 'ruffian' (*WBY*, 169), Yeats's own sympathy and affection for the Land Leaguer, whom he had met at the Contemporary Club in 1885, increased progressively over the years culminating in his first ever letter of admiration to a politician.[42] He had been deeply moved by 'the nobility' of Davitt's resignation speech in parliament and wrote to convey his regard.[43] The letter once again highlights the point that, for Yeats, the post-split vulgarity that he found so repellent was not the preserve of any one side. His sniping at Healy's anti-Parnellite 'underbred and untruthful articles and speeches' (*CL1*, 373) before a Parnellite *UI* audience carries as much significance as his preaching insurrection and devaluing Parnell in favour of the more militant Emmet before a Clan na Gael audience in America.[44] Similarly, his criticising Parnellite politics for having swamped the nation's intellect and silenced her muses was as much in the future as his stifled barb at Dillon: 'Had Zimri peace who slew his master?' (*Auto*, 366). In 1897 Yeats successfully solicited subscriptions for the Irish National Theatre from Parnellites and anti-Parnellites. Healy's charming response – 'I gather you ask my support to some Irish project, & as I am sure you are not connected with anything that is not meant for the elevation of the country put me down for any sum you think reasonable' (*WBY*, 184–5) – gives no indication of any offence given or taken in the past, save the trouble caused by Yeats's illegible handwriting. A little later both sections rallied to help change the theatre licensing laws and once again Healy sent in a friendly reply to Yeats's request.[45] Around the turn of the century, Yeats solicited Dillon's help in thwarting Frank Hugh O'Donnell's mischief and was surprised by Dillon's 'honourable' (*Mem*, 116) behaviour:

> I was very much struck by my reception for I was promised that
> he would prevent if possible Frank Hugh O'Donnell ever getting
> a seat, and a little later the Party refused a large subscription from
> O'Donnell. That man [Dillon] was Maud Gonne's political oppo-
> nent [over the Paris funds], I think she had attacked him person-
> ally and certainly he was our opponent. (*CL2*, 711)

Yeats's mythologising of Parnell as a haughty Protestant aristocrat was a later creation; in December 1890 he was as little inclined, intellectually and emotionally, to the Parnellites as he was to the anti-Parnellites. Why then did he align himself with Parnell? Part of the answer lies in the influence exerted by those around him. O'Leary was a Parnellite, as was Tynan. Maud Gonne, who 'had never been enthusiastic about Parnell, had, when Gladstone ordered the Irish people to go against him, become violently Parnellite'.[46] The fact that most southern Protestant nationalists (Oldham, T. W. Rolleston, Gwynn) sided with Parnell was also a significant factor. Even among southern unionists, there was a distinct softening in attitude towards the fallen leader owing to the Independent Party's determined efforts to woo unionists in the three elections after the split, to the new *entente cordiale* between the *UI* and the unionist media, to their own pride in having produced yet another leader of the Catholic masses and to his vilification by the Catholic clergy. Callanan points out that the *Kilkenny Moderator's* unionism was 'tempered by a deep susceptibility to Parnell'; the *St Stephen's Review* lauded his 'unflinching stand against the pack of curs that are yapping round him, bent on his destruction'; and the *Dublin Daily Express* confessed to being unable to withstand 'a certain admiration for the man who fought so strenuously against great odds'. Edward Dowden described him in Miltonic terms as 'one who, compared with the pigmy forces whom he has left behind, seems hardly less in stature than the Archangel ruined'; and, perhaps most significantly of all, the organ of the Church of Ireland, the *Irish Ecclesiastical Gazette*, declared on Parnell's death that '"Parnellism" has lately come to mean a "Home Rule" which is not "Rome Rule" '.[47] Yeats was not immune to this sense of caste pride and it would have played a significant role, along with the above-mentioned factors, in his decision. But this is one only part of the answer. The other part lies in the timing of his first public declaration of Parnellite allegiance. Why did he wait until July 1891 before committing himself?

To seek an answer based on ideology or principle is to search for tropical fruit in temperate climes; it was not ideology but expedience and practicality that determined many of Yeats's actions and professed opinions. From the beginning of his journalistic career, he had flaunted his nationalist credentials before nationalist audiences. Given that his own political views were ambivalent at best, it is fair to say that these articles affected a nationalist fervour that was not entirely sincere. There were practical advantages to be reaped, as the nationalist media had a larger readership than any other in Ireland and therefore aligning with them resulted in wider coverage. His work thus far in the *Boston Pilot, Providence Sunday Journal, Scots Observer, Dublin University Review* and *UI* shows that he always had more than one pack and played his cards depending on his audience's political loyalties. He had realised early that the 'alliance of politics and literature that marked the '48 movement resulted in so great a popularity for the poets' (*UP1*, 215), whereas the later writers, 'lacking the great wind of politics to fill their sails' (216), lived and wrote in oblivion. For Yeats, politics was precisely that: a great wind to fill his sails. He told Tynan that he had reason to be optimistic about *Oisin*: 'the present state of English opinion' (*CL1*, 56) would help his sales. 1888–89 was the honeymoon period of the Union of Hearts and he saw quickly enough that this would be to his advantage. Sensing the readers' mood, he also made a few positive references to the English connection in his reviews and even endorsed a poem, twice, because Gladstone had praised it.[48] A year later, sensing another change in mood, he attacked the English connection.

After the split, with the *UI* once again in Parnell's control, Yeats's fortunes improved considerably. For two-and-a-half years after his Blunt essay in January 1888 he had failed to get other *UI* commissions. During that period, he had established his reputation in England through numerous book publications (*Oisin*, 'Dhoya', *Countess Kathleen*, *Fairy and Folk Tales*, *Stories from Carleton*, *Representative Irish Tales*), his association with W. E. Henley and his own journalistic output (17 periodical publications in 1889 and 16 in 1890). After the split, D. J. O'Donoghue, whom Yeats had known as an enthusiastic Southwark Literary Club organiser, became the *UI*'s London-based literary correspondent and helped Yeats in many ways. Edmund Leamy, the erstwhile literary editor, took over the paper's editorship and John McGrath took over Leamy's job. Like O'Donoghue, McGrath had a serious interest in literature and was to prove a boon companion to Yeats's literary endeavours. He had moved to the *UI* from the *Freeman* when the latter defected to the anti-Parnellites, highlighting once again the fact that the Parnellite split ran through all sections of society and opinion, rendering neutrality impossible. He penned the topical 'North & South' column and the famous attacks on the anti-Parnellites ('Done to Death' and 'The Dead Chief', 10.10. 91, 4) accusing them of Parnell's murder. In the *UI,* the split had also resulted in a greater coverage of literature. Bereft of political news, the paper, as Yeats was soon to realise, had become extremely welcoming to writers and 'anxious for literary articles' (*CL1*, 261).

Before the Kilkenny defeat, literature was virtually non-existent in the paper and aligning with the Parnellites at this stage would have been of no particular advantage to Yeats. Immediately after the defeat, the *UI* began devoting an unprecedented amount of space to literature. During this two-month period of literary enthusiasm, the fervour and zeal that the paper had initially devoted to its political campaigns were now transferred to literature and the Literary Revival. While self-consciously propagating 'an Irish Literary *Renaissance*' (28.2.91, 1), every opportunity was taken to bemoan literary anglicisation, the lack of a national literature and the neglect of Irish writers by the Irish public. The *UI*'s response to the American Copyright Act is illustrative:

> But what, you will perhaps ask me, has all this to do with Ireland, a country which, practically speaking has no literature at all? Well, indeed, not much. But won't we have some literature in the

future? Certainly, if we make up our minds to have it. And, indeed, this new international copyright arrangement ought to spur our Irish writers to new exertions. They have a great field in the States – probably a much better one than their brothers of the quill over in England. So let them be up and doing now! (14.3.91, 1)

The North Sligo election blocked out everything but political propaganda, but only for five issues. After the second Parnellite defeat, Yeats was one of the immediate beneficiaries of the *UI*'s shortage of political news and its resultant focus on literature. On 2.5.91, the paper commended his 'courageous as well as interesting' (1) *Boston Pilot* article where he had regurgitated the *UI*'s views on John Francis O'Donnell and Ellen O'Leary.[49] The paper also quoted a long extract where Yeats praised Hyde and expressed optimism about the future of Irish literature. Two issues later, he received the biggest boost of his career to date. In a one-and-a-half column (30 inches) review of his *Representative Irish Tales*, the paper described him 'as rapidly emerging into the upper strata of Irish authorship' and his Introduction as being 'short, but admirably to the point' and 'marked by sound judgement and taste':

> He works quietly and unostentatiously, like a true literary labourer; but when he gives us a book – and he is already responsible for several – we look for something worth more than a mere passing attention. (16.5.91, 5)

The review also quoted a long (three pages of *P&I*) extract from his Introduction and summarised the remainder. It also quoted his prophecy apropos of the Revival being at hand and hoped that it 'may be fulfilled'. Two issues later, D. J. O'Donoghue, probably at Yeats's prompting, inserted a few notes updating readers on Yeats's projected book of 'Irish adventurers' and gave it a puffing up: 'In hands like his this indeed must prove a work of unique interest to us all' (30.5.91, 5). The following note remarked that though 'Mr Yeats looks the ideal poet' his dreamy and mystical aspect is belied by his capacity for 'hard and practical work.' The last note pointed out some errors of ascribed authorship in *Representative Irish Tales*.

Though the Carlow election again interrupted the *UI*'s literary coverage, it was quite clear now that the paper would soon have to backtrack. The Parnellites were losing and the *UI* would once again have difficulties filling up the pages. Besides, it had aggressively begun championing the Revival. This, along with its very extensive and very flattering coverage of Yeats's own work, played an important and perhaps decisive role in tipping the scales in favour of the Parnellites and finally convincing Yeats that an alliance with them would be more beneficial to his literary career. The timing of Yeats's declaration of Parnellite allegiance – the fact that it was made at least six months after most peoples' – merits attention and inquiry. This, coupled with the fact that he made it in the *UI* at a time when the paper was backing Irish literature, the Literary Revival and, perhaps more significantly, Yeats, makes the convergence of events seem too thought out and orchestrated to be merely coincidental. This impression is reinforced by Yeats's *Memoirs*, where while referring to this period he speaks of taking 'advantage of that swing ['of the pendulum'] to found my own movement' (82). Having decided his post-split political allegiance, he wrote and submitted to the *UI* his Tod-hunter article right in the middle of the Carlow election campaign, on or about 20 June.[50] It was published in the issue immediately following the defeat of the Parnellite candidate, which, as in the previous two cases (Kilkenny and Sligo), signalled both the curtailment of political news and an increased coverage of literature.

The events of the next two weeks would have confirmed him in his actions. Between 17 and 22 July, he visited the *UI*'s offices and was warmly welcomed. This contrasted radically with his first experiences with the *UI* and was significant enough for him to mention it in two consecutive letters written at least a week apart.[51] He had clearly sensed an opportunity, for in these letters he also mentions detecting an over-eagerness and urgency in McGrath for literary articles. He was too sharp not to realise that the *UI*, being hard-up for admissible political news, was now anxiously searching for other ways to fill the pages. Besides, this realisation would have also been brought home to him by a casual perusal of the paper after the Kilkenny election. Within a few days of this reconnaissance, he read an anti-Parnellite attack on Tynan and, cannily, predicted that the 'papers on your own side will be made all the more favourable by this attack' (*CL1*, 259). Foster's biography repeatedly stresses that Yeats's actions were significantly influenced by his per-ception, in most cases accurate, of how things would look in the future. His prediction to Tynan is another case in point, for it wasn't long before the *UI* gallantly rallied to her defence.

Yeats had enough experience of Irish journalism to know that political considerations often determined literary evaluation. He had effectively manipulated this in the past to his advantage, but to continue doing so he would have to take sides. Neutrality would have aroused suspicion all round, leaving him open to attacks from both quarters. Of the two, an alliance with the Parnellites seemed the most advantageous. His visit to the *UI* offices was perhaps a way of confirming this impression and testing the waters. Having found them welcoming and hospitable, he plunged right in. The gains were immediate. Not only were his own essays published promptly, but his work in other periodicals was also noticed, his books were reviewed favourably, his literary activities were reported, his forthcoming books were announced, and his candidature as the Irish representative at the forthcoming International Folklore Conference in London was championed.[52] Moreover, Yeats also orchestrated a few fillips for others as well. This was largely done through O'Donoghue. At Yeats's behest, he inserted notices in the weekly about Maud Gonne's activities and whereabouts and about Jack Yeats's paintings. With a view to *UI* publicity, Yeats kept him abreast with his own work, informed him in advance of the forthcoming lectures and publications (*Book of the Rhymers' Club, Irish Fairy Tales* and *Countess Kathleen*), requested a notice of 'The Countess Kathleen's' first performance for copyright purposes and asked O'Donoghue to reveal his authorship of *John Sherman and Dhoya* to readers.[53] In these letters Yeats continually stressed his Irish and national credentials, his attempts to write a national drama and his preoccupation with and loyalty to Irish subjects. He was achieving what he had set out to do, namely 'influence newspapers' (*Mem*, 50).

Having declared himself a Parnellite, Yeats went the whole hog and paraded his sympathy with the physical force movement.[54] O'Leary's dictum, ratified by his own experiences, had taught him that if he could not have the Church he must have the Fenians on his side.[55] Their support being crucial to his future plans, they were, for Yeats, 'the instruments we had been looking for' (*Mem*, 83). Before a Parnellite audience he defended Parnell, attacked his detractors and the anti-Parnellite media, criticised the Gladstonian alliance and the tame version of Home Rule desired by the 'seceders', claimed that the Parnellites were the 'real' nationalists and that he considered them rather than the anti-Parnellites to be his true audience.[56] The depth of feeling or conviction underlying these claims can be gauged by his response to Parnell's death. The feelings expressed by his lament, 'Mourn – And Then Onward!' (*VP*, 737–38) – mourning, sadness, fear and gloom – do not in any way correspond to the feelings expressed in the accompanying letter to his sister. Instead there is a sense of having carried out a *coup*. And indeed he had. Parnell died just before midnight on Tuesday, 6 October 1891. The news would have reached Ireland only on Wednesday, the very day that the *United Ireland* was published, and was too late to be put on the cover page. Only pages 4 and 5 covered the event and Yeats's dirge was printed on page 4, immediately above 'Done to Death', McGrath's bitter attack on the anti-Parnellites that reverberated for years thereafter. That issue of the *UI* would have sold even faster than Andrew Morton's biography after Princess Diana's death. Yeats had indeed made a splash and, what's more, had beaten others to it. He thus had the privilege of being the sole poet mourning the Chief in the Chief's own newspaper. Other Parnellite rhymesters were caught napping, or mourning, and only in the following issue could ten of them vent their grief before the

Poetry.

MOURN — AND THEN ONWARD!

YE on the broad high mountains of old Eri,
  Mourn all the night and day,
The man is gone who guided ye, unweary,
  Through the long bitter way.

Ye by the waves that close in our sad nation,
  Be full of sudden fears,
The man is gone who from his lonely station
  Has moulded the hard years.

Mourn ye on grass-green plains of Eri fated,
  For closed in darkness now
Is he who laboured on, derided, hated,
  And made the tyrant bow.

Mourn—and then onward, there is no returning
  He guides ye from the tomb ;
His memory now is a tall pillar, burning
  Before us in the gloom !

W. B. YEATS.

TERMS OF SUBSCRIPTION.

(Free by Post.)

	s. d.
Three Months,	1 8
Six Months,	3 3
Twelve Months,	6 6

UNITED IRELAND will be sent at above rate to any part of Ireland and Great Britain. To the United States of America, Canada, France, Spain, Germany, Australia, &c., &c.—Three Months, 2s 2d; Six Months, 4s 4d; Twelve Months, 9s 0d; India, Twelve Months, 11s 0d (including Extra Double Numbers).

. All Cheques, Post Office Orders, &c., to be made payable to the Manager of UNITED IRELAND

UNITED IRELAND.

DUBLIN: SATURDAY, OCT. 10, 1891.

"DONE TO DEATH."

ON this Thursday morning as we go to press a human body lies stiff and cold in Brighton. It is the body of CHARLES PARNELL. It lies there to-day, soulless ; stark and soulless. Does Ireland know what this means ? Does Ireland know that the mightiest intellect which has given itself to her cause for two hundred years, has ceased to think and plan for her ? Ah, fellow-countrymen, you turned upon him in his hour of trial. Do you feel happy this morning as the news flashes over the hills of Ireland that *he is dead ?* DEAD ? Good GOD, kind and merciful GOD, can it be true that CHARLES PARNELL's mind has ceased to think for us ? Can it be true that his heart has ceased to beat for us ? Ah, brothers, brothers, what have you rest of the nation. Tynan, perhaps to compensate for her slow start, went twice the distance and published two laments. Yeats's hastily composed obituary on Parnell, written, as he told his sister, 'the day he died, to be in time for the press that evening', had certainly 'been a success' (*CL1*, 265). But not a literary success. Thirty years later, when he saw the poem blazed across a banner, he initially mistook it for a biblical quotation; when the penny dropped, he was horrified.[57] Yeats's response to Parnell's death indicates not only his detachment from what Parnellites – and at this time he was counted among them – considered a national tragedy, but also what Conor Cruise O'Brien calls his 'eye for an opportunity – a politician's eye, and a politician's sense of timing' ('Passion and Cunning', 219).

V

As we have seen in Chapter 1, Yeats's article on Blunt and his American journalism adopted a style of literary criticism-cum-political propaganda characteristic of the pre-split *UI*. Both preached the same nationalist aesthetic, drew upon the same stock of literary and racial stereotypes, attacked English literature in similar terms, demanded that literature should foster nationalism, advocated parochialism and derided modernism as well as 'thin-blooded' cosmopolitanism. These features remained integral both to the post-split *UI* and, consequently, to Yeats's literary criticism. The changes that resulted from the split were a greater emphasis on Irishness and the role of literature in nation-building. Yeats had anticipated this. His American journalism repeatedly stressed that Irish writers should draw on Irish themes and study Ireland's history and literature; it also repeatedly stressed that literature had an important role to play in achieving political freedom and in preparing the people for it.[58] While emphasising these aspects more strongly in his post-split *UI* articles, he also espoused the paper's altered literary and political agenda.

Irish literature, Yeats averred in a letter to the *UI*, 'must be applied to the needs of Ireland' (*UP1*, 224). These needs, as he clarified, pertained as much to the 'lyre' as to the 'pike-head' and could be best fulfilled by 'books on subjects ranging from Fenianism to the Education Question, from Oisin to Robert Emmet'. He reiterated the old formula about nationality and literature in a context that perforates the thin veneer of 'nationality' and casts about it the stronger glare of nationalism:

> Let it be the work of the literary societies to teach to the writers
> on the one hand, and to the readers on the other, that there is no
> nationality without literature and no literature without national-
> ity. In the old days when Davis sang there was no need to teach

it, for then Apollo struck his lyre with a pike-head, but now he
has flung both pike-head and lyre into the sea. (*UP1*, 224)

Allingham was criticised for not 'stirring our blood with great emotions' and
'writing of the joys and sorrows of the Irish people, as Davis, and Ferguson,
and Mangan have done' (212). He 'was no national poet', and hence was criticised for not being a nationalist, an equation that Yeats had made use of in
the past and would do so again. At his behest, the *UI* reported on his lecture,
'Nationality and Literature', delivered to the Clapham Branch of the Irish
National League of Great Britain.[59] The lecture, as with most such lectures,
began by attacking English literature and its influence. Yeats proclaimed that
Irish literature was 'in the period of great and hopeful youth' while 'that of
England has passed the stage of vigorous development and glided into its era
of old age' (23.1.92, 3). Among other things, the literature of old age was elaborate, skilled, technically accomplished and complex. These, for Irish poets,
were vices; the corresponding virtues were simplicity, sincerity and direct-
ness. They were advised that 'Irish literature should be careful to avoid English standards and modes of thought – youth cannot imitate old age with
success.' He then highlighted 'the connection which should exist between
nationality and literature' and explained how Irish literature through the ages
had always articulated the 'National idea'. His instancing of 'the Gaelic bards,
the Jacobite singers, the local and less known songsters, the Young Irelanders,
and others to our own day' who 'were thoroughly impressed with the idea
of Irish unity' once again indicates that in using 'National' instead of 'nationalist' he was merely paying lip-service to political secularism. His zeal did not
go unrewarded. While reviewing the *Book of the Rhymers' Club*, the paper
announced that it 'has become almost superfluous to praise Mr Yeats's poetry'
and instanced him as one among those who have benefited by not being
'afraid to declare their intense Nationalism in all places and under all circumstances' (5.3.92, 5–6). Such notices, of course, were part of the benefits,
however uneasily they may sit besides Yeats's contributions to Henley's
Observer.

During this period, both in the *UI* as well as in his American journalism,
Yeats's literary criticism was distinctly anglophobic. Despite his repeated insistence that criticism should be as international as possible, his own criticism
was as parochial as possible. Neither did his verse conform to his dictum of
literature being as national as possible. His '90s poems ('Rosa Mundi', 'The
Peace of the Rose', etc.), mostly written for Henley's periodicals and collected in *The Secret Rose* and *The Wind Among the Reeds*, were as esoteric and
international as possible, or, as O'Leary caustically remarked of his '80s writings, 'Irish in everything but the name' (*CL1*, 19, n.3). It is hardly surprising
therefore that, in the ten years of Yeats's association with the *UI* (1888–97),

he submitted only one poem for publication in the first instance to the newspaper. His articles drew on the *UI*'s register of polemics and racial and literary stereotypes to attack England and English literature in no uncertain
terms. Wilde was found to be 'Irish of the Irish' and his work was 'an extravagant Celtic crusade against Anglo-Saxon stupidity' (*UP1*, 203–4). In keeping with the *UI*, Yeats also continually advocated a parochialism and
disparaged English influence as being deracinating, modern and 'cosmopolitan'. English literature was something to be wary of and readers were told that
they 'need not concern themselves – unless they be very ardent readers' (*UP1*,
216) with Allingham's 'English' – i.e. non-Irish – poetry. Similarly, Todhunter's
non-Irish verse was felt to be a 'mistake', and something that could be safely
excluded from 'the present Irish edition with advantage to the book' (217).
In these articles, technical indifference was presented as being a positive Irish
attribute. The superiority of Todhunter's Irish poems lay in their being
'extremely simple and almost rough in their strain [*sic*] for primeval utterance', 'at times too matter-of-fact and bald, like the old stories themselves'.
Robert James O'Reilly's *Songs of Arcady* was praised for similar reasons: his
poems were 'simple, sincere and lucid', 'anything but experimental' using only
'the oldest and the simplest forms of verse', and all the more delightful
because they were 'wholly without ambition and as quiet and unobtrusive as
[their] tasteful brown paper cover' (230). Technical mastery was still too cosmopolitan and English an attribute. Though Yeats stressed the necessity of
practising an international and disinterested brand of literary criticism,[60] he
consistently weighed a writer's merits in relation to the 'Irishness' of his
theme rather than the manner or quality of its execution. While compiling
one of his many book lists in the *UI*, he explained his slanted methodology:

> Irish writers of equal or greater merit there have been whom I
> have not mentioned, because they did not make Ireland their sub-
> ject-matter, but united with the main stream of English literature.
> They have no special claim upon us . . . But those writers who
> have made Ireland their study have a peculiar claim on our affec-
> tions. (*UP1*, 208)[61]

To praise things Celtic at the expense of things Saxon was a principle that
informed Yeats's literary journalism, his book lists and his society-founding
sprees. It also informed the peculiar view of literary history that he preached
for a while.

Despite his numerous and robust assertions that literature should be serviceable to the national cause, Yeats was quite clearly an uneasy bedfellow
with the *UI*'s unmitigated and aggressive literary nationalism. Never 'quite
certain that one should be more than an artist, that even patriotism is more

than an impure desire in an artist' (*E&I*, 4), he had adopted the *UI* line partly to win its support and partly also to assert his own nationalist credentials in the only way the paper recognised. Given its narrow view of what constituted literary Irishness, and that Yeats, as a Protestant, would, in all likelihood, fall outside it, his assertions had to be that much more vociferous; he had to show himself to be more Irish than the Irish Catholic nationalists. Also, in such a situation, a defence and safeguard against marginalisation by a bigoted and oppressive criterion was to appropriate for himself the mantle of deciding who is and who isn't Irish. In doing so Yeats not only perpetuated the intolerance and bigotry that later so embittered him, but he also lashed others with the very scourge that could so easily have descended on him.

His treatment of Edward Dowden and George Savage-Armstrong exemplifies this. The former has already been dealt with by others and so it might be profitable to focus more on the latter.[62] For Yeatsians, Dowden and Savage-Armstrong have much in common: both were unionist littérateurs, Professors of English and old friends of J. B. Yeats who had encouraged his son in the past and were to be subjected to strongly worded public attacks by him in the future.[63] One of the most moving passages in the *Autobiographies* was probably written with them in mind and explains Yeats's hostility towards such figures:

> When I look back upon my Irish propaganda of those years I can see little but its bitterness. I never met with, or but met to quarrel with, my father's old family acquaintance; or with acquaintance I myself might have easily found, and kept among the prosperous educated class, who had all the great appointments at University or Castle; and this I did by deliberate calculation. If I must attack so much that seemed sacred to Irish Nationalist opinion, I must, I knew, see to it that no man suspect me of doing it to flatter Unionist opinion. Whenever I got the support of some man who belonged by birth and education to University or Castle, I would say, 'Now you must be baptised of the gutter.' (233)

Most of Yeats's Irish propaganda was in the *UI*, and indeed the phrase 'gutter journalism' springs quickly to mind while thinking of that nationalist weekly. 'Baptism of the gutter' was also a phrase that he had used in the past in a letter to Lady Gregory to describe the deliberate and systematic self-soiling that is a prelude to winning acceptance among the lower orders: 'In a battle, like Irelands, which is one of poverty against wealth, one must prove ones sincerity, by making oneself unpopular to wealth. One must accept the baptism of the gutter' (*CL2*, 512). He was to use the same phrase again later in his *Auto-*

biographies while describing a series of attacks he had made on establishment opinion, one of which involved Savage-Armstrong.[64] Hence, it is reasonable to infer that in the above-quoted passage from *Autobiographies* Yeats could well have been referring to the same person. Here, he confesses to distancing himself from his own class interests and making scapegoats out of unionists and establishment figures, not out of any ideological antagonism, but so that his own nationalist credentials could pass muster with Catholic nationalists. From Yeats's perspective, his Protestant background, at least initially, was a hostage to fortune and an impediment to his literary enterprise. Given the *UI*'s Catholic chauvinism, its narrow view of Irishness and its uncompromising attitude towards nationalism which brooked no half-measures – c.f. its reply to Rolleston: 'he who is not with us is against us, and must expect to be dealt with accordingly' (11.12.86, 6) – Yeats's fears were quite justified.

The context which provoked Yeats's attack on Savage-Armstrong is interesting because it links up with the above-quoted extract from *Autobiographies* and illuminates the motives underlying his attacks on the unionist establishment. The context also explains what exactly the 'baptism of the gutter' entails. According to Roy Foster, Yeats's Savage-Armstrong review was a response to Hyde's de-anglicising address:

> His [Yeats's] answer appeared in *United Ireland* on 17 December 1892, and argued unequivocally that Irish literature could be written in English, but in a Gaelic mode: Hyde's own translations were adduced as proof, and the Irish language identified with 'the snows of yesteryear.' But this put him in awkward company (Dowden? Mahaffy?), so he simultaneously proved his credentials as a hammer of the Unionist establishment by a vituperative review of George Savage-Armstrong's collected works. As a professor of English literature, Armstrong 'cut himself off from the life of the nation', and therefore doomed himself to literary futility. (*WBY*, 126)

Foster is right in interpreting Yeats's attack as a bid to strengthen his nationalist credentials. His explanation of Yeats's motives looks credible but is actually mistimed and anachronistic. In attacking Savage-Armstrong, Yeats could not possibly have been responding to either Hyde's address or the potential embarrassments arising out of his own response to it in the *UI*; both events occurred more than four months after his review of Savage-Armstrong.[65] In attacking Savage-Armstrong, Yeats was responding to something much closer to the bone.

The context for Yeats's attack on Savage-Armstrong is not Hyde's 'De-anglicising' lecture, but the *UI*'s 'Intellectual Capital' debate which Yeats claims to have helped engineer,[66] but which, like so many of his endeavours during this period, boomeranged on him. The debate, carried on in the *UI* between 7.3.92 and 9.7.92, was triggered by an article in the London *Daily Telegraph* arguing that, since the Irish spoke English, it is 'eminently fitting' (7.3.92, 4) that London and not Dublin should be the seat for an Irish Literary Society. The *UI* had retorted that it did not see any reason 'why we should regard London as the centre of our intellectual life. To do so would be to compromise our position as intelligent Nationalists, and to acknowledge that Ireland has no future' (12.3.92, 5). This, and the paper's subsequent statements (quoted earlier, see pp. 198–9, 211) indicate that its initial intention in engineering the debate was to impose the Parnellite agenda on the Revival and brand it with its stamp. During the debate, the paper asserted the intellectual independence of Irishmen, the centrality of Dublin over London and the link between Parnellite nationalism and the Literary Revival. The paper also demanded that Irish writers return to Dublin. The protests that this provoked among London's Irish émigrés widened the debate's focus to include ways in which Irish literature could be promoted in Ireland so that expatriate writers could be lured back, as well as the latters' reasons for living in London. They answered that should they return they would starve 'beautifully' and that Irish literature commanded more respect by the Thames than by the Liffey. Gradually, the debate provoked assertions of a more sensitive nature: true patriotism lies in staying at home; expatriate writers lacked the patriotism of resident Irish writers; the former had exploited and then turned against their people 'in their hour of need' (9.4.92, 5); they had sold out by writing for English readers and catering to their prejudices; their work was therefore not Irish.[67] Almost all of this applied to Yeats. He was acutely sensitive to such attacks and in his contribution to this debate had even tried to ward them off by denouncing anglicisation. His letter of 14.5.92 to the *UI* claimed that 'Ireland is between the upper and nether millstone – between the influence of America and the influence of England, and which of the two is denationalising us more rapidly it is hard to say' (*UP1*, 223). He also claimed that the purpose of the ILS was to 'arrest this denationalisation' rather than make London Ireland's intellectual capital. Out-righting his own right-wing critics, he asserted that Irish writers who had 'turned to any rather than Irish purposes' (224) and who had been 'compelled to make their pens the servants of a foreign literature and foreign inspirations' would never prosper until they applied themselves to Irish needs. But this wasn't quite enough.

While the debate was still in progress, the *UI* published an extensive report of a National Literary Society meeting at the Rotunda in Dublin. After reiterating that literature was instrumental in the 'preservation of the nation's dignity, and the guarding of the nation's independence' (18.6.92, 5), the paper commented on Yeats's speech:

Mr Yeats in his speech declared that the means in this matter [the literary Revival] were nobler and better than the end; but as Mr John Augustus O'Shea said a few weeks ago in these columns, let us not put too much faith in books. Thomas Davis was fond of literature, *qua* literature, as any man, but when he wrote for Ireland it was not the book he was thinking of, but what the book might do. We are most certainly for the end. (18.6.92, 5)

Yeats had already been worsted in a clash with O'Shea over the origin of the *Countess Kathleen* story. By invoking the latter's views to criticise Yeats, the *UI* was adding salt to injury. Coming as the culmination of the 'Intellectual Capital' debate which would have already touched a few raw nerves about Yeats's own expatriate and anglicised condition, not to mention his catering to English tastes and prejudices, the *UI*'s criticism put him in the dock along with cosmopolitans, Decadents and *fin de siècle* aesthetes who subscribed to the pernicious *l'art pour l'art* doctrine. It also contrasted unfavourably the pedantry and effeminacy, or, in other words, the un-Irishness that for the *UI* was entailed by being bookish, with the vigour and spirit of a Thomas Davis. More seriously still, it called Yeats's patriotism into question. Four issues later, Yeats made amends and reaffirmed his credentials by slating Savage-Armstrong's poetry in characteristically nationalist vocabulary and attacking him for being a unionist and an *anglicised* Irishman.[68]

His principle criticism of Savage-Armstrong's 'Collected Works' was that their author 'has tried to be an Englishman and to write as an Englishman, instead of reflecting the life that is about him' (*UP1*, 229). Having dissociated himself from the national life, he is ignorant of 'Celtic feelings and the Celtic traditions'. His 'false philosophy of life' has laid waste 'his innate poetic faculty' and condemned him to 'being the beater of the air all his days'. Of the nine volumes, only Savage-Armstrong's lone 'Irish' book met Yeats's stringent nationalist criterion but that too was touched with 'that conventionality of feeling which seems inseparable with West Britonism'. The literary merits of his work received little mention. When Yeats attacked Savage-Armstrong, he made him a scapegoat and did so by 'deliberate calculation' in order to ratify his own impugned nationalist credentials before the *UI* readers. That it was convenience rather than conviction, context rather than content that determined Yeats's *UI* article on Savage-Armstrong is highlighted by a comparison with another review of Savage-Armstrong's works that Yeats wrote about the same time.[69] Free from the compulsions and considerations determining his *UI* article, his review of Savage-Armstrong, published in the *Bookman's* September issue, addressed itself primarily to the literary aspects of the works and not at all to their author's politics. As a result, instead of one, Yeats finds two 'very readable and pleasant works' (*UP1*, 238), one of which deals with

Greek topics, and these contain 'a very fairly bulky collection of more or less interesting verse'. Further, though Savage-Armstrong lacks the 'imaginative impulse' he is praised for the courage of his conviction and for taking 'the world and his own mission very seriously'. After the triflers and dilettantes, Yeats is pleased to find a poet who is in his element while dealing with 'weighty themes and in the most lofty metrical forms'. In a single paragraph, 'lofty' and 'great' are used twice to describe Savage-Armstrong's poetry. Yeats's conclusion indicates how radically the pressures of literary propaganda before a nationalist audience affected his literary style and critical pronouncements: '[the Wicklow poems] will commemorate for a generation or two Mr Armstrong's name *and keep him a king among his own people*' (239; emphasis added). A *UI* reader of this *Bookman* article might well have wondered who were Armstrong's own people, who were Yeats's people, and what happened to 'the beater of the air'?

By 1892–93, the slipshod and rough-and-ready style of Davis and the Young Irelanders had become the object of Yeats's most strenuous attacks. However, his attempts to court popular favour which accompanied these attacks ended up ratifying the very prejudices that undermined his attempts at de-Davisising Irish literature. Though he attacked technical indifference, he also claimed it as being a typically Irish characteristic, as opposed to decadent or cosmopolitan. What further undermined his whole de-Davisisation project was that each time he attacked technical indifference and shoddy execution he provoked a counter-attack accusing him of being anglicised, decadent and cosmopolitan, for these were the very qualities that the *UI*, and Yeats, had associated with technical accomplishment. 'For how could I prove by argument that certain wavering rhythms, for instance, are nearer to the soul than the resolute rhythm of political oratory, or even that such a question had any importance? I had by taking to propaganda estranged the artist's only friend, Time, who brings to his side the purified senses of men' (*Mem*, 57).

At this stage, Yeats could not afford to lose his Irish readership; at the same time he felt it incumbent on him to reform their tastes and create the standards by which his own work should be judged. As a result, his critical writings of this period are riven with contradictions borne out of the desire to both pander to popular literary prejudices as well as to dispel them. They are also characterised by the insecurity of one anxious to be accepted as 'one of us' lest he be left on the margins. His article, 'Hopes and Fears for Irish Literature', and his lecture of 19.5.93, 'Nationality and Literature' (not to be confused with the identically entitled lecture reported on 23.1.92, 3), exemplify this. They also exemplify his attempts to accommodate and mediate between the conflicting sides of his public and private selves: Irish writer and London resident; a propagandist of literary nationalism and a *fin de siècle*

aesthete; an Irish nationalist and a Protestant; an anglophobe and cosmopolitan; a Celticist and an anglophone. His article, published in the *UI* on
15.10.92, begins by remarking on the astonishing difference between cultivated people in Ireland and in England. In England, he states, they are more
numerous and see art as an end in itself and the most important thing in life.
Under French influence, they have divorced poetry from life and privileged
it over morality and philosophy. 'Music of cadence and beauty of phrase'
(*UP1*, 248) was all. For them, 'literature had ceased to be the handmaid of
humanity, and become instead a terrible queen, in whose services the stars
rose and set, and for whose pleasure life stumbles along in the darkness'. He
states, however, that there is much to be learned from them, namely the desire
to write as well as possible, and the refusal to 'bow to the prejudices of the
multitude'. This does not conflict with literary nationalism. But then by
asserting that 'he who writes well and lives badly is usually of more service
to the world at large than he who writes badly and lives well, and he is always
better than the crowd who do both indifferently' (248–9), he privileges literature over life and action, thereby contradicting his own professed belief in
the subservience of literature to national ends. He first criticises aestheticism
from an Irish standpoint, and then demands that the Irish become aesthetes.

This see-sawing goes on throughout the article. Irish literature is shown
to be radically different to the aestheticism of the English and French poets:

> When I talk to people of literary ambition here in Ireland, I find
> them holding that literature must be the expression of convic-
> tion, and be the garment of noble emotion and not an end in
> itself. I found them most interested in the literary forms that give
> most opportunity for the display of great characters and great pas-
> sions. (249)

To clarify his own loyalties before a nationalist audience, he recalls the irritation that he provoked among 'a noted gathering of the younger English
imaginative writers' – his fellow members of the Rhymers' Club – when he
tried to explain his 'philosophy of poetry . . . and to show the dependence, as
I conceived it, of all great art and literature upon conviction and upon heroic
life' (248). Having differentiated Irish literature from English and French aestheticism on the basis of whether or not one believes in *l'art pour l'art*, Yeats,
in the later part of his essay, demands that artists show a religious devotion to
their art and, Buddha-like, renounce the world:

> Yet, he who would write a memorable song . . . must give to his
> art the devotion the Crusaders of old gave to their cause and be
> content to be alone among men, apart alike from their joys and
> their sorrows, having for companions the multitude of his dreams

and for reward the kingdom of his pride. He who would belong to things eternal must for the most part renounce his allotted place amid the things of time. (249–50)

However, the care and workmanship that he now demands have already been described as decadent and quintessentially un-Irish qualities in the earlier part of the essay:

> for he who writes well and lives badly . . . is always better than the crowd who do both indifferently. But one thing cannot be said. It is not possible to call a literature produced in this way the literature of energy and youth. The age which has produced it is getting old and feeble, and sits in the chimney-corner carving all manner of curious and even beautiful things upon the staff that can no longer guide its steps. Here in Ireland we are living in a young age, full of hope and promise – a young age which has only just begun to make its literature. It was only yesterday that it cut from the green hillside the staff which is to help its steps upon the long road. There is no carving upon the staff, the rough bark is still there, and the knots are many upon the side. (249)

Yeats's literary polarities cater to his audience's sense of national identity and fulfil what has in a way become a prerequisite and prelude to any kind of literary lecture. By mouthing these standard platitudes and pandering to popular prejudices, he ingratiates himself to his listeners so that they might be more receptive to his views on the necessity of literary workmanship and technique. However, his argument against the politicisation of art is in itself a cleverly masked political argument. Its crux, pithily summarised by Terry Eagleton, is that 'an art too closely geared to political action fails precisely as art, and so fails to move in some more deep-seated, politically fertile way':

> His position on nationalist art around the turn of the century was admirably adroit: by serving some immediate political cause, Irish writers have failed to evolve a tradition of their own, a task which demands time and patience, and so surrendered themselves meekly to English literary forms. Yeats can thus assail propagandist nationalist verse while covering his political back, out-lefting and de-politicising simultaneously.

Eagleton also quite rightly points to the nationalist and modernist bases of Yeats's hostility to the Young Ireland poetic tradition: 'nationalist because England was the home of debased popular literature, modernist because modernism is among other things a resistance to the mass culture which was born alongside it'.[70] However, Yeats undermines his own case by soaking his sops in the *UI*'s concoction of anglophobic racial dichotomies according to which his own de-Davisisation enterprise is decadent and un-Irish. What he doesn't seem to realise is that stereotypes cannot be invoked in isolation; willy-nilly they come as a package: buy one and you get the others free. And it is not merely by association that they make their presence felt, but by actual instancing, as we see in the above example. The antagonism that is posited is both racial as well as literary: age versus youth; feebleness versus energy; decay versus freshness; complexity and beauty versus hope and promise; finesse versus roughness; aestheticism versus literary nationalism. It is all very well to say that English literature is different from Irish literature and that in some ways the latter is better. But when even a few of the characteristics ascribed to the former take on pejorative racial connotations, all get tainted by the same brush by the power of association. Technical accomplishment and literary workmanship, qualities Yeats would want to see in Irish writing, are put into the enemy's camp; they are the products of old age, debility and decadence. On the other hand, social and political utility, literary didacticism, crudity and technical indifference, qualities which Yeats is militating against, are seen as being preeminently Irish and hence desirable. To now expect Irish writers to learn technique from their English counterparts is to undercut the very bedrock of his Irish propaganda and of the posited difference between literary Irishness and Englishness or cosmopolitanism. Yeats's metaphorising of literature as a staff indicates this perfectly. Decadent literature, though crafted beautifully with care and effort, is peripheral to life; it 'sits in the chimney-corner' effete and ineffectual: it cannot guide or direct its age. In stark contrast, Irish literature is young, fresh, idealistic and in the service of the community, even though it has not been polished or refined. To desire the polish and the refinement as Yeats does would be to swap Irish characteristics for English ones lock, stock and barrel. Not surprisingly, the following week, a reader, signing his name in Gaelic, rejected Yeats's 'appeals for more form in our Irish productions' (29.10.92, 1–2). Averring that art should be a 'handmaid to life', the indignant nativist attacked what he saw as Yeats's art for art's sake attitude and criticised him for attempting to divorce literature from human concerns.

Yeats's 'Nationality and Literature' address, published in the *UI* on 27.5.93, is even more ambivalent about his own literary standing and consequently embodies even more such contradictions and back-and-forth manoeuvres. He begins as usual by positing some governing racial differences between the Saxons and the Celts. The former are practical, utilitarian and materialistic while the latter are philosophic, idealistic and spiritual. Moreover, Irish literature is not utilitarian and has never 'served the material needs of the race' as its counterpart has done. After giving his audience a rather flattering image of themselves, he reverts to his theory of literary genealogy delineating the increasing degeneration, debility and complexity of older literatures.[71] He claims that not only are English and Irish literatures in different stages of their development, but also that they are 'as different as the beach [*sic*] tree from the oak' (*UP1*, 269). (Needless to add, the qualitative difference between the beech and the oak reflects the qualitative differences between the two literatures.) He then suggests that there are things that the oak could learn from the beech.

Yeats goes on to divide a nation's literature into three phases – epic, dramatic and lyric – and asserts that, like a tree in its development, literature as it moves from the epic to the lyric phase gradually becomes more complex, sophisticated, decadent and divorced from humanity. Ireland is in its epic phase and England in its lyric. Greek literature is instanced as an example of literary degeneration: Homer (epic) was followed by Aeschylus and Sophocles (dramatic) who in turn were followed by 'the [lyric] poets known to us through the Greek anthology' (*UP1*, 269). Contemporary English poetry is also cited as another example of such degeneration. He asserts that one of the disadvantages of the poetry of the lyric age is that it 'steps aside further and further from the general life' (270) and hence is of little use to the nation. (Earlier in the lecture he criticised English literature for being utilitarian and serving the 'material needs of the race'.) On the other hand, Irish literature, being in its pure epic age, 'deals with great national events' and deploys 'those literary forms that . . . [give] opportunity for the display of great character and great passions' (249). Such easy formulations give rise to absurd classifications: *In Memoriam*, in Yeats's view, can have no connection with human affairs because of its provenance in a lyrical age, and 'Down by the Salley Gardens' and 'The Lake Isle of Innisfree' are epics dealing with great national events because they emanate from an epic age. To force his point about English poetry being in the throes of a lyric epidemic, Yeats classifies Browning as a lyricist. Not one to shy away from a challenge, he asserts that the 'form of Browning is more commonly than not dramatic or epic, but the substance is lyrical'. He then adduces 'Paracelsus' and 'Sordello'– poems as far from being epic as they are from being lyric – and concludes magisterially, 'The very names of these writers and of these poems are enough to prove my case. The tree has come to greatest complexity of leaf and fruit and flower' (272).

Yeats's theory of literary genetics and mutation, a theory that portrayed the Celt in ascendancy and the Saxon in decline, was intended to flatter nationalist sentiment and anticipate slurs of 'Decadent' and 'Aesthete' that inevitably greeted his suggestion that Irish writers should take their craft more seriously. In this lecture, lyric, for Yeats, was a bad thing and therefore the English poets were lyricists. It dealt not with national character or great events as epic or drama did but with nationless moods and passions. It was cosmopolitan. Further, unlike Irish poetry which was national, lyrics were 'made by the few for the few' (271). They were also full of 'subtlety, obscurity and intricate utterance' (271). But forty years later, when he had realised his own lyric genius, he boasted that, while a lyric was an aberration in Victorian poetry, he and his friends had 'tried to write like the poets of the Greek Anthology' (*E&I*, 495):

> [In the Victorian era] A short lyric seemed an accident, an interruption amid more serious work. Somebody has quoted Browning as saying that he could have written lyrics had he thought them worth the trouble. The aim of my friends, my own aim, if it sometimes made us prefer the acorn to the oak, the small to the great, freed us from many things that we thought an impurity. (*E&I*, 494–5)

In Ireland during the 1890s nationalist literature was ostensibly Yeats's measure of excellence and he devised various criteria to assert its superiority over English poetry. It is superior, Yeats stresses in his lecture, because it is the product of a national spirit, not of an individual vision. He argues that Irish literature, unlike 'cosmopolitan' English poetry, is national and rooted in the populace; it expresses 'its loves and its hates, its likes and its dislikes . . . it deals with great National events. Our poetry is still a poetry of the people in the main, for it still deals with the tales and thoughts of the people' (*UP1*, 273). The ideal he espouses is that of a populist and national literature, or, in other words, the Irish antithesis to English poetry.

Nearing the end of the lecture, Yeats begins administering the sugar-coated pill which undermines much of what had gone before. At this stage his contradictions follow each other rapidly. He declares that the Irish must 'foster and protect' a distinct school of Irish literature whose 'foundation is sunk in the legend lore of the people and in the National history' (273). However, the latter would excuse the versified political propaganda that so often passed for literature, and so in the very next sentence Yeats backtracks with some attempts at obfuscation: 'The literature of Greece and India had just such a foundation, and as we, like the Greeks and the Indians, are an idealistic people, this foundation is fixed in legend rather than in history' (273–4). Then, having already denigrated the Victorian lyric poets for their aestheticism and their art-for-art's-sake philosophy, Yeats now advocates a similar approach for Irish writers:

> We must learn, too, from the old nations to make literature almost the most serious thing in our lives if we would understand it properly, and quite the most serious thing if we could write it well. (274)

> How often do I not hear in this country that literature is to be
> achieved by some kind of mysterious visitation of God, which
> makes it needless for us to labour at the literary art, and hearing
> this long for one hour among my books with the great Flaubert,
> who talked of art, art and again art . . .

A year earlier, he had warned Irish writers that they 'should be careful to
avoid English standards and modes of thought – youth cannot imitate old age
with success' (23.1.92, 3). Moreover, at the beginning of this lecture, he had
criticised lyric poetry for its obscurity and praised Irish poetry for its rugged
simplicity. But now, towards the end of the lecture, he defends obscurity as
being inevitable 'unless much that is more profound in thought and feeling
is to be left out of poetry'. Does that imply that, for Yeats, Irish poetry lacks
profundity in thought and feeling?

When Yeats pitted nationalist literature against lyric poetry, he indicted the
Rhymers along with the Victorians. While doing so, he chose to forget his
own involvement with the Rhymers' Club and his contributions to its first
anthology published just eight months earlier.[72] A few years later it was these
very theories that were to be forgotten when Yeats enthusiastically reviewed
books by the Rhymers, defended 'Decadence' and placed numerous articles
in the *Yellow Book* and the *Savoy*, including one on Verlaine's visit to London.
He would then define the Victorian age, not as an age of lyric poetry, but one
'of scientific and political thought'.[73] The Rhymers, though now placed
firmly in the enemy camp along with the Victorians, would later be rehabilitated into the ranks of Yeats's anti-Victorian brigade. For 'they, too, were in
reaction against everything Victorian' (*E&I*, 494). While Yeats's schema of literary evolution served his purpose – to push English literature to a lower
level than Irish literature – it trapped him in all sorts of contradictions and
distortions. In December 1892, he had asserted (to an English audience in the
Bookman) that all writers, 'the great no less than the small among them, have
been heavily handicapped by being born in a lyrical age' (*UP1*, 251). By May
of 1893 (to a *UI* readership), he claimed that only England was in the lyric
age; Ireland remained uncontaminated in its pristine epic glory. Then in 1895,
Ferguson, though an 'epic' figure, was relegated to the lyric age.[74] By 1898,
however, when Yeats was championing Arthur Symons and symbolism, lyri-
cism was, apparently, ubiquitous.[75]

Yeats derived his tree analogy and much of his theory of literary history
from Arthur Hallam. While defending lyric poetry, and Tennyson in particular, against hostile utilitarian criticism, Hallam had charted the development of literature and advanced the principles of the movement which he
felt Tennyson represented.[76] In England and Ireland, Yeats selectively
expounded Hallam's principles for directly contrary ends. It is therefore

important to differentiate between Yeats's use of Hallam's literary historiography and his application of Hallam's defence of Tennyson and his principles (which Yeats termed 'aestheticism').[77] In English literary journals, lyric poetry and aestheticism were espoused by citing Hallam's defence; in Ireland, however, they were disparaged on the authority of Hallam's literary history. By defining a nationalist literature in opposition to lyric and decadent poetry, and by privileging the former over the latter, Yeats imposed a political burden on Hallam's classification of literary periods and gave his own 'Irish' aesthetic a patriotic aspect in the public eye. Yeats's Irish and English literary criticism also differed radically on *l'art pour l'art*, which was attacked in Ireland and defended in England. While in England, he raised the call for a literature and criticism that was 'pure and unalloyed', in Ireland he advocated nationalist literature.

Only two months after the lecture on 'Nationality and Literature', and in his very next article,[78] but now to an English audience, Yeats praised pure lyric poetry in terms which, in someone not Janus-faced, would suggest an abrupt transformation. Hallam's essay was presented as being a defence 'of the first principles of a school' (*UP1*, 277) whose artistic purity and aestheticism did not find favour with lay readers accustomed to populist and didactic literature. Yeats highlighted the persistence of such a malaise, and argued that 'Any who adopt their [populist and didactic] principles . . . share their popularity' (*UP1*, 277). Quoting Hallam's conclusion in italics –

> *Hence, whatever is mixed up with art, and appears under its semblance, is always more favourably regarded than art free and unalloyed.* Hence, half the fashionable poems in the world are mere rhetoric, and half the remainder are not liked by the generality for their substantial merits.

– he adduced it as 'the best explanation we have seen of the popularity of the didactic poets and of the anecdotists of all ages' (277–8). What with the widespread popularity enjoyed by Tennyson and Browning, and the stigma attached to decadent literature, Yeats, in this review, did not have to name either the modern-day beneficiaries of Hallam's plea or the objects of his attack. He skilfully superimposed the image of the Rhymers onto the school of Tennyson (as defined and defended by Hallam) and then expelled Tennyson along with Browning into the enemy ranks.[79]

The hitherto professed ideal of a literature 'of the people in the main', a literature which is 'the expression of conviction' dealing 'with great national events' and facilitating 'the display of great characters and great passions' would now be denounced as 'the lusts of the market place' (*UP2*, 131) and as merely good rhetoric:

all good literature is made out of temperaments. To be preoccupied with public conduct is to be preoccupied with the ideas and emotions which the average man understands or can be made to understand, and out of the ideas and emotions of the average man you can make no better thing than good rhetoric. (*UP2*, 34)

What was advanced in place of a nationalist and popular literature was the antithesis of Yeats's earlier ideal, a poetry that 'steps aside further and further from the general life'. In a complete *volte face*, he averred in 1898–99 that the poet must 'liberate the arts from "their age" and from life' (*UP2*, 131), pursue 'a dangerous delight in beauty for the sake of beauty' (*UP2*, 194) and 'draw one's imagination as far as possible from the complexity of modern life and thought' (*E&I*, 190).

In the two months (27 May to 22 July 1893) between propagating his theory of literary nationalism to the National Literary Society and to *UI* readers, and expounding the concept of pure art to readers of the *Bookman*, Yeats had not undergone a sudden change of heart. His own facility with the lyric had become increasingly clear to him since his association with the Rhymers in the early nineties. However, lyric was a cosmopolitan art form and therefore not suitable for Irish literature. An adept rhetorician with ten years of journalistic propaganda behind him, he modified his arguments *mutatis mutandis* to keep abreast of the change in his readers. The ones he was addressing in the *Bookman* were more literary, and less liable than the readers of the *UI* to be either gulled by simplistic literary theories or to be won over by caricatures of English character and literary tastes. Hence he used Hallam to advance the very same avant-garde aesthetic that he had denounced in Ireland with Hallam's help.

The contradictory literary gospels Yeats preached in England and Ireland were reflected in the opposition between his poetic practice and his public pronouncements. The very themes that his English criticism disparaged as being unsuitable for literature – public themes, philosophy, morality and history – his *UI* criticism validated as being essentially Irish. On the other hand, though in Ireland Yeats had criticised 'the nature description of most modern poets' as being mere 'masks behind which go on the sad soliloquies of a nineteenth-century egotism' (*UP1*, 103), he was equally guilty of the same faults. As his poetry of the 1880s and '90s testifies, he was prone to expressions of soul sickness amid scenes 'Where drops of dew in myriads fall, / And tangled creepers every hour / Blossom in some new crimson flower' ('The Wanderings of Oisin', *VP*, 16). Early reviews of his poetry were quick to seize on his self-indulgence.[80] His most famous and much anthologised early lyric, 'The Lake Isle of Innisfree', exemplified the same sad soliloquies that Yeats found so distasteful in English nature poetry. Similarly, when Yeats, in his schema of literary history, espoused the genetically superior form of nation-alist epic over the decadence of lyric poetry, he ignored the fact that he had earned his reputation as a writer of lyrics, not of epics. That during this period he continued exploring the potentialities of the lyric form indicates how lit-tle heed he paid to his own literary propaganda.

The insincerity necessitated by his work in the *UI* and the strain of hav-ing to constantly say things he did not agree with began taking its toll. Reply-ing to Alice Milligan's criticisms, he wrote to the paper saying that a writer, regardless of his political passions and convictions, must 'endeavour to become a master of his craft, and be ever careful to keep rhetoric, or *the ten-dency to think of his audience* rather than of the Perfect and the True, out of his writings' (*CL1*, 371; emphasis added). This was entirely unprovoked, because Milligan had accused Yeats not of being insincere or of playing to the galleries but of forsaking politics for literature. A year later, while protesting against the *UI*'s vaunted 'adamantine indifference' to non-Irish literary criticism, Yeats argued that such provinciality hindered literary development. He also defended Irish critics who, because of such an attitude, were 'forced to crit-icise Irish books in English papers' (*CL1*, 417) and repeated his slogan about the necessity for criticism to be as international as possible. The paper, how-ever, stuck to its guns, insisting that literary criticism outside Ireland was big-oted and insensitive. This, as we have seen earlier (see p. 130), was precisely the same defence Yeats had made some years earlier in a *Boston Pilot* article.[81]

That the *UI*, which was the prime mover in the Literary Revival, viewed literature as a means to an end and not as an end in itself, as Yeats did, often created a clash of opinions. His attempts to argue against this view were strongly rebuked, as Dr McBride's letter to the *UI* illustrates. Similarly, Yeats's efforts to refine Irish literary tastes and shift the focus away from politics and patriotism to literature and literary criticism met with stiff *UI* opposition. He wrote to the paper suggesting that it was inappropriate for the National Musical Festival to be dedicated to Moore, whose literary reputation had been denuded over time.[82] He also argued that such indifference to critical opinion would repel rather than attract educated people and perpetuate the 'artificiality', 'insincerity' and 'uncritical enthusiasm' that has entangled Irish literature and kept 'patriotic fire' away from the 'dim corners of West Briton-ism'. While he stressed the role of 'national literature' and 'history' in build-ing up patriotism, he insisted that these would be of no avail unless the Irish learn to 'set truth above the national glory'. His letter displays an awareness of the fact that in criticising the patriotic considerations underlying Moore's popularity, he was leaving himself open to charges of West Britonism. Once again his predictions were accurate and the *UI*'s response was swift and cut-ting. A few weeks later, a long lampoon of thirteen quatrains, entitled 'A

Poetaster's Soliloquy on Moore' and clearly directed at Yeats, appeared in the first column of the cover page. It attacked Yeats for sycophantically following English opinion and attributed his dislike of Moore to professional jealousy. Yeats's nationalism, it suggested, was self-serving.[83] The matter did not end there and a few weeks the paper published an extract of T. O. Russell's speech to the ILS defending Moore's 'genius and patriotism' (1.6.95, 4): 'Mr Russell said that he "counted all joy" whenever he saw Moore dispraised by the English and by their *shoneen* imitators in Ireland.'

Yeats was often a victim of the paper's overriding preoccupation with political ends. In a *Bookman* review he had criticised Duffy's selection of *The Patriot Parliament* as more becoming of a 'learned society' than a literary one:

> Pages upon pages of Acts of Parliament may be popular literature on the planet Neptune, or chillier Uranus, but our quick-blooded globe has altogether different needs. (*UP1*, 333)

The *UI* attacked him for this even though it largely agreed with his views on Duffy's selection. Its opposition was directed at Yeats's criticism of an Irish production in an English publication. It printed his above-quoted remark about Neptune and Uranus and commented:

> What, by the way, our quick-blooded globe has to do with the case I do not know; for I was under the impression that the Library was written and published for our own quick-blooded Ireland. (18.8.94, 1)

Not only was this harking back to the issue of 'adamantine indifference' over which Yeats and the *UI* had already clashed swords, but it was also obliquely asking Yeats to decide as to which constituency of readers and, consequently, standard of literary criticism he owed his loyalty. Later, his *Bookman* article of August 1895, in which he described the Revival as consisting of 'a school of men of letters united by a common purpose, and a small but increasing public who love literature for her own sake and not as the scullery-maid of politics', was found to be 'not worthy of him':

> We sincerely wish that the hope may be fulfilled, but we are of the opinion that if ever Irish Literature is loved for its own sake it must be at a time when the people have no concern with politics. That, we fear, is a long way off. While the struggle for our National rights goes on politics is indispensable. It might be best for the cause of Literature if its votaries so fostered it that it would tend to make the National struggle short. Davis made it serve that purpose. (17.8.95, 1)

The one-and-a-half column cover-page review went on to criticise Yeats's 'very pernicious doctrine', which it attributed to the influence of 'the eccentric philosophy of Oscar Wilde'. The fact that this was written in the wake of the Queensbury trial would explain why Wilde is denied the courtesy of a 'Mr', something generally accorded to even Balfour at his coercive worst. The rebuke also indicates the *UI*'s own deep-seated opposition to anything that diverted attention away from the nationalist agenda.

However, Yeats's efforts at de-Davisising Irish literature did not go entirely unrecognised by the *UI*. In December 1895, while reviewing his *Poems*, the weekly hailed him as the leader of the Irish literary revolution. Because this article was particularly gratifying to him, an extended quotation is perhaps justifiable:

> But nothing, we dare say, could better illustrate the backward condition of Irish opinion with reference to literature than the fact that the notion [that the Young Irelanders were the greatest poets] has lasted for almost fifty years and that it is dying a very slow death even at the present moment, with all the new literary forces and movements of the day knocking at its gates with Cyclopean hammers. It is dying, however; and to no one person – or perhaps we should say to no half dozen of persons – is the fact so much due as to Mr W. B. Yeats. For over ten years Mr Yeats was a voice crying in the wilderness. He was ridiculed for his literary peculiarities, and laughed at for his critical eccentricities. Men who had grown grey in the conventionalities of Irish verse shrugged their shoulders at this queer and piquant person. Yet, time has been with Mr Yeats. Nay, perhaps we should, in justice, put the matter more directly by saying that Mr Yeats has been the leader of an Irish literary revolution. Certainly no Irish literary man of our day has done so much to lift Irish poetry out of what we may justly call the ruck of Young Ireland rhetoric, and place it, so to speak, without prejudice, on the floor of English and international literature. (14.12.95, 5)[84]

During 1892–95 Yeats had begun to strain against the restraints of a stringent literary nationalism partly perpetuated by himself. De-anglicisation as advocated by Yeats – read only Irish books, write about only Irish things – resulted in a narrow parochialism. This, when yoked to literary nationalism, especially as the *UI* interpreted it, made patriotic Irishness the only yardstick of literary talent. Further, in toeing the *UI* line, Yeats's emphasis on de-anglicisation and parochialism was distinctly anglophobic and politically motivated. This once again put literature in thrall to a political cause. Anglicisation, cosmopolitanism, decadence and aestheticism had been portrayed as vices, just as Irishness, provincialism and literary nationalism were their corresponding virtues. By propounding this opposition between Irish and non-Irish qualities in such stark terms, Yeats left no allowance for the possibility that a hair-breadth could divide one from the other. He also ended up condemning his own literary instincts and tastes, especially those fostered at the Cheshire Cheese with the Rhymers. Technique, which for Yeats was a desirable quality (by 1893), had been damned as non-Irish and cosmopolitan. Similarly, Irishness too was a virtue, but taken to its extreme, especially while disregarding literariness, it resulted in propaganda or mere patriotism parading as literature of the Young Ireland variety. So also *l'art pour l'art* was something Yeats would have liked to endorse, but it was a decadent and *fin de siècle* characteristic and directly conflicted with the nationalist agenda by recognising no higher law. The whole dilemma can be summarised in the basic formula: literature should be an end in itself but it should also be typically Irish, national and patriotic. The problem was that Irishness, as the *UI* and Yeats had defined it, was intrinsically opposed to literariness, just as de-anglicisation was opposed to de-Davisisation.

When referring to this period of his *UI* propaganda, his autobiographical writings speak of how 'one part of me looked on, mischievous and mocking, and the other part spoke words which were more and more unreal, as the attitude of mind became more and more strained and difficult' (*E&I*, 249). His literary proselytising and its compromises bred self-loathing and unease: 'I had come to think of societies and movements to encourage literature, or create it where it was not, as absurd – is not the artist always solitary?' (*Mem*, 50). Though his own instincts ran counter to his proclamations, a clean break was impossible. Caught in this gutter of his own choosing and steep't in so far, returning were as tedious as going o'er.

APPENDIX II

Date	Contents	Political Events
20.12.90	First issue under Parnell after the split.	
20.12.90 to 10.1.91	Dominated by politics. Coverage of the split and of the North Kilkenny by-election.	Parnellite split and North Kilkenny by-election called.
3.1.91.	New column 'The Farm' started on 3. League reports significantly reduced.	
17.1.91 to 21.3.91	An average of 1 col. of literature often on cover.	Parnellite candidate defeated.
21.2.91	New column 'Beyond the Seas' started on 1. Literature increased to about 4 columns.	
28.2.91	New column 'North & South' started on 1 and 'The Gael' on 5.	
28.3.91 to 25.4.91	Dominated by politics. Almost no literature.	North Sligo election called.
2.5.91 to 30.5.91	Politics reduced and literature increased on 1 and 5.	Parnellite candidate defeated.
6.6.91 to 4.7.91	Dominated by politics. Almost no literature	Carlow election called.
11.7.91 to 8.8.91	Politics curtailed. Literature back on 1 and 5.	Parnellite candidate defeated.
15.8.91 to 22.8.91	International news on cover, literature on 5.	
12.9.91	5 dominated by literature and 6 by international news.	
19.9.91	History on cover. No political news on cover. Article on Irish art on 2, and international news on 6.	

26.9.91	Literature on 5 and international news on 6.	
10.10.91	Literature on cover. 4–5 Parnell.	Parnell died just before midnight on 6.10.91
17.10.91	Whole issue on Parnell.	
24.10.91 to 31.10.91	Mainly Parnell; literature and international news curtailed.	
7.11.91	Literature dominates 5.	
7.11.91	Literary serial interrupted by Cork election propaganda.	
14.11.91	Whole issue on political events.	Redmond defeated in Cork.
21.11.91	International news on cover; serial on 5, but no literary articles.	
28.11.91 to 12.12.91	Literature on 5.	
19.12.91 to 2.1.92	Only political news.	Waterford election.
9.1.92 to 6.2.92	Literature back on 5.	
13.2.92	Literature on 1 and dominates 5; also 'Irish Wit and Humour' on cover.	
20.2.92	Only politics on cover.	Parliament convened.
25.6.92 to 16.7.92	Only politics in full issue.	Election campaigning.
23.7.92	Literature back on page 5.	Parnellite MPs reduced from 23 to 9.
30.7.92	Literature dominates cover and 5.	
20.8.92	Literature dominates cover and 5.	
27.8.92	Only politics in the whole issue.	Gladstone tables Home Rule Bill.
3.9.92	Literature on 2 and 5.	

10.9.92	Literature dominates cover.	
1.10.92	Literature dominates cover.	
8.10.92	Only politics in whole issue.	Parnell anniversary.
15.10.92	Literature on 5.	
22.10.92	Literature on cover.	
7.1.93 to 21.1.93	Only politics in whole issue.	Home Rule Bill imminent.
28.1.93	Literature on 2 and 5.	
4.2.93 to 25.2.93	Only politics in whole issue.	Parliament convened and Home Rule Bill introduced.
11.3.93	Literature on cover and 5.	
30.12.93	Literature dominates cover and 5.	
14.4.94 to 2.6.94	Literature dominates cover; politics on 5.	
2.6.94 to 14.7.94	India debate on cover; very little literature.	
21.7.94 to 28.7.94	Literature dominates cover.	
4.8.94	Literature on cover replaced by Davitt Debate, Irish Gossip, war coverage.	Japan–Korea War.
18.8.94	Literature back on cover.	
6.10.94 to 13.10.94	Only politics in whole issue.	Parnell anniversary.
10.11.94 to 24.11.94	Literature dominates cover.	
1.12.94	Only literature on cover.	
8.12.94	Mainly literature on cover. No politics.	
29.12.94	Very little politics in this issue and none on 1–2 which is mainly literature.	

5.1.95	Mostly international news and literature in issue; no politics. 'Gossip' on cover.	
19.1.95 to 2.2.95	Only literature on cover. Out of total of 56 columns literature has 19, news and politics has 18, Advertisements have 16, Miscellaneous Notes has 1 and 'Irish Gossip' has 1.	
9.2.95	Only literature on cover. Opening of parliament and Queen's speech relegated to 2.	
16.2.95	Literature dominates cover.	
23.2.95 to 20.4.95	Mainly literature on cover and 5.	
27.4.95	Mostly politics on cover.	East Wicklow election propaganda.
4.5.95	Election results, international news and literature on cover.	
18.5.95	Literature dominates cover. Only Athletics on 3.	
25.5.95 to 22.6.95	No politics on cover which is made up of travelogues, tourist guides, reviews of periodicals and other newspapers, 'Irish Folk Lore', and 'Miscellaneous Items'.	
29.6.95	Only politics on cover. No literature in whole issue	Fall of Liberal government and Cork elections.
13.7.95	Politics dominates cover, 4 and 5; takes over 3 from Athletics.	Election campaigning.
20.7.95	Literature dominates cover; Athletics on 3.	Parnellites trounced in elections.
27.7.95	Only literature on cover.	

APPENDIX III

To the Editor, *United Ireland*, 16.2.95.

'Thomas Moore and the National Music Festival'

Sir —

I see by your issue of last Saturday that the National Musical Festival is to be held, if possible, on the anniversary of the birth of Moore; and is intended, I gather from the general tone of the article, to be a kind of annual proclamation of his greatness. I urge the committee, if this be so, to consider the change that has taken place in the attitude of the best critics towards the greater portion of his works. As the fame of Keats, Shelley and Wordsworth has risen, the fame of Southey, Campbell, and Moore has declined, and if this change of opinion be justified, a 'Musical Festival' permanently connected with his name will repel more strongly every year many educated people whom it might otherwise attract; for it is not possible to celebrate his unquestionable service to Irish music without also celebrating his more questionable service to literature. The writer of the article I refer to seems to consider that only English opinion, and the opinion of those Irishmen who despise Irish literature — at least so I understand him — refuse to Moore the title of a great poet. You, sir, can settle the matter in a way which will be interesting, and at the same time help to draw attention to the projected Festival, by asking the Irishmen who have most excelled in the making as in the criticism of imaginative literature — Mr O'Grady, Mr Stopford Brooks, Mr King, Mr Johnson, Mr Graves, and their fellow-workers — to send you for publication in UNITED IRELAND a short expression of their opinion. It is, of course, possible, though always unlikely, that the cultivated people of a particular age may be wrong, but the only court of appeal from their judgement is time. Should their verdict be against Moore, it would be easy to find some other date, such as the anniversary of Carolan's death, if it be known, or of the death of one of the old Gaelic musicians, which would be full of national suggestion, and perpetuate no uncritical enthusiasm. I only press this matter because I believe that Irish literature, if it disentangle itself from artificiality and insincerity, will in the next few years penetrate all classes in Ireland, and bring something of patriotic fire into even the dim corners of West Britonism. Every one of the small nationalities of Europe has gone through the struggles we are now passing through; and in almost all it has been national literature and history which have filled the educated classes with patriotism, but in none were they able to do so until they learned to set truth above the national glory.

Yours truly,

A STUDENT OF IRISH LITERATURE.

'A Poetaster's Soliloquy on Moore'

Bad scran to that jaynius, Tom Moore,
For the run on my poethry fails.
An' I'm thryin' to write somethin' new,
But he takes the win' out o' my sails.

No matther how much I abuse him
The people 'ill stick to him still;
But 'tis harder to get them to read me
Than to make wather run up a hill.

I'm doin' my best to belie him –
I folly the Englishman's thrack–
An' whinever it lies in my power,
I'm down on his fame wid a whack.

I'm tellin' the poor foolish craythurs,
That glory in all that he wrote,
That they're asses whinever they praise him,
For he's only a drawin' room pote

I show them how foolish an' artful
His verses are cast in their mowld;
But for all that they're willin' to read them,
An' lave mine outside in the cowld.

All my beautiful poems on fairies,
On sheeogues and leprechauns small,
Are the same as if written in Hebrew,
For the divil attintion they'll call.

An' whin spakin' ov Ireland's glory,
An' the hope that's afore her still –
Sure I don't care a button for Ireland,
But I want to bring grist to my mill –

I'm met by such songs as the 'Bright Lamp
That shone in Kildare's holy fane',
An' I feel like a woman in muslin,
Whin she's ketched in a shower o' rain;

For I'm knocked out clane by its beauty,
An' I'm like a man ready to die;
If the wings of my muse were an eagle's,
She never could flutter so high.

An' whin tryin' to spake ov the hayroes,
That in ould times for Ireland fell,
I spind near a month on aich poem,
In ordher to have it done well;

An' whin it's wrote out an' quite finished,
An' whin I'm fatayged to the bone,
I'll hear somebody singin' the verses
That Moore made on Emmet and Tone;

An' my heart thin sinks down in my body,
As deep as a man's heart can go,
For I see that my poethry's rubbish,
An' my pride as a poet's laid low.

Threth, I'm thinkin' I made a big blundher
Whin I put up my poems for sale;
I'll rise out o' this business ov poet,
An' go dailin' in flour or mail.

                    FINNOOLA (13.4.95, 1)

CONCLUSION

I

This book has focused on the relationship between Yeats, Irish literary nationalism and the publishing industry of late Victorian Britain and Ireland and tried to comprehend the dynamics of late nineteenth-century Irish politics and literature through the bibliographical and socio-historical context surrounding Yeats and the Revival. It has also examined the intellectual, bibliographical and political environment surrounding the primary publication of Yeats's work during the 1880s and '90s. In the process the preceding chapters have re-read Yeats's texts, not just as aesthetic artefacts but as documents of their time, caught in the complexities of Irish political and literary affairs and influenced by fiercely partisan editorial advocacy and agendas. They have shown that the pressures of the marketplace and Yeats's relationship with powerful and mutually antagonistic editors and journals were key components in the development of his early poetry and criticism, his political affiliations and the political and cultural personality of the Revival. They have also shown that meanings, embedded in a text's historical and bibliographical context of publication and taken for granted by both author and readers, are often eliminated when the text is republished, and that these meanings are often crucial to understanding these texts, their reception and their function.

Having demonstrated how Yeats adapted and revised his writing to coincide with his periodical (in both senses of the term) allegiances, and having shown how a contextually informed approach can fundamentally alter our understanding of Yeats and of Yeatsian texts, this book advances the claim that no balanced judgement can be made about Yeats's work, his politics or his aesthetics without an awareness of the original bibliographical and socio-historical contexts of his publications. In the preceding chapters I have high-lighted the importance of these contexts by showing that they invariably influence the making of a text, that they almost always influence its reception and that they very often contain meanings sanctioned or authorised by Yeats. Locating a text within the original context from which it has been subsequently extracted restores the 'aura' and immediacy it formerly possessed. It also sheds new light on the text's composition, its author's intentions and its meaning, which are beyond conventional and formalistic approaches.

For instance, between pages 267 and 275 of *UP1*, one sees Yeats advancing the view that the lyric is a bad thing which should be shunned. It is obscure and cosmopolitan, it is indifferent to human concerns and it represents the literary degeneration of a culture. As an alternative, he suggests, literature should be rooted in the populace, express 'its loves and its hates, its likes and its dislikes' (273), instil patriotism and deal with 'great national events' (249). From page 276 onwards, in Yeats's very next article, which was written less than two months after the earlier one, one sees Yeats suggesting that the lyric is *the* quintessential literary form and infinitely superior to populist and didactic literature. That this contradiction has thus far been ignored indicates our willingness to accept Yeatsian utterances uncritically and at face value. It also indicates a widespread tendency to see Yeatsian texts in isolation and not in relation to each other or in their individual socio-historical and bibliographical contexts. Assuming for a moment that a scholar's attention was drawn to this contradiction, what would he make of it? A deconstructionist might explain this as yet another instance of the untenability of 'metaphysical' categories (lyric and epic), and see his proof in the fact that Yeats's *volte face* deconstructs his own opposition. While not incorrect in itself, does such an explanation advance our understanding of Yeats or clarify his views on the lyric? Another example is Yeats's early work. Historians of poetic influence, particularly those specialising in romantic poetry (Bloom, Bornstein), have recognised the allegorical nature of 'The Two Titans' and 'The Island of Statues', but have given it short shrift. They have insisted on a non-allegorical and Shelleyan reading and claimed that the political elements in these texts are inchoate. Their claim is correct, but a study of these poems' bibliographical environment shows that their nationalist elements had to be toned down, as they were published in a periodical that catered to a Protestant readership and was (at that particular stage) avowedly non-political. Consequently, the political elements in these poems assume greater importance. The very fact that these poems are only inchoately political becomes in itself politically significant. Such an understanding can only be arrived at once we study these texts in their original contexts of publication, focus on their historical testimony, the value systems brought to bear on them and the meanings produced thereby.

Writers often remark that their work is not shaped solely by imagination, and that imagination itself is 'the slave of stolid circumstance', 'conditioned by its surroundings like a river-stream'.[1] By neglecting these 'surroundings', scholarship has ignored the influence of socio-historical contexts on literary creation. In an age saturated with politics and the Irish question in particular, periodicals had their own political allegiances and agendas and expected contributors to toe the editorial line. As a young writer trying to establish himself in the literary marketplace, Yeats had to make opportunistic choices and concessions in his dealings with periodicals. It is important to understand just how significantly periodical publication constrained and determined his literary output by demanding conformity to particular political programmes and prevalent literary tastes. The fact that fiction sold better than poems influenced Yeats's own forays into the market for short stories, as is indicated by his letter to Tynan about promoting 'John Sherman': 'Do what you can for it – for a success with stories would solve many problems for me & I write them easily' (*CL1*, 257). The preceding chapters have shown that much of Yeats's work during the late 1880s and the 1890s was influenced by the context in which it was meant to appear. This influence extends not merely to individual texts but also to larger groupings within Yeats's overall *oeuvre*. To secure Henley's backing, he tailored his work to suit Henley's political and literary tastes, and in so doing restricted all his contributions to fairy tales and folklore. This raises the question about the extent to which Henley influenced, determined, consolidated or fuelled Yeats's own interests in these subjects. A similar question arises with respect to the *United Ireland*'s championing of the Revival and Yeats's Parnellite allegiance.

Corkery's complaint – that Yeats (and other Anglo-Irish writers he disapproves of) 'would have written quite differently if extra-mural influences, such as the proximity of the English literary market . . . had not misled them from the start'[2] – is valid in as much as readers' tastes influenced Yeats's work. Moreover, his particular grievance about the tastes of English readers 'misleading' Yeats is vindicated by Yeats's publications in Henley's *Observer*. The degree of revision evident in Yeats's writings on Carleton – the introduction of new material and the exclusion of 'unacceptable opinions' – bespeaks a willingness to vary and modulate his literary expressions in order to accommodate the tastes and prejudices of his prospective readers. However, when viewed in the broader context of Yeats's work as a whole, particularly his publications in *United Ireland* and the *Boston Pilot*, Corkery's views seem a little blinkered, for the 'extra-mural' influences that 'misled them from the start' were not merely English but very Irish as well, which should not make them any less 'extra-mural'. Nor does Yeats being Anglo-Irish have anything to do with his being particularly vulnerable to the influence of English tastes. Tynan, as we have seen, was quite willing to play the Irish Biddy to Henley's manly union-ist readers. Moreover, to say that Yeats and other writers were misled presumes that there was a right path from which they strayed. I hope that the preced-ing chapters have shown that if 'authenticity' (whatever that may mean) is the yardstick, and readers' tastes the corrupting 'extra-mural' factor, then Yeats's work for English periodicals cannot be presumed to be less authentic than his work for Irish ones, for both were influenced by readers' tastes.

Just as a text's production is subject to socio-historical and non-literary influences, so also is its reception. Meaning – both intended and received – is invariably linked to cultural contexts, and the significance and value of utterances depend on the context and the predispositions of the audience for whom they are intended. Authors generally do their utmost to ensure that the form, timing and readers of their publications will produce readings compat-ible with their intentions. By ignoring the context of primary publication of 'September 1913' and the background of its intended audience, literary schol-arship has also ignored the meanings derived by its original audience, mean-ings sanctioned to a large extent by Yeats himself by the very act of his choosing a particular time, place and readership for the reception of his poem. Jeffares, Ellmann, Cullingford et al. might have reappraised their own understanding of this poem had they taken cognisance of the fact that it was written for and endorsed by a Protestant unionist readership.

Yet another example of how conventional approaches to Yeats are under-mined by ignorance of a text's original context is Said's reading of Yeats as a poet of decolonisation. It is unlikely that he would have advanced such a view had he read in the context of Henley's Observer the 'Rose' poems he adduces as proof of Yeats's 'cartographic impulse'. The same applies to Michael North's contention that 'The Lake Isle of Innisfree' – also published in Henley's Observer – 'represents the call of the Fenian brotherhood, a call not just to a particular place, but to a particular time'.[3] The aesthetic standards bequeathed to the Revival and to twentieth-century Irish writing by Yeats's Celticism can be radically revised by a closer examination of his immediate political and bibliographical environment. For example, what Seamus Heaney calls Yeats's 'noble reclamation' of Irish place names, I show to be Yeats's strategic deploy-ment of a depoliticised Irishness in order to sell himself to powerful union-ist editors and, ultimately, to the English reading public. Understanding this difference alters our perception of Yeats's nationalism and of the Revival's political underpinnings.

One of the by-products of this investigation has been a highlighting of what Joyce called Yeats's 'treacherous instinct of adaptability'.[4] Doubtless, Yeats was promiscuous in his ideological affiliations and used these to further his lit-erary career. The incongruity of running with the hares and hunting with the hounds, of writing simultaneously for O'Brien's *United Ireland* and Henley's *Observer*, is striking. Moreover, one also realises to what extent Yeats modulated his writings to suit the tastes of his intended audiences. Therefore, in examining Yeats's political and literary identities and their acquiescence in contemporary discourses of literary unionism or militant nationalism, it becomes necessary to take cognisance of the place, time and intended readership of Yeats's publications, since these factors often played an important role in influencing the content of his work, its reception and its intended function. The point is not to depoliticise Yeats. Admittedly, he is the most political of writers. Rather, the evidence presented in this book suggests that through ignorance of context scholars have often misunderstood, or, at the very best, not fully understood, the nature of Yeats's politics and his political allegiances.

It is one thing to recognise, as most of us do, that time, place and forms of publication mediate meaning and carry an interpretative burden, and that the message cannot be uncoupled from the medium. However, it is another thing altogether – and this is seldom done – to incorporate the implications of this recognition into our study of authors and their texts. The implications of this truth are of importance to all readers of texts, regardless of the approach they individually espouse. The fact that Yeats in 1895 suddenly gave a 'firm command' to his publishers that his books 'be not green & have no shamrocks' (*CL1*, 434) says something about the way he wished his poetry to be read henceforth. It also says something about the way he wished his poetry to be read earlier and thus provokes inquiry into this sudden change of heart. This in turn leads to the issue of his disillusionment with the Revival, the reasons for that and how it affected his work.

How a text is presented, and by whom, when and where it is read, are issues to which authors pay close attention. Hence Yeats, having written 'Easter 1916', 'Sixteen Dead Men' and 'The Rose Tree' within a year of the Rising itself, published them only four years later, even though the first of these, completed by his own account on 25 September 1916, could have been included in *The Wild Swans at Coole* (1919). Why was it not?[5] A comparison of the first publication of 'September 1913' with its publication immediately after the Easter Rising shows that republication of texts, especially with Yeats, is a means of manipulating and controlling the view posterity takes of an author, the context in which his work is read and the range of meanings generated by his texts. The shifts effected in the meaning and significance of 'Romantic Ireland' and thereby of 'September 1913' through republication and the accompanying annotations have misled critics about the purpose and function of that poem. By linking 'Romantic Ireland' and 'September 1913' with the Rising, Yeats has so successfully represented himself as a romantic revolutionary that this has dominated academic perceptions of him and sanitised many of his most political and Protestant-sectarian poems into a kind of serial romanticism. Yeats was the first of many powerful and influential readers of his work, and other powerful and influential readers have accepted his readings at face value. Nevertheless, these myths could have been exploded by an examination of the bibliographical and socio-historical contexts of his work and a realisation that republication is often a means of controlling meaning and influencing interpretation.

Another instance of such control over textual meaning and one's future reputation – but through non-publication rather than republication – is Yeats's attempt to restrict consideration of his literary and political journalism of the 1880s and '90s, downplay their relationship to his *oeuvre* and minimise their influence on posterity's understanding of his life and work. From 1906 onwards Yeats began selecting and revising work with a view to its publication in a collected edition, 'a collection of precisely those things I wish to be my permanent self' rather than 'a collection of odds and ends including some that should not have been published' (*L*, 575–6). In the published edition, he emphasised the importance of his editorial decisions *vis-à-vis* his self-image:

> The friends that have it I do wrong
> When ever I remake a song,
> Should know what issue is at stake:
> It is myself that I remake.
>
> (*VP*, 778)

However, in addition to revising previous work, these editorial decisions through which he would remake himself for the future also involved burying some of the past that contradicted Yeats's view of 'my permanent self':

> Accursed who brings to light of day
> The writings I have cast away!
> But blessed he that stirs them not
> And lets the kind worm take the lot!
>
> (*VP*, 779)

He was also quite clear about which texts would be allowed to contribute to this self-image and which 'cast away'. In a letter to A. H. Bullen, the publisher of his collected works, Yeats remarked that '[a]ccident has given the work written before I was thirty [i.e. before 1895], all the public attention I get'. What was the nature of this 'Accident' which made his work of the 1880s and '90s the cynosure of readers' judgement? And why was he in 1913 so uncomfortable with it? In a biography written during 1914–15 with Yeats's co-operation and approval, Joseph Hone used the same word – 'accident' –

to describe Yeats's conversion to Irish nationalism: 'Almost by accident he fell into the company of a group of Nationalists.'[6] He mentions Yeats's work in *United Ireland* but shifts attention away to Yeats's more literary and less political work:

> Very little of this work has been reprinted; but in later writings when re-interpreting his own career, he often alludes to the temper out of which it came. Another part of him, he says, looked on half mockingly – the other part of him which was engaged in a monumental work on William Blake, and to which we owe the 'Rose' poems. (32)

He then goes on to describe Yeats's attempts at de-Davisising Irish literature and his quarrel with the nationalists, 'who defined their object, Irish political freedom, as all-important, [and] demanded logically enough that the poet – if he also wanted the title of patriot – should put his song directly into the service of the Fatherland'. This was precisely the demand Yeats had repeatedly made of Allingham and numerous other poets. Hone was subsequently authorised to write the full-length biography published in 1943. While working on that he published an essay in which he averred, apropos of Yeats's quarrel with 'all the little semi-literary and semi-political clubs and societies out of which the Sinn Fein movement grew', that Yeats had never claimed 'that the criterion by which Irish work should be judged was its . . . power to shoulder an idealistic conception of Irish character and provide useful political thoughts'.[7] We have seen that this was the burden of much of his work for *United Ireland* and the *Boston Pilot*.[8] This would perhaps explain Yeats's discomfort in 1913 at the prospect of it returning like a ghost from the past to contradict and undermine the image of 'my permanent self' he was then remaking for the future. Hone's comment on Yeats's work nicely summarises some of the themes explored in this book. The underlined section is true (though this was not what Hone meant) of the bibliographical and socio-historical influences evident in the primary context of Yeats's publications. Seen thus, it also gives the lie to the italicised section, which is how Yeats wished to be remembered.

> *Not that there is anything hidden away in old files of which Mr Yeats really needs to be ashamed. He was never a journalist in the sense that he would turn his mind to any topic of the moment;* <u>and in all that he has written, however fugitive in appearance, we discover something of the influences that shaped his mind and art</u>.[9] (italics and underlining added)

II

Often an ignorance of a text's context has significantly impaired and distorted readings of key Yeatsian poems. On the odd occasion, it has led to absolute howlers. More often than not, it has lead to scholarly inaccuracies, which are less flagrant but more damaging and influential for that reason. These pertain not merely to individual poems, but sometimes to our understanding of seminal events in a writer's life or even of important historical movements. Roy Foster's dating of the Revival is a case in point, as is also his dating of Yeats's Parnellism. By relocating Yeatsian texts to their original contexts, this book discovers new facets to these texts, to Yeats's political allegiances and to the social and political underpinnings of the Revival that contradict the views of an established body of scholarly opinion. It thus also highlights the efficacy and need of a bibliographical approach to Yeats's work.

I am not suggesting that texts should be studied only in their original editions. That would put an end to literary studies in most parts of the world, including my own country, where even reprints of many primary texts are difficult to come by. But I do think it is necessary for scholars teaching and studying these texts to be familiar – either through first-hand experience or through secondary material – with their different versions, the environments that produced them and in which they were first published or subsequently reprinted, the type of audience they were addressed to and the purposes they served. Neither am I suggesting that bibliographical and historical contexts completely control and determine textual meaning, or that textual meaning is produced by forces that exclude the author and over which she or he is powerless. My central thesis is that an awareness of the primary context of a text's publication significantly enhances our understanding of an author and that text. To recognise that Yeats, like the rest of us, worked under personal, social and institutional constraints and pressures is not to say that those constraints could not be subverted or those pressures withstood or that Yeats was not a free agent. Neither does such a recognition deny agency to an author or personality to his utterance. On the contrary, it restores to literary studies a human dimension often lacking in many intellectually rarefied theories. But I do make my arguments forcefully, and in attempting to emphasise a point one always risks over-emphasising it. However, the point needs to be made forcefully because the critical framework that I have used is not as yet established in contemporary criticism.

This book is part of an emerging practice of reading texts in the contexts for which they were first written. Relocating a text in this environment casts a new light on it and often poses such radical challenges to dominant interpretations that it offers itself as one of the most promising and invigorating critical methodologies. Reinserting Yeats's work into its original bibliographic, cultural and political contexts can fundamentally alter our understanding of his *oeuvre* and of those contexts to such an extent that even time-honoured and canonical texts such as 'September 1913' and seminal historical events such as the Irish Literary Revival can be seen to have new aspects which challenge commonly accepted views. Such an approach is all the more promising because, unlike excessively theoretical or subjective approaches, this one has the advantage of being backed up by solidly empirical methods. It is hoped that this work will provide a modest example of what ought to be done to a greater degree with Yeats, and indeed with other writers.

List of Works Cited

Works by W. B. Yeats

Autobiographies. London: Macmillan, 1955.

The Collected Letters of W. B. Yeats, vol. I, ed. John Kelly. Oxford: Clarendon Press, 1986.

The Collected Letters of W. B. Yeats, vol. II, eds. Warwick Gould, John Kelly and Deirdre Toomey. Oxford: Clarendon Press, 1997.

The Collected Letters of W. B. Yeats, vol. III, eds. John Kelly and Ronald Schuchard. Oxford: Clarendon Press, 1986.

Essays and Introductions. London: Macmillan, 1961.

Explorations, ed. Mrs. W. B. Yeats. London: Macmillan, 1962.

'Four Lectures by W. B. Yeats: 1902–1904', ed. Richard Londraville. *YA* 8 (1991) 78–122.

The Letters of W. B. Yeats, ed. Allan Wade. London: Hart-Davis, 1954.

Letters to the New Island, eds. George Bornstein and Hugh Witemeyer. London: Macmillan, 1989.

'The Literary Movement in Ireland' and 'A Postscript', *Ideals in Ireland*, ed. I. A. Gregory. London: Unicorn, 1901, 85–102, 103–7.

Memoirs, ed. Denis Donoghue. London: Macmillan, 1972.

'Modern Ireland: An Address to American Audiences 1932–33'. *Massachusetts Review* V (Winter 1964) 256–68.

Plays in Prose and Verse. London: Macmillan, 1922.

Prefaces and Introductions, ed. William H. O'Donnell. London: Macmillan, 1988.

Senate Speeches, ed. Donald R. Pearce. Bloomington: Indiana University Press, 1960.

Tribute to Thomas Davis. Oxford: Basil Blackwell, 1947.

Uncollected Prose, vol. 1, ed. John P. Frayne. New York: Columbia University Press, 1970.

Uncollected Prose, vol. 2, eds. John P. Frayne and Colton Johnson. New York: Columbia University Press, 1975.

Variorum Edition of the Poems of W. B. Yeats, eds. Peter Allt and Russell K. Alspach. New York: Macmillan, 1957.

Books edited by W. B. Yeats

A Book of Irish Verse. London: Methuen, 1895.

Fairy and Folk Tales of the Irish Peasantry. London: Scott, 1888.

The Oxford Book of Modern Verse. Oxford: OUP, 1936.

Representative Irish Tales. Gerrard's Cross: Colin Smythe, 1979.

Stories from Carleton. London: Walter Scott, 1889.

Books Containing Contributions by Yeats

Book of the Rhymers' Club. London: Elkin Mathews, 1892.
Poems and Ballads of Young Ireland. Dublin: M. H. Gill and Sons, 1888.

Periodicals

Blackwoods Magazine
Dublin University Magazine
Dublin University Review
Freeman's Journal
Irish Monthly
Irish Times
National Observer
National Press
New Review
Saturday Review
Scots Observer
The Times
United Ireland

Secondary Material

Albright, Daniel, ed. *W. B. Yeats: The Poems*. London: Dent, 1990.

Altick, Richard. *The Presence of the Present: Topics of the Day in the Victorian Novel*. Columbus: Ohio State University Press, 1991.

Anonymous. 'Sir Samuel Ferguson: In Memoriam'. *The Irish Monthly* (October 1886), 529–36.

Anesko, Michael. *'Friction with the Market': Henry James and the Profession of Authorship*. New York: OUP, 1986.

Arnold, Matthew. 'On the Study of Celtic Literature'. *The Complete Prose Works of Matthew Arnold*. vol. 3, ed. R. H. Super. Ann Arbor: University of Michigan Press, 1962 291–395.

Arnold-Foster, Florence. *Florence Arnold-Foster's Irish Journal*, eds. T. W. Moody, Richard Hawkins, Margaret Moody. Oxford: Clarendon Press, 1988.

Beckett, J. C. 'The Irish Writer and his Public in the Nineteenth Century'. *Yearbook of English Studies* 11 (1981), 102–16.

Beerbohm, Max. 'A Letter to the Editor'. *Yellow Book* 2 (July 1894), 283.

Beetham, Margaret. 'Open and Closed: The Periodical as a Publishing Genre'. *Victorian Periodicals Review* 22 (1989), 96–100.

Benjamin, Walter. *Illuminations*, ed. Hannah Arendt, trans. Harry Zohn. London: Jonathan Cape, 1970.

Bennett, Arnold. *The Truth about an Author*. New York: George H. Doran, 1911.

Besant, Walter. *The Pen and the Book*. London: T. Burleigh, 1899.

Bishop, Edward. 'Re:Covering Modernism – Format and Function in the Little Magazines', eds. Ian Willison *et al.*, 287–319.

Bloom, Harold. *Yeats*. New York: OUP, 1972.

Blunt, Wilfred Scawen. *The Land War in Ireland*. London: Stephen Swift, 1912.

— *My Diaries*. London: M. Secker, 1920.

Bodkin, M. M. *Recollections of an Irish Judge*. London: Hurst and Blackett, 1914.

Bornstein, George. *Yeats and Shelley*. Chicago: University of Chicago Press, 1970.

— *The Early Poetry: Mosada and* The Island of Statues. Ithaca: Cornell University Press, 1987.

— 'Yeats and Textual Reincarnation: "When You Are Old" and "September 1913"' . *The*

Iconic Page in Manuscript, Print and Digital Culture, eds. George Bornstein and Theresa Tinkle. Ann Arbor: University of Michigan Press, 1998, 223–48.

Bourdieu, Pierre. *Distinction: A Social Critique of the Judgement of Taste*, trans. Richard Nice. Cambridge, MA: Harvard University Press, 1984.

— *The Field of Cultural Production: Essays on Art and Literature*, ed. Randal Johnson. Cambridge: Polity Press, 1993.

Bourke, Marcus. *John O'Leary: A Study in Irish Separatism*. Tralee: Anvil Books, 1967.

Boyd, E. A. *Ireland's Literary Renaissance*. London: Maunsel & Co., 1916.

Brake, L. 'Literary Criticism and Victorian Periodicals'. *Yearbook of English Studies* 16 (1986), 92–116.

—, A. Jones and L. Madden, eds. *Investigating Victorian Journalism*. London: Macmillan, 1990.

Brown, Malcolm. *The Politics of Irish Literature*. London: George Allen and Unwin, 1971.

— *Sir Samuel Ferguson*. Lewisburg: Bucknell University Press, 1973.

Brown, Terence. *Ireland's Literature: Selected Essays*. Mullingar: Lilliput Press, 1988.

— *The Life of W. B. Yeats: A Critical Biography*. Oxford: Blackwell, 1999.

Buckland, Patrick. *Irish Unionism: The Anglo-Irish and the New Ireland, 1885–1922*. Dublin: Gill and Macmillan, 1972.

Buckley, Jerome Hamilton. *William Ernest Henley: A Study in the Counter-Decadence of the 'Nineties*. Princeton: Princeton University Press, 1945.

Callanan, Frank. *The Parnell Split*. Cork: Cork University Press, 1992.

Carleton, William. *The Autobiography of William Carleton*, ed. Patrick Kavanagh. London: MacGibbon & Lee, 1968.

Chalmers, Patrick R. *Kenneth Grahame: Life, Letters and Unpublished Work*. London: Methuen, 1933.

Charvat, William. *The Profession of Authorship in America, 1800–1870: The Papers of William Charvat*, ed. Matthew J. Bruccoli. Columbus: Ohio State University Press, 1968.

Chaudhry, Yug Mohit. 'Yeats, Victorianism and Irish Nationalism'. Unpublished M.Phil. thesis. University of Oxford, 1996.

Cole, Richard Cargill. *Irish Booksellers and English Writers: 1740–1800*. London: Mansell, 1986.

Colles, Ramsay. *In Castle and Courthouse*. London: T. Werner Laurie, 1911.

Connell, John. *W. E. Henley*. London: Constable, 1949.

Conrad, Joseph. *The Collected Letters of Joseph Conrad*, 5 vols, eds. Frederick R. Karl and Laurence Davies. Cambridge: CUP, 1983–1996.

Corkery, Daniel. *Synge and Anglo-Irish Literature: A Study*. Cork: Cork University Press, 1931.

Cross, Nigel. *The Common Writer: Life in Nineteenth-Century Grub Street*. Cambridge: CUP, 1985.

Cullingford, Elizabeth. *Yeats, Ireland and Fascism*. London: Macmillan, 1981.

Daly, Dominic. *The Young Douglas Hyde*. Dublin: Irish University Press, 1974.

Davis, Lloyd. 'Journalism and Victorian Fiction'. *Victorian Journalism: Exotic and Domestic: Essays in Honour of P. D. Edwards*, eds. Barbara Garlick and Margaret Harris. St Lucia: Queensland University Press, 1998, 197–211.

de Vere, Aubrey. *Essays Chiefly Lyrical and Ethical*. London: Macmillan, 1889.

Dowden, Edward. *Letters of Edward Dowden and his Correspondents*. London: Dent, 1914.

Dunleavy, Janet Egleson and Gareth W. Dunleavy. *Douglas Hyde: A Maker of Modern Ireland*. Berkeley: University of California Press, 1991.

Dunlop, Andrew. *Fifty Years of Irish Journalism*. Dublin: Hanna and Neale, 1911.

Dunne, Tom. 'Haunted by Irish History: Irish Romantic Writing 1800–50'. *Romanticism in National Context*, eds. R. Porter and M. Teich. Cambridge: CUP, 1988, 68–91.

Eagleton, Terry. *Criticism and Ideology*. London: New Left Books, 1976.

— *Heathcliff and the Great Hunger: Studies in Irish Culture*. London: Verso, 1995.

Ellmann, R. *The Identity of Yeats*. London: Faber and Faber, 1964.
— *Yeats: The Man and the Masks*. London: Penguin, 1987.
Everett, Edwin Mallard. *The Party of Humanity: The* Fortnightly Review *and its Contributors 1865–1874*. New York: Russell & Russell, 1971.

Fagan, H. S. *The Government of Ireland: Will Home Rule Be Rome Rule?* National Press Leaflet no. 70. London: National Press Agency, 1886.
— *The Government of Ireland: Are We Utter Fools?* National Press Leaflet no. 71. London: National Press Agency, 1886.
— *The Government of Ireland: Who Are the 'Persecuted Minority'?* National Press Leaflet no. 72. London: National Press Agency, 1886.
Ferguson, Mary. *Sir Samuel Ferguson and the Ireland of his Day*. 2 vols. London: William Blackwood, 1896.
Ferguson, Samuel. 'A Dialogue Between the Head and Heart of an Irish Protestant'. *Dublin University Magazine* II (November 1833), 586–93.
— 'Hardiman's Irish Minstrelsy I'. *Dublin University Magazine* III (April 1834), 456–78.
— 'Hardiman's Irish Minstrelsy II'. *Dublin University Magazine* IV (August 1834), 152–67.
— 'Hardiman's Irish Minstrelsy III'. *Dublin University Magazine* IV (October 1834), 447–67.
— 'Hardiman's Irish Minstrelsy IV'. *Dublin University Magazine* IV (November 1834), 514–42.
Fleming, Deborah. *A Man Who Does Not Exist: The Irish Peasant in the Work of W. B. Yeats and J. M. Synge*. Ann Arbor: University of Michigan Press, 1995.
Foster, John Wilson. 'Getting the North: Yeats and Northern Nationalism'. *YA* 12 (1996), 180–212.
Foster, Roy. *Modern Ireland, 1600–1972*. London: Penguin, 1989.
— 'Anglo-Irish Literature, Gaelic Nationalism and Irish Politics in the 1890s'. *Ireland After the Union*. London: British Academy, 1989, 61–82.
— 'Protestant Magic: W. B. Yeats and the Spell of Irish History'. *Proceedings of the British Academy* LXXV (1989), 243–66.
— *W. B. Yeats: A Life*, vol. 1. Oxford: OUP, 1997.
Freedman, Jonathan. *Professions of Taste: Henry James, British Aestheticism, and Commodity Culture*. Stanford: Stanford University Press, 1990.

Gabler, Hans Walter. 'Introduction'. *Contemporary German Editorial Theory*, eds. Hans Walter Gabler, George Bornstein, Gillian Borland. Ann Arbor: University of Michigan Press, 1995, 1–16
Gatrell, Simon. *Hardy the Creator: A Textual Biography*. Oxford: Clarendon Press, 1988.
Gill, T. P. 'William O'Brien: Some Aspects'. *Studies* XVII (December 1928), 605–20.
Glandon, Virginia E. 'The Irish Press and Revolutionary Irish Nationalism'. *Eire–Ireland* XVI, 1 (Spring 1981), 1–33.
Goldsmith, Oliver. 'The Traveller'. *Collected Works of Oliver Goldsmith*, 5 vols, ed. Arthur Friedman. Oxford: Clarendon Press, 1966, vol. 4, 245–69.
Gonne, Maud. *The Autobiography of Maud Gonne: A Servant to the Queen*, eds. Anna MacBride White and A. Norman Jeffares. London: Hutchinson, 1992.
— and W. B. Yeats. *The Gonne–Yeats Letters 1893–1938*, eds. Anna MacBride White and A. Norman Jeffares. London: Hutchinson, 1992.
Gould, Warwick. '"Playing at Treason with Miss Maud Gonne": Yeats and his Publishers in 1900'. *Modernist Writers and the Marketplace*, eds. Ian Willison, Warwick Gould and Warren Chernaik. London: Macmillan, 1996, 36–80.
— and Deirdre Toomey. '"Take Down This Book": *The Flame of the Spirit*, Text and Context'. *YA* 11 (1995), 124–137.
Green, Peter. *Kenneth Grahame*. London: John Murray, 1959.

Gregory, I. A., ed. *Ideals in Ireland*. London: Unicorn, 1901.

— *Sir Hugh Lane: His Life and Legacy*. Gerrards Cross: Colin Smythe, 1973.

— *Seventy Years: Being the Autobiography of Lady Gregory*, ed. Colin Smythe. Gerrards Cross: Colin Smythe, 1974.

Griest, Guinevere L. *Muddie's Circulating Library and the Victorian Novel*. Bloomingdale: Indiana University Press, 1970.

Gwynn, Stephen. *Garden Wisdom*. Dublin: Talbot Press, 1921.

— *Ireland*. London: Ernest Benn, 1924.

— *A Student's History of Ireland*. London: Longman, 1925.

— *Experiences of a Literary Man*. London: Thornton Butterworth, 1926.

— *Ireland's Literature and Drama*. London: Thomas Nelson, 1936.

Hallam, Arthur. 'On Some of the Characteristics of Modern Poetry, and on the Lyrical Poems of Alfred Tennyson'. *The Writings of Arthur Hallam*, ed. T. H. Vail Morter. London: Modern Language Association of America, 1943, 87–139.

Hansard. *Parliamentary Debates* 294 (4.12.84), 613.

Harbinson, John F. *The Ulster Unionist Party, 1882–1973*. Belfast: Blackstaff Press, 1973

Hardy, Thomas. 'Candour in English Fiction'. *Thomas Hardy's Personal Writings: Prefaces, Literary Opinions, Reminiscences*, ed. Harold Orel. London: University Press of Kansas, 1966, 125–33.

Hayley, Barbara. 'A Reading Thinking Nation: Periodicals as the Voice of Nineteenth-Century Ireland'. *Three Hundred Years of Irish Periodicals*, eds. Barbara Hayley and Edna McKay. Gigginstown: Lilliput Press, 1987, 29–48.

— and Terence Brown, eds. *Samuel Ferguson: A Centenary Tribute*. Dublin: Royal Irish Academy, 1987.

— 'A Detailed Bibliography of Editions of William Carleton's *Traits and Stories of the Irish Peasantry* Published in Dublin and London During the Author's Lifetime'. *Long Room* 32 (1987), 29–55.

Henley, W. E. 'When You are Old'. *A Book of Verses*. London: David Nutt, 1888, 164–5.

— Unpublished ALS to Charles Whibley, 10.1.89, Pierpont Morgan Library, New York.

— Unpublished ALS to Charles Whibley, 15.1.89, Pierpont Morgan Library, New York.

— 'The Song of the Sword' and 'What I Have Done for You, England, my England'. *The Song of the Sword*. London: David Nutt, 1892, 1–12, 101.

— 'The Tory Press and the Tory Party'. *National Review* (May 1893), 371.

— 'To R. F. B'. *Poems*. London: David Nutt, 1898.

— *Views and Reviews*. London: Macmillan, 1921.

— *The Selected Letters of W. E. Henley*, ed. Damian Atkinson. Aldershot: Ashgate, 2000.

Henn, T. R. *The Lonely Tower*. London: Methuen, 1965.

Hind, C. Lewis. *Authors and I*. New York: John Lane, 1921.

Hodder, William. 'Ferguson: His Literary Sources'. *Sir Samuel Ferguson: A Centenary Tribute*, eds. Barbara Hayley and Terence Brown. Dublin: Royal Irish Academy, 1987, 57–66.

Hogan, J. J. 'W. B. Yeats'. *Studies* XXVIII (1939), 35–48.

Holdeman, David. *Much Labouring: The Texts and Authors of Yeats's First Modernist Books*. Ann Arbor: University of Michigan Press, 1997.

Hone, J. M. *William Butler Yeats: The Poet in Contemporary Ireland*. Dublin: Maunsel, nd.

— 'Yeats as Political Philosopher'. *London Mercury* 39 (March 1939), 492–6.

— *W. B. Yeats 1865–1939*. London: Macmillan, 1942.

Horne, Philip. 'Henry James and the Economy of the Short Story'. *Modernist Writers and the Marketplace*, eds. Ian Willison, Warwick Gould and Warren Chernaik. London: Macmillan, 1996, 1–35.

Houghton, Walter, ed. *Wellesley Index to Victorian Periodicals 1824–1900*. 4 vols. Toronto: University of Toronto Press, 1972.

Hueffer, Ford Madox. *Ancient Lights and Certain New Reflections*. London: Chapman and Hall, 1911.

Hulbert, William Henry. *Ireland under Coercion: The Diary of an American*. 2 vols. Edinburgh: David Douglas, 1888.

Hutchinson, John. *The Dynamics of Cultural Nationalism*. London: Allen and Unwin, 1987.

Irish Loyal and Patriotic Union Prospectus, The (nd).

Jeffares, A. Norman. *W. B. Yeats: Man and Poet*. London: Keegan Paul, 1949.

— *A New Commentary on the Poems of W. B. Yeats*. London: Macmillan, 1984.

— ed. *Yeats's Poems*. London: Macmillan, 1989.

Joyce, James. 'The Day of the Rabblement'. *The Critical Writings of James Joyce*, eds. Ellsworth Mason and Richard Ellmann. London: Faber and Faber, 1959, 68–72.

Karl, Frederick R. *Joseph Conrad: The Three Lives*. New York: Farrar, Straus, and Giroux, 1979.

Kearns, Michael. 'The Material Melville: Shaping Readers' Horizons'. *Reading Books: Essays on the Material Text and Literature in America*, eds. Michale Moylan and Lane Stiles. Amherst: University of Massachusetts Press, 1996, 52–74.

Kelleher, John V. 'Matthew Arnold and the Celtic Revival'. *Perspectives of Criticism*, ed. Harry Levin. Cambridge, MA: Harvard University Press, 1950, 197–221.

Kelly, John. 'The Fall of Parnell and the Rise of Anglo-Irish Literature: An Investigation'. *Anglo-Irish Studies* ii (1976), 1–23.

— 'Aesthete among the Athletes: Yeats's Contributions to *The Gael*'. *Yeats: An Annual of Critical and Textual Studies* II (1984), 75–143.

— '"Song of the Spanish Insurgents": A Newly Discovered Poem by Yeats'. *Yeats Annual* 3 (1985), 179–81.

— 'Yeatsian Magic and Rational Magic: An Uncollected Review of W. B. Yeats'. *Yeats Annual* 3 (1985), 182–9.

— 'Parnell in Irish Literature'. *Parnell in Perspective*, eds. D. George Boyce and Alan O'Day. London: Routledge, 1991, 242–83.

Kiberd, Declan. *Inventing Ireland*. London: Jonathan Cape, 1995.

Kinsella, Thomas, 'Irish Poetry and the Nineteenth Century'. *Davis, Mangan, Ferguson? Tradition and the Irish Writer*, ed. Roger McHugh. Dublin: Dolmen Press, 1970, 67–70.

Kipling, Rudyard. *Something of Myself*. London: Macmillan, 1937.

Laird, J. T. *The Shaping of* Tess of the D'Urbervilles. Oxford: Clarendon Press, 1975.

Leavis, Q. D. *Fiction and the Reading Public*. London: Chatto and Windus, 1932.

Legg, Marie-Louise. *Newspapers and Nationalism: The Irish Provincial Press, 1850–1892*. Dublin: Four Courts Press, 1999.

Londraville, Richard. 'Four Lectures by W. B. Yeats: 1902–1904'. *Yeats Annual* 8 (1991), 78–122.

Loughlin, James. 'The Irish Protestant Home Rule Association and Nationalist Politics, 1886–93'. *Irish Historical Studies* XXIV (May 1985), 341–60.

Lycett, Andrew. *Rudyard Kipling*. London: Weidenfeld & Nicolson, 1999.

Lyons, F. S. L. *Ireland Since the Famine*. Bungay, Suffolk: Collins/Fontana, 1979.

— *Culture and Anarchy in Ireland*. Oxford: Clarendon Press, 1979.

— 'Yeats and Victorian Ireland'. *Yeats, Sligo and Ireland*, ed. A. Norman Jeffares. Gerrards Cross: Colin Smythe, 1980.

— *Charles Stewart Parnell*. London: Fontana, 1991.

Macken, Mary M. 'W. B. Yeats, John O'Leary and the Contemporary Club'. *Studies* XXVIII (March 1939), 136–42.

Maguire, Thomas. *England's Duty to Ireland as Plain to a Loyal Irish Roman Catholic.* Dublin: Wm. McGee, 1886.

— *Reasons Why Britons Should Oppose Home Rule.* Dublin: Wm. McGee, 1886.

Mahaffy, J. P. 'Sir Samuel Ferguson'. *Athenaeum* (14 April 1886), 205.

Maidment, Brian. 'Readers Fair and Foul: John Ruskin and the Periodical Press'. *The Victorian Press: Samplings and Soundings,* eds. Joanne Shattock and Michael Wolff. Leicester: Leicester University Press, 1982, 29–58.

Marcus, Philip. *Yeats and the Beginnings of the Irish Renaissance.* Ithaca: Cornell University Press, 1970.

May's British and Irish Press Guide. London: May and Co., 1880.

McCann, P. J. O. 'The Protestant Home Rule Movement, 1885–95'. Unpublished MA thesis, University College, Dublin, 1972.

MacDonagh, Michael. *The Life of William O'Brien.* London: Ernest Benn, 1928.

McDonald, Peter. 'Three Authors and the Magazine Market: The Influence of the Periodical Press, 1890–1914'. Unpublished D. Phil. Thesis, Oxford, 1994.

— *British Literary Culture and Publishing Practice 1880–1914.* Cambridge: CUP, 1997.

McDowell, R. B. and D. A. Webb. *Trinity College Dublin, 1592–1952: An Academic History.* Cambridge: CUP, 1982.

McGann, Jerome. 'Introduction'. *Historical Studies and Literary Criticism,* ed. Jerome McGann. Maddison: University of Wisconsin Press, 1985, 3–21.

— 'How to Read a Book'. *The Library Chronicle of the University of Texas at Austin* 20 (1990), 12–37.

— 'What is Critical Editing?' *Text* 5 (1991), 15–29.

— *The Textual Condition.* Princeton: Princeton University Press, 1991 (B).

— *Black Riders: The Visible Language of Modernism.* Princeton: Princeton University Press, 1993.

McKenzie, D. F. *Bibliography and the Sociology of Texts.* London: The British Library, 1986.

Mercier, Vivien. *Modern Irish Literature: Sources and Founders.* Oxford: Clarendon Press, 1994.

Meredith, George. *The Collected Letters of George Meredith,* ed. C. L. Cline. 3 vols, Oxford: Clarendon Press, 1970.

Moloney, Patrick. 'A Survey of the Development of Dublin Daily Newspapers, 1850–1914'. Unpublished MA thesis, National University of Ireland, 1952.

Moore, George. *Hail and Farewell, Vale.* Leipzig: Bernard Tauchnitz, 1914.

Nelson, James G. *The Early Nineties: A View from the Bodley Head.* Cambridge, MA: Harvard University Press, 1971.

Nevinson, Henry W. *Changes and Chances.* London: Nesbit, 1923.

North, Michael. *The Political Aesthetic of Yeats, Eliot and Pound.* Cambridge, CUP, 1990.

Nowell-Smith, Simon, ed. *Letters to Macmillan.* London: Macmillan, 1967.

O'Brien, Conor Cruise. *Parnell and his Party, 1880–90.* Oxford: Clarendon Press, 1957.

— 'Passion and Cunning: An Essay on the Politics of W. B. Yeats'. *In Excited Reverie: A Centenary Tribute to William Butler Yeats, 1865–1939,* eds. A. Norman Jeffares and K. G. W. Cross. London: Macmillan, 1965, 207–78.

O'Brien, Joseph V. *William O'Brien and the Course of Irish Politics, 1881–1918.* London: University of California Press, 1976.

O'Brien, R. Barry. *Charles Stewart Parnell.* 2 vols. London: Smith Elder, 1898.

O'Brien, William. *Recollections.* London: Macmillan, 1905.

Ó Buachalla, Breandán. 'The Gaelic Background'. *Samuel Ferguson: A Centenary Tribute,* eds. Barbara Hayley and Terence Brown. Dublin: Royal Irish Academy, 1987, 27–47.

Ó Dúill, Gréagóir. 'Sir Samuel Ferguson, Administrator and Archivist'. *Irish University Review* 16, 2 (1986), 117–40.

O'Grady, Standish. *Selected Essays and Passages*, ed. Ernest A. Boyd. Dublin: Phoenix Publishing Co., 1918.

O'Hagan, J. 'The Poetry of Sir Samuel Ferguson'. 2 Parts. *Irish Monthly* (May and August 1884), 217–34, 379–401.

Oldham, Charles Hurbert. *The Record of Ulster in Irish Patriotism*. Dublin: Sealy, Bryers and Walker, 1888.

— *Dublin Executive of the IPHRA: Address to its Members*. Dublin: Sealy, Bryers and Walker, 1886.

— *Address to the Protestants of Ireland*. Dublin: Sealy, Bryers and Walker, 1893.

Oram, Hugh. *The Newspaper Book: A History of Newspapers in Ireland, 1649–1983*. Dublin: MO Books, 1983.

Patten, Eve. 'A "General Crowd of Small Singers": Yeats and Dowden Reassessed'. *Yeats Annual* 12 (1994), 29–44.

Patten, Robert L. *Charles Dickens and his Publishers*. Oxford: Clarendon Press, 1978.

Paulin, Tom. *Minotaur*. London: Faber and Faber, 1992.

Rabinowitz, Peter J. *Before Reading: Narrative Conventions and the Politics of Interpretation*. Ithaca: Cornell University Press, 1987.

Rainey, Lawrence. *Institutions of Modernism: Literary Elites and Public Culture*. New Haven: Yale University Press, 1998.

Regan, Stephen. 'W. B. Yeats and Irish Cultural Politics in the 1890s'. *Cultural Politics at the Fin de Siècle*, eds. Sally Ledger and Scott McCracken. Cambridge: CUP, 1995, 66–84.

Roberts, Frank C, compiler. *Obituaries from* The Times *1951–1960*. Reading: Newspaper Archive Developments, 1979.

Rolleston, C. H. *Portrait of an Irishman: A Biographical Sketch of T. W. Rolleston*. London: Methuen, 1939.

Rolleston, T. W. 'The Archbishop in Politics'. *DUR* II (February 1886), 92–103.

Sadleir, Michael. '*Dublin University Magazine*: Its History, Contents and Bibliography'. *The Bibliographical Society of Ireland* V, 4 (1938), 59–81.

Said, Edward. 'Yeats and Decolonization'. *Nationalism, Colonialism and Literature*, ed. Seamus Deane. Minneapolis: University of Minnesota Press, 1990, 67–95.

— *Culture and Imperialism*. London: Chatto and Windus, 1993.

Sell's Directory. London: Sell, 1887–90.

Shillingsburg, Peter. 'Text as Matter, Concept, and Action'. *Studies in Bibliography* 44 (1991), 31–82.

— *Pegasus in Harness: Victorian Publishing and W. M. Thackeray*. Charlottesville: University Press of Virginia, 1992.

— 'Polymorphic, Polysemic, Protean, Reliable, Electronic Texts'. *Palimsest: Editorial Theory in the Humanities*, eds. George Bornstein and Ralph G. Williams. Ann Arbor: University of Michigan Press, 1993, 29–43.

— *Resisting Texts: Authority and Submission in Constructions of Meaning*. Ann Arbor: University of Michigan Press, 1997(A).

— *Scholarly Editing in the Computer Age*. Ann Arbor: University of Michigan Press, 1997(B), 3rd ed.

— 'The Faces of Victorian Fiction'. *The Iconic Page in Manuscript, Print and Digital Culture*, eds. George Bornstein and Teresa Tinkle. Ann Arbor: University of Michigan Press, 1998, 141–56.

Special Commission Act, The, 1888: Report of the Proceedings before the Commissioners Appointed by the Act. Reprinted from *The Times*. 4 vols. London: George Edward Wright, 1890.

Stephen, Herbert. 'William Ernest Henley as a Contemporary and an Editor'. *London Mercury* (February 1926), 387–400.

Stevenson, Robert Louis. *The Letters of Robert Louis Stevenson*. eds. Bradford A. Booth and Ernest Mehew. 8 vols. London: Yale University Press, 1994–95.

Sullivan, Alvin, ed. *British Literary Magazines: The Victorian and Edwardian Period, 1837–1913*. London: Greenwood Press, 1984.

Sutherland, John. 'Fiction and the Erotic Cover'. *Critical Quaterly* 33 (1991), 3–18.

Thorpe, James. 'The Aesthetics of Textual Criticism'. *Bibliography and Textual Criticism*, eds. O. M. Brack and Warner Barnes. Chicago and London: University of Chicago Press, 1969, 102–38.

Torchiana, Donald T. *W. B. Yeats and Georgian Ireland*. Evanston: Northwestern University Press, 1966.

— and Glenn O'Malley, eds. 'Some New Letters from W. B. Yeats to Lady Gregory'. *A Review of English Literature* 4, 3 (July 1963), 9–47.

Tynan, Katharine. 'William O'Brien'. *Catholic World* (November 1888), 151–61.

— *Twenty-five Years: Reminiscences*. London: Smith, Elder and Co., 1913.

— 'Recent Irish Poetry'. *Studies* 6 (June 1917), 200–11.

Unterecker, John. *A Reader's Guide to W. B. Yeats*. London: Thomas and Hudson, 1959.

Wade, Allan, ed. *A Bibliography of the Writings of W. B. Yeats*. London: Rupert Hart-Davis, 1968.

Ward, A. W. and A. R. Waller, eds. *The Cambridge History of English Literature*, vol. 14. Cambridge: CUP, 1916.

Warwick-Haller, Sally. *William O'Brien and the Irish Land War*. Dublin: Irish Academic Press, 1990.

Watson, George. *Irish Identity and the Literary Revival*. London: Croom Helm, 1979.

Webb, Alfred. *The Opinions of Some Protestants Regarding their Irish Catholic Fellow-Countrymen, with the Address of the Irish Protestant Home Rule Association*. London: Irish Press Agency, 1887.

Webb, T. E. *The Irish Question: A Reply to Mr. Gladstone*. Dublin: Hodges and Figgis, 1886.

— *Ipse Dixit or the Gladstonian Settlement of Ireland*. Dublin: Hodges and Figgis, 1886.

Williamson, Kennedy. *W. E. Henley: A Memoir*. London: Harold Shaylor, 1930.

Willey, Todd G. 'The Conquest of the Commodore: Conrad's Rigging of "The Nigger" for the Henley Regatta'. *Conradiana* 7, 3 (1985), 163–82.

Willison, Ian, Warwick Gould and Warren Chernaik, eds. *Modernist Writers and the Marketplace*. London: Macmillan, 1996.

Wolff, Robert Lee. *Ireland: From the Act of Union to the Death of Parnell*. New York: Garland, 1978.

Yeats, J. B. *Letters to his Son, W. B. Yeats and Others, 1869–1922*, ed. Joseph Hone. London: Faber and Faber, 1944.

— *Further Letters of John Butler Yeats*, ed. Lennox Robinson. Dundrum: Cuala Press, 1920.

Notes

INTRODUCTION

1 Walter Benjamin, *Illuminations*, 223, 225.

2 Pierre Bourdieu, *The Field of Cultural Production*, 31–2.

3 Terry Eagleton, *Criticism and Ideology*, 48.

4 Quoted in Philip Horne, 'Henry James and the Economy of the Short Story', 2.

5 For a discussion on the relevance of a text's primary publication, see Edward Bishop, 'Re:Covering Modernism', 287–319; Jerome McGann, *Historical Studies and Literary Criticism*, 3–21, 80; Jerome McGann, *The Textual Condition*, 60–1.

6 Ian Willison, 'Introduction', *Modernist Writers and the Marketplace*, xvi; and Horne, 22.

7 Richard Ellmann sees the poem built around 'a contrast between the sordid present and a past heroic for the simplicity of its blood sacrifice'; *The Identity of Yeats*, 143; cited hereafter as *Identity*. Elizabeth Cullingford reads the poem as Yeats's 'satiric attack on modern cowardice' and a lament for the demise of 'Romantic nationalism' and the 'belief in the possibility of armed insurrection'; *Yeats, Ireland and Fascism*, 4, 90.

8 Malcolm Brown, *The Politics of Irish Literature*, 170.

9 George Moore, *Hail and Farewell, Vale*, 154–7.

10 Allan Wade, ed., *A Bibliography of the Writings of W. B. Yeats* 114; cited hereafter as *Bibl.*

11 The *Irish Times* was also a very genteel, high-society paper which regularly published the 'Court Circular' and other columns such as 'Fashionable Intelligence' focusing on the activities of the royal family, where they would holiday and whether the Prince would enrol in the navy or a German university; society gossip such as the Duchess of Connaught's health and the prosecution against the Countess of Desart; and other articles ('The Liffey as a Salmon River', 'Richard Wagner: His Ideals, His Achievements') of general interest for a cultivated, 'quality' readership.

12 Gun-running had already begun and culminated in April 1914 with the landing of 25,000 firearms and three million rounds of ammunition; R. F. Foster, *Modern Ireland, 1600–1972*, 467.

13 *Modern Ireland*, 459.

14 *Modern Ireland*, 459, 467; F. S. L. Lyons, *Ireland since the Famine*, 303; cited hereafter as *Famine*.

15 *Famine*, 298.

16 *IT*, 8.9.1913, 6–8.

17   W. B. Yeats, *Essays and Introductions*, 246; cited hereafter as *E&I*.

18   A. Norman Jeffares, *A New Commentary on the Poems of W. B. Yeats*, 110.

19   R. F. Foster, *W. B. Yeats*, vol. 1, 190, 367; cited hereafter as *WBY*.

20   30.4.92, 4; 7.5.92, 4, 5; 14.5.92, 4.

21   'One windy night I saw a fisherman staggering, very drunk, about Howth Pier and shouting at somebody that he was no gentleman because he had not been educated at Trinity College, Dublin' (*Collected Letters of W. B. Yeats*, ed. John Kelly, vol. 1, 296; cited hereafter as *CL1*).

22   *Uncollected Prose*, vol. 1, 233; cited hereafter as *UP1*.

23   See also *UI*, 31.1.85, 1; 21.3.85, 4; 10.6.93, 1; 14.7.94, 1.

24   *The Times*, 24.12.80, 8; 21.4.82, 5; 20.1.85, 5; 25.8.85, 4; 16.9.91, 7.

25   A. Norman Jeffares, ed., *Yeats's Poems*, 543–44.

26   Jeffares, *Commentary*, 110.

27   A. Norman Jeffares, *W. B. Yeats: Man and Poet*, 171–2.

28   T. R. Henn, *The Lonely Tower*, 90; John Unterecker, *A Reader's Guide to W. B. Yeats*, 118. Harold Bloom sees the poem anticipating 'the bewildering excess of love in the revolutionary martyrs of "Easter 1916"'. See *Yeats*, 172.

29   A TCD graduate, married to the sister of Dr E. H. Alton, Provost of TCD, he retained close contact with his *alma mater* (which graced him with an honorary degree) and his tutor, J. P. Mahaffy, to whom he regularly turned for guidance and whose will he administered. He became the Dublin correspondent for *The Times* in 1899, and the editor of the *Irish Times* in 1907 and retained both positions till his death in 1934. A galaxy of dignitaries, ambassadors and TCD dons attended his funeral. He was survived by his wife and two sons, both serving in the RAF; 'John Edward Healy', *The Times* (31.3.34, 19; 4.6.34, 17).

30   Jerome McGann, 'How to Read a Book', 26; Peter Shillingsburg, 'The Faces of Victorian Fiction,' 142. For an analysis of how British publishing houses between 1920 and 1950 similarly coded their paperback covers to target a particular audience, see John Sutherland, 'Fiction and the Erotic Cover', 3–18. Peter J. Rabinowitz, *Before Reading*, 2, 3; see also Michael Kearns, 'The Material Melville: Shaping Readers' Horizons', 53. Margaret Beetham, 'Open and Closed: The Periodical as a Publishing Genre,' *Victorian Periodicals Review*, 22 (1989), 98–9.

31   W. B. Yeats, 'Introduction', *A Book of Irish Verse*, xxvii.

32   'A Book of Irish Verse', *United Ireland*, 23.3.95, 1.

33   W. B. Yeats, *The Letters of W. B. Yeats*, ed. Allan Wade (London: Hart-Davis, 1954), 474; cited hereafter as *L*.

34   Jerome McGann, 'What is Critical Editing', 20.

35   Peter Shillingsburg, *Scholarly Editing in the Computer Age*, 34–5; Jerome McGann, 'Introduction', *Historical Studies and Literary Criticism*, 17. See also, Hans Walter Gabler, 'Introduction', *Contemporary German Editorial Theory*, 1–16.

36   Benjamin, *Illuminations*, 223, 225, 226, 227.

37   Daniel Albright, ed., *W. B. Yeats: The Poems*, 528.

38   Marcus Bourke, *John O'Leary*, 37–8; Dominic Daly, *The Young Douglas Hyde*, 72; R. F. Foster, 'Anglo-Irish Literature, Gaelic Nationalism and Irish Politics in the 1890s', 70.

39   *Famine*, 110.

40   J. M. Hone, *William Butler Yeats: The Poet in Contemporary Ireland* (Dublin: Maunsel, nd, Bodleian copy marked 7 July 1916), 37–40. Foster says that this book was being written in 1914 (*WBY*, 528).

41   Richard Altick, *The Presence of the Present*.

42 Elizabeth Cullingford, *Yeats, Ireland and Fascism*, 4, 90.

43 See Donald T. Torchiana, *W. B. Yeats and Georgian Ireland*, 23.

44 Quoted in Torchiana, *Georgian Ireland*, 25, from a speech given in 1898.

45 W. B. Yeats, *Explorations*, 346-7; cited hereafter as *Ex*.

46 *Uncollected Prose*, vol. 2, 313; cited hereafter as *UP2*.

47 W. B. Yeats, *Memoirs*, 212, 271; cited hereafter as *Mem*.

48 Torchiana, *Georgian Ireland*, 66-7.

49 Paudeen, a diminutive of Patrick (or Padraig) – stock Irish Catholic names – was often used by Yeats, especially during this period, to refer to the Catholic middle classes. See 'Paudeen' (*VP*, 291), also written in 1913. The title of 'The Gift' was subsequently altered to 'To a Wealthy Man . . .' (*VP*, 287).

50 Letter to Lane, 1.1.1913; John Kelly typescript.

51 To Augusta Gregory 14.1.1913 (ALS Northwestern). John Kelly's typescript has 'very vaguely'; Donald T. Torchiana and Glenn O'Malley ('Some New Letters from W. B. Yeats to Augusta Gregory', 16) read it as 'on enquiry'. On 4.1.1913 Yeats had written to Hone inviting him to dinner in order to discuss the article. (ALS Kenyon, [Kelly typescript]).

52 For a photograph of this page, see *WBY*, 480.

53 Joseph Hone, *W. B. Yeats*, 265.

54 Conor Cruise O'Brien, 'Passion and Cunning', 234.

55 *Autobiographies*, 381; cited hereafter as *Auto*.

56 For example, see the leading front-page article in *Sinn Fein* on 18.1.1913 and the *Leader's* lampoon, 'The Playboy and the Gallery' (5.4.1913, 177).

57 See also Augusta Gregory's letter of 12.8.1913 to John Quinn, quoted in *WBY*, 495.

58 The story goes that the tops of the newspaper's pages were left uncut as most readers had butlers. Hugh Oram, *The Newspaper Book*, 68.

59 In July 1861, the paper announced that its 'circulation now exceeds by several thousand that of any other newspaper in Ireland, and also that of any conservative newspaper in the United Kingdom'.

60 For revenue, circulation and advertisement figures in Irish newspapers, see Patrick Moloney, 'A Survey of the Development of Dublin Daily Newspapers, 1850-1914'.

61 Torchiana and O'Malley, 32.

62 Though Foster dates the inception of the idea to July (*WBY*, 295), it is likely that Yeats started thinking about the poem a few months earlier, as his letter of 24 January to Augusta Gregory indicates: 'I've a couple more poems in my head to be written if the Gallery falls through' (Torchiana and O'Malley, 22).

63 Torchiana and O'Malley, 16-40.

64 Torchiana and O'Malley, 20-37; letter to Augusta Gregory, 18.5.1913 (ALS Berg, Kelly typescript); letter to Craig, 28.5.1913 (Kelly typescript).

65 See Frank Callanan, *The Parnell Split*, 116.

66 John Kelly, 'Parnell in Irish Literature', 253.

67 Torchiana, 94.

68 Torchiana and O'Malley, 32, 39-40.

69 Hone's later affinities with Yeats are also highlighted by the obituary. It goes on to add:

> Hone, the biographer of the eighteenth-century golden age in Ireland, settled down to live in Dublin in that second golden age, when a group of brilliant writers tried, in his words to bring the aristocratic and Protestant tradition of Swift, Berkeley and Burke in to line with modern 'Gaelic' nationalism. Ireland had not seemed too small a stage for their endeavours

. . . (Frank C. Roberts, compiler, *Obituaries from* The Times *1951–1960*, 361.)

70   Hone, 267.

71   Peter Shillingsburg, *Resisting Texts*, 88, 105, 154, 155; and 'Text as Matter, Concept, and Action', 74. I would disagree with Shillingsburg's view that 'utterance is reduced to sentence in written works' and argue that each publication is a separate utterance attended as it is by its own context, purpose and bibliographic codes.

72   Shillingsburg, *Resisting Texts*, 105.

73   For just such a reading, see Elizabeth Cullingford, *Yeats, Ireland and Fascism*, 90.

74   'Did that play of mine send out / Certain men the English shot?', 'The Man and the Echo', *VP*, 632.

75   Harold Bloom is a notable instance of Yeats's success. He sees 'September 1913' as anticipating 'the bewildering excess of love in the revolutionary martyrs of "Easter 1916" '(*Yeats*, 172).

76   George Bornstein, 'Yeats and Textual Reincarnation', 236.

77   The *Edinburgh Review*, the official organ of the Whigs, was dressed in its party colours (buff and blue) and its motto – *Judex damnatur cum nocens absolvitur* – further reiterated its partisan nature. See Edwin Mallard Everett, *The Party of Humanity*, 3–4. See also Lloyd Davis, 'Journalism and Victorian Fiction', 197–211; L. Brake, A. Jones and L. Madden, eds., *Investigating Victorian Journalism*.

78   Torchiana and O'Malley, 22, 37.

79   I. G. Gregory, *Sir Hugh Lane*, 95. For an account of the whole controversy, see 84–109.

80   For an equally unconvincing, politically correct attempt to 'associate [Yeats's] poetic works with phenomena that modernists often are attacked for failing to embrace, including collaboration, feminism . . .' see David Holdeman, *Much Labouring*, 23. For Cuchulain in Loyalist iconography, see John Wilson Foster, 'Getting the North', 180–1.

81   According to McGann, Cuala's typographical style
      is closer to the Bodley Head press than it is to Kelmscott. That is to say, the books from Yeats's press are not closely printed in faces that recall medieval manuscripts and tight fifteenth-century printing styles. The Dun Emer/Cuala typeface is a modern Caslon, and the lines of text are generously leaded to deliver – in contrast to Kelmscott books – an easily read page. [Jerome McGann, *Black Riders*, 16]

82   Quoted in Tom Paulin, *Minotaur*, 150.

83   William Charvat, *The Profession of Authorship in America, 1800–1870*, 285, 286, 288–9.

84   Thomas Hardy, 'Candour in English Fiction', 130. See also Guinevere L. Griest, *Mudie's Circulating Library and the Victorian Novel*; Simon Gatrell, *Hardy the Creator*; J. T. Laird, *The Shaping of* Tess of the D'Urbervilles.

85   Quoted respectively in Horne, 7, and Michael Anesko, *'Friction with the Market'*, 144, 169.

86   Arnold Bennett, *The Truth about an Author*, 100–1; Walter Besant, *The Pen and the Book*, 8–10.

87   Peter Shillingsburg, *Pegasus in Harness*; Robert L. Patten, *Charles Dickens and his Publishers*.

88   For an analysis of artistic disavowals of economic motives in the context of modernism and British aestheticism, see respectively, Lawrence Rainey, *Institutions of Modernism*, and Jonathan Freedman, *Professions of Taste*.

89   Warwick Gould, ' "Playing at Treason with Miss Maud Gonne" ', 40–1.

90   Terence Brown, *Ireland's Literature: Selected Essays*, viii.

91   Q. D. Leavis, *Fiction and the Reading Public*, 20.
92   Nigel Cross, *The Common Writer*, 219.
93   See *CL1*, 217, 250.
94   Brian Maidment, 'Readers fair and foul', 29–58.
95   Besant, 132–44, 252.
96   Anesko, 168–9, *WBY*; 94–5.
97   *WBY*, 95.
98   Thorpe supports his assertion with an impressive array of examples of editors amending an author's contribution, in one case composing the final instalments of a serial after the author had refused to co-operate until he had been paid his dues. James Thorpe, 'The Aesthetics of Textual Criticism', 110–11.
99   Laurel Brake, 'Literary Criticism and Victorian Periodicals', 102, 104.
100 D. F. McKenzie, *Bibliography and the Sociology of Texts*, 10–20.

CHAPTER ONE

1   The magazine ran from February 1885 to June 1887. Though it changed proprietors on at least two occasions, it assumed an entirely different aspect after its resurrection in February 1887 following a collapse in December 1886. It is clear that C. H. Oldham, who founded and managed this magazine, did not align himself with the new management, and for the purposes of this study the life of the magazine is taken to be co-extensive with his involvement, i.e. February 1885 to December 1886.
2   Katharine Tynan, *Twenty-five Years*, 141-3; Maud Gonne, *The Autobiography of Maud Gonne*, 88; *CL1*, 270, n.17; Daly, 70-1; Janet Egleson Dunleavy and Gareth W. Dunleavy, *Douglas Hyde*, 152.
3   There are diverging views on the club's life span. According to Foster (*WBY*, 41), it lasted till about 1915; however, Mary M. Macken, in an article written in 1939 ('W. B. Yeats, John O'Leary and the Contemporary Club', 137), claimed that the Club was still functioning under the presidency of Senator Rowlette and had recently celebrated its Golden Jubilee. For further information on the club, see *CL1*, 481. For editorial work, see Daly, 56-88, Dunleavy and Dunleavy, 120, and *Auto*, 92–3. A comparison of Hyde's diaries and the *DUR*'s contents illuminates the relationship between the club and the magazine.
4   For the *DUM*, see Walter E. Houghton, ed., *Wellesley Index to Victorian Periodicals 1824–1900*, IV, 195.
5   For a fuller discussion of the impetus behind the *DUM*'s founding, see John Hutchinson, *The Dynamics of Cultural Nationalism*, 79, 90; Michael Sadleir, '*Dublin University Magazine*', 62–6; Houghton, 194.
6   For Butt, see Lyons, *Famine* 147–50; Oldham's political position is indicated by his *DUR* articles published in July 1885 (158) and June 1886 (457–68), by his pamphlets (*The Record of Ulster in Irish Patriotism*), by his IPHRA (Dublin) leaflets (*Dublin Executive of the IPHRA*), and by newspaper accounts of his speeches (*UI*: 4.6.87, 3; 30.10.91, 2; 29.4.93, 3).
7   R. B. McDowell and D. A. Webb, *Trinity College Dublin, 1592–1952*, 323; Lyons, *Famine*, 94.
8   This account of TCD is derived from a description given by the eminent Irish historian and sometime Provost of Trinity, F. S. L. Lyons (*Famine*, 93-4, 179).
9   *The Irish Loyal and Patriotic Union Prospectus*; see also John F. Harbinson, *The Ulster Unionist Party, 1882–1973*, 9; Lyons, *Famine*, 291–2.

10   See his *The Irish Question* and *Ipse Dixit or the Gladstonian Settlement of Ireland.*

11   Edward Dowden, *Letters of Edward Dowden and his Correspondents*, 383.

12   See for instance his *England's Duty to Ireland as Plain to a Loyal Irish Roman Catholic*; and *Reasons Why Britons Should Oppose Home Rule.*

13   James Loughlin, 'The Irish Protestant Home Rule Association and Nationalist Politics, 1886–93', 341.

14   For Hyde's encounters with this bias, see Dunleavy and Dunleavy, 200–1. For Mahaffy, see W. B. Yeats, *Tribute to Thomas Davis*, 6.

15   See *WBY*, 41; *CL1*, 127; Daly, 203; Anna MacBride White, 'Prologue', in *Maud Gonne and W. B. Yeats, The Gonne–Yeats Letters 1893–1938*, 11.

16   See Alfred Webb, ed., *The Opinions of Some Protestants*; Loughlin, 342; and P. J. O. McCann, 'The Protestant Home Rule Movement', 1885–95'.

17   Loughlin, 354–5.

18   Quoted in Loughlin, 354.

19   Loughlin, 355.

20   William Henry Hulbert, *Ireland under Coercion*, II, 294.

21   This letter is also interesting because Rolleston's public stand on the Land League was quite different; see his *DUR* article, 'The Archbishop in Politics', February 1886, 92–103.

22   Stephen Gwynn, *Experiences of a Literary Man*, 56.

23   McCann, 22–3.

24   Patrick Buckland, *Irish Unionism*, xxv.

25   See *Freeman's Journal*, 23.6.86, 3; *UI*, 4.6.87, 3, and 31.10.91, 2.

26   Quoted in Loughlin, 347.

27   Buckland, xiv, xx. In the north, Protestants constituted 60% of the population.

28   Quoted in Sadleir, 70.

29   For a short list of *DUR* contributors, see Appendix I.

30   Lyster helped Yeats revise the *Island of Statues*, taught him to correct proofs and directed his reading in Elizabethan literature (*UP2*, 470–2). Yeats sought his advice as late as 1902 (*Collected Letters of W. B. Yeats*, eds. John Kelly and Ronald Schuchard, Vol. III, 166; cited hereafter as *CL3*) and acknowledged his debt generously while chairing the Lyster Memorial Committee (*UP2*, 305). However, he also thought him 'too West British' (*CL1*, 125) to review *PBYI.*

31   F. S. L. Lyons, *Culture and Anarchy in Ireland*, 103.

32   P. J. Smyth (1826–1885): associate of T. F. Meagher; member of the Repeal Association and of Young Ireland; participated in the abortive 1848 insurrection and escaped to the USA; helped rescue John Mitchell from jail in Tasmania; returned to Ireland in 1856; proprietor of the advanced nationalist newspaper, the *Irishman*; elected MP in 1871 on Butt's Home-Rule ticket; disapproved of Parnell's extreme policies, opposed the Land League and retired from parliament in 1882.

33   The substance and sentiments of this article were to be later echoed by Yeats. His own 'Grattanism,' though vaunted only in the next century, also had its basis in a similar sense of Protestant patriotism and superiority:

>   when we think of the whole history of Ireland for the last seven hundred years, there is perhaps only one epoch that we look upon with entire joy and pride – the ten or fifteen years of the Irish Parliament.
>
>   During that brief period the manufactures of Ireland awoke; prosperity began to come upon the land. (*UP2*, 312–13)

34   See the note welcoming the introduction of Irish history in the intermediate school syllabus (June 1885, 105–6).

35   November 1886, 958.

36   See Yug Mohit Chaudhry, 'Yeats, Victorianism and Irish Nationalism'.

37   Daly, 59–69.

38   Stephen Gwynn (*Garden Wisdom*, 12) repeatedly adverts to the significance of this periodical whose copies he has preserved. The *Cambridge History of English Literature* (ed. A. W. Ward and A. R. Waller, vol. 14, 211) claimed that 'Collectors now give high prices for single copies' of the *DUR*.

39   See, for example, Daly, 59–60. For Yeats's admission see *VP*, 841.

40   See *Auto*, 199 and 559.

41   According to the *United Ireland*, the *DUR* was a periodical of 'high character' (10.4.86, 6), provided a 'continuance of readable and high-class prose and poetical matter' (4.9.86, 3), and promised to be 'an important focus of higher thought in Ireland' (10.10.85, 5). It was rated above the English monthlies.

42   Barbara Hayley, 'A Reading Thinking Nation', 29–48.

43   See, for instance, L. Ginnell's response to T. W. Rolleston (editor) (March 1886, 181–91); Frederick Gregg (member of the editorial team) and C. H. Oldham's responses to T. W. Russell (March 1886, 234–6, and June 1886, 457–68, respectively).

44   For *Island of Statues* and 'Epilogue' see *VP*, 645 and 65, respectively.

45   These are excerpts from Robert Atkinson and Mahaffy's reports to the Intermediate Education Council in 1899 and the controversy that followed. Although not contemporary with the *DUR*, they reflect TCD's abiding attitude towards Gaelic in the nineteenth century. For a summary of this debate, and for Yeats's intervention, see *UP2*, 148–52.

46   George Bornstein, ed., *The Early Poetry*, 11.

47   Bornstein, *Early Poetry*, 12.

48   'The Two Titans', subtitled 'A Political Poem', was published in the *DUR* (March 1886).

49   See 'The Rose Tree' (*VP*, 396), 'Three Songs to the One Burden: III' (608), 'Three Marching Songs' (613), 'Vacillation: VI' (502).

50   Richard Ellmann, *Yeats: The Man and the Masks*, 51.

51   See John Kelly, ' "Song of the Spanish Insurgents" ', 179–81.

52   Quoted by Malcolm Brown, *The Politics of Irish Literature*, 297.

53   Consequently, the location of Oldham's lodgings, the Contemporary Club and the offices of the *DUR* were shifted from 29 Trinity College to 116 Grafton Street. An insert in the November issue announced this re-location with regard to Oldham and the review. Both Mary Macken (137) and Henry W. Nevinson (*Changes and Chances*, 206) attribute Oldham's dismissal from Trinity to his Home Rule activities.

54   *UI*, 10.10.85, 5.

55   Buckland, 4–6.

56   Foster, *Modern Ireland*, 62.

57   Though TCD's obduracy occasionally had disastrous consequences for its tenants – the rack-renting Earl of Leitrim was murdered in 1878 – it eventually paid rich dividends, for, under the Wyndham Act, the college's lands were bought over on the basis of the unrealistic rentals it had maintained undiminished. See McDowell and Webb, 244, 279.

58   McDowell and Webb, 509–10.

59   See his *Home Rule for Ireland under a Parnellite Government* discussed in the *DUR* (May 1886, 456).

60   The new *DUR* cover in January 1886 replacing the TCD arms with those of Dublin city, provoked further fears that the magazine had gone over to the nationalists. To explain the change and clarify these 'misconceptions', the *DUR*'s February issue (168) printed TCD's letter:

14th December, 1885.

Sir, – I am directed by the Board to inform you that they have passed a resolution as follows: – 'That it is not desirable that the publishers of the
DUBLIN UNIVERSITY REVIEW should use the College Arms on the
cover of that publication, inasmuch as the authorities of the College have no
control over the articles inserted in it.'

I am, Sir, your obedient servant,

Thoaas [*sic*] Stack, Registrar.

61 Another change following the receipt of TCD's letter, perhaps even resulting from
    it, was that John Beare's (Junior Fellow at TCD) and Rolleston's names no longer
    appeared as classical editor and editor respectively alongside Oldham's as proprietor.
    Such timidity was characteristic of Rolleston, who remained editor of the periodi-
    cal till the end of 1886 as is borne out by his son's biography (C. H. Rolleston, *Por-
    trait of an Irishman*, 25), Hyde's diaries (Dunleavy and Dunleavy, 123) and his own
    self-advertisement in a pamphlet (Webb, ed., *The Opinions of Some Protestants*, 20).
    Yeats's description of Rolleston – '"an intimate enemy"; without passion . . . "a hol-
    low image"' (*Mem*, 51) – though tinged with some rancour, is justified apropos of
    Rolleston's lack of courage and conviction.

62 Contemporary Club member and Secretary to the Royal Commission on Irish pub-
    lic works; later, President of the Statistical Society of Ireland, Privy Counsellor, Gov-
    ernor of the National Gallery and one of the Irish Land Commissioners. He was
    later a shareholder in the Abbey and one of the witnesses in the hearings which
    secured the Abbey's patent. Lady Gregory dedicated her *New Irish Comedies* to him
    as 'Counsellor, Peacemaker, Friend'.

63 Another instance is his role in the New Irish Library Scheme; see *CL1*, 304–58.

64 January 1886, 71–2.

65 See his *The Government of Ireland: Will Home Rule Be Rome Rule?*, *The Government of
    Ireland: Are We Utter Fools?* and *The Government of Ireland*.

66 Bourke, 195.

67 *UP1* 81–87 and 87–104. While the first, a shorter piece, was published in the *Irish
    Fireside* (9.10.86), the second, a fuller length review, was published in the *DUR*
    (November 1886). While discussing Yeats's views on Ferguson, I concentrate on the
    DUR article while occasionally referring to its companion piece. Such references are
    indicated by ★.

68 Letter to Allingham, 8 June 1885. Quoted in Lady Mary Ferguson, *Sir Samuel Fergu-
    son and the Ireland of his Day*, vol.1, 361; cited hereafter as *SSF*.

69 To Aubrey de Vere, 21.2.48. Quoted in Gréagóir Ó Dúill, 'Sir Samuel Ferguson,
    Administrator and Archivist', 121.

70 To Larcom, 15 July 1874. Quoted in Ó Dúill, 135.

71 Breandán Ó Buachalla, 'The Gaelic Background'; Ó Dúill, 117; Hutchinson, 90.

72 Quoted in William Hodder, 'Ferguson: His Literary Sources', 60.

73 See Tom Dunne, 'Haunted by Irish History: Irish Romantic Writing 1800–50', 83–4.

74 Quoted in Hodder, 62.

75 Richard Londraville, 'Four Lectures by W. B. Yeats: 1902–1904', 114.

76 W. B. Yeats, *The Senate Speeches of W. B. Yeats*, 99.

77 *Congal*, 'Mesgedra', 'The Healing of Conall Carnach' and 'The Burial of King Cor-
    mac' are instances of the first kind of interpolation and 'The Death of Dermid' and
    'Conary' of the second. See Philip Marcus, *Yeats and the Beginnings of the Irish Renais-
    sance*, 233; Malcolm Brown, *Sir Samuel Ferguson*, 90–6.

78 Cited in Marcus, 233.

79   Marcus, 233.

80   Malcolm Brown, *Ferguson*, 91–2.

81   For Ferguson's letter see (Anonymous) 'Sir Samuel Ferguson: In Memoriam'.

82   Before the publication of the *Wanderings of Oisin*, Yeats's journalistic offerings more often than not remained on the editors' desks for a long while before being blackened by the printer's ink (see *UP1*, 21.) His letter to Katharine Tynan of June 1888 bemoans the 'ever-multiplying boxes of unsalable MSS' (*CL1*, 71).

83   W. B. Yeats, *Letters to the New Island*, 48; cited hereafter as *LNI*. See also his *Book of Irish Verse*, xxi.

84   For de Vere's letter see *SSF*, vol.2, 229–30 and for de Vere's essay see *Essays Chiefly Lyrical and Ethical*, 98–125.

85   'The Poetry of Sir Samuel Ferguson'. For corroboration of the authorship of this article, see *SSF*, vol.1, 128.

86   Quoted in *SSF*, vol.2, 225.

87   J. P. Mahaffy, 'Sir Samuel Ferguson'.

88   Quoted in Malcolm Brown, *Ferguson*, 18.

89   'I never wrote for the "Nation". To say that I have upborne their banner is more than I would like to vouch' (*SSF*, vol.1, 254).

90   *DUM*, February 1847, 194–5.

91   Quoted in Malcolm Brown, *Ferguson*, 34.

92   I. A. Gregory, ed., *Ideals in Ireland*, 106.

93   Thomas Kinsella, 'Irish Poetry and the Nineteenth Century', 69–70.

94   February 1886, 170; April 1886, 297–300; and December 1885, 392, respectively.

95   The advertisements under the new owners made an even more concerted bid to attract Protestants, 'the richest people in this country, and . . . throughout Great Britain' (insert, February 1887). Though the review avoided current politics, it consistently displayed a unionist bias through editorial notes on Dublin Castle, the activities of the British army and poems on the Primrose League (see June 1887, 229). However, the fact that Irish politics was not primary on the agenda ensured the early demise of this endeavour, and the *DUR* folded finally in June 1887.

96   In a famous case that Gladstone made much of in parliament, Rev. Samuel Sandys of Donnybrook was expelled by popular demand from his curacy for being a Protestant Home Ruler. See Loughlin, 348–9, 357–9.

CHAPTER TWO

1   *UI*, 10.10.85, 5.

2   Not all of Yeats's early publications have survived and occasionally one reads of new discoveries. In addition to Wade's *Bibl* and Frayne's *UP1*, I have drawn upon the following articles by John Kelly to arrive at a more complete list of Yeats's nineteenth-century periodical publications: 'Aesthetes Among the Athletes', 75–143; '"Song of the Spanish Insurgents"', 179–81; 'Yeatsian Magic and Rational Magic', 182–9.

3   His work appeared in the *North & South* (two poems), the *Gael* (one letter, two articles and at least two poems), the Catholic *Irish Monthly* (two poems) and the *Irish Fireside* (two articles and two poems). The first two were media organs of the IPHRA and the Gaelic Athletic Association (GAA) respectively; the remaining two periodicals were low-brow purveyors of cheap and wholesome religious writing. The *North & South* featured financial news, political and social comment, and poetry. According to John Kelly, it had a relatively small circulation and was often badly produced. See

his article, 'Song of the Spanish Insurgents'. For the *Gael*, a 'magazine founded for, and predominantly read by, beefy athletes of the Gaelic Athletic Association', see 'Aesthetes'.

4   *May's British and Irish Press Guide* (1880), 146; cited hereafter as *May's*.

5   Kelly, 'Aesthetes', 81.

6   *Gael*: 1 letter, two poems; *Irish Fireside*: 1 poem; *Irish Monthly*: 1 poem; *United Ireland*: 1 article.

7   'The history of *United Ireland* is an epic in itself. Since the *Nation* of Thomas Davis there had been no paper like it in Ireland, and there has been none since. It instantly became a power. It was an entirely novel and original production . . . From the first it made history.' (T. P. Gill, 'William O'Brien: Some Aspects', 614).

8   For Pigott, see F. S. L. Lyons, *Charles Stewart Parnell*, 162 (cited hereafter as *Parnell*); and William O'Brien, *Recollections*, 301. For Chief Secretary Trevelyan, see Sally Warwick-Haller, *William O'Brien and the Irish Land War*, 73.

9   *The Special Commission Act, 1888*, vol. 3, 204. cited hereafter as *PSC*.

10   *May's* (1883) provides the following data:

Affiliation	Dailies	Other
Conservative	7	33
Liberal/Conservative	2	11
Liberal	6 (includes *Freeman's Journal*)	32
Nationalist	–	16

11   For a lucid account of this dissension and for Parnell's reasons for starting a newspaper, see Warwick-Haller, 43–5; R. Barry O'Brien, *Charles Stewart Parnell*, 190–301.

12   *PSC*, vol. 2, 778.

13   Michael MacDonagh, *The Life of William O'Brien*, 53.

14   Florence Arnold-Foster, *Florence Arnold-Foster's Irish Journal*, 268.

15   'I read the rebel papers. The new one *United Ireland* is the cleverest of all of them. Very violent about the Ch. Sec's letter to the Ulster deputation: calling him every kind of opprobrious name, and indulging generally in language worthy of Billlingsgate whenever having occasion to allude to him' (Arnold-Foster, 248). See also Warwick-Haller, 73.

16   Quoted in Joseph V. O'Brien, *William O'Brien and the Course of Irish Politics, 1881–1918*, 17.

17   MacDonagh, 53.

18   M. M. Bodkin, *Recollections of an Irish Judge*, 150.

19   *PSC*, vol. 1, 32.

20   *PSC*, vol. 2, 61–81.

21   A similar anti-English sentiment, though with a more convoluted logic, prompted Yeats in 1937 to aver apropos of the Spanish War: 'I am an old Fenian and I think the old Fenian in me would rejoice if a Fascist nation or government controlled Spain, because that would weaken the British empire, force England to be civil to Indians, perhaps to set them free and loosen the hands of English finance in the far East of which I hear occasionally' (*L*, 881).

22   *PSC*, vol. 1, 32, 70, 79, 452–6, 789; vol. 2, 61–81, 725, vol. 3, 66; vol. 4, 269, 316, 514–7; Hansard, *Parliamentary Debates*, 294 (4.12.84), 613; '[Father says] a prohibition or a prosecution would only give it a new lease of life' (Arnold-Foster, 318).

23   *PSC*, vol. 3, 257; MacDonagh, 54, 85. For a similar claim regarding the paper's readership, see J.V. O'Brien, 15. It was customary for newspapers to pass from one hand to another and, because of the low literacy levels, they were often read out aloud for the benefit of others. See Virginia E. Glandon, 'The Irish Press and Revolutionary

Irish Nationalism', 21. For other newspapers, see *Sell's Directory*, 1887, 370–3; 1889, 581–601.

24 William O'Brien, 379–84; *PSC*, vol. 2: 335, vol. 3: 212, 769.

25 Conor Cruise O'Brien, *Parnell and his Party, 1880–90*, 80.

26 The cartoon of 28.8.86 depicted Parnell swinging a noosed rope over a lamp-post and a policeman ordering a quivering Lord Randolph Churchill to approach the makeshift gallows; in the background an angry mob is pelting stones. That of 27.11.86 depicted a figure called 'Landlordism' being roasted over a fire called 'Plan of Campaign'.

27 18.8.94, 1.

28 See for instance 1.2.90, 3; 16.8.90, 6; 17.4.86, 6. 17.4.86, 6; *PSC*, vol. 1, 452–3, 456, 461. For similar instances, see vol. 2, 242–3 (cattle killed for hiring machinery to boycotted people).

29 *PSC*, vol. 2, 456.

30 The following are the advertisement rates in Irish newspapers as listed in *Sell's Directory* (1887: 369–73; 1889: 581–601). Those in parenthesis refer to weeklies and all but the first are unionist organs circulating among the more affluent classes:

Name	Business Advertisements per inch				Official per line	
	Once	78 (13)	156 (26)	312 (52)		
United Ireland	(3/6)	(3/-)	(3/-)	(3/-)	1/-	
Irish Times	3/6	2/6	2/3	2/-	1/-	
Dublin Daily Express	3/-	2/-	2/-	2/-	6d	9d
Dublin Evening Mail	2/-	1/6	1/3	1/-	6d	1/-
Union	(2/-)	(1/9)	(1/6)	(1/-)		
Sligo Independent	(3/-)	(1/3)	(1/-)	(1/-)		
Armagh Standard	(2/-)	(1/-)	(-/9)	(-/6)	6d	1/-

31 See, for instance, 23.4.87, 1.

32 Examples are J. G. Swift McNeill's *How the Union Was Carried* (26.3.87, 5) and *English Interference with Irish Industries*; M. Thomas's *Paddy's Dream and John Bull's Nightmare* (1.5.86, 5–6); William Dillon's *Life of John Mitchell* (16.6.88, 4).

33 See also 18.8.88, 3, and 10.5.90, 5.

34 See also 1.5.86, 5–6; 2.7.87, 6; 19.5.88, 3; 16.6.88, 4; 18.8.88, 3.

35 T. S. Cleary's *Lays of the Irish Land War* was fortunate enough to have been attacked by the unionist *Dublin Evening Mail* thus meriting a spirited defence and a second review by the *United Ireland*. See 19.5.88, 3, and 23.6.88, 6.

36 6.4.89, 6 and 27.4.89, 6.

37 Andrew Dunlop, *Fifty Years of Irish Journalism*, 270–1.

38 See for instance 17.6.93, 5, where the duality is presented in very stark terms.

39 See 24.1.91, 5.

40 O'Reilly, a Fenian ex-convict who had escaped to America and started the *Boston Pilot*, was also a poet. He was reviewed on at least half-a-dozen occasions and when he died he received about twice the space given to Cardinal Newman, who also died the same week (16.8.90).

41 15.5.86, 6.

42 See W. S. Blunt, *The Land War in Ireland*, 335–6; 345–55.

43 See, for instance, 5.11.87, 5, 6; 17.12.87, 6; 7.1.88, 1; 11.1.88, 1–3; 28.1.88, 3.

44 29.10.87, 4; and *UP1*, 128.

45 W. B. Yeats, ed., *Oxford Book of Modern Verse*, v–vi; cited hereafter as *OBMV*.

46 This letter, though not in *CL1*, is mentioned in a letter to Tynan (14.3.88; *CL1*, 55) and its receipt is acknowledged by the *UI*.

47   *CL1*, 58.

48   *CL1*, 17, 73, 269, 273, 276, 281.

49   *CL1*, 102, 141.

50   *CL1*, 61, 68, 282, 295.

51   See *CL1*, 174, 186 n. 4.

52   *LNI*, xiv. References to Yeats's American journalism are taken from *LNI*.

53   See also: 'The man when he sold them to me did so timidly, mistaking me, most evidently, for one of the loyal minority' (*LNI*, 55). 'By the by . . . Mr O'Grady is seeing the error of his ways and growing into a good Nationalist after all' (34). 'Your Celt has written the greater bulk of his letters from the capital of the enemy' (64).

54   *LNI*, 11, 76.

55   Yeats's penchant for linguistic bravado has also been noticed by Roy Foster, 'Anglo-Irish Literature', 73, and Stephen Regan, 'W. B. Yeats and Irish Cultural Politics in the 1890s', 79–80.

56   *LNI*, 32, 67.

57   Terence Brown, *Ireland's Literature*, 4.

58   Compare *United Ireland*, 11.4.91, 1 ('In art, eclecticism means loss of character . . .', see pp. 196–7), with *LNI*, 103–4.

59   *E&I*, 519.

CHAPTER THREE

1   See *CL1*, 47, 48, 50, 51, 56, 71, 92.

2   For example, 'Popular Ballad Poetry of Ireland', submitted on (approximately) 15 July 1887, was published in November 1889, i.e. two years and four months later; and 'Irish Fairies', submitted on 12 February 1888, was published in October 1890, i.e. two years and eight months later. Both articles had been commissioned by the *Leisure Hour*. See *CL1*, 25, 46, 47, 53, 56–7.

3   Yeats's income from his American publications was instrumental in keeping the family afloat and the bulk of his earnings from November 1889 to November 1890 came from the *Providence Sunday Journal* and the *Boston Pilot*. See *WBY*, 94.

4   *Mem*, 31, *Auto*, 136. According to John Kelly, Yeats earned about 6s a month from this source and Lolly's diary entries of his earnings mention regular receipts till May 1890. See *CL1*, 48, n.3, 158, 160; *WBY*, 94; and *Bibl*, 11.

5   These were published in the *Girl's Own Paper* on 8 June and 6 July 1889. He neither reprinted nor included them in the Collected Works. See *VP*, 735–6.

6   In December 1890 the *Scots Observer* shifted to London and was re-christened *The National Observer* (*NO*). There is some misapprehension as to when exactly Henley took up this assignment. Alvin Sullivan (ed., *British Literary Magazines*, 393) holds that the 'editorship of W. E. Henley from the *Observer*'s premiere on 24 November 1888 to 24 March 1894 is undisputed'. More recently, Peter McDonald (*British Literary Culture and Publishing Practice 1880-1914*, 32) has used the same starting point. However, John Connell's claim made in 1949 that Henley took over the editorship only after the first few issues is the correct one. (John Connell, *W. E. Henley*, 141.) It is borne out by Henley's letter to Whibley of 10.1.89 – 'I have taken over the *Scots Observer*, a sixpenny weekly some six or seven numbers new' (unpublished ALS, Pierpont Morgan Library, NY) – and by his letter of 28.1.89 to William Archer announcing that the issue of 26.1.89 was the second under his command (W. E. Henley, *The Selected Letters of W. E. Henley*, 84). This makes it quite

clear that Henley's first issue was that of 19.1.89. However, Yeats's letter of 21.12.88 to Tynan (*CL1*, 117) indicates that Henley was connected in some influential way with the journal even before January 1889. This is reconfirmed by Stevenson's letter of 9.10.88 to Henley about inserting 'Christmas at Sea' in the *SO*. It was eventually published on 22.12.88, 131 (Robert Louis Stevenson, *The Letters of Robert Louis Stevenson*, vol. 6, 210). I am grateful to Dr Damian Atkinson for typescripts of Henley's unpublished letters.

7   C. Lewis Hind, *Authors and I*, 131, 132; Patrick R. Chalmers, *Kenneth Grahame*, 55; Max Beerbohm, 'A Letter to the Editor', 283; Peter McDonald, *British Literary Culture*, 51; Peter Green, *Kenneth Grahame*, 111.

8   Andrew Lycett, *Rudyard Kipling*, 292.

9   Subsequently though, Kipling would sell to the highest bidder the serial rights of his novel, *Captains Courageous*, even though Henley was among the interested editors.

10   Jerome Hamilton Buckley, *William Ernest Henley*, 152, 153, 166; Patrick R. Chalmers, 63; Ford Maddox Hueffer, *Ancient Lights and Certain New Reflections*, 174, 239; Herbert Stephen, 'William Ernest Henley as a Contemporary and an Editor', 388, 390; Rudyard Kipling, *Something of Myself*, 82; George Meredith, *The Collected Letters of George Meredith*, vol. 3, 1600; Joseph Conrad, *The Collected Letters of Joseph Conrad*, vol. 1, 322–3, 329, 344, 408; Frederick R. Karl, *Joseph Conrad*, 561; Todd G. Willey, 'The Conquest of the Commodore', 163–82.

11   Henley, *Selected Letters*, 200.

12   W. E. Henley, 'What I have done for you, England, my England', *The Song of the Sword*, 101.

13   Buckley, 156; Connell, 212; Kennedy Williamson, *W. E. Henley*, 133; W. E. Henley, *Views and Reviews*, 39.

14   W. E. Henley, 'The Song of the Sword', *Song*, 1–12. For similar examples, see 'To R. F. B.', *Poems*, 211–13. Compare with Yeats's 'The Statues':
     We Irish, born into that ancient sect
     But thrown upon this filthy modern tide
     And by its formless, spawning, fury wrecked . . .
     (*VP*, 611)

15   W. E. Henley, 'The Tory Press and the Tory Party', 271.

16   However, this did not prevent Henley wanting to cash in on the Master's prestige. As editor of the *Magazine of Art*, he had written to James pleading for a short story and refusing to 'take no for an answer' (Henley, *Selected Letters*, 105). He later published *What Masie Knew* in the *New Review*. Connell, 316. For Churchill, see *New Review*, September, October 1895, 250, 372.

17   On Wilde's conviction for homosexuality, Henley wrote gleefully to Whibley:
     Yes: the Bugger at Bay was on the whole a pleasing sight. The air is alive with rumours, of course; but I believe no new arrests will be made, & that morality will be satisfied if Oscar gets two years; as of course he will. Why he didn't stay at Monte Carlo, once he got there, God alone knows . . . Be this as it may, he is mad no more. Holloway & Bow St. have taken his hair out of curl in more senses than one. And I am pretty sure that he's having a damn bad time. (Henley, *Selected Letters*, 245)
     For his attacks on the *Yellow Book*, see *NO*, 10.2.94, 313; *New Review* (May 1895), 526; for those on Wilde, see *SO*, 5.7.90, 181, and the issues over the next two months; also Connell, 187–193.

18   Yeats was to make similar statements about Pater and his influence on the 1890s generation:

...and yet I began to wonder if it [*Marius the Epicurian*], or the attitude of mind of which it was the noblest expression, had not caused the disaster of my friends. It taught us to walk upon a rope tightly stretched through serene air, and we were left to keep our feet upon a swaying rope in a storm. (*Auto*, 302–3)

I will then describe a debate at Oxford a few years ago when I felt so much pity for that young brilliant man full of feminine sensitiveness. Surely the ideal of culture expressed by Pater can only create feminine souls. (*Auto*, 477)

19   Stephen, *London Mercury*, 393. Apropos of Parnell's affair with Kitty O'Shea and his use of aliases, Stephen recalls that Henley 'printed between two of the leaders' a parody entitled 'The Statesman and the Fire-escape':

> 'I want to know of all the six
> Who best enjoyed the run,
> And which amused himself the most?'
> But answer there was none,
> And this was really *very* odd
> Because the six were one.

For other examples in a single year, see, *SO*, 2.2.89, 292; 9.2.89, 318–19; 16.2.89, 345; 2.3.89, 406, 456; 23.3.89, 491; 30.3.89, 519; 13.4.89, 574; 22.6.89, 116; 13.7.89, 206; 3.8.89, 289; 17.8.89, 340.

20   Ford Madox Hueffer found it surprising that Henley's periodicals were not subsidised by the Tory party:

> And I have always considered that the final proof that the Tory Party is really the stupid party – the damning and final proof was that it never subsidised Henley and never provided him with an organ. Had Henley been a Liberal, he would have had half-a-dozen papers at his feet. The Tory party without a qualm let die alike the *National Observer* and the *New Review*. (*Ancient Lights*, 174–5)

21   For other anti-Parnell articles and lampoons, see 9.3.89, 433, 436; 20.4.89, 609; 11.5.89, 683; 22.2.90, 368; 1.3.90, 400; 6.12.90, 57, 58, 60–4; 5.9.91, 392–93.

22   For other such attacks in its first year see *SO*, 1.12.88, 34; 8.12.88, 62; 22.12.88, 118; 5.1.89, 175; 12.1.89, 202; 19.1.89, 229; 2.2.89, 285; 16.2.89, 341; 23.2.89, 369; 2.3.89, 406, 436; 13.4.89, 570; 27.4.89, 622; 1.6.89, 34, 94; 20.7.89, 235; 28.9.89, 505; 5.10.89, 534; 9.11.89, 674.

23   For other examples see, *SO*, 16.2.89, 345; 10.5.90, 695–6.

24   For other examples, see *SO*, 19.1.89, 251; 6.7.89, 187–88; 12.10.89, 581; 19.7.90, 229, and *NO*, 1.8.91, 278–9.

25   Quoted in Willey, 169, from Wilfred Scawen Blunt, *My Diaries*.

26   See also *SO*, 1.12.88, 353; 3.8.89, 300; 21.9.89, 493; *NO*, 5.11.92, 630.

27   For Henley's attacks and lampoons on Morris, see *SO*, 30.11.89, 46; 7.12.89, 65; Connell, 195; for his aversion to the Pre-Raphaelites, see *Auto*, 125, Hueffer, *Ancient Lights*, 228, and *SO*, 28.12.89, 158–9; for Blake and Villiers de L'Isle-Adam see *SO*, 19.10. 89; 605; 22.3.90; 499–500; and for Pater see *NO*, 2.5.91; 608–9, and *Mem*, 38.

28   See also Buckley, 128. Subsequently, the *New Review* carried the following announcement pertaining to a change in editors:

> in one sole respect will tradition be maintained: while it will welcome all that is good and new, as heretofore, its politics, as heretofore, will be steadily Imperialist and Conservative. (*New Review*, Insert, December 1897)

29   For Yeats's views on Henley's gatherings, see *CL1*, 91, 97, 99, and *Mem*, 252.

30   Though Foster claims that Henley paid a pound per column (*WBY*, 95), the figures from Lolly's diary (94) indicate that it was a guinea. This is also borne out by a letter

from Henley to Whibley of 15.1.89 (unpublished ALS, Pierpont Morgan) inviting him to be a contributor and informing him of the rate of payment.

31 James G. Nelson, *The Early Nineties*, 246–7, 309; Peter Green, 309.

32 See *CL1*, 157–8, 283.

33 See also *CL1*, 356.

34 *CL1*, 151, 152, 247, 271, 272, 273, 389.

35 Years later, Yeats himself would become a symbolic banker and use his cultural capital to promote other writers (Rabindranath Tagore, Charles Peguy, Lennox Robinson, James Joyce). See Simon Nowell-Smith, ed., *Letters to Macmillan*, 288, 290–4. See also, Pierre Bourdieu, *Distinction*, 2, 483; Peter McDonald, 'Three Authors and the Magazine Market', 2; and Willey, 167.

36 I have examined the 500-odd letters that make up Henley's correspondence to Whibley, and Damian Atkinson's edition of Henley's selected letters. Dr Atkinson informs me that he cannot recall a reference to Yeats in any of Henley's letters that he has seen. Yeats's article, 'Scots and Irish Fairies' (*SO*, 2.3.89, 410), was reprinted under the revised title 'A Remonstrance with Scotsmen for Having Soured the Disposition of their Ghosts and Fairies' in *The Celtic Twilight* (1893). The *SO* advertisements can be seen in the issues of 25.5.89, 27 and 15.6.89, iii.

37 'Tis the privilege of editors now & then to stumble upon a *writer*. And it is a very great pleasure to me to reflect that, with a single exception ('East & West'), all R.K.'s best numbers have been passed out through me . . . [As a postscript] I don't mind confessing that R.K. has given me a new interest in life. (W. E. Henley, *Selected Letters*, 203)

38 Buckley, 128.

39 This is discussed in Willey, 176.

40 For Henley's authorship of this review, see *CL1*, 152.

41 Declan Kiberd, *Inventing Ireland*, 104. For a fuller treatment, see Deborah Fleming, *A Man Who Does Not Exist*.

42 '. . . no doubt the sensibility of the Celtic nature, its nervous exaltation, have something feminine in them, and the Celt is thus peculiarly disposed to feel the spell of the feminine idiosyncrasy; he has an affinity to it; he is not far from its secret.' Matthew Arnold, 'On the Study of Celtic Literature', 347.

43 Oliver Goldsmith, 'The Traveller', 269.

44 His heavy figure and powerful head . . . his eyes steadily fixed upon some object in complete confidence and self-possession, and yet as in half-broken reverie . . . He was most human – human, I used to say, like one of Shakespeare's characters – and yet pressed and pummelled, as it were, into a single attitude, almost into a gesture and a speech as by some overwhelming situation . . . he was like a great actor of passion . . . and an actor of passion will display some one quality of soul, personified again and again . . . He terrified us . . . (*Auto*, 124–7)

45 Edward Said, 'Yeats and Decolonization', 77, 79. A revised version appears in *Culture and Imperialism*, 27.

46 John V. Kelleher, 'Matthew Arnold and the Celtic Revival', 197–221.

47 *CL1*, 166, 175, 264.

48 See *LNI*, 12, 25, 45–6.

49 See *UP1*, 256–8. 'It is exceedingly simple, both in thought and expression. Its very simplicity and sincerity have made it, like much Irish verse, unequal; for when the inspiration fails, the writer has no art to fall back upon. Nor does it know anything about studied adjective and subtle observation' (258).

50   See John Kelly, 'Parnell in Irish Literature', 242–83; and R. F. Foster, 'Anglo-Irish Literature', 61–82.

51   Kennedy Williamson, 177. W. E. Henley, *A Book of Verses*, 164–5.

52   Before its publication in 1892, Yeats had the previous year inscribed the poem along with six others in an ornate notebook called *The Flame of the Spirit* and presented it to Maud Gonne. In March 1892 he had included it in a letter to Tynan offering it to her for her anthology, *Irish Love-Songs*, published in December 1892. She declined the offer. See Warwick Gould and Deirdre Toomey, ' "Take Down This Book" ', 124–37; *CL1*, 288–9.

53   For a possible example of such revisions, see Hone, 63.

54   *Fairy and Folk Tales* was published well before any of the others were even commissioned and therefore is not germane to my argument.

55   *CL1*, 28–228.

56   Many of the facts, opinions and phrases in the *SO* article and the Introduction to the Carleton section of the *Representative Irish Tales* are similar and often identical to those in the Introduction to *Stories from Carleton*. See also headnote, *UP1*, 142. References hereafter to the Introduction to *Representative Irish Tales* are meant to refer to the Introduction to the Carleton section only.

57   Material that figures in both *Stories from Carleton* and *Representative Irish Tales* but not in the *SO* review is indicated by (★).

58   *W. B. Yeats: Prefaces and Introductions*, ed. William H. O'Donnell, 23; cited hereafter as *P&I*. Yeats's quotation of Carleton's mother's words is a largely accurate rendering from Carleton's *Autobiography*. For a comparison, see William Carleton, *The Autobiography of William Carleton*, 20.

59   Carleton, 16.

60   *SO*, 1.12.88, 34; 5.1.89, 175.

61   The agitation carried on until the autumn of 1891.

62   See *Freeman's Journal*, 8 January, 26 June and 19 March 1891.

63   Bourke, 5, 45, 195–9.

64   Of *Valentine M'Clutchy*, 'where half the characters are devils', he goes on to say that 'the artist has passed and only the politician remains.' The novel 'would be intolerable but for its wild humour and the presence of the village madman in whose half-inspired and crazy oratory Carleton seems to pour himself out'. Yeats finds its satire against proselytising Protestant clergymen inconsistent, 'coming strangely from a new convert like Carleton' (*SO*, 608; *UP1*, 145).

65   For *Valentine M'Clutchy*, see *CL1*, 174, n.4.

66   James Joyce, 'The Day of the Rabblement', 71.

67   Robert Lee Wolff, *Ireland*, 22; Vivien Mercier, *Modern Irish Literature*, 53, 55; Barbara Hayley, 'A Detailed Bibliography of Editions of William Carleton's *Traits and Stories of the Irish Peasantry* Published in Dublin and London During the Author's Lifetime', 29–55.

CHAPTER FOUR

1   Lyons, *Parnell*, 535–47.

2   10.10.91, 6; 31.1.92, 4; 21.5.92, 3.

3   *UI*, 15.8.91, 1.

4   15.8.91, 1; 22.8.91, 1 and 19.9.91, 1.

5   Appendix I.

6   The general election coverage between May and June 1892 interrupted the TCD debate; in 1895 it appropriated page 3 from 'Athletics'; the Parnell anniversary in 1892 and 1894 interrupted the Irish Constitution and Davitt debates respectively. See Appendix II.

7   4.8.95 and 5.1.95.

8   The *National Press* had claimed that Tynan lacked:

the sobriety of imagination . . . the staidness and gravity of thought and of language which such themes of their nature demand. She has, in fact, a plentiful lack of nearly all the qualifications requisite for the work she undertook, except enthusiasm; and the enthusiasm she possesses is too apt at times to degenerate into gush' (*National Press*: 23.7.91, 6).

A few months later when the *UI* dismissed Tynan's *Ballads and Lyrics* (9.1.92, 5) as old hat and described her as a poet who had stagnated, John O'Leary accused the paper of being, ironically enough, 'ungallant' (16.1.92, 5).

9   24.12.92, 5; 2.12.93, 1; 24.12.94, 1.

10   30.4.92, 1.

11   See also 30.4.92, 1 reprinted from *Kilkenny Moderator* (Conservative).

12   See, for example, 22.8.91.

13   See also 'Wanted: An Irish Novelist' (11.7.91, 1), 'Wanted: An Irish Dramatist' (14.4.94, 1) and 'Wanted: A National Drama' (14.4.94, 1).

14   14.2.91, 5.

15   9.4.92, 5.

16   16.5.91, 5; 23.5.91, 5.

17   For other instances of the *United Ireland* exhorting its readers, see 9.4.92, 5; 23.4.92, 1; and 30.4.92, 1; for publishers, 30.10.91, 1; 11.6.92, 1; for booksellers 21.10.93, 1; for newspapers editors 14.2.91, 5; 28.3.91, 1; 23.4.92, 1; for scholars 3.10.91, 1. For a non-political criticism, see 11.11.93, 1; 11.8.94, 1; 18.8.94, 1.

18   24.1.91, 5; 14.2.91, 5; 14.3.91, 1; 11.4.91, 1; 1.8.91, 1; 22.8.91, 1; 10.10.91, 2; 12.3.92, 5; 14.4.94, 1.

19   *UP1*, 208.

20   See for landscape poetry, 12.3.92, 5; for realism, 22.8.91, 1; for transcendentalism, 2.7.87, 6 and 24.12.87, 1; for *fin de siècle* 17.6.93, 5; 2.9.93, 1.

21   28.2.91, 1.

22   See for instance 23 and 30.4.92, 1. A note on 11.4.91, 1 commended the anti-Parnellite *Freeman's Journal* for beginning to take literature seriously and devoting three columns to literary reviews.

23   23.4.92, 1; 30.4.92, 21.5.92, 5; 1.10.92, 4. These cannot be fictitious letters written by the editor for the names appended to them belong to well-known literary personalities of the day such as John T. Kelly and Frank MacDonagh.

24   C. H. Rolleston, 16; E. A. Boyd, *Ireland's Literary Renaissance*, 27.

25   This claim is supported by other contemporary accounts; Katharine Tynan, 'Recent Irish Poetry', 200–11; Stephen Gwynn, *Experiences of a Literary Man*, 11, 62; *A Student's History of Ireland*, 288; *Ireland*, 115, 119; *Ireland's Literature and Drama*, 122. Ramsay Colles (*In Castle and Courthouse*, 19–27) takes a contrary view, and supports Foster's contention. He claims that the Revival began around 1886 and, like Foster, instances the *DUR* as an example.

26   John Kelly, 'The Fall of Parnell and the Rise of Anglo-Irish Literature', 1–23.

27   Foster, 'Anglo-Irish literature', 63, 67.

28   The modern literature of Ireland, and indeed all that stir of thought which prepared for the Anglo-Irish war, began when Parnell fell from power in

1891. A disillusioned and embittered Ireland turned from parliamentary politics; an event was conceived; and the race began, as I think, to be troubled
by that event's long gestation. (*Auto*, 559)

29   18.6.92, 5 and 10.9.92, 2.

30   *Mem*, 57.

31   Joseph Chamberlain, Sir Charles Dilke and G. J. Shaw Lefevre resigned because of
this. See Lyons, *Famine*, 180.

32   The table of yearly agrarian outrages in J. V. O'Brien's Appendix (250–1) makes this
clear.

33   J. V. O'Brien's table (253) indicates that evictions too reduced significantly only in
1888.

34   *WBY*, 113.

35   His previous letter to O'Leary exemplifies this. The latter had sent him extracts of a
Freeman's Journal article reporting a meeting between Arthur 'Bloody' Balfour, the
nationalist MP J. G. S. MacNeill, and a deputation from Dungloe town who wanted
both to avail of the economic assistance the coercionist Chief Secretary was proffer-
ing and fulfil their patriotic duty by presenting him with an address denouncing him
in violent language. (For a hilarious account of this episode, see *CL1*, 234.) MacNeill
and the nationalist deputation had ended up with egg on their faces, which is probably why O'Leary, ever-contemptuous of parliamentary politicians and weak-kneed
patriotism, sent Yeats the report. While replying, Yeats dutifully commented on how
'rediculously' MacNeill and the delegation had behaved but added, 'However, all
roads lead to Rome I suppose even those of McNeil and McSweeny.' Having written
this, he must have immediately realised that O'Leary advocated a different path and
recognised the validity of no other, and hence the following sentence: 'I meen that
they are Nationalists of a kind & intend right things.' Oh Reader, what a falling off
was there!

36   Lyons, *Parnell*, 547.

37   Conor Cruise O'Brien, 'Passion and Cunning', 217. He detects a note of 'gleeful
excitement' rather than genuine concern or worry in Yeats's letter of 4 December.

38   Letter of 22.12.90; quoted in Lyons, *Parnell*, 544.

39   'It is in fact conceivable that a native legislature of a certain character . . .' (9.4.92, 5).
See pp. 198–9.

40   Kelly, 'The Fall of Parnell', 17.

41   J. B. Yeats, *Letters to his Son, W. B. Yeats and Others, 1869–1922*, 126; J. B. Yeats, *Further
Letters of John Butler Yeats*, 69–70; See also Malcolm Brown, *Politics of Irish Literature*,
230–31, 242–43.

42   For Yeats's sympathy for and identification with Davitt, see *Auto*, 356–7.

43   *Collected Letters of W. B. Yeats*, eds. Warwick Gould, John Kelly and Deirdre Toomey,
vol. 2, 464–5; cited hereafter as *CL2*.

44   *UP2*, 310–27.

45   *CL2*, 227.

46   Maud Gonne, *Autobiography*, 84.

47   Callanan, 47, 173, 177, 265.

48   *LNI*, 25, 78.

49   While the former was criticised for his anglicisation, for reading 'much English literature' (*LNI*, 47) and for choosing English rather than Irish literary models, the latter's simplicity and sincerity were praised and her Fenian connections highlighted.
Compare with *United Ireland* articles 24.1.91, 5 and 31.1.91, 6.

50   *CL1*, 250.

51   *CL1*, 260–3.

52   3.10.91, 5.

53   For example, *CL1*, 295 and *CL2*, 635 resulted in notes on Maud Gonne on 2.7.92, 1; 9.4.92, 1; 23.4.92, 1 and 18.6.92, 4. For Jack Yeats see *CL1*, 264 n.3 and 3.12.91, 1. For Yeats, compare *CL1*, 282 with 23.1.92, 1; *CL1* 295 with 14.5.92, 1 and *CL2* 635–7 with 9.4.92, 1.

54   *UP1*, 206, 208, 214, 218–19, 222–5; *CL1*, 298–9, 315, 370, 373.

55   *Auto*, 209.

56   *UP1*, 206–8, 218–9; *CL1*, 315, 369–74.

57   I. A. Gregory, *Seventy Years*, 128.

58   *LNI*, 20–1, 30, 55, 77–8.

59   *CL1*, 282.

60   'To the Editor of *United Ireland*', 10 November 1894, *L*, 238.

61   See also *UP2*, 360.

62   Eve Patten, 'A "General Crowd of Small Singers"', 29–44; Roy Foster, 'Protestant Magic', 258; Terrence Brown, *Ireland's Literature*, 29–48; F. S. L. Lyons, 'Yeats and Victorian Ireland', 115–38.

63   For Savage-Armstrong, see *CL1*, 303–4, n. 7, *CL2*, 231–2.

64   *Auto*, 410.

65   Yeats's review was printed in the issue of 23.7.92; Hyde's lecture was delivered on 25.11.92 and covered by the paper in two issues over 3.12.92 and 10.12.92; Yeats's response, 'The De-Anglicising of Ireland', was published on 17.12.92.

66   *Mem*, 57.

67   In his *Memoirs*, Yeats tried to sanitise the whole debate by reducing it to a 'matter of morals. Was not it the duty of Irishmen to consider Dublin their intellectual capital, and then always to accept its leadership?' (57–8).

68   This did not save him from future allegations about his anglicisation. Though he sent another letter reiterating his belief in Dublin as Ireland's intellectual capital, the *United Ireland* was not pacified:

   We know, and fully recognise, that there are literary Irishmen in London whose patriotism is as pure as our own mountain rills; but we are equally certain that the influences a successful Irish literary man has to withstand in London will, nine times out of ten, modify and often shatter the ideals he has cherished in connection with his country. (30.7.92, 5)

69   *CL1*, 303.

70   Terry Eagleton, *Heathcliff and the Great Hunger*, 240.

71   Yeats had been promulgating this theory from 1889 onwards to project an inherent difference between Irish and English literature, and to emphasise the genetic superiority of the former. He first outlined it in a *Boston Pilot* article on Todhunter's poems (10.2.89; *LNI*, 89), developed it in an earlier lecture on 'Nationality and Literature' (23.1.92, 3) and referred to it in 'Hopes and Fears for Irish Literature'. He published his address to the National Literary Society in the *United Ireland* on 27.5.93, 1–2. See *UP1*, 266–75.

72   *The Book of the Rhymers' Club*.

73   *UP1*, 276–9, 373–5, 397–9; *UP2*, 38–42, 70–3, 88–91, 91–4, 115–8; and *E&I*, 189–94.

74   *A Book of Irish Verse*, xix.

75   *E&I*, 191.

76   Arthur Hallam, 'On Some of the Characteristics of Modern Poetry, and on the Lyrical Poems of Alfred Tennyson', 87–139; cited hereafter as *AH*. For Hallam's use of the tree metaphor, see 98–9 and for his views on the three ages of literature and their

characteristics, see 102–7. For Yeats's use of Hallam's tree metaphor and theory of literary history in another context, see George Bornstein, *Yeats and Shelley*, 31–39.

77   I am indebted to Nicholas Shrimpton's observation that Hallam never used the word
'aesthetic' or 'aestheticism'. Yeats, quite characteristically, has foisted it onto Hallam
for his own purposes.

78   *UP1*, 276–9.

79   The terms 'Decadents' and 'Aesthetes' were often used interchangeably by Yeats and
he frequently presented the Rhymers as encompassing both. (See *UP2*, 38–42 and
E&I, 189–94.) For the sake of brevity I have followed his example without meaning
to obscure the differences between these groups.

80   The *Nation* review of 'Oisin' (25 May 1889) criticised 'this sense of unreality, of
remoteness from living interests which makes the general effect of Mr Yeats's poetry
pall'. The *Evening Telegraph* of 6 Feb. 1889, commented on 'the sense of remoteness
characteristic of his verse'. See *CL1*, 128, 132, 144.

81   *UI*, 24.11.94, 1.

82   This letter, published in the *United Ireland* on 16.2.95, 1, has not been collected and
can be found in Appendix III.

83   Appendix III.

84   Yeats described this piece by McGrath as 'the most important article on my work'
(*CL2*, 14).

CONCLUSION

1   Thomas Hardy, 'Candour in English Fiction', 125.

2   Daniel Corkery, *Synge and Anglo-Irish Literature*, 26.

3   Michael North, *The Political Aesthetic of Yeats, Eliot, and Pound*, 23.

4   James Joyce, 'The Day of the Rabblement,' 71.

5   For an answer, see Paulin, 133–40; Conor Cruise O'Brien, 'Passion and Cunning,'
238–41; Terence Brown, *The Life of W. B. Yeats*, 234–6; 275–7.

6   Hone, *William Butler Yeats: The Poet in Contemporary Ireland*, 16.

7   Hone, 'Yeats as Political Philosopher', 493.

8   For example: 'To the greater poets everything they see has its relation to the national
life . . . nothing is an isolated artistic moment . . .'; 'By the by . . . Mr O'Grady is
seeing the error of his ways and growing into a good Nationalist after all'; 'Can we
not unite literature to the great passion of patriotism and ennoble both thereby?'; '. . .
and may not we men of the pen hope to move some Irish hearts and make them
beat true to manhood and to Ireland?'; 'Political doctrine was not demanded of them
[Allingham, Lover and Lever], merely nationalism' (*LNI*, 78, 34, 65, 65, 78); 'Until it
[Irish talent] . . . [is] applied to the needs of Ireland it will never do anything great
in literature' (*UP1*, 224).

9   Hone, *William Butler Yeats: The Poet in Contemporary Ireland*, 34–5.

Index